Lecture Notes of the Institute for Computer Sciences, Social Informatics and Telecommunications Engineering 504

The LNICST series publishes ICST's conferences, symposia and workshops.

LNICST reports state-of-the-art results in areas related to the scope of the Institute. The type of material published includes

- Proceedings (published in time for the respective event)
- Other edited monographs (such as project reports or invited volumes)

LNICST topics span the following areas:

- General Computer Science
- E-Economy
- E-Medicine
- Knowledge Management
- Multimedia
- Operations, Management and Policy
- Social Informatics
- Systems

Ao Li · Yao Shi · Liang Xi

Editors

6GN for Future Wireless Networks

5th EAI International Conference, 6GN 2022
Harbin, China, December 17–18, 2022
Proceedings, Part I

 Springer

Editors
Ao Li
Harbin University of Science and Technology
Harbin, China

Yao Shi
Harbin Institute of Technology
Shenzhen, China

Liang Xi
Harbin University of Science and Technology
Harbin, China

ISSN 1867-8211   ISSN 1867-822X (electronic)
Lecture Notes of the Institute for Computer Sciences, Social Informatics
and Telecommunications Engineering
ISBN 978-3-031-36010-7   ISBN 978-3-031-36011-4 (eBook)
https://doi.org/10.1007/978-3-031-36011-4

This Springer imprint is published by the registered company Springer Nature Switzerland AG
The registered company address is: Gewerbestrasse 11, 6330 Cham, Switzerland

Preface

We are delighted to introduce the proceedings of the 5th EAI International Conference on 6G for Future Wireless Networks (6GN 2022). This conference brought together researchers, developers, and practitioners around the world who are leveraging and developing 6G technology for a smarter cellular network with spectacular speeds and almost non-existent latency, extreme connectivity and sensing, comprehensive and reliable coverage, and unparalleled energy efficiency. The theme of 6GN 2022 was "6G for Future Wireless Networks".

The technical program of 6GN 2022 consisted of 60 full papers which cover multiple technical fields such as wireless communication networks, edge computing, and artificial intelligence. The conference tracks were: Track 1 - Resource Allocation for 6G Networks; Track 2 - Security and Privacy for 6G Networks; Track 3 - Big data mining and pattern analysis techniques for 6G Networks; Track 4 - Artificial intelligent techniques for 6G Networks; Track 5 - Mobile Edge Computing for 6G Networks; and Track 6 - Unmanned Aerial Vehicle Communication for 6G Networks. Aside from the high-quality technical paper presentations, the technical program also featured two keynote speeches. The two keynote speeches were from Xinwang Liu from National University of Defense Technology (NUDT), China and Yong Wang from Harbin Institute of Technology (HIT), China.

Coordination with the Steering Chair, Imrich Chlamtac, was essential for the success of the conference. We sincerely appreciate his constant guidance and all the support from the Steering Committee. It was also a great pleasure to work with the excellent Organizing Committee led by General Chair Deyun Chen, and Co-Chairs Emad Alsusa and Gongliang Liu. In particular, we offer up our thanks to the Technical Program Committee led by Ao Li, Yao Shi, and Liang Xi, who completed the peer-review process of technical papers and made a high-quality technical program. We are also grateful to Conference Manager Ivana Bujdakova for her support and to all the authors who submitted their papers to the 6GN 2022 conference.

We strongly believe that the 6GN 2022 conference provided a good forum for all researchers, developers, and practitioners to discuss all science and technology aspects that are relevant to 6G networks. We also expect that the future 6GN conference will be as successful and stimulating, as indicated by the contributions presented in this volume.

Ao Li
Yao Shi
Liang Xi

Organization

Steering Committee

Imrich Chlamtac   University of Trento, Italy

Organizing Committee

General Chair

Deyun Chen   Harbin University of Science and Technology, China

General Co-chairs

Emad Alsusa   University of Manchester, UK
Gongliang Liu   Harbin Institute of Technology, China

TPC Chair and Co-chairs

Ao Li   Harbin University of Science and Technology, China
Yao Shi   Harbin Institute of Technology, China
Liang Xi   Harbin University of Science and Technology, China
Ruofei Ma   Harbin Institute of Technology, China

Sponsorship and Exhibit Chair

Ao Li   Harbin University of Science and Technology, China

Local Chairs

Yuan Cheng   Harbin University of Science and Technology, China
Shuo Shi   Harbin Institute of Technology, China

Workshops Chair

Qiang Guan   Kent State University, USA

Publicity and Social Media Chair

Xiaomeng Wang   Harbin Institute of Technology, China

Publications Chairs

Emad Alusa   University of Manchester, UK
Shibiao Xu   Beijing University of Posts and
                                       Telecommunications, China

Web Chair

Hailong Jiang   Kent State University, USA

Posters and PhD Track Chairs

Wanlong Zhao   Harbin Institute of Technology, China
Song Li   Harbin University of Science and Technology,
                                       China

Panels Chairs

Mohammed W. Baidas   Kuwait University, Kuwait
Jiguang Zhang   Institute of Automation, Chinese Academy of
                                       Sciences, China

Demos Chairs

Jingchao Li   Shanghai Dianji University, China
Xinlu Li   Huizhou Engineering Vocational College, China

Tutorials Chairs

Hailu Yang   Harbin University of Science and Technology,
                                       China
Jianyue Zhu   Nanjing University of Information Science and
                                       Technology, China

Contents – Part I

Security and Privacy for 6G Networks

Big Data Mining and Pattern Analysis Techniques for 6G Networks

Contents – Part II

Mobile Edge Computing for 6G Networks

Unmanned Aerial Vehicle Communication for 6G Networks

Resource Allocation for 6G Networks

OLSR Protocol Optimization Based on Node and Link Stability

Xi Wang[1]([✉]), Shuo Shi[1,2], and Meng Wang[1]

[1] Harbin Institute of Technology, Harbin 150001, Heilongjiang, China
wangxi_chn@foxmail.com, crcss@hit.edu.cn
[2] Network Communication Research Centre, Peng Cheng Laboratory, Shenzhen 518052, Guangdong, China

Abstract. As UAV (unmanned aerial vehicle) formation is more and more widely applied in the real environment, how to effectively organize a communication network between UAVs is the main research hotspot and difficulty at present. The characteristics of UAVs, such as flexible movement, limited load and limited communication distance, pose great challenges to the design of communication protocols. After years of development, unmanned aerial vehicle Ad hoc network has gradually become the key technology in this field. This paper focuses on the classical routing protocol in the UAV Ad hoc network, optimizes the Link State routing protocol (OLSR), and further optimizes and tests the advantages and disadvantages of it. The optimized routing protocol is more suitable for the complex environment of UAV, and further improves the network transmission performance.

Keywords: UAV · FANETs · OLSR · MPR

1 Introduction

With the rapid development of electronic devices, sensors and communication technology, more and more unmanned aerial vehicles (UAVs) are coming into people's sight. These systems are capable of flying autonomously and can carry out special missions without any intervention from external operations. Because of their versatility, flexibility, ease of installation, and minimal operational costs for redeployment, the use of UAVs offers a new approach for several military and commercial applications. For example, map exploration, target search, network relay [1], disaster monitoring, remote sensing and traffic management [2]. While the systems for single UAVs are fairly mature and have been developed for decades, the development and deployment of a fleet of small UAVs is just beginning. There are many advantages to operating a large unmanned aerial vehicle. However, with the broader application, there are challenges unique to multi-UAV systems. Prominent among the challenges is the design of communication networks between multiple UAVs.

In this paper, Flying Ad-hoc Networks (FANETs), a proprietary network architecture of UAVs is adopted. This Ad hoc network between UAVs is considered as a new form

© ICST Institute for Computer Sciences, Social Informatics and Telecommunications Engineering 2023
Published by Springer Nature Switzerland AG 2023. All Rights Reserved
A. Li et al. (Eds.): 6GN 2022, LNICST 504, pp. 3–13, 2023.
https://doi.org/10.1007/978-3-031-36011-4_1

of networks. The unique structure and characteristics of UAVs Ad hoc network have aroused close attention to its solutions and a series of open research. FANETs is able to use the wireless device on the drone as a mobile terminal, but also let the terminal function as a router, without the help of infrastructure such as base stations for network communication. Each node on the network is automatically configured to connect to each other, enabling dynamic networking and rapid deployment. This complex distributed network provides a new solution for designing a flexible and powerful data transmission network.

Because FANETs is restricted by UAV cluster carriers and functions, the routing protocols used in traditional MANETs and VANETs usually cannot directly adapt to the scenarios where FANETs topology and routing information change strongly, thus affecting the communication performance of the whole network. Therefore, it is necessary to design a routing protocol suitable for FANETs scenario to support the communication function of UAV formation. At present, a series of drafts on Ad-hoc routing published officially provide developers and researchers with reference to design the best routing protocol suitable for different application scenarios [3].

This paper focuses on the Optimized Link State Routing (OLSR) protocol for mobile Ad-hoc networks and its implementation and improvement in the context of UAV networks. By optimizing the classical link algorithm and combining with the actual demand of mobile Ad hoc network, the expert group designed the OLSR routing protocol. It inherits the stability of the original link-state algorithm and uses table-driven management scheme. OLSR is an active routing protocol. In the process of transmission, the nodes of the network will exchange the network information in their information base with the surrounding nodes at a fixed frequency. The routing overhead of OLSR protocol is large but relatively fixed, but its overhead is related to the size of the network. Using active routing to establish routing table and maintain it in real time, the end-to-end delay performance in the network is better. Therefore, it is more suitable for the QoS requirements of communication networks in FANETs scenarios.

2   Related Work

As the root of FANETs, MANETs technology has gone through a long process of research. DAERA was the first to design and research mobile Ad hoc networks on behalf of the U.S. government. In June 1997, the Internet Engineering Task Force (IETF) established the MANET Working Group. The establishment of the MANET enabled the commercial process to move forward quickly.

With the deepening of MANET research, its combination with unmanned aerial vehicle network has gradually emerged in the sight of researchers. S. Temel and Bekmezci designed the architecture for the combination of High-Altitude Platform (HAP) and FANETs to become one of the most promising technologies for military and civilian near space wireless networks in [4]. The HAP system resides in the stratosphere and solves the challenging problem of identifying the location of neighboring UAVs in FANETs. It plays an important role in reliability, security and conflict avoidance, and then proposes a media access control (MAC) protocol.

S. Temel and Iens. Bekmezci argue in [5] that interference brought by simultaneous transmission in FANETs limits the maximum amount of concurrent communication, so the deployment of traditional omnidirectional antennas cannot effectively improve the spatial reuse rate. In this regard, they put forward a scheme to set up directional antennas to increase the space reuse rate and network capacity of FANETs. An analysis model is proposed to analyze the influence of different UAV flight types and different flight scenarios on the transmission information between communication nodes. K. Singh and A. K. Verma proposed the application of OLSR routing protocol in FANETs scenario in [6], and also focused on the network performance of OLSR under different mobility models of UAVs, and put forward guidance on how to continue to optimize. Y. Mostafaei and S. Pashazadeh analyzed the problems caused by the direct application of OLSR routing protocol in FANETs, and pointed out that the OLSR routing protocol did not fully consider the mobility of nodes in the process of MPR selection, leading to link disruption in [7].

In this paper, a new selection method is proposed, in which as many as possible nodes that are prevented from moving violently are selected as relay nodes. According to the simulation results, this method increases the network lifetime. Alamsyah et al. established the wireless network model of health monitoring system in [8]. The performance of AODV, DSDV and OLSR routing protocols is compared by simulation, and the performance of the three protocols in different scenarios is evaluated by delay, throughput and packet delivery rate. Through research, it is found that OLSR has better performance in the mobile terminal, especially when the node of the mobile terminal is above 50. Therefore, OLSR routing protocol is more suitable in FANETs scenario.

3   Problem Description

The problems related to flooding are collectively called Broadcast Storm Problem. In the OLSR routing protocol, three schemes are adopted to avoid broadcast bursts in AD hoc networks [9]:

1) The protocol selection adopts the multi-point relay technology, that is, only the MPR relay node selection algorithm is used to select the nodes with high connectivity to forward the control packets sent by the source nodes, avoiding the waste of network resources caused by unrestricted replay in the flooding mechanism.

2) According to the protocol, only selected MPR nodes are allowed to generate link-state information to participate in the calculation and generation of routing tables, which can effectively reduce the number of control packets transmitted in the network and reduce the control overhead of network protocols.

3) MPR nodes selected by the algorithm can choose to broadcast only the link information between themselves and their MPR selectors, so as to further reduce the control overhead.

By analyzing the MPR set selection algorithm in RFC3626 specification of OLSR routing protocol, it is not difficult to see that OLSR protocol, as a link-state based first response routing, can effectively reduce the network control overhead because of the MPR set generation and selection process [10]. The nodes in the network will select multiple appropriate relay nodes in their one-hop neighbor table by the algorithm, and each node is independent of each other in this process. Whether the relay node selection is optimal is whether all the two-hop neighbors under this selection can be covered by nodes in the MPR node set. The MPR selection scheme in the original OLSR protocol uses a greedy selection algorithm. The greedy algorithm has a fast convergence rate and requires fewer computing resources. However, in the greedy strategy adopted by MPR algorithm in OLSR routing protocol, the generation of MPR sets depends on the connection degree of nodes in the one-hop neighbor table. In this way, an appropriate MPR relay node can be quickly selected, which greatly reduces the transmission of control packets in the network, reduces the flooding of link information when routing information is broadcast, and gives full play to the advantages of OLSR protocol.

However, for the existing operational network architecture of unmanned aerial vehicles, the movement speed of the UAV itself is an important factor that cannot be ignored. The current UAV speed is up to hundreds of km/h. If the multi-point relay MPR set selection algorithm in the original protocol is still adopted, the update frequency of network topology information may not catch up with the change frequency of network topology structure. Under the influence of the drastic change of network topology, the UAV is likely to move out of the communication range before completing the transmission task, resulting in the unreachable network.

Therefore, an optimized MPR set selection algorithm should be designed. The consideration of this algorithm is not only based on the connectivity of one-hop neighbor nodes and the willingness of nodes, but also the moving speed of current nodes, link change rate and other factors affecting network transmission. In the MPR selection algorithm, the emphasis of the original OLSR on node willingness is changed to the emphasis on node quality. Nodes can get indicators to describe whether they are suitable as relay nodes by sensing the changes in the surrounding topology. Based on the size of this metric, the source node will decide whether to add it to the MPR node or participate in the comparison consideration with other nodes. In this way, a comprehensive selection algorithm is implemented, which makes FANETs more capable of resisting the impact of drastic changes in network topology and link breaks on transmission.

4 Proposed Algorithm

From the above analysis, we can know that OLSR limits the scale of message flooding in the network through its unique MPR mechanism. Therefore, when selecting which nodes can be used as MPR relay nodes, relatively stable nodes and links can be selected in advance, which plays a key role in improving the transmission performance of the network. In this paper, it is defined as a measure of FANETs node mobility, which includes node stability and link stability.

Node stability is defined as the degree of change of the neighbor set between a node and all its neighbors. The higher the stability is, the lower the relative mobility of its neighbors, the smaller the change of the surrounding topology of the node, the smaller the impact on routing performance, and the shorter the time of routing recovery after route breakage. Link stability is defined as the remaining lifetime of a link. The higher the stability is, the longer the link can guarantee the transmission link, which plays a key role in the stability of the path. When establishing a complete stability evaluation mechanism, node stability and link stability should complement each other. Node stability can only estimate the topological changes of neighboring nodes quantitatively, while link stability can obtain the moving direction and speed of nodes by GPS devices, and estimate the remaining life time of links accordingly, so that nodes can select stable links in advance.

4.1 Stability Evaluation Mechanism Based on Node

In order to measure the neighbor changes of each node in FANETs, the concept of node stability is introduced. The basic idea of the algorithm is to measure the rate of change of the neighboring nodes through the stability of the node, so as to obtain the description of the stability degree of the node. The basic idea is to evaluate the stability by the HELLO packets passed between nodes and the rate of change of neighbor table entries of nodes. The neighbor stability of node I is defined in Eq. (1).

$$NS_i = \frac{\left| S_{i_t} \cap S_{i_{t+\Delta t}} \right|}{\left| S_{i_t} \cup S_{i_{t+\Delta t}} \right|} \tag{1}$$

where S_{i_t} is the neighbor set of node i at time t, after time Δt, that is, the neighbor set of node i at time $t + \Delta t$ is $S_{i_{t+\Delta t}}$. The value of NS_i is between 0 and 1, that is, the stability of node i is between 0 and 1.

Based on the evaluation method of node stability, the first optimization scheme of OLSR protocol is proposed. In this optimization protocol, a weight model of node stability is proposed, which takes both node stability and connectivity as greedy strategies to participate in the MPR node screening algorithm, and to participate in the mechanism of evaluating whether the node is suitable for MPR node. The comprehensive link evaluation index L is calculated by formula (2).

$$L(y_i) = NS_i * D(y_i), i \in [nb] \tag{2}$$

The comprehensive link evaluation index L is used as the standard to evaluate whether the adjacent node is suitable to join the MPR node.

4.2 Stability Evaluation Mechanism Based on Link Mobility Prediction

To properly assess the lifetime of a communication link between two nodes, we need to make additional assumptions about how each node is configured. It is assumed that any two UAV nodes can communicate bidirectionally in FANETs, and the radius of communication transmission range of each node is R. Moreover, each network node is equipped with GPS, and the node can perceive the position, speed and time information and periodically send its coordinates, speed and other information to the neighbor node. At this time, each node receives the message sent by the neighbor node and extracts the geographical location information according to the received information to predict the remaining lifetime of each link, so as to obtain the link stability of the node. The survival time of the two nodes is calculated as follows.

The initial distance of two nodes M and N is d, and the link life cycle is estimated as shown in Fig. 1. Calculating the remaining time of link MN is to estimate the time of node N within the transmission radius R of node M. The relative motion of two nodes

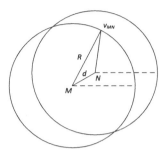

Fig. 1. Link lifetime estimation between two nodes

can be regarded as one node being stationary and the other node moving. In this way, the position of node M relative to node N can be calculated as the following Eq. (3).

$$(x_{MN}, y_{MN}) = (x_N - x_M, y_N - y_M) \tag{3}$$

In this case, the distance between M and N is shown in Eq. (4).

$$d = \sqrt{x_{MN}^2 + y_{MN}^2} \tag{4}$$

Since the two nodes are in relative motion, after time t, the position of node M relative to node N is

$$
\begin{aligned}
x'_{MN} &= x_{MN} + |v_{MN}|t\cos\theta_{MN} \\
y'_{MN} &= y_{MN} + |v_{MN}|t\sin\theta_{MN}
\end{aligned}
\tag{5}
$$

In Eq. (5), θ_{MN} is the velocity angle between node M and node N, and v_{MN} is the velocity between node M and node N. When the distance between them is R, the link is broken.

$$d' = \sqrt{x'^2_{MN} + y'^2_{MN}} = R \tag{6}$$

Substitute Eq. (5) into Eq. (6) to obtain the following Eq. (7).

$$|v_{NM}|^2 t^2 + 2|v_{NM}|(x_{NM}\cos\theta_{NM} + y_{NM}\sin\theta_{NM})t + d^2 - R^2 = 0 \tag{7}$$

$$
\begin{aligned}
v_M &= (|v_M|\cos\theta_M)i + (|v_M|\sin\theta_M)j \\
v_N &= (|v_N|\cos\theta_N)i + (|v_N|\sin\theta_N)j
\end{aligned}
\tag{8}
$$

$$v_{NM} = v_N - v_M = (|v_N|\cos\theta_N - |v_M|\cos\theta_M)i + (|v_N|\sin\theta_N - |v_M|\sin\theta_M)j$$

$$|v_{NM}| = \sqrt{(|v_N|\cos\theta_N - |v_M|\cos\theta_M)^2 + (|v_N|\sin\theta_N - |v_M|\sin\theta_M)^2} \tag{9}$$

$$\theta_{NM} = \tan^{-1}\left(\frac{|v_N|\sin\theta_N - |v_M|\sin\theta_M}{|v_N|\cos\theta_N - |v_M|\cos\theta_M}\right) \tag{10}$$

In Eq. (10), θ_M is the moving direction of node M, θ_N is the moving direction of node N, v_M is the speed of node M, and v_N is the speed of node N. Since t cannot be negative, it can be evaluated as Eq. (11).

$$t = \frac{\sqrt{R^2 - (x_{MN} \sin \theta_{MN} - y_{MN} \cos \theta_{MN})^2} - (x_{MN} \cos \theta_{MN} + y_{MN} \sin \theta_{MN})}{|v_{MN}|} \tag{11}$$

The link stability is defined as Eq. (12).

$$LS_{MN} = \frac{t}{t_{max}} = \frac{t}{\frac{R}{|v_{MN}|}}$$

$$= \frac{\sqrt{R^2 - (x_{MN} \sin \theta_{MN} - y_{MN} \cos \theta_{MN})^2} - (x_{MN} \cos \theta_{MN} + y_{MN} \sin \theta_{MN})}{R} \tag{12}$$

In Eq. (12), x_{MN} is the difference of abscissa between node M and node N, y_{MN} is the difference of ordinate between node M and node N, the value of LS_{MN} is between 0 and 1 when the two nodes are gradually away from each other, and greater than 1 when the two nodes are gradually close to each other.

Based on the evaluation method of the link stability, a second OLSR protocol optimization scheme is proposed. In this optimization protocol, a weight model that can refer to the link stability between nodes is proposed, and a greedy strategy is taken into consideration of link stability and node connectivity to participate in the MPR node screening algorithm, which is involved in the mechanism of evaluating whether the node is suitable for MPR node. The comprehensive link evaluation index L can be calculated by the calculation formula, see Formula (13).

$$L(y_i) = \sum LS_{y_i s_j}, i \in [nb], j \in [nb2hop] \tag{13}$$

The comprehensive link evaluation index L is used as the standard to evaluate whether the adjacent node is suitable to join the MPR node.

4.3 Evaluation Mechanism of Integrated Node Stability and Link Stability

The comprehensive stability of nodes and links can be obtained by integrating the two mechanisms: the rate of change of nodes' neighbors and the prediction of the remaining lifetime of link MN, as shown in Eq. (14).

$$PS_{MN} = \lambda_1 NS_N + \lambda_2 LS_{MN} \tag{14}$$

In the formula, λ_1 and λ_2 are the change rate of node neighbors and the selection coefficient of link stability respectively, which are between 0 and 1, and their value is dynamically adjusted according to the network type and state. The value of PS_{MN} will directly affect whether the node is suitable as a relay node in MPR. The proposed algorithm can comprehensively consider node stability, link stability and node connectivity to obtain a comprehensive link evaluation index L. The calculation method is shown in Eq. (15).

$$L(y_i) = \lambda_1 \overline{LS_{y_i s_j}} + \lambda_2 NS_i, i \in [nb], j \in [nb2hop] \tag{15}$$

5   Simulation Results

We use NS2 to simulate the OLSR protocol and its optimization part. Both node stability and link stability are integrated to test the final impact of MPR node selection algorithm on the network performance of OLSR routing protocol after the design of weighted comprehensive link evaluation mechanism. By comparing the experiment with the original protocol, when the maximum moving speed of the node is between 5 m/s and 30 m/s, the simulation interval is 5 m/s, and the control overhead (Fig. 2), end-to-end delay (Fig. 3) and packet loss rate (Fig. 4) vary with the moving speed of the node:

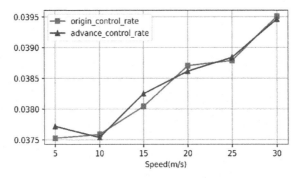

Fig. 2. Comparison of network control overhead between original and optimized protocols

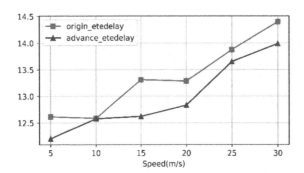

Fig. 3. Comparison of network end-to-end delay between original and optimized protocols

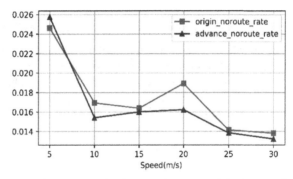

Fig. 4. Comparison of network packet loss rate between original and optimized protocols

At the same time, this paper also considers the influence of protocol optimization on network throughput. We focus on the network throughput changes over time when the number of network nodes is 20, the maximum moving speed of nodes is 20 m/s, and the moving range of nodes is 500 m*500 m. The link evaluation mechanism protocol, which integrates node stability and link stability, is compared with the original protocol, as shown in Fig. 5.

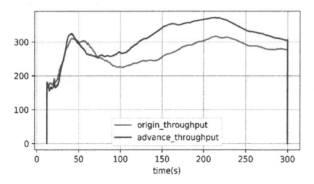

Fig. 5. Network throughput comparison between original and optimized protocols

According to the experimental results, we can see that the routing protocol that integrates two optimization schemes of node stability and link stability can improve the network performance in end-to-end delay and packet loss rate without increasing the network control overhead. In the experimental results of throughput change, we can see that when the network is just established and in the node exploration link exploration stage, there is basically no difference in throughput between the two protocols. After a period of time, when the network topology is basically established and data transmission service is the main work, the throughput performance of the optimized protocol is significantly better than that of the original protocol. Therefore, it can be confirmed that the scheme achieves the purpose of MPR node selection optimization algorithm.

6   Conclusion

This paper focuses on the MPR node selection algorithm of standard OLSR protocol, and points out that the greedy strategy adopted in the greedy algorithm is not completely suitable for FANETs mobile scenario. A link stability evaluation mechanism based on node stability and link prediction is proposed. The design principle of the evaluation mechanism is pointed out in detail. After the OLSR routing protocol using this mechanism is investigated, the network performance indexes of routing cost, end-to-end delay, packet delivery rate and throughput rate are investigated. Through comparison, it is found that the end-to-end delay, packet delivery rate and throughput rate are improved to a certain extent without significantly increasing the routing overhead.

Acknowledgement. This work has been supported by the National Natural Science Foundation of China under Grant 62171158. The research leading to these results has received the funding from Research Fund Program of Guangdong Key Laboratory of Aerospace Communication and Networking Technology under Grant 2018B030322004.

References

1. de Freitas, E.P., et al.: UAV relay network to support WSN connectivity. In: International Congress on Ultra Modern Telecommunications and Control Systems, pp. 309–314, IEEE, Moscow (2010)
2. Semsch, E., Jakob, M., Pavlíček, D., Pechoucek, M.: Autonomous UAV surveillance in complex urban environments. In: 2009 IEEE/WIC/ACM International Joint Conference on Web Intelligence and Intelligent Agent Technology, pp. 82–85, IEEE, Milan (2009)
3. AlKhatieb, A., Felemban, E.: Performance evaluation of ad hoc routing protocols in (FANETs). In: 2019 International Conference on Advances in the Emerging Computing Technologies (AECT), pp. 1–6, IEEE, Seoul (2020)
4. Temel, S., Bekmezci, I.: On the performance of flying ad hoc networks (FANETs) utilizing near space high altitude platforms (HAPs). In: 2013 6th International Conference on Recent Advances in Space Technologies (RAST), pp. 461–465. IEEE, Istanbul (2013). https://doi.org/10.1109/RAST.2013.6581252
5. Temel, S., Bekmezci, I.: Scalability analysis of flying ad hoc networks (FANETs): a directional antenna approach. In: 2014 IEEE International Black Sea Conference on Communications and Networking (BlackSeaCom), pp. 185–187. IEEE, Odessa (2014). https://doi.org/10.1109/BlackSeaCom.2014.6849036
6. Singh, K., Verma, A.K.: Applying OLSR routing in FANETs. In: 2014 IEEE International Conference on Advanced Communications, Control and Computing Technologies, pp. 1212–1215. IEEE, Ramanathapuram (2014). https://doi.org/10.1109/ICACCCT.2014.7019290
7. Mostafaei, Y., Pashazadeh, S.: An improved OLSR routing protocol for reducing packet loss ratio in ad-hoc networks. In: 2016 Eighth International Conference on Information and Knowledge Technology (IKT), pp. 12–17. IEEE, Hamedan (2016). https://doi.org/10.1109/IKT.2016.7777778
8. Alamsyah, M.H., Purnama, I.K.E., Setijadi, E.: Performance of the routing protocols AODV, DSDV and OLSR in health monitoring using NS3. In: 2016 International Seminar on Intelligent Technology and Its Applications (ISITIA), pp. 323-328. IEEE, Lombok (2016). https://doi.org/10.1109/ISITIA.2016.7828680.

9. Singh, K., Verma, A.K.: Applying OLSR routing in FANETs. In: 2014 IEEE International Conference on Advanced Communications, Control and Computing Technologies, pp. 1212–1215. IEEE, Ramanathapuram (2014)
10. Leonov, A.V., Litvinov, G.A.: Considering AODV and OLSR routing protocols to traffic monitoring scenario in FANET formed by mini-UAVs. In: 2018 XIV International Scientific-Technical Conference on Actual Problems of Electronics Instrument Engineering (APEIE), pp. 229–237. IEEE, Novosibirsk (2018)

Dynamic Computation Offloading and Resource Allocation for Multi-access Edge Computing Networks

Meng Wang[1(✉)], Shuo Shi[1,2], and Xi Wang[1]

[1] School of Electronic and Information Engineering, Harbin Institute of Technology, Harbin 150001, Heilongjiang, China
wangmeng_hit@163.com, crcss@hit.edu.cn
[2] Peng Cheng Laboratory, Network Communication Research Centre, Shenzhen 518052, Guangdong, China

Abstract. This paper studies the computation offloading and resource allocation of Multi-access Edge Computing Networks (MEC) networks under stochastic task arrivals and imperfect channle state conditions (CSI). We aim to minimize the energy consumptions of all mobile users (MUs) while satisfying the stability of all MUs' queues by optimizing the transmit power, computational frequency and offloading ratio. The problem is modeled as a a long-term average stochastic optimization problem which cannot be solved trivially. To address this, we firstly apply the Lyapunov framework to transform the long-term average optimization problem into a series of per-slot optimization subproblems, and then an iterative optimization method is proposed to decompose the perslot optimization subproblem into three toy problems. The simulation results demonstrate the convergence and performance of the proposed algorithm.

Keywords: multi-access edge computing · computation offloading · resource allocation · imperfect CSI

1 Introduction

With the continuous demand for emerging services such as virtual reality, augmented reality, ultra-high-definition video live broadcast, and ultra-low-latency online games, mobile terminals need to run more and more tasks that are both latency-sensitive and consume a lot of computing resources [1]. However, the growth of the battery capacity of MUs is far from meeting the requirements for handling those tasks [2]. To address this, the European Telecommunications Standards Institute (ETSI) proposed a new paradigm namely Multi-access Edge

This work is supported by the National Natural Science Foundation of China under Grant 62171158 and the Research Fund Program of Guangdong Key Laboratory of Aerospace Communication and Networking Technology under Grant 2018B030322004.

A. Li et al. (Eds.): 6GN 2022, LNICST 504, pp. 14–25, 2023.
https://doi.org/10.1007/978-3-031-36011-4_2

Computing (MEC) in 2016. By deploying computing servers at the edge of the network which are close to MUs, MEC allows MUs to offload computational sensitive tasks to the MEC server, thereby greatly reducing the computing burden on the user side [3]. Meanwhile, compared with the high latency of mobile cloud computing (MCC) to complete tasks, MEC allows MUs to offload tasks to MEC servers through wireless interfaces (4G, 5G, WIFI, etc.), thereby reducing the transmission delay between users and servers. However, it should be noted that although MEC can greatly improve the MUs' quality of experience, it faces many technical challenges in the actual implementation process. The computation offloading and resource allocation strategy of MEC is the core problem among many theoretical problems to be solved [4]. Specifically, the objective of computation offloading is to design a strategy which aims to solve the problem of "Where to execute". Moreover, the objective of resource allocation is to solve the problem of "How to Execute" [1–4]. The connotation of the successful completion of the task has two aspects. One is that the task can be completed within the specified delay, the other is the MUs' queue can be kept stable during the long-term task execution process. The performance of MEC can be greatly improved by jointly optimizing the computation offloading and resource allocation strategy [5]

At present, many scholars have made contributions in this field [6] is a pioneering work in this direction. Sardellitti et al. considered the resource allocation problem in multi-cell MEC for the first time, respectively in single-user and multi-user scenarios. The objective is to minimize the total energy consumption, and the optimal strategy is obtained by the convex optimization method under the condition of satisfying the task processing delay. However, in [6], all tasks are processed by the edge server by default, and all MUs are considered to process only one fixed task without considering the dynamic task arrivals [7] further considers the queue stability problem caused by the dynamic arrival of tasks. Jeongho et al. introduced Lyapunov optimization into the joint offloading and resource allocation of MEC for the first time, and proposed the DREAM algorithm, which reduced the energy consumption by 35% compared with the benchmark algorithm. However, the mobile cloud computing scenario considered in [7] does not consider the fading effect brought by the wireless uplink. In [8], under the premise of considering the wireless uplink, considering the singleserver multi-user scenario, an online joint optimization strategy is designed by optimizing the offload ratio, computational frequency, transmit power and spectrum allocation strategy, and the average queue length and energy consumption are considerd. Simulation results demonstrate the relationship between average queue length and energy consumption. In [9], the terminal is further extended from the smart phone to the IoT device. First, the problem is modeled as a longterm average optimization problem, and the online joint computing and resource allocation algorithm is designed using Lyapunov optimization. The simulation results prove the convergence and effectiveness of the algorithm.

As can be seen from the previous review, the current research in this direction mainly considers using the Lyapunov optimization framework to reduce the energy consumption of all users while ensuring queue stability. However, although the Lyapunov optimization framework does not rely on the priori distribution of the channel state, it relies on the accurate CSI at the current moment. Due to the sophisticated communication scenario, MUs cannot guarantee to obtain a perfect CIS at each moment [10]. In [11], the CSI at each moment is defined as the channel estimation value plus an estimation error, where the estimation error is a random variable. Therefore, the channel state at each moment is also a random variable. There is no work to prove whether the Lyapunov optimization framework can still obtain the trade-off between queue stability and energy consumption when the channel state is unknown at the current moment. Based on the above two points, the main contributions of this paper can be summarized as follows.

– This paper considers the joint computing offloading and resource allocation of a single cell MEC system under the premise of imperfect CSI between MUs and base stations, the problem is modeled as a long-term average stochastic optimization problem. We prove that the Lyapunov optimization framework can still maintain the stability of the queue and obtain a trade-off between the average energy comsumptions and the queue stability by applying Jenson's inequality.
– Then, the Lyapunov optimization framework is applied to transform the long-term average optimization problem into a per-slot optimization problem, and the corresponding per-slot optimization problem is solved by an iterative optimization method. Specifically, by dividing the original problem into sub-problems of calculation frequency optimization, offloading ratio optimization, and optimization of transmission power, each subproblem is solved separately.
– The simulation results show the convergence and performance superiority of the algorithm. It confirms the tradeoff relationship between average queue length and total energy consumptions in Lyapunov optimization under imperfect CSI. Moreover, we compare the performance of the proposed method with three benchmark algorithms.

The rest of the paper is organized as follows. Section 2 presents the system model and formulate the problem as long-term average optimization problem. Section 3 converts the problem into a per-slot optimization problem by applying the Lyapunov optimization framework, and propose an iterative optimization method to solve the per-slot optimization problem. Section 4 gives the numerical results of the proposed method. Finally, this paper is conclued in Section 5.

2 System Model and Problem Formulation

2.1 Network Model

Figure 1 gives an illustration of the considered network model. Specifically, we consider a single-cell network consists of one MEC server located in the BS and N MUs. We assume the tasks in this paper can be offloaded to the BS in the partial offloading manner, where tasks can be executed simultaneously both in MEC server and local processor under an offloading ratio [12]. We consider a discrete time slot system $\mathcal{T} = \{1, 2, 3, \cdots, T\}$ and ΔT denotes the time interval of a single time slot. In each time slot $t \in \mathcal{T}$ tasks arrive dynamically with $\mathbb{E}\{A_i(t)\} = \lambda, \forall i \in [1, N]$, where $A_i(t) = (S_i(t), C_i(t), L_i(t))$. $S_i(t), C_i(t)$ and $L_i(t)$ denote the size (bits), CPU cycles per bit and the maximum tolerant latency, respectively. Each MU has a local execution queue and a remote offloading queue to buffer the incoming computational tasks.

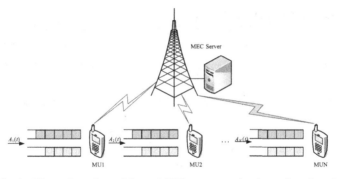

Fig. 1. An illustration of a multi-user MEC system under dynamic task arrivals.

2.2 Communication Model

In the beginning of each time slot, MUs offload the task to the MEC server through wireless uplink. In this paper, we assume the imperfect CSI between MUs and the BS, which is given by

$$h_i(t) = \hat{h}_i(t) + \phi, \forall i \in [1, N] \tag{1}$$

where $\hat{h}_i(t)$ is the channel estimate value of i-th MU, which considers the large scale fading and small scale fading. ϕ is the channel estimation error denoted by $\phi \sim \mathcal{CN}\left(0, \sigma_z^2\right)$, where σ_z^2 is the variance. According to [14], the uplink transmission rate can be given by

$$R_i(t) = \frac{B}{N} \log_2\left(1 + \frac{|h_i(t)|^2 p_i(t)}{|\phi|^2 p_i(t) + \frac{N_0 B}{N}}\right), \forall i \in [1, N] \tag{2}$$

where B denotes the bandwidth of MUs, $p_i(t)$ is the transmit power, N_0 is the white noise spectrum density. In this paper, we assume the bandwidth is equally allocated to N MUs, the spectrum resource allocation issue will be discussed in our future work. The probability density function (PDF) of $|\phi|^2$ can be formulated as

$$p\left(|\phi|^2 = r\right) = \frac{1}{2\sigma_z^2} \exp\left(-\frac{r}{2\sigma_z^2}\right), 0 < r < \infty. \tag{3}$$

The uplink transmission time between i-th MU and the BS can thus be modelled as:

$$T_i^U(t) = \frac{\beta_i(t)S_i(t)}{R_i(t)}, \forall i \in [1, N]. \tag{4}$$

The transmit energy consumption in each time slot can thus be given as:

$$E_i^U(t) = p_i(t)T_i^U(t), \forall i \in [1, N]. \tag{5}$$

According [4], we do not consider the downlink transmission time in this paper, the reason is that compared with the uplink offloading process, the size of the result after processing can be neglected, and therefore the downlink transmission time is negligible.

2.3 Computational and Queueing Model

According to [5], the computational energy consumption of i-th MU can be given as

$$E_i^L(t) = \epsilon(1 - \beta_i(t))C(t)f_i(t)^2, \tag{6}$$

where ϵ is the compuataion coefficient the CPU, $f_i(t)$ is the computation frequency of i-th MU. In this paper, we focus on the energy consumption in the MUs' side, and thus the energy consumption in the MEC server is not taken into consideration. Moreover, we assume the computation capacity in the MEC server is sufficient so that the exeuction delay in MEC server is negligiable. Therefore, the local execution delay can be given as

$$T_i^L(t) = \frac{(1 - \beta_i(t))C_i(t)S_i(t)}{f_i(t)} \tag{7}$$

According to [15], the local execution queue can be modeled as

$$Q_i^l(t + 1) = \max\left[Q_i^l(t) + I_i^l(t) - O_i^l(t), 0\right], i \in [1, N], \tag{8}$$

where $I_i^l(t) = (1 - \beta_i(t))\sum_{k=1}^{A_i(t)} S_k$ represents the input data in t-th time slot.

$O_i^l(t) = \frac{f_i(t)\Delta T}{C_i}$ represents the output data in t-th time slot. Similarly, the remote offloading queue can be modeled as

$$Q_i^r(t + 1) = \max\left[Q_i^r(t) + I_i^r(t) - O_i^r(t), 0\right], i \in [1, N], \tag{9}$$

where $I_i^r(t) = \sum_{k=1}^{A_i(t)} S_i\beta_i(t), O_i^r(t) = R_i(t)\Delta T$.

2.4 Problem Formulation

According to the communication and computational model, the total energy consumption in a single time slot can be given as

$$E_i^T(t) = E_i^U(t) + E_i^L(t) \tag{10}$$

The total execution delay in time slot t can be given as

$$T_{total}(t) = \max(T_U(t), T_l(t)) \tag{11}$$

Therefore, the long-term average energy-efficient computation offloading problem can be formulated as

$$\mathbf{P1} \min_{f(t),\boldsymbol{\beta}(t),p(t),\, T\to\infty} \frac{1}{T}\sum_{t=0}^{T-1}\sum_{i=1}^{N}\left\{E_i^T(t)\right\} \tag{12a}$$

$$s.t. 0 \leq f_i(t) \leq f_{\max}, \forall t \in [1, T], \forall i \in [1, N] \tag{12b}$$

$$0 \leq p_i(t) \leq p_{\max}, \forall t \in [1, T], \forall i \in [1, N] \tag{12c}$$

$$0 \le \beta_{i,k}(t) \le 1, \forall t \in [1, T], \forall i \in [1, N], \forall k \in [1, A(t)] \tag{12d}$$

$$\frac{(1 - \beta_{i,k}(t))C_i(t)S_i(t)}{f_i(t)} \le L_i(t), \forall t \in [1, T], \forall i \in [1, N], \forall k \in [1, A(t)] \tag{12e}$$

$$\Pr\left(\frac{\beta_{i,k}(t)S_i(t)}{R_i(t)} > L_i(t)\right) < \eta, \forall t \in [1, T], \forall i \in [1, N], \forall k \in [1, A(t)] \tag{12f}$$

$$\lim_{T \to \infty} \frac{E\{|Q_i^l(t)|\}}{T} = 0, \lim_{T \to \infty} \frac{E\{|Q_i^r(t)|\}}{T} = 0 \tag{12g}$$

The objective is to minimize the average total energy consumption of all MUs while satsifying the queue stability constraints. Specifically, (12b) and (12c) gives the constraints on computational frequency and transmit power of MUs, respectively. (12d) gives the constraint on local execution time. (12e) gives the constraint on remote offloading time, since $R_i(t)$ is a random variable, (12e) is given in the probability form. (12f) gives the constraint on queue stability [15]. **P**1 is a stochastic optimization problem and cannot be solved directly through conventional optimization technique [8].

3 Proposed Iterative Optimization Method

To solve **P**1, we first apply Lyapunov optimization framework. Specifically, according to [15], we first define the Lyapunov function as follows

$$L(Q(t)) = \frac{1}{2}\sum_{i=1}^{N}\left(Q_i^l(t)^2 + Q_i^r(t)^2\right) \tag{13}$$

Then we can define the Lyapunov Drift which is given by

$$L(Q(t+1)) - L(Q(t)) = \frac{1}{2}\sum_{i=1}^{N}\left(\Delta Q_i^l(t) + \Delta Q_i^r(t)\right) \tag{14a}$$

$$\Delta Q_i^l(t) = \max\left[Q_i^l(t) + I_i^l(t) - O_i^l(t), 0\right]^2 - Q_i^l(t)^2 \tag{14b}$$

$$\Delta Q_i^r(t) = \max\left[Q_i^r(t) + I_i^r(t) - O_i^r(t), 0\right]^2 - Q_i^r(t)^2 \tag{14c}$$

The conditional Lyapunov Drift is then expressed as

$$\Delta Q(t) = \{L(Q(t+1)) - L(Q(t))|Q(t)\} \tag{15}$$

By applying

$$\max[x - y + z, 0]^2 \le x^2 + y^2 + z^2 + 2x(z - y) \tag{16a}$$

$$\mathbb{E}\{A_i(t)|Q(t)\} = \{A_i(t)\} = \lambda_i \tag{16b}$$

We can given an upper bound of $\Delta Q(t)$, which is given by

$$
\Delta(\boldsymbol{Q}(t)) \leq K + \sum_{i=1}^{N} \lambda_i \left(Q_i^l(t) + Q_i^r(t) \right)
$$
$$
- \left\{ \sum_{i=1}^{N} Q_i^l(t) O_i^l(t) + Q_i^r(t) O_i^r(t) | Q(t) \right\}
\tag{17}
$$

where K is a constant. To obtain a tradeoff between energy consumption and queue length, we define the Lyapunov Drift-Plus-Penalty function as follows.

$$
\Delta(\boldsymbol{Q}(t)) + V \left\{ E_i^T(t) | \boldsymbol{Q}(t) \right\} \leq K + V \{ \hat{e}((t)) | \boldsymbol{Q}(t) \}
$$
$$
+ \sum_{i=1}^{N} \lambda_i \left(Q_i^l(t) + Q_i^r(t) \right) - \left\{ \sum_{i=1}^{N} Q_i^l(t) O_i^l(t) + Q_i^r(t) O_i^r(t) | \boldsymbol{Q}(t) \right\}
\tag{18}
$$

According to the max-weight algorithm proposed in [15], we can convert the long-term stochastic optimization problem into per-slot optimization problem by minimizing the following term in each time slot.

$$
\omega(\mathbb{X}(t)) = V \left(E_i^T(t) \right)
$$
$$
- \sum_{i=1}^{N} Q_i^l(t) \left(\hat{b}_i^l(\mathbb{X}(t)) - I_i^l(t) \right) - \sum_{i=1}^{N} Q_i^r(t) \left(\hat{b}_i^{r'}(\mathbb{X}(t)) - I_i^r(t) \right)
\tag{19}
$$

where $\mathbb{X}(t) = [\boldsymbol{f}(t), \boldsymbol{\beta}(t), \boldsymbol{p}(t)]$, $\hat{b}_i^l(\mathbb{X}(t)) = f_i(t)\Delta T$ and $\hat{b}_i^{r'}(\mathbb{X}(t)) = \Delta T Q_i^r(t) R_i(t)$.
Thus, $\boldsymbol{P}$ can be transformed into

$$
\textbf{P2} \min_{f(t), \boldsymbol{\beta}(t), \boldsymbol{p}(t),} w(\mathbb{X}(t))
\tag{20a}
$$

$$
s.t. 0 \leq f_i(t) \leq f_{\max}, \forall t \in [1, T], \forall i \in [1, N]
\tag{20b}
$$

$$
0 \leq p_i(t) \leq p_{\max}, \forall t \in [1, T], \forall i \in [1, N]
\tag{20c}
$$

$$
0 \leq \beta_{i,k}(t) \leq 1, \forall t \in [1, T], \forall i \in [1, N], \forall k \in [1, A(t)]
\tag{20d}
$$

$$
\frac{\left(1 - \beta_{i,k}(t)\right) C_i(t) S_i(t)}{f_i(t)} \leq L_i(t), \forall t \in [1, T], \forall i \in [1, N], \forall k \in [1, A(t)]
\tag{20e}
$$

$$
\Pr\left(\frac{\beta_{i,k}(t) S_i(t)}{R_i(t)} > L_i(t) \right) < \eta, \forall t \in [1, T], \forall i \in [1, N], \forall k \in [1, A(t)]
\tag{20f}
$$

However, **P2** is still a non-convex optimization problem due to (20a) and (20f). To address this, we propose an iterated optimzation method to optimize $\mathbb{X}(t)$ separately. Specifically, the computation frequency optimization subproblem can be formulated as

$$
\textbf{P3}: \min_{f(t)} \Delta T V \sum_{i=1}^{N} \left(\varepsilon f_i(t)^3 \right) - \sum_{i=1}^{N} Q_i^l(t) \left(\frac{f_i(t)\Delta T}{C_i(t)} \right)
\tag{21a}
$$

$$\text{s.t.} 0 \le f_i(t) \le f_{\max}, \forall i \in [1, N] \tag{21b}$$

$$\frac{\left(1 - \beta_{i,k}(t)\right)C_i(t)S_i(t)}{f_i(t)} + \frac{Q_i^l(t-1)}{f_{\max}} \le L_i(t), \forall i \in [1, N], \forall k \in [1, A(t)] \tag{21c}$$

Note that $f(t)$ can be decoupled in **P3**, we can define the component-wise objective function as follows

$$F_1(f_i(t)) = \varepsilon \Delta T V f_i^3(t) - Q_i^l(t)\Delta T f_i(t)/C_i(t) \tag{22}$$

By taking the first derivative, we can find the stationary point $f_i^*(t) = \sqrt{\frac{Q_i^l(t)}{3\varepsilon V C_i(t)}}$ (21c) can be rearranged as

$$f_i(t) \ge \frac{\left(1 - \beta_{i,k}(t)\right)C_i(t)S_i(t)}{L_i(t) - \frac{Q_i^l(t-1)}{f_{\max}}} \triangleq \Omega \tag{23}$$

The optimal $f^*(t)$ is then determined by the relationship of $f_i(t)$ between Ω and $f_{\max}$. Specifically, when $\Omega \le f_{\max}$, (21b) can be rewritten as $\Omega \le f_i(t) \le f_{\max}$. Then, when $f_i^*(t) \in [\Omega, f_{\max}]$, we have $f^*(t) = f_i^*(t)$. When $f_i^*(t) \notin [\Omega, f_{\max}], f^*(t) \in \{\Omega, f_{\max}\}$, $F^* = \min\{F_1(\Omega), F_1(f_{\max})\}$. Furthermore, when $\Omega > f_{\max}$, (21c) can be ignored. By letting $\Omega = 0$ in the previous results, we can obtain $f^*(t)$ when $\Omega > f_{\max}$.

Now we consider the offloading ratio optimization subproblem, which is formualted as

$$\textbf{P4} : \min_{(t)} \sum_{n=1}^{N} Q_i^l(t)\left(\sum_{k=1}^{A_i(t)} \left(1 - \beta_{i,k}(t)\right)S_i(t)\right) + \sum_{n=1}^{N} Q_i^r(t)\left(\sum_{k=1}^{A_t(t)} S_i(t)\beta_{i,k}(t)\right) \tag{24a}$$

$$\text{s.t.} 0 \le \beta_{i,k}(t) \le 1, \forall k \in [1, A_i(t)], \forall i \in [1, N] \tag{24b}$$

$$\frac{\left(1 - \beta_{i,k}(t)\right)C_i(t)S_i(t)}{f_i(t)} + \frac{Q_i^l(t-1)}{f_{\max}} \le L_i(t), \forall k \in [1, A_i(t)], \forall i \in [1, N] \tag{24c}$$

$$\Pr\left(\frac{\beta_{i,k}(t)S_i(t)}{R_i(t)} + \frac{Q_i^r(t-1)}{R_{\max}(t)} \ge L_i(t)\right) \le \eta, k \in [1, A_i(t)], \forall i \in [1, N] \tag{24d}$$

It is not difficult to observed that (24a) is a convex objective function, (24b) and (24c) are convex constraints. According to (3), (24d) can be reformulated as

$$\beta_{i,k}(t)S_i(t) + \frac{x_1 \log_2(1+c)B_g}{N} < \frac{\log_2(1+c)BL_i(t)}{N} \tag{25}$$

where $x_1 = \frac{Q_i^r(t-1)}{R_{\max}(t)}, c = \frac{|h_i(t)|^2}{\frac{N_0 B}{N p_i(t)} - 2\sigma_z^2 \ln \eta}$ are not related to $\beta_{i,k}(t)$. Therefore, (24d) is also a convex constraint, which shows **P4** is a convex optimization problem, which can be solved by optimization toolbox, e.g., CVX.

Finally, we focus on the transmit power optimization problem, which is given by

$$\textbf{P5}: \min_{p(t)} \Delta TV \sum_{i=1}^{N} (p_i(t)) - \sum_{i=1}^{N} Q_i^r(t)(\Delta T(R_i(t))) \tag{26a}$$

$$\text{s.t.} 0 \leq p_i(t) \leq p_{\max}, \forall i \in [1, N], \forall t \in [1, T] \tag{26b}$$

$$\Pr\left(\frac{\beta_{i,k}(t)S_i(t)}{R_i(t)} + \frac{Q_i^r(t-1)}{R_{\max}(t)} \geq L_i(t)\right) \leq \eta, k \in [1, A(t)], \forall i \in [1, N] \tag{26c}$$

Note that (26a) has random variables, therefore we can only minmize its expectation. Furthermore, since $R_i(t)$ is a convex function with respect to $|\phi|^2$, therefore we can apply Jenson's equality to convext (26a) into

$$\Delta TV \sum_{i=1}^{N} (p_i(t)) - \sum_{i=1}^{N} Q_i^r(t)\left(\Delta T\left(\frac{B}{N}\log_2\left(1 + \frac{|h_i(t)|^2 p_i(t)}{2\sigma_z^2 p_i(t) + \frac{N_0 B}{N}}\right)\right)\right) \tag{27}$$

It is trivial to prove that (27) is a convex function with respect to $p_i(t)$, $\forall i \in [1, N]$ Moreover, (26c) can be converted as

$$\frac{\beta_{i,k}(t)S_i(t)}{L_i(t)B} - \frac{1}{N}\log_2\left(1 + \frac{p_i(t)\left|h_g^i(t)\right|^2}{N_0 B_g/N - p_i(t)2\sigma_z^2 \ln \eta}\right) \leq 0 \tag{28}$$

By taking the second derivative of (28) with respect to $p_i(t)$, we can prove (28) is a convex constraint. Therefore, **P5** now can be solved by minimizing its upper bound. Until now, we can solve **P2** in an iterative fashion.

4 Simulation Results

The main simulation parameters of this paper are given in Table 1. The simulation results are averaged over 10000 slots. Figure 2 shows the impact of V on the total average energy consumptions when $N = 5$, $\lambda = 3$. It is observed that the total energy consumptions decreases with the increase of V. When $V = 1e9$, we have the minimum energy consumption $3.4337e$ 6j and the algorithm converges. The reason is that when V becomes larger, the optimization goal foucus more on energy consumptions thereby resulting in a lower average energy consumptions which is consistent with the results in [15].

Figure 3 shows the impact of V on the total average queue length when $N = 5$, $\lambda = 3$. It is observed that the total average queue length increases with the increase of V. This results is consistent with the result of Fig. 2, which shows that by applying the Lyapunov optimization framework, we can obtain a $[O(1/V), O(V)]$ tradeoff. Therefore, we can dynamically adjust the value of V to acheive diffrent optimzation objectives.

Table 1. Parameters settings

Parameters	Values
Bandwidth B	$2*10^6$
Noise power density N_0	-174 dBm/Hz
Data input size $S(t)$	500–2000 KB
Maximum tolerant delay $L(t)$	0.01–0.1s
Maximum CPU frequency of MUs f_{max}	1 GHz
Maximum transmit power p_{max}	23 dBm
Computation factor $C(t)$	40
The variance of the channel estimation error σ_Z^2	10^{-7}
Computation energy coefficient ϵ	10^{-26}
The successful transmission rate η	0.001
The threshold of the iterative method ξ	0.001

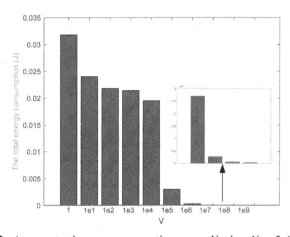

Fig. 2. Average total energy consumption versus V when $N = 5$, $\lambda = 3$.

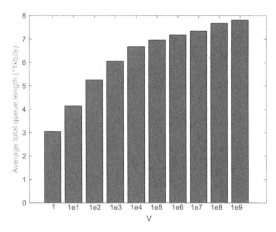

Fig. 3. Average total queue length versus V when $N = 5$, $\lambda = 3$.

5 Conclusion

In this paper, we mainly studied the dynamic computation offloading and resource allocation problem of a single cell MEC networks. Considering the stability of the queue, the problem is modeled as a long-term average stochastic optimization problem. In order to solve this problem, we leverage the Lyapunov optimization framework to obtain the trade-off between queue stability and total energy consumption under the condition of imperfect channel state. Specifically, Lyapunov optimization is used to transform the long-term average problem into a single-time optimization problem, which is solved iteratively by decomposing the optimization problem into three sub-problems. In order to deal with the non-convex constraint in the transmit power optimization subproblem, we relax the non-convex objective function by applying Jenson's equality, and transforms the non-convex problem into a convex optimization problem. Finally, simulation results verify the convergence and effectiveness of the algorithm.

References

1. Abbas, N., Zhang, Y., Taherkordi, A., et al.: Mobile Edge Computing: a Survey. IEEE Internet Things J. **5**(1), 450–465 (2018)
2. Mach, P., Becvar, Z.: Mobile edge computing: a survey on architecture and computation offloading. IEEE Commun. Surv. Tutor. **19**(3), 1628–1656 (2017)
3. Mao, Y., You, C., Zhang, J., Huang, K., Letaief, K.B.: A survey on mobile edge computing: the communication perspective. IEEE Commun. Surv. Tutor **19**(4), 2322–2358 (2017)
4. Dinh, T.Q., Tang, J., La, Q.D., Quek, T.Q.S.: Offloading in mobile edge computing: task allocation and computational frequency scaling. IEEE Trans. Commun. **65**(8), 3571–3584 (2017)
5. Chen, X., Jiao, L., Li, W., Fu, X.: Efficient multi-user computation offloading for mobile-edge cloud computing. IEEE/ACM Trans. Networking **24**(5), 2795–2808 (2016)
6. Sardellitti, S., Scutari, G., Barbarossa, S.: Joint optimization of radio and computational resources for multicell mobile-edge computing. IEEE Trans. Sig. Inf. Process. Over Netw. **1**(2), 89–103 (2015)

7. Kwak, J., Kim, Y., Lee, J., et al.: DREAM: dynamic resource and task allocation for energy minimization in mobile cloud systems. IEEE J. Sel. Areas Commun. **33**(12), 2510–2523 (2015)

8. Mao, Y., Zhang, J., Song, S.H., et al.: Stochastic joint radio and computational resource management for multi-user mobile-edge computing systems. IEEE Trans. Wireless Commun. **16**(9), 5994–6009 (2017)

9. Chen, Y., Zhang, N., Zhang, Y., et al.: Dynamic computation offloading in edge computing for internet of things. IEEE Internet Things J. **6**(3), 4242–4251 (2019)

10. Yang, Z., Ding, Z., Fan, P., et al.: On the performance of non-orthogonal multiple access systems with partial channel information. IEEE Trans. Commun. **64**(2), 654–667 (2016)

11. Fang, F., Wang, K., Ding, Z., et al.: Energy-efficient resource allocation for NOMAMEC networks with imperfect CSI. IEEE Trans. Commun. **69**(5), 3436–3449 (2021)

12. Mao, Y., Zhang, J., Song, S.H., Letaief, K.B.: Stochastic joint radio and computational resource management for multi-user mobile-edge computing systems. IEEE Trans. Wireless Commun. **16**(9), 5994–6009 (2017)

13. Guo, K., Gao, R., Xia, W., Quek, T.Q.S.: Online learning based computation offloading in MEC systems with communication and computation dynamics. IEEE Trans. Commun. **69**(2), 1147–1162 (2021)

14. Xie, R., Tang, Q., Liang, C., Yu, F.R., Huang, T.: Dynamic computation offloading in IoT Fog systems with imperfect channel-state information: a POMDP approach. IEEE Internet Things J. **8**(1), 345–356 (2021)

15. Neely, M.: Stochastic network optimization with application to communication and queueing systems. Morgan & Claypool (2010)

Technical Design of an Ad-Hoc Network Topology Simulation System

Zhongyu Yin[1(✉)] and Shuo Shi[1,2]

[1] School of Electronic and Information Engineering, Harbin Institute of Technology,
Harbin 150001, Heilongjiang, China
a87557766@163.com, crcss@hit.edu.cn
[2] Peng Cheng Laboratory, Network Communication Research Centre, Shenzhen 518052,
Guangdong, China

Abstract. In order to study the adaptation of Ad-hoc networks to different topologies at the network layer, this paper designs a platform based on Raspberry PI hardware to meet the demand of hardware-in-the-loop networking simulation of Ad-hoc networks on the desktop. Firstly, this paper will demonstrate the importance of physical topology scenario simulation in Ad-hoc network technology development and deployment. Secondly, this paper will propose a physical topology scene control and performance monitoring scheme based on the Netfilter module used for network layer data processing in Linux system. This scheme will be programmed and deployed to Raspberry PI node, and then automatically executed by a set of graphical control system on Ubuntu 20.04 host. Finally, this paper will rely on the above system to simulate the representative network topology in certain practical applications, and test the performance indexes of OLSR and its evolved version OLSR V2 respectively, so as to evaluate the performance of the two protocols in specific systems.

Keywords: Ad-hoc · Network Simulation · OLSR

1 Source and Purpose of the Project

The proliferation of electronic devices and corresponding communication technologies has become a sign of The Times we live in. Taking the ground mobile communication network as an example, people can easily achieve long-distance, low-delay and high-rate wireless communication through mobile phones and base stations all over the continent. In general, such networks, which rely on base stations for access and grids for power supply, are convenient, fast and reliable. However, under special circumstances, the mobile communication network that depends on the infrastructure is deficient in reliability [1]. Relating to this topic, on the other hand, self-organizing network technology as a kind of network mode is different from the ground mobile communication network, does not depend on infrastructure [2], can adapt to different topologies and jump forward network technology, more because of its anti-damage ability showed its emergency communication [3], military police and other special value in the field of communications [4].

A. Li et al. (Eds.): 6GN 2022, LNICST 504, pp. 26–37, 2023.
https://doi.org/10.1007/978-3-031-36011-4_3

Therefore, the embodiment of this technology at the network layer, that is, the adaptation of Ad-hoc network routing protocol to different topologies, is worth further research and testing.

The so-called Wireless Ad-hoc Network refers to a Wireless communication Network with the following characteristics [5]:

(1) No center. All nodes participating in the network have equal rights in principle, and there is no dispatching node as the control center, which is also the source of strong damage resistance of Ad-hoc networks.
(2) Independent networking. After the nodes are powered on and running, they independently form an independent network according to the pre-written protocol logic.
(3) Multi-hop routing. The communication between two nodes outside the direct communication distance can be relayed and forwarded by multiple ordinary intermediate nodes. Each intermediate node is called a hop, and the whole route process can be multiple hops.
(4) Dynamic topology. Firstly, topology generally refers to network topology in the field of communication, which belongs to the category of graph theory in theory. It is a concept that abstracts the physical devices participating in the network as points and the direct links between devices as chains to describe the connection relationship between physical devices in the network. However, in Ad-hoc networks, nodes can join or exit at any time, and the original direct connection between any two neighbor nodes may be interrupted due to factors such as movement or occlusion, which leads to dynamic network topology [6].

The term topology needs a little more explanation here. In this paper, the term topology can be divided into two categories:

(1) Physical topology, especially the communication links and topological associations in the physical channels of actual communication;
(2) Protocol topology, especially the network topology detected by routing protocols.

In normal cases, the protocol topology detected by the routing protocol of Ad-hoc networks is the actual topology, which is also the basis for routing protocol to select routes. In the simulation environment, the physical topology can be easily specified by simulation scenarios, but in the experiment of the actual system development stage, in order to test the performance of routing protocols under different topologies [7], it is necessary to physically create the specified topology by means of pulling distance, occlusion, shielding, etc., which is extremely inconvenient.

On this basis, the research focus of this paper is to design a platform based on Raspberry PI hardware, and realize the simulation of Ad-hoc networking in different topology scenarios on the desktop.

Therefore, in the design of this paper, a new topology is artificially added between the above two topologies, that is, the simulation scene topology. The system topology association after the addition is shown in Fig. 1:

As shown in Fig. 1, in a development environment, the physical topology of each simulated node can be considered fully connected due to its close proximity. Based on this fully connected physical topology, different simulated scene topologies can be artificially

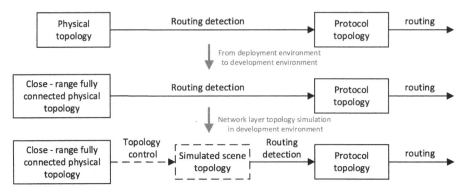

Fig. 1. The connection of several topologies in this article.

created by filtering incoming packets in the Linux network layer. For routing protocols, the simulated scene topology generated by masking is equivalent to the physical topology, so it can replace the pull test to simulate the behavior of routing protocols in different topology scenarios and test their performance, which is also the meaning and goal of this design topic.

2   Overview of Topology Simulation Principles

2.1   Description of Topology

A common mathematical description of network topology is the adjacency matrix. Adjacency matrix is a matrix representation of graph in graph theory.

In this paper, since there is no unidirectional link in the network topology between nodes, the network topology can be abstracted as an undirected graph $G(V,E)$, and its matrix expression, that is, the undirected adjacency matrix G [8], is a square matrix with the following properties:

(1) G is a real symmetric square matrix of order N with diagonal element 0;
(2) Each element of G can be 0 or 1 only;
(3) G_{ij} represents the topological connection between node i and node j. If the topology exists, that is, there is a direct link, then $G_{ij} = 1$;
(4) If no direct link exists, $G_{ij} = 0$. In this case, the corresponding data packets need to be masked in the system.

For example, in the case of three points, $\begin{bmatrix} 0 & 1 & 1 \\ 1 & 0 & 1 \\ 1 & 1 & 0 \end{bmatrix}$ said the connection topology

relationship, and $\begin{bmatrix} 0 & 1 & 0 \\ 1 & 0 & 1 \\ 0 & 1 & 0 \end{bmatrix}$ said chain topology relationship.

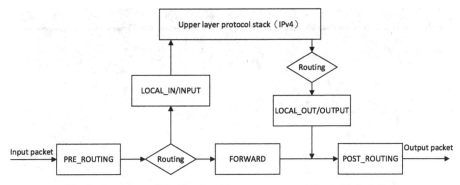

Fig. 2. Location of Netfilter/iptables processes and Hooks/linked lists.

2.2 Topology Control and Performance Monitoring Principle Based on Netfilter

Aiming at the network layer topology control method, this paper proposes a topology control scheme based on Netfilter module of network layer of Linux system:

In principle, Netfilter/iptables is a processing mechanism with firewall function introduced into network layer data flow processing after Linux2.4.x [12]. From the perspective of implementation, Netfilter/iptables is a subsystem of Linux kernel. It consists of three parts: Netfilter framework, iptables linked list and iptables command line tool. Netfilter is fully compatible with the IP protocol and provides users with functions such as filtering, address translation, and processing before data is delivered to the IP protocol for processing [9]. Netfilter sets a total of 5 hook points on the IPv4 protocol stack, and several functions can be set on each hook point according to the priority to realize the processing of packets flowing through. Their positions are shown in the Fig. 2.

On this basis, the topology control tool selected in this paper is the iptables command line tool provided by Netfilter in the application layer. Simply put, the iptables command line tool and the principle behind it abstracts each Hook node through which Netfilter data flows as a chain, and the data processing functions in the chain are encapsulated in the form of a rule table that can be added and modified. In particular, iptables defines up to four tables with different functions on each chain, namely:

(1) Filter table: responsible for filtering the packets flowing through according to the rules to realize the firewall function;
(2) NAT table: Network address translation to realize network address translation;
(3) Mangle table: disassemble packets, modify them and repackage them;
(4) RAW: Disables the connection tracing mechanism on the NAT table.

It can be seen that the implementation of the filter function is the filter table. However, since the PRE_ROUTING chain does not provide filtering function for data security, discarding data can only be transferred to the INPUT chain and FORWARD chain. The reason why the data in the OUTPUT chain is not filtered is that the specific destination IP or MAC address cannot be identified due to the presence of UDP broadcast packets.

After the above analysis, it can be determined that the data on the INPUT and FORWARD chains is all the data flowing into the local machine. However, for the sake of rigor, an additional question needs to be answered, that is, the data flowing through

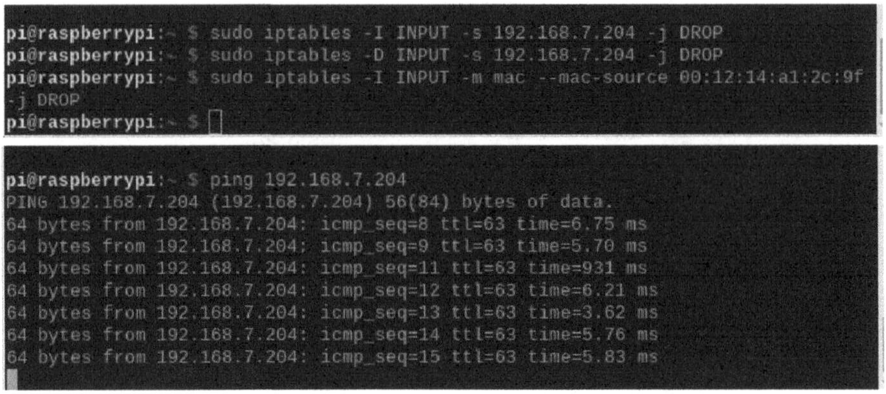

```
pi@raspberrypi:~ $ sudo iptables -I INPUT -s 192.168.7.204 -j DROP
pi@raspberrypi:~ $ sudo iptables -D INPUT -s 192.168.7.204 -j DROP
pi@raspberrypi:~ $ sudo iptables -I INPUT -m mac --mac-source 00:12:14:a1:2c:9f
-j DROP
pi@raspberrypi:~ $ []
```

```
pi@raspberrypi:~ $ ping 192.168.7.204
PING 192.168.7.204 (192.168.7.204) 56(84) bytes of data.
64 bytes from 192.168.7.204: icmp_seq=8 ttl=63 time=6.75 ms
64 bytes from 192.168.7.204: icmp_seq=9 ttl=63 time=5.70 ms
64 bytes from 192.168.7.204: icmp_seq=11 ttl=63 time=931 ms
64 bytes from 192.168.7.204: icmp_seq=12 ttl=63 time=6.21 ms
64 bytes from 192.168.7.204: icmp_seq=13 ttl=63 time=3.62 ms
64 bytes from 192.168.7.204: icmp_seq=14 ttl=63 time=5.76 ms
64 bytes from 192.168.7.204: icmp_seq=15 ttl=63 time=5.83 ms
```

Fig. 3. Topology control based on MAC addresses.

the INPUT chain is routed and the destination address is the data on the local machine. Does this mean that the INPUT chain is already behind the routing protocol process?

However, it can be found that protocol software such as OLSRD and OLSRD2 run completely on the application layer by combining with the related research on the implementation principle of typical OLSR routing protocol. In the process of running, it will act as a background application of the system to maintain the routing table of the system through UDP protocol, such as broadcast detection, instead of directly modifying the data flow.

The experiment also proves the validity of this topology control principle for OLSR protocol. In Iptables tool, developers can mask nodes by physical address, that is, MAC address. The command format is: "sudo iptables -A INPUT -m mac --mac-source <MAC Address>-j DROP" [10].

The topology control test results are shown in Fig. 3:

In addition to filtering, the linked lists of Iptables also count the number of packets in bytes and the size of packets in bytes when the rules match successfully. Iptables starts counting from the time a rule is added and stops until the rule is deleted or the result is emptied when an instruction with a "-z" argument is received. When receiving a command with the "-nvx-l" parameter, iptables will output the statistics to the console terminal through the standard input-output pipeline. With this method, we can monitor the link performance indicators in real time by adding matching rules for MAC addresses and port numbers, and clean up the data after the simulation.

3   Design of Ad-Hoc Network Topology Simulation System Based on Raspberry PI

3.1   System Architecture and Development Environment

After completing the research on topology representation and control principle in the previous chapter, the next topic will shift from theoretical analysis to the design and engineering implementation of the overall topology simulation system. The work of this

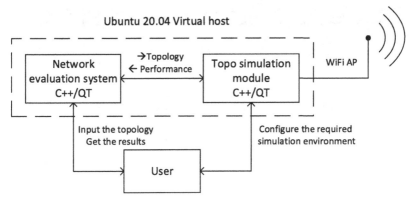

Fig. 4. Topology simulation system scheme diagram of the host.

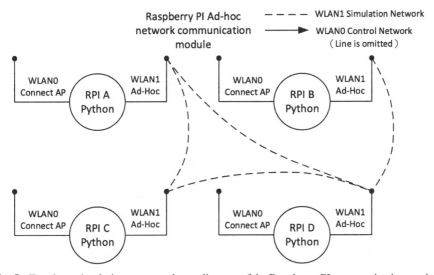

Fig. 5. Topology simulation system scheme diagram of the Raspberry PI communication module.

chapter is how to integrate the preceding independent functions into a system through a set of programs running on the host and Raspberry PI, so that users only need to interact with the graphical interface of the host, and can realize the topology control, communication behavior and real-time performance data return on the node with a simple click. To this end, I first give the specific scheme diagram:

Figure 4 and Fig. 5 show the scheme diagram of the control host program and the communication simulation module of Raspberry PI Ad-hoc network respectively. Two features of this design can be seen from it:

First, this design is not completely merged with the upper network performance evaluation system, but exists in the form of loadable modules. The upper-layer network evaluation platform is responsible for providing the interface for users to deploy topology

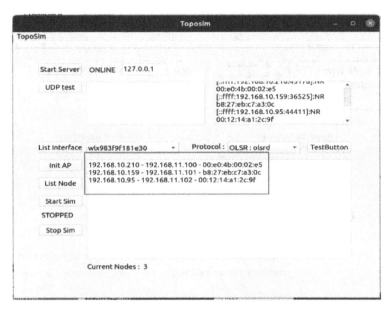

Fig. 6. Nodes probe and simulate network IP assignment results.

and dynamically detect performance statistics, while the topology simulation module acts as a computing engine and only provides necessary control functions related to physical simulation.

Second, as shown in Fig. 5, in order to simultaneously realize the transmission of control information and performance data between the host and Raspberry PI, as well as the Ad-hoc network simulation communication between Raspberry PI and Raspberry PI, two sets of networks are constructed on Raspberry PI with two network cards in this system:

(1) Raspberry PI built-in network card WLAN0: used to connect to the open WiFi hotspot of the host, forming a "control network". On this basis, the two ends of the program to transfer control data and performance data to each other by UDP protocol;
(2) Raspberry PI external network adapter WLAN1: The model of network adapter chip selected in this design is RT3070, which can run in AP mode and Ad-hoc mode after testing. This NIC is used to run Ad-hoc networking protocols to form an analog network among raspberry Pies.

The purpose of adopting the two-layer network scheme in this design is mainly to consider the IP assignment problem when the Ad-hoc network protocol is running. Before the traditional Ad-hoc network devices go online, they need to be configured with different IP addresses for each node in the same network segment. In real objects, this means that different nodes are equipped with different firmware programs, which requires manual configuration one by one. Expanding the number of nodes is time-consuming and laborious, but not flexible and convenient. After adopting the two-layer network, the DHCP service deployed by the host when establishing the WiFi hotspot enables each Raspberry PI with identical firmware to get automatically assigned IP address on the control network, and then respond to the node probe message of the host in this network to get the temporary simulated network IP address assigned by the host.

The control interface of the host is as shown in Fig. 6, this program interface is divided into three display boxes, in which the upper left is used to display key process prompts and error information, the upper right is the UDP communication data status monitoring bar, and the lower display bar is used to display the current scanned physical node status. In this figure, three nodes have been simulated, and their information from left to right are respectively the IP address of the control network, the assigned IP address of the simulated network and the MAC address of the network adapter used for simulation.

Up to now, the topology simulation system has been built, and the simulation test of OLSR and OLSR V2 protocols can be carried out based on this system.

4 Test the Performance of OLSR and OLSR V2 Routing Protocols

4.1 Scenario Classification and Deployment

The first step in the simulation is to specify a specific scenario. In this article, the test scenarios are divided into three categories:

(1) Equal networking:

The equal networking scenario is a scenario with fully connected physical topology between nodes. All nodes are neighbors and no additional topology control is required.

The adjacency matrix of the equal networking is: $\begin{bmatrix} 0 & 1 & 1 & 1 \\ 1 & 0 & 1 & 1 \\ 1 & 1 & 0 & 1 \\ 1 & 1 & 1 & 0 \end{bmatrix}$, which can test the single-hop performance.

(2) Hierarchical networking:

In this scenario, networking devices are divided into upper and lower layers, and the two layers are independently networked in Ad-hoc networking mode. Generally, the lower layer network uses a node in the upper layer network as the default forwarding node, making the lower layer network not completely equal. The adjacency matrix of the hierarchical network is as follows: $\begin{bmatrix} 0 & 1 & 1 & 1 \\ 1 & 0 & 0 & 0 \\ 1 & 0 & 0 & 0 \\ 1 & 0 & 0 & 0 \end{bmatrix}$, which can test the two-hop performance.

(3) Multi-hop relay forwarding:

The multi-hop relay is generally used to communicate through the hop-by-hop relay of multiple Ad-hoc network nodes when the physical distance between the sender and the receiver is too long or the direct link is blocked or interfered. The adjacency matrix

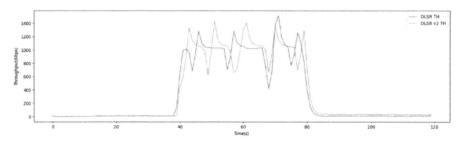

Fig. 7. Throughput curve of the egalitarian networking scenario.

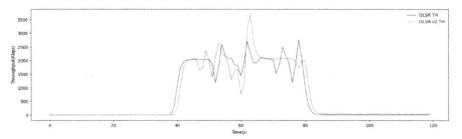

Fig. 8. Throughput curve of hierarchical networking (minimum unit) scenario.

of the multi-hop relayed forwarding scenario is as follows: $\begin{bmatrix} 0 & 1 & 0 & 0 \\ 1 & 0 & 1 & 0 \\ 0 & 1 & 0 & 1 \\ 0 & 0 & 1 & 0 \end{bmatrix}$, which can test

the triple hop performance.

4.2 The Test Results

Throughput. In this section, the simulation results of throughput performance index of OLSR protocol and OLSR V2 protocol are analyzed qualitatively according to their trends in different scenarios. The measured data in each scenario are shown in Fig. 7, 8 and 9.

Considering the impact of link congestion and performance fluctuation, the throughput curves in this chapter are averaged within three seconds. As shown in the figure above, when the hardware performance meets the test service rate, the throughput statistics obtained by OLSR and OLSR V2 at the network layer in the same scenario are approximately the same. During the execution of the test service, the typical throughput in the three scenarios increases in turn, and the ratio is approximately 1:2:3, which is consistent with the global throughput generated by the 1Mbps test service in the three scenarios of 1-hop, 2-hop and 3-hop, which can prove the effectiveness of the design of the topology simulation system from the side.

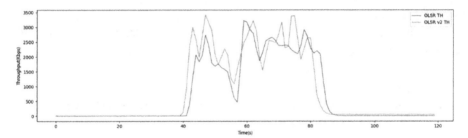

Fig. 9. Throughput curve of the multi-hop relay forwarding (three-hop) scenario.

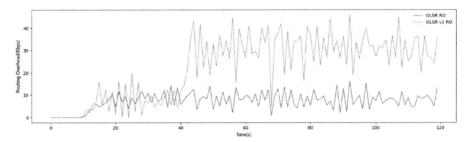

Fig. 10. Routing cost curve in egalitarian networking scenario.

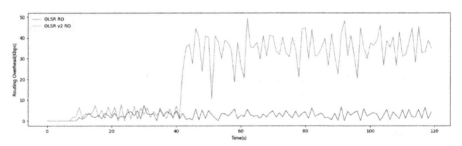

Fig. 11. Routing cost curve in hierarchical networking (minimum unit) scenario.

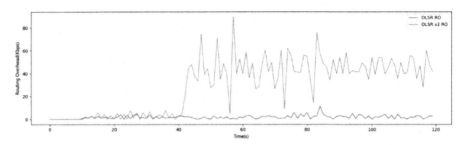

Fig. 12. Route cost curve in the multi-hop trunk forwarding (3-hop) scenario.

Rrouting Overhead. In this section, the simulation results of routing cost index will be qualitatively analyzed in different scenarios. The measured data are shown in Fig. 10, 11 and 12.

As can be seen from the figure, the routing packet sending of OLSR V2 seems to be significantly close to the traffic load. That is to say, only when the simulation time reaches 40s and a large number of traffic demands are generated, OLSR V2 will send a large number of packets to maintain the routing.

5 Conclusion

In this paper, the author theoretically discusses the implementation of topology simulation scheme, and according to the Linux operating system kernel, the Netfilter module has made research and analysis, put forward a set of topology control scheme based on Netfilter application layer interface iptables tool. After analysis and experiment, the author makes clear the meaning of iptables linked list rules, the way of node identification in the process of topology masking, and the universality of this scheme for the implementation of the selected protocol in this paper. At the end of this paper, using the developed system, the author conducted a hardest-in-kind simulation of OLSR and OLSR V2 protocols on the basis of control variables for three typical scenarios in Ad-hoc networks, namely, equal networking, hierarchical networking (minimum network unit) and multi-hop relay forwarding, and verified the effectiveness of the system designed in this paper.

Acknowledgement. This work is supported by the National Natural Science Foundation of China under Grant 62171158 and Research Fund Program of Guangdong Key Laboratory of Aerospace Communication and Networking Technology under Grant 2018B030322004.

References

1. Lei, L.: Application of wireless Ad-hoc network technology in emergency communication network. Heilongjiang Sci. **10**(14) (2019)
2. Ajith Kumar, S.P., Sachdeva, R.: Wireless adhoc networks: performance analysis considerations for AODV routing protocols. In: 2019 6th International Conference on Computing for Sustainable Global Development, INDIACom, pp. 140–144. IEEE (2019)
3. Leite, J.R.E., Martins, P.S., Ursini, E.L.: Planning of AdHoc and IoT Networks under emergency mode of operation. In: 2019 IEEE 10th Annual Information Technology, Electronics and Mobile Communication Conference, IEMCON, pp. 1071–1080. IEEE (2019)
4. Miao, Y., Sun, Z., Wang, N., Cruickshank, H.: Comparison studies of MANET-satellite and MANET-cellular networks integrations. In: 2015 International Conference on Wireless Communications & Signal Processing, WCSP, pp. 1–5. IEEE (2015)
5. Hanzo, L., Tafazolli, R.: A survey of QoS routing solutions for mobile ad hoc networks. IEEE Commun. Surv. Tutor. **9**(2), 50–70 (2007)
6. Toutouh, J., Garcia-Nieto, J., Alba, E.: Intelligent OLSR routing protocol optimization for VANETs. IEEE Trans. Veh. Technol. **61**(4), 1884–1894 (2012)

7. Taleb, T., Sakhaee, E., Jamalipour, A., Hashimoto, K., Kato, N., Nemoto, Y.: A stable routing protocol to support ITS services in VANET networks. IEEE Trans. Veh. Technol. **56**(6), 3337–3347 (2016)
8. Min, Z., Jiliu, Z.: A new dynamic routing protocol of wireless ad hoc network. In: 2009 Asia-Pacific Conference on Computational Intelligence and Industrial Applications, PACIIA, pp. 447–450. IEEE (2009)
9. Wang, B., Lu, K., Chang, P.: Design and implementation of Linux firewall based on the frame of Netfilter/IPtable. In: 2016 11th International Conference on Computer Science & Education, ICCSE, pp. 949–953. IEEE (2016)
10. Voronkov, A., Martucci, L.A., Lindskog, S.: Measuring the usability of firewall rule sets. IEEE Access **8**, 27106–27121 (2020)

Electromagnetic Propagation Path and Signal Attenuation Prediction Based on DEM Electronic Map

Ziqi Sun[1], Shengliang Fang[2], Weichao Yang[3], Gongliang Liu[1], and Ruofei Ma[1](✉)

[1] Harbin Institute of Technology, Weihai 264200, Shandong, China
maruofei@hit.edu.cn
[2] School of Space Information, Space Engineering University, Beijing 101416, China
[3] China Academy of Space Technology (Xi'an), Xi'an 710100, Shanxi, China

Abstract. With the development of information technology, the advantages of information warfare have become increasingly obvious. Wireless communication is the main means of communication in modern warfare. In military wireless communication where the electromagnetic environment of the battlefield is quite complex, the problem of electromagnetic prediction is particularly prominent. Based on the multi-domain grid of the battlefield environment with the help of Digital Geographic Elevation Model (DEM) data, combined with the accurate wireless propagation model, it can make predictions more accurately, and provide data support for wireless network coverage prediction and the discovery of communication blind spots. The main research is the ITU.RP-526 accurate prediction model, which divides obstacles into knife-edge type and round type, and calculates the total propagation attenuation of the path based on the modified free-space attenuation prediction formula. By comparing with Okumura model and Egli, COST model which considers terrain correction factor, it is verified that the calculation accuracy of this design algorithm is high and the result is reasonable. Complete point-to-point radio wave prediction and field strength coverage.

Keywords: Electromagnetic Prediction · DEM · ITU.RP-526 · Propagation Attenuation

1 Introduction

In military communications, both the transmitting antenna and the receiving antenna have the characteristics of movement, and the height of the receiving antenna is often extremely low, and the propagation of radio waves will often be constantly affected by terrain obstacles, buildings and surface vegetation. Applying the traditional artificial field strength prediction method to obtain the field strength prediction map as the basis for network design, not only the workload is large, the efficiency is low, and the results are somewhat random. Therefore, it is necessary to use Digital Elevation Model (DEM) data to obtain geographic information with a certain accuracy, and then through the analysis

A. Li et al. (Eds.): 6GN 2022, LNICST 504, pp. 38–51, 2023.
https://doi.org/10.1007/978-3-031-36011-4_4

of application scenarios and actual conditions, compare various existing radio wave propagation models. Prediction under the premise of good, this can further improve the efficiency of field strength prediction. Compared with traditional paper maps, electronic maps have the advantages of fast storage and display, realization of animations, and the ability to modify and supplement topographic and landform information at any time. With the informatization of wars, military digital maps will play an important role. Therefore, it is of great significance to study the electromagnetic attenuation prediction based on the electronic map under special terrain.

At present, the prediction of electromagnetic radiation is mainly based on ray tracing technology in indoor or urban research. The ray tracing method has become an important tool for propagation prediction due to its high precision [1–5]. The algorithm is mainly divided into four modules, namely the ray-plane intersection calculation module, ray information module, calculation module and ray path tracing module. The four modules can call each other. The ray path tracing module will return all qualified ray path information. Literature [6] proposed grid-based electromagnetic prediction of urban environment, using distributed grid computing to reduce the workload and speed up the calculation, but it did not reflect the accuracy and reliability of the prediction.

There have been many achievements in the research of radio wave propagation theory, and many radio wave propagation models have been established. Divided by research methods, including empirical model, deterministic model and semi-empirical semi-deterministic model. The empirical model is a formula summed up by a large amount of measurement data after statistical analysis. Typical examples include the Egli model, the Okumura-Hata model, the CCIR model, and the COST 231-Hata model. The empirical model does not require detailed environmental information, and can only adapt to the field strength prediction of a specific environment, and the prediction results have large errors. Semi-empirical and semi-deterministic models require environmental information to obtain predicted values. When the environment is not too complex, the prediction accuracy is higher, such as the Longley-Rice model. The deterministic models are all based on electromagnetic wave theory and do not rely on measurement results. Instead, a large number of terrain and architectural details are required for accurate electromagnetic wave path loss prediction and field strength distribution. Typical examples are: ITU-R P.368, ITU-R P.526, ITU-R P.452, Durkin model, Johnson-Gierhart model, etc.

2 Electromagnetic Diffraction Theory

2.1 ITU.RP-526 Model Algorithm

In free space, the propagation of electromagnetic waves is a relatively simple natural phenomenon, but due to the diversity of the surface environment, the prediction of the propagation of electromagnetic waves on the surface is a relatively complicated process. Electromagnetic waves also have different propagation processes in different ground environments, and exhibit different propagation mechanisms such as reflection, refraction, diffraction, transmission and scattering [7]. The main channel of radio wave propagation is an ellipsoid with the transmitting and receiving antenna as the focal point, that is, the first Fresnel zone in space. In this paper, the ITU-R P 526 model and the field strength prediction algorithm in the presence of side obstacles jointly predict the field strength attenuation under special terrain. The algorithm of the ITU-RP.526 model mainly includes ground type analysis, line-of-sight determination, obstacle type determination, obstacle number calculation, and loss calculation for various scenarios, as shown in Fig. 1.

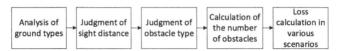

Fig. 1. Algorithm flow chart of the model ITU.RP-526

2.2 Attenuation Calculation Applied to Different Scenarios

The calculation method for different scenarios is more complicated. For details, please refer to Recommendation ITU-RP.526-11 issued by the International Telecommunication Union [7].

Diffraction Within A Smooth Spherical Line-of-Sight Range
The transmission loss is

$$L(\text{X}) = \begin{cases} 11 + \log(X) - 17.6X \\ -20\log(X) - 5.6488X^{1.425} \end{cases}$$

(1)

Among them, X is the distance of the path between the transmitting and receiving antennas.

Diffraction Within The Horizon of a Smooth Spherical Surface
Find the minimum distance between the transmitting and receiving antenna line and the surface of the earth, as shown in Fig. 2:

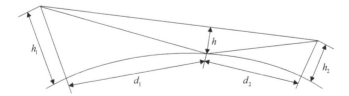

Fig. 2. Schematic diagram of the minimum point of transmission clearance

The calculation formula of the minimum distance h is:

$$h = \frac{\left(h_1 - \frac{d_1}{2a_e}\right)d_2 + \left(h_2 - \frac{d_2}{2a_e}\right)d_1}{d}$$

(2)

The threshold distance h_{req} of diffraction loss is:

$$h_{req} = 0.552\sqrt{\frac{d_1 d_2 \lambda}{d}} \tag{3}$$

If $h \geq h_{req}$, it means that the diffraction loss of transmission is zero, and the diffraction calculation ends, otherwise the following operations continue. The calculation of the attenuation L_{req} of the diffracted transmission at the smooth earth horizon is:

$$L = (1 - h/h_{req})L_{req} \tag{4}$$

Diffraction of Independent Peak-Shaped Obstacles

The ideal scenario is shown in Fig. 3:

$$v = 0.0816h \left[\frac{f(d_1 + d_2)}{d_1 d_2} \right] \tag{5}$$

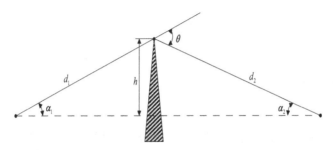

Fig. 3. Ideal spike-shaped obstacle diagram

In the formula, v is the normalized geometric parameter used to mark obstacles; h is the Fresnel clearance, which may be a negative value, in m; f is the signal frequency in MHz; d_1 and d_2 are the path length, in units km.

The mathematical relationship between the diffraction attenuation $J(v)$ and v is:

$$J(v) = -20\log\left(\frac{\sqrt{[1 - C(v) - S(v)]^2 + [C(v) + S(v)]^2}}{2} \right) \tag{6}$$

The following formulas are often used in actual calculations:

$$J(v) = \begin{cases} 6.9 + 20\log\left(\sqrt{(v - 0.1)^2 + 1} + v + 0.1\right) & v > -0.78 \\ 0 & v \leq -0.78 \end{cases} \tag{7}$$

Diffraction of Two Consecutive Peak-Shaped Obstacles

The ideal scenario is shown in Fig. 4:

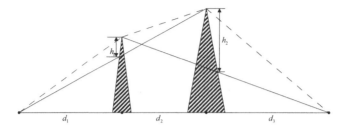

Fig. 4. Two consecutive spike-shaped obstacles

For the diffraction of two peak-shaped obstacles, it can be calculated by splitting into two independent peak-shaped obstacles. The diffraction attenuation generated by the two obstacles is superimposed, and finally the correction item can be used to correct it. Then, the key to this scenario calculation is whether the correction term is accurate.

Two consecutive peak obstacles are divided into two situations, one is that the two obstacles are basically the same, and the other is that the obstacles have obvious primary and secondary differences. When the two peak-shaped obstacles are basically the same, the formula for the correction term:

$$T_c = 10\log\left[\frac{(d_1 + d_2)(d_2 + d_3)}{d_2(d_1 + d_2 + d_3)}\right] \tag{8}$$

When two peak-shaped obstacles have obvious primary and secondary differences, the correction term calculation formula:

$$T_c = \left[12 - 20\log_{10}\left(\frac{2}{1 - \alpha/\pi}\right)\right]\left(\frac{q}{p}\right)^{2p} \tag{9}$$

$$p = \left[\frac{2(d_1 + d_2 + d_3)}{\lambda d_1(d_2 + d_3)}\right]^{\frac{1}{2}} h_1 \tag{10}$$

$$\tan\alpha = \left[\frac{d_2(d_1 + d_2 + d_3)}{d_1 d_3}\right] \tag{11}$$

The total diffraction loss is:

$$L = L_1 + L_2 - T_c \tag{12}$$

Diffraction of Cascading Spike-Shaped Obstacles

Represents the scene that occurs when the signal transmission path passes through multiple spike-shaped obstacles connected together. The calculation method of diffraction in this scenario is somewhat similar to that of the double peak. First, find the main peak of diffraction, that is, find the maximum point n of the geometric parameter v, and calculate the diffraction loss $J(v_n)$ according to the method of single-peak diffraction. At that time, the diffraction losses $J(v_{tn})$ and $J(v_{nr})$ between the transmitter and n points and between n points and the receiver were calculated respectively. The mathematical expression is:

$$L = \begin{cases} J(v_n) + T[J(v_{nr}) + J(v_{tm}) + C] & v_n > -0.78 \\ 0 & v_n \le -0.78 \end{cases} \tag{13}$$

Diffraction of a Single Circular Obstacle

The circular obstacle is different from the blade shape. The geometric shape of the obstacle is similar to that of a semicircle. The ideal scene is as follows (Fig. 5):

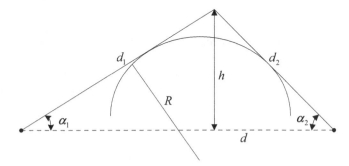

Fig. 5. Schematic diagram of an ideal cylindrical obstacle

The diffraction loss in this scenario is:

$$L = J(v) + T(m, n) \tag{14}$$

In the formula, $J(v)$ is the attenuation caused by the equivalent peak-shaped obstacle at the apex, and $T(m,n)$ is the attenuation related to the curvature of the occlusion.

$$T(m, n) = \begin{cases} 7.2m^{1/2} - (2 - 12.5n)m + 3.6m^{3/2} - 0.8m^2 & mn \le 4 \\ -6 - 20\log(mn) + 7.2m^{1/2} - (2 - 17n)m + 3.6m^{3/2} - 0.8m^2 & mn > 4 \end{cases} \tag{15}$$

$$m = R\left[\frac{d_1 + d_2}{d_1 d_2}\right] \bigg/ \left[\frac{\pi R}{\lambda}\right]^{1/3} \tag{16}$$

$$n = h\left[\frac{\pi R}{\lambda}\right]^{2/3} \bigg/ R \tag{17}$$

2.3   Attenuation Prediction of Electromagnetic Propagation

The attenuation prediction of electromagnetic propagation mainly considers line-of-sight propagation, diffraction propagation, tropospheric scattering propagation, atmospheric

Table 1. Calculation of total attenuation in different scenarios

Path type	Calculation formula
Line-of-sight propagation path	$L_b(p) = L_{b0}(p) + A_{ht} + A_{hr}$
Diffraction propagation path	$L_b(p) = L_{b0}(p) + L_{ds}(p) + A_{ht} + A_{hr}$
Tropospheric scattering path	$L_b(p) = -5\log\left(10^{-0.2L_{bs}} + 10^{-0.2L_{bd}} + 10^{-0.2L_{bam}}\right)$ $+A_{ht} + A_{hr}$

reflection, additional scattering loss, etc. The specific attenuation calculations are shown in Table 1.

$L_{ds}(p)$ is the predicted transmission loss of time p% given by the partial diffraction path of the diffraction propagation model. L_{bs} is the basic transmission attenuation caused by the tropospheric scattering model. L_{bd} is the basic transmission attenuation caused by the diffraction propagation model. L_{bam} is the corrected attenuation caused by atmospheric reflection. All the above attenuation parameters can be calculated from the empirical formulas in the ITU. RP. 526 recommendations.

3 Model Establishment

Digital elevation model (DEM) refers to a collection of geographic elevation data within a certain range to describe the spatial distribution of actual terrain features. Digital elevation model is an important format of electronic map, which has a wide range of applications in the fields of national economy and national defense construction, as well as humanities and natural sciences. The standard definition of a digital elevation model is a combination of three-dimensional vectors representing the attributes of the surface space, represented by (x, y, z), where (x, y) represents the location information, and z represents the elevation information of the location, in discrete points Build a model to describe the continuous topography. In practical applications, DEM is usually expressed as a raster data, but it is different from ordinary image information raster data. An ordinary image pigment point is just a simple discrete point, which only represents the attribute information of the point. There is no topological relationship between points, and DEM elevation data not only express the elevation information of the corresponding point, but also express the elevation information of the area between the points through the topological relationship between the points. The data source of this article is SRTM data, and the accuracy of the data is 3arc-seconds. First, download the SRTM data through the Internet, and then convert it to the required DEM data format through the Global mapper software.

When obtaining the path profile data between the transmitter and the receiver, after determining the position of the transmitter and the receiver, you need to determine the number of points that need to be taken for the entire path according to the accuracy requirements, and adopt the method of sampling at equal intervals, and each sampling point the position of can be calculated. Since the sampling points cannot completely correspond to the geographic elevation data points, elevation interpolation is required for each sampling point and two endpoints, so as to obtain the elevation data at equal intervals on the entire path, based on which the profile curve can be obtained. There are many interpolation methods, including high-order polynomial interpolation, spline function interpolation, bilinear interpolation, spline function fitting interpolation, polynomial fitting interpolation, moving surface fitting method, and weighted average method. The elevation data in this paper adopts regular grid data, so the bilinear polynomial interpolation method can simplify the calculation and have higher accuracy. The bilinear polynomial interpolation uses the four other known elevation data points that are closest to the unknown elevation point and surrounds it to perform surface fitting. The schematic diagram is shown in Fig. 6. For each sampling point P, four points A, B, C, and D with known elevations around it can be found. Their elevation values are H_a, H_b, H_c, H_d, and the elevation value of point P is:

$$H_p = (1 - dx)(1 - dy)H_c + dx(1 - dy)H_d + dxdyH_b + (1 - dx)dyH_a \qquad (18)$$

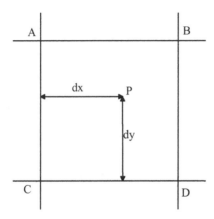

Fig. 6. Schematic diagram of bilinear polynomial interpolation

4   Example of Different Scenario Analysis

The attenuation of electromagnetic signal strength is mainly affected by the signal frequency, distance and obstacles. In this part of the simulation, the signal frequency is fixed to 460 MHz. In practical applications, the radar needs to detect the frequency of the received signal and use the frequency as the input for calculation. The reference points affected by obstacles are mainly ground reference points, and the reference points in the air are regarded as free space propagation loss during simulation, so only the signal vector of the ground reference point is considered when the monitoring stations are deployed later. The test results of the electromagnetic signal attenuation prediction algorithm are as follows. The test is carried out for different terrain conditions, and the simulation results of multiple propagation paths and propagation attenuation are obtained.

The following simulation diagrams show the comparison between the path profiles and the calculation results of the attenuation program under different conditions and a variety of classical wave propagation models. When it is determined that there is no obstacle on the path, as shown in Fig. 7, it is considered to be a smooth earth, and the free space attenuation is calculated, and the running result of the program is close to the classical model.

When it is determined that there is a single spike-shaped obstacle on the path, as shown in Fig. 8, when the electromagnetic signal passes through the obstacle, it can be seen that there is obvious attenuation, and the total attenuation after passing through the obstacle through diffraction is about 20dB higher than that of the classical model. This is consistent with the previous understanding of obstacle diffraction and has higher accuracy.

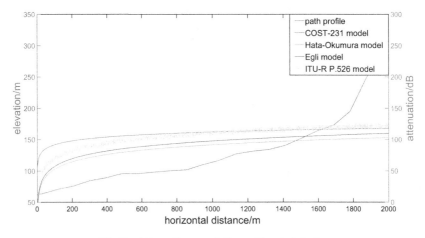

Fig. 7. Attenuation prediction without obstacles

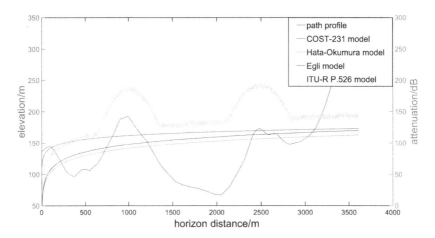

Fig. 8. Attenuation prediction in the case of a single spike-shaped obstacle

When it is determined that there is a single circular obstacle on the path, as shown in Fig. 9, when the electromagnetic signal passes through the obstacle, it can be seen that there is obvious attenuation, but the attenuation is significantly smaller than the diffraction attenuation of the spike-shaped obstacle, and the electromagnetic signal passes through the obstacle. The total attenuation behind the obstacle is close to the classical model. It can be seen that the circular obstacle has little influence on the diffraction attenuation, and the attenuation can be approximately ignored when the width of the obstacle is small compared to the length of the entire path.

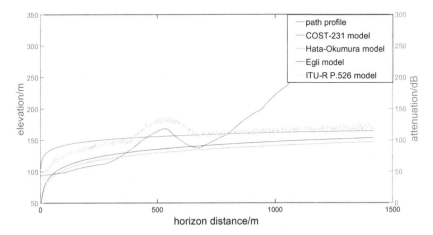

Fig. 9. Attenuation prediction in the case of a single circular obstacle

When it is determined that there are multiple cascading obstacles on the path, as shown in Fig. 10, according to the decomposition principle mentioned above, the previous obstacle vertex is used as the electromagnetic radiation source for the subsequent diffraction calculation, and the multiple levels The connected obstacles are decomposed into multiple separate obstacles for processing. It can also be seen from the figure that the electromagnetic signal undergoes multiple stages of attenuation. After passing through an obstacle, the next diffraction value does not return to the original attenuation value. Calculated, the final total attenuation also superimposes the attenuation value of multiple diffractions, and the gap with the classical model is larger than that of a single obstacle, and the specific increase depends on the number of cascaded obstacles.

Through the simulation test, it can be seen that the electromagnetic prediction program can roughly simulate the propagation path and propagation loss of the electromagnetic radiation signal when it is diffracted by various obstacles on various terrains. Since the propagation path of the electromagnetic signal is predicted and more Factors affecting the propagation and attenuation of electromagnetic signals, the final signal attenuation value calculated by this algorithm is generally higher than the traditional propagation attenuation algorithm, and the signal path and attenuation prediction effect is ideal.

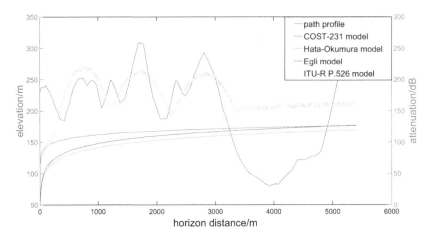

Fig. 10. Attenuation prediction in case of cascading obstacles

Using the elevation data of parts of Shandong, China, set the transmitter positions as E121.0574 and N37.2188, and the receiver positions as E121.7379 and N37.2561, as shown in Fig. 11. Obtain the path profile data according to the above method, and draw the path profile as shown in Fig. 12.

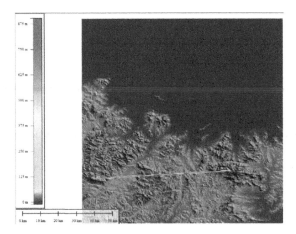

Fig. 11. Determining the position of transmitter and receiver in digital map

The program initialization input parameters are shown in Table 2.

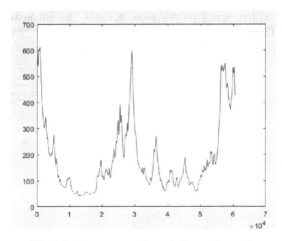

Fig. 12. Electromagnetic radiation path profile

Table 2. Input parameter settings

Enter parameter name	Input parameter value
Percentage of time p_w	50
Mean atmospheric refractive index gradient ΔN	45
Sea level refractive index N_0	325
Signal frequency f (MHz)	460
Transmit antenna height h_t (m)	10
Receiving antenna height h_r (m)	10
Transmit antenna gain G_t (dBW)	30
Receive antenna gain G_r (dBW)	30
Transmitting antenna position	E121.0574, N37.2188
Receiving antenna position	E121.7379, N37.2561

The simulation result of the program is shown in Fig. 13, which includes the topographic profile of the propagation path, the attenuation curve calculated according to the ITU-R P.526 model, and the Okumura-Hata model, Egli model and COST-231 model are set as a comparison. The attenuation value at the receiving antenna calculated according to the ITU-R P.526 model is 201.6587 dB. Because of the diffraction loss and the attenuation in various scenarios, the calculated attenuation value is slightly higher than the attenuation value obtained under the empirical model. Electromagnetic wave propagation is line-of-sight propagation. It can be seen that when obstacles pass through the propagation path, the attenuation value increases significantly. As the distance increases and the height of the receiving point increases, the attenuation value will continue to decrease to similar to free space propagation, but still The attenuation value will be higher due to the influence of obstacles.

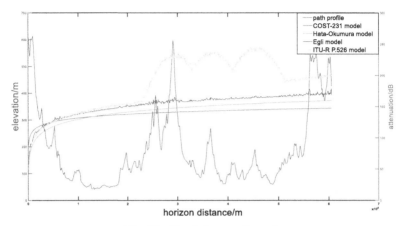

Fig. 13. Simulation result graph

5   Conclusion

Aiming at the complex and changeable terrain of the battlefield, this paper uses digital geographic elevation model data combined with the deterministic model of wireless diffraction propagation to classify and calculate the obstacles in the terrain, predict the electromagnetic environment of the battlefield, and calculate the target position The propagation path and attenuation value at the location. By comparing with Okumura model and Egli, COST model considering the terrain correction factor, it is concluded that the calculated attenuation value is slightly higher than the attenuation value obtained under the empirical model, and the electromagnetic wave propagation is line-of-sight propagation. When passing obstacles on the path, the attenuation value increases significantly. As the distance increases and the height of the receiving point increases, the attenuation value will continue to decrease to similar to free space propagation, but it will still be affected by the obstacles and make the attenuation value higher. Therefore, when the signal is blocked by a mountain, the attenuation value increases sharply, and the electromagnetic wave propagation link should avoid mountain blocking as much as possible. Therefore, when deploying a monitoring station, it should be deployed in a higher altitude area as much as possible. It has been verified that the calculation accuracy of the algorithm in this paper is high and the results are reasonable. It can be applied to the prediction of the electromagnetic environment of the battlefield, which is of great significance to the future electromagnetic spectrum warfare.

References

1. Rizk, K., Wagen, J.-F., Gardiol, F.: Two-dimensional ray-tracing modeling for propagation prediction in microcellular environments. J. IEEE Train. Veh. Technol. **46**, 508–518 (1997)

2. kreuzgruber, P., Unterberger, P., Gahleitner, R.: A ray splitting model for indoor radio propagation associated with complex geomehies. In: Conference Proceedings of the 1993 43rd IEEE Vehicular Technology Conference, pp.227–230. IEEE (1993)
3. McKown, J.W., Hamilton Jr., R.L.: Ray tracing as design tool for radio networks. J. IEEE Network Mag. S, 27–30 (1991)
4. Seidel, S., Rappaport, T.: A ray-tracing technique to predict path loss and delay spread inside buildings. Conf. IEEE Globecom 92, 649–653 (1992)
5. Valenzuela, R.A.: A ray-tracing approach to predicting indoor wireless transmission. In: Conference Proceedings of the 1993 IEEE 43rd Vehicular Technology Conference, Piscataway, NJ, pp. 214–218. IEEE Press (1993)
6. Coco, S., Laudani, A., Pollicino, G.: GRID-based prediction of electromagnetic fields in urban environment. J. IEEE Trans. Magnet. 45(3) (2009)
7. ITU International Telecommunication Union. Recommendation TU-R P.526–11. http://www.itu.int/pub1/R-REC/en

Multi-object Tracking Based on YOLOX and DeepSORT Algorithm

Guangdong Zhang⬤, Wenjing Kang$^{(\boxtimes)}$ ⬤, Ruofei Ma⬤, and Like Zhang⬤

Harbin Institute of Technology, Weihai 264209, Shandong, China
{kfjqq,maruofei}@hit.edu.cn

Abstract. The implementation of 5G/6G network provides high-speed data transmission with a peak transmission rate of up to 10 Gbit/s, which solves the problems of blurred video and low transmission rate in monitoring systems. Faster and higher-definition surveillance images provide good conditions for tracking multiple targets in surveillance video. In this context, this paper uses a two-stage processing algorithm to complete the multi-target tracking task based on the surveillance video in the 5G/6G network, realizing the continuous tracking of multiple targets and solving the problem of target loss and occlusion well. The first stage uses YOLOX to detect the target and passes the detection data to the DeepSORT algorithm of the second stage as the input of Kalman Filtering, and then use the deep convolutional network to extract the features of the detected frames and compare them with the previously saved features. The algorithm can better continuously track multiple targets in different scenarios and achieve the real-time effect of the processing of monitoring video, which has certain significance for solving the problems of large-scale dense pedestrian detection and tracking and pedestrian multi-object tracking for pedestrians in the future 5G/6G video surveillance network.

Keywords: Multi-object tracking · YOLO · Deep convolutional neural network · Kalman filter

1 Introduction

1.1 MOT Method

At present, there are mainly two kinds of multi-object tracking (MOT) methods, Tracking by Detection (TBD) and Detection Free Tracking (DFT) [1]. Figure 1 clearly shows the difference between the two types of algorithms. DFT is similar to single target tracking. It is necessary to manually mark the target in the first frame of the video when initializing the target, and then detect while tracking. The incompleteness of manual annotation may cause instability of tracking results, so compared with DFT, TBD is more efficient which is commonly used and is the most effective paradigm for MOT in current. The MOT based on the TBD strategy includes an independent detection process, a process in which detection results and tracker trajectories are connected. Number of TBD tracking

A. Li et al. (Eds.): 6GN 2022, LNICST 504, pp. 52–64, 2023.
https://doi.org/10.1007/978-3-031-36011-4_5

targets and types are related to the results of the detection algorithm, usually the detection results are unpredictable, so the performance of TBD basically depends on the quality of the detection results. Simple Online Realtime Tracking with Deep Association Metric (DeepSORT) [2] is a MOT algorithm based on the TBD strategy which implements tracking by designing an association strategy for detection results and tracking prediction results.

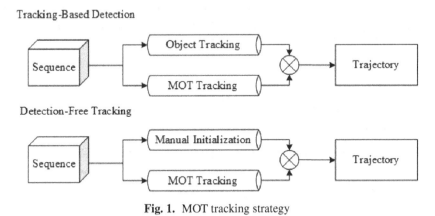

Fig. 1. MOT tracking strategy

1.2 Related Work

Figure 2 shows that the vast majority MOT algorithm consists of four steps. The two key components of MOT are object detection and data association. The estimated bounding box is realized by detection, while the identity is realized by association.

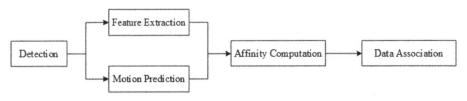

Fig. 2. MOT algorithms key steps

Many methods use detectors with higher performace to obtain higher tracking performance. A lot of methods used CenterNet [3] due to its simplicity and efficiency. A large number of methods [4] used the YOLO series detectors [7] because of its balance of accuracy and speed. The detection box on a single image is used to complete the tracking task by most methods This practice can also help to obtain a more accurate detection box. There are many other methods [9] to enhance the feature representation of subsequent frames by tracking the boxes in the previous frame. Several methods used transformer-based [12] detectors [10] because it has the powerful ability to propagate boxes between frames.

As the core of multi-target tracking, the process of data association first computes the similarity, which is the basis for matching, between tracklets and detection boxes. The way of combining location and motion cues used by SORT [6] is very simple. Firstly, Kalman Filter [8] is used to predict the position of the trajectory in the new frame. Then the Intersection over Union (IOU) between the detection frame and the prediction frame is calculated as the similarity. The way that Sort matches the check boxes with the tracklets is once matching. The first step of MOTDT [5] is to match through appearance similarity, and the second part uses IOU similarity to match the previously mismatched trajectories.

2 Target Detecting Based on YOLOX

2.1 ConvNeXt

The structure of YOLOX network (Fig. 3) mainly consists of four parts including Imput, Backbone, Neck and Prediction. YOLOX's Backbone actually is a convolutional neural network which adopts Darknet53 network structure. It is used to forms image features and aggregate different fine-grained images.

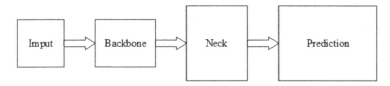

Fig. 3. YOLOX-Darknet53 structure

In this paper, the convolutional network in Backbone is replaced by ConvNeXt. In ConvNeXt, its optimization strategy draws on Swin-Transformer. Specific optimization strategies include: increase the number of training Epochs from 90 to 300, change the optimizer from SGD to AdamW, more complex data augmentation strategies including Mixup, CutMix, RandAugment, Random Erasing and so on, add regularization strategies, such as random depth [13], label smoothing [14] and so on.

Starting from ResNet-50, the five perspectives of macro design, ResNeXt, MobileNet v2, large convolution kernel, and detailed design are drawn from the ideas of Swin Transformer in turn, and then carried out on ImageNet-1K Training and evaluation, and finally get the core structure of ConvNeXt. In the macro design, the improvement of ConvNeXt is to adjust the ratio of the blocks of each Stage of ResNet-50 to 1:1:3:1, and the final number of blocks is (3, 3, 9, 3). This improvement increases the accuracy of ResNet-50 from 78.8% to 79.4%. ResNeXt is a more compromised solution, which improves the computational speed of the model by grouping convolutions (grouping channels and then convolving in groups). Similarly, the Self-Attention of Swin-Tranformer is also an operation unit in units of channels. The difference is that the separable convolution is a learnable convolution kernel, and Self-Attention is a weight dynamically calculated according to the data.

In ConvNeXt, the idea of grouped convolution is also introduced. It replaces 3*3 convolutions with 3*3 grouped convolutions, which reduces GFLOPs from 4.4 to 2.4, but it also reduces accuracy from 79.5% to 78.3%. To compensate for the drop in accuracy, it increases the base channel count of ResNet-50 from 64 to 96. This operation increases GFLOPs to 5.3, but improves the accuracy to 80.5%. ConvNeXt also uses the structure of the inverse bottleneck layer. The bottleneck layer is a structure with a small middle and large ends, which was first used in the residual network. In MobileNet v2, a structure with large middle and small ends is used, which can effectively avoid information loss.

2.2 FPN and PAN

A series of network layers constitute the main structure of Neck. The function of this part is mixing and combining image features and transmit image features to the prediction layer. The neck structure of YOLOX-X is mainly composed of FPN and PAN (Fig. 4).

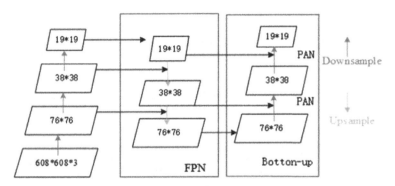

Fig. 4. FPN and PAN structure

Semantic information is transmitted by FPN from high-dimensional to low-dimensional. From top to bottom, FPN conveys strong semantic features at the high level, and enhances the whole pyramid, but only enhances semantic information and does not transmit location information. Aiming at this point, PAN adds a bottom-up pyramid behind FPN to complement FPN and transmits the powerful localization features of the underlying layer and semantic information from low-dimensional to high-dimensional again.

2.3 Decoupled Head

The Prediction part of the YOLOX structure, which Decoupled Head belongs to, can predict image features to generate boundary boxes and prediction categories. Compared with Yolo Head, Decoupled Head has faster convergence and higher accuracy. However, it should be noted that decoupling the detection head will increase the complexity of the operation. After a trade-off between speed and performance, a 1x1 convolution is used for dimensionality reduction first, and two 3x3 convolutions are used in each of the latter two branches to adjust the network parameters to only increase a little. Decoupling the detection head has a deeper importance: YOLOX's network architecture can be integrated with many algorithmic tasks.

Extract the Decoupled Head 1 in Yolox-Darknet53 (Fig. 5). Passing through the previous Neck layer, the length and width of the Decoupled Head 1 input is 20*20. There are three branches in front of Concat:

(1) cls_output: Mainly for the category of the target box, predict the score. Because the COCO data set has a total of 80 categories, and it is mainly N two-category judgments, it becomes 20*20*80 size after being processed by the Sigmoid activation function.
(2) obj_output: It mainly judges whether the target frame is foreground or background, so it is processed by Sigmoid and becomes 20*20*1 size.
(3) reg_output: It mainly predicts the coordinate information (x, y, w, h) of the target frame, so the size is 20*20*4.

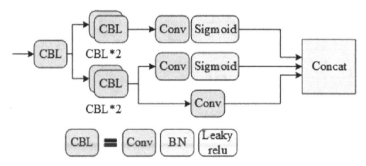

Fig. 5. Decoupled Head 1 structure

The last three outputs are fused together by Concat to obtain 20*20*85 feature information. Similarly, Decoupled Head 2 outputs feature information and performs Concat to obtain 40*40*85 feature information. Decoupled Head 3 outputs feature information and performs Concat to obtain 80*80*85 feature information. Then, perform the Reshape operation on the three pieces of information of Decoupled Head 1, 2 and 3, and perform the overall Concat to obtain the prediction information of 8400*85. After a Transpose, it becomes a two-dimensional vector information of 85*8400 size. Here 8400 refers to the number of prediction boxes, and 85 is the information of each prediction box (Fig. 6):

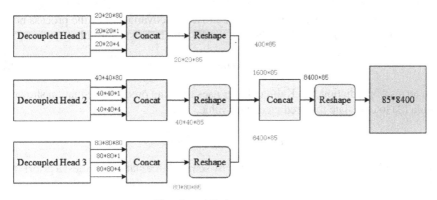

Fig. 6. Prediction structure

3   Target Tracking Based on DeepSORT Algorithm

3.1   Kalman Filter

DeepSORT is a very efficient classical MOT algorithm based on TBD strategy, which completes the task of identifying multiple targets according to the detection results and uses the detection recognition mechanism to help the tracker predicting the trajectory to achieve the function of connecting and distinguishing targets in adjacent images. Since DeepSORT recognizes multiple targets based on the detection algorithm, the tracking effect of DeepSORT is related to the result of target detection, and different detectors can achieve different tracking effects.

In the DeepSORT algorithm, the Kalman Filter is used to realize the tracker's prediction function of the motion trajectory, and the Hungarian Algorithm is used to realize the optimal distribution function of the detection results and the tracker's prediction results.

As a method of optimal state estimation, Kalman Filter plays an irreplaceable role in automatic control systems that need to be pre-judged. On the one hand, Kalman Filter has certain effects on system parameters containing noise and inaccurate observations. The fault tolerance of, on the other hand, is due to the overall performance of the prediction step of the Kalman Filter as far as possible to achieve the optimal estimation of the state value of the dynamic system. Tracking predicts the future state based on the current trajectory of the target, so the Kalman Filter is an essential part of the tracking algorithm.

Formula (1) represents a mathematical model of Kalman Filter that satisfies the basic assumptions of a discrete linear dynamic system.

$$x_k = \mathbf{A} * x_{k-1} + \mathbf{B} * u_k + w_{k-1} \quad z_k = \mathbf{H} * x_k + v_k \tag{1}$$

where x_k is the system state matrix, $\mathbf{A}$ is the state transition equation, $\mathbf{H}$ is the state observation matrix, and w_{k-1} is the process noise. z is the observed amount of the state matrix obtained by the actual measurement, which corresponds to the state x_k obtained by the system simulation. $\mathbf{B}$ is the control input matrix. Two noise parameters, process noise and measurement noise, are introduced to achieve the fault tolerance of the Kalman filter. v_k is the Gaussian measurement white noise, the covariances of the process noise w_{k-1} and the measurement noise v_k are $\mathbf{Q}$ and $\mathbf{R}$, which Satisfy formula (2).

$$p(w) \in N(0, \mathbf{Q}), p(v) \in N(0, \mathbf{R}) \tag{2}$$

In terms of prediction, the Kalman Filter uses the state prediction equation shown in formula (3) to calculate the predicted state value.

$$x_k^- = \mathbf{A} * x_{k-1}^- + \mathbf{B} * u_k \tag{3}$$

Kalman Filter performs state estimation by setting three state quantities: a priori state predicted value x_k^-, a posteriori optimal estimated value x_k and the actual value x_k. $\mathbf{K}$ is the gain for Kalman, which Indicates the proportion of prediction error to measurement error. The state update equation is used to calculate the optimal estimated value x_k of the state, as shown below:

$$x_k = \mathbf{K}(z_k - \mathbf{H} * x_k^-) \tag{4}$$

The cost function is calculated by the state estimation covariance shown below:

$$\mathbf{P}_k = \mathbf{P}_k^- - \mathbf{KHP}_k^- - \mathbf{P}_k^- \mathbf{H}^T \mathbf{K}^T + \mathbf{K}(\mathbf{HP}_k^- \mathbf{H}^T + \mathbf{R})\mathbf{K}^T \tag{5}$$

where $\mathbf{P}_k^-$ is the covariance of the true value and the predicted value, $\mathbf{P}_k$ is the covariance between the true value and the optimal estimated value. The Kalman gain matrix $\mathbf{K}$ under the optimal estimation condition is calculated by formula (6), and the estimation error variance matrix is calculated as formula (7). The calculation of the prediction covariance matrix $\mathbf{P}_k^-$ is shown in formula (8).

$$\mathbf{K} = \mathbf{P}_k^- \mathbf{H}^T (\mathbf{HP}_k^- \mathbf{H}^T + \mathbf{R})^{-1} \tag{6}$$

$$\mathbf{P}_k = (\mathbf{I} - \mathbf{KH}) * \mathbf{P}_k^- \tag{7}$$

$$\mathbf{P}_{k+1}^- = \mathbf{AP}_k \mathbf{A}^T + \mathbf{Q} \tag{8}$$

3.2 Hungarian Algorithm

The Hungarian Algorithm is a method to find the optimal allocation. Its classical mathematical model is the assignment problem, and its general form is shown in formula (9), where c_{ij} is the efficiency matrix.

$$\begin{cases} min\ z = \sum_{i=1}^{n} \sum_{j=1}^{n} c_{ij} x_{ij} \\ s.t. \sum_{j=1}^{n} x_{ij} = 1, j = 1, 2, ..., n \\ \sum_{i=1}^{n} x_{ij} = 1, i = 1, 2, ..., n \\ x_{ij} = 0\ or\ 1, i, j = 1, 2, ..., n \end{cases} \tag{9}$$

In order to solve the allocation problem of detection and tracking results in Deep-SORT, the Hungarian Algorithm is used to find an optimal allocation with the least cost between the detection results of the detector and the tracking trajectories of the tracker. DeepSORT adopts the weighted Hungarian Algorithm to track the association between objects frame by frame, and uses the IoU distance as the weight of the Hungarian Algorithm. The setting of the IoU threshold also has a certain tolerance for short-term occlusion, but it can only be established when the obstacle is slightly larger than the target.

When DeepSORT works, the tracker first estimates the location of each target in the next image through Kalman Filtering, and then calculates the IoU with the prediction result of the tracker according to the recognition result of each detector in the next image. The IoU is taken as the cost matrix of the Hungarian Algorithm. The Hungarian algorithm is used to optimize the distribution of the trajectory of each target. When the overlap between the detection frame and the prediction frame is less than the IoU threshold, it refuses to match the two.

3.3 Algorithm Flow

DeepSORT reduces the frequency of ID-Switch by integrating appearance information. As can be seen from the Fig. 7, DeepSORT adds a cascade matching strategy based on the SORT algorithm, while considering the target distance and feature similarity, and adopts a verification mechanism for the newly generated tracking trajectory to eliminate erroneous prediction results. The core process of DeepSORT is consistent with SORT, and it follows the combination of prediction, observation, and update. In this paper, the convolutional network in this algorithm is replaced by OSNet for better performance.

The DeepSORT matching process is divided into the following situations:

(1) Kalman predicting and detecting match successfully.

After each frame of image in the video is predicted by Kalman filter, the predicted trajectory bounding box of all objects in the current frame is generated, and the detected and predicted bounding boxes are data-related according to the detection results of the detector in the current frame.

The estimated tracking trajectory bounding box is updated for the Kalman filter prediction result that has the corresponding detection result to be matched, and then the next frame is tracked, and the process of observation, prediction, and matching update is performed cyclically.

(2) Kalman predicting and detecting match unsuccessfully.

When the detection is missed, it is easy to lead to the situation that some tracking trajectories do not match the detection results, that is, the matching of the tracking trajectories is missing. At the same time, there is also a situation where the detection result lacks the matching tracking trajectory, which is easy to occur in the scene where a new target enters the camera's field of view. Since the new object entering the field of view has no past trajectory for Kalman filter prediction, the tracking trajectory is missing, resulting in the lack of detection matching. In addition, when an object is occluded for a long time and exceeds the life limit of consecutive matching failures, the algorithm will

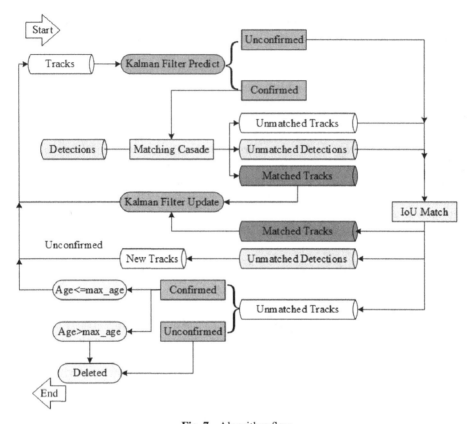

Fig. 7. Algorithm flow

consider that it will no longer appear in the lens and delete the object trajectory, which will also lead to a lack of detection matching.

For the prediction and detection bounding boxes that fail to match, DeepSORT will calculate the IoU again for secondary matching, and re-match the failed matching caused by interference factors such as calculation errors through secondary matching, so as to reduce the remaining detection and tracking results as much as possible. For the detection of secondary matching failure, a new trajectory is established and marked as an unreal trajectory.

After three matching inspections, if the matching is successful three times in a row, it is modified and marked as a real trajectory, and added to the trajectory set. For the tracking box that fails to be matched again, consider the case where the detector misses detection. If the track is marked as untrue, delete its track. If it is marked as true, set a lifetime for it. If the track is marked as true, it will still fail to match within the lifetime. The target has moved out of the shot, so the track is deleted.

4 Experiments

4.1 Setting

The detector is YOLOX-X whose backbone is replaced by ConvNeXt network. There is no doubt that the key point is to train the improved detector. The feature extraction threshold τ_f is set to 0.85 and matching threshold is 0.13. The input image size, the shortest side, the optimizer and other parameters used during multi-scale training adopte what is described in [11].

Training was performed on NVIDIA GTX2080Ti GPU for 80 epochs using a combined training schedule containing multiple datasets including Cityperson, ETHZ, MOT17 and CrowdHuman. Mosaic and Mixup are included in data augmentation.

After the training is completed, four videos are tested on the NVIDIA GTX1080 GPU. The loss function of the COVNeXt after training is as Fig. 8. Moreover, we evaluate the integrated tracker on MOT17 datasets under the "private detection" protocol. Both datasets contain training sets and test sets.

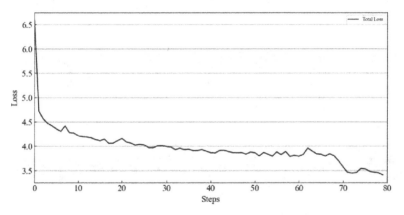

Fig. 8. Iterative loss value

4.2 Visualization Results

Four surveillance videos in different scenes including living area, teaching area and intersection, which are recorded by the camera in the format of 1080P and 30 FPS, are tracked using this algorithm. The algorithm can achieve the mission of tracking multiple targets. When occlusion occurs and the occluded object reappears, the algorithm can still identify and track the target according to the original identity information of the target, give the same ID at the same time (Fig. 9).

Scene 1 is two frames of images taken in the living area. It can be seen that the algorithm can effectively track almost all visible targets, and the targets can be re-identified and tracked after being occluded, and the same detection frame is given. The tracking effect of other scenes is also similar to scene 1. In the very dense environment of scene 3, a good tracking effect is also achieved.

Scene 1

Scene 2

Scene 3

Scene 4

Fig. 9. Visualization results in different scenarios

We compare the integrated tracker with state-of-the-art trackers on the test set of MOT17. The evaluate results are shown in Table 1. Our tracker achieves state-of-the-art performance under the "private detector" protocol. We get 74.9 MOTA, 67.0 IDF1 and 12819 FP.

Table 1. Comparison of the state-of-the-art methods under the "private detector" protocol.

Tracker	MOTA↑	HOTA↑	IDF1↑	FP↓	FN↓	IDs↓	Frag↓
PermaTrackpr	73.8	55.5	68.9	28998	115104	3699	6132
OCSORT	78.0	63.2	77.5	15129	107055	1950	**2040**
GSDT	66.2	55.5	38.7	43368	144261	3318	8046
StrongSORT	79.6	**64.4**	**79.5**	27876	86205	**1194**	1866
ByteTrack [11]	**80.3**	63.1	77.3	25491	**83721**	2196	2277
TraDes	69.1	52.7	63.9	20892	150060	3555	4833
Ours	74.9	58.1	67.0	**12819**	125874	3165	3474

5 Conclusion

Based on the realization and application of 5G/6G technology, this paper realizes multi-target tracking in different complexity scenarios through YOLOX detector and Deep-SORT algorithm. The algorithm can better track a large number of targets continuously and solve the problem of target occlusion and loss to a certain extent. It has certain value in solving the multi-object tracking problem in surveillance video under 5G/6G network.

Acknowledgement. This work was supported partially by National Natural Science Foundation of China (Grant Nos. 61971156, 61801144), Shangdong Provincial Natural Science Foundation (Grant No. ZR2019QF003, ZR2019MF035, ZR2020MF141), the Fundamental Research Funds for the Central Universities, China (Grant No.HIT.NSRIF.2019081) and the Scientific Research Innovation Foundation in Harbin Institute of Technology at Weihai (Grant No. 2019 KYCXJJYB06).

References

1. Luo, W., Xing, J., Zhang, X.: Multiple object tracking: A literature review. Artif. Intell. **293**, 103448 (2021)
2. Wojke, N., Bewley, A., Paules, D.: Simple online and real-time tracking with a deep association metric. In: Proceedings of the 2017 IEEE International Conference on Image Processing, Beijing, China, pp. 3645–3649 (2017)
3. Zhou, X., Wang, X., Krähenbühl, P.: Objects as points. arXiv preprint arXiv:1904.07850 (2019)
4. Wang, Z., Zheng, L., Liu, Y., Li, Y., Wang, S.: Towards real-time multi-object tracking. In: Vedaldi, A., Bischof, H., Brox, T., Frahm, J.-M. (eds.) ECCV 2020. LNCS, vol. 12356, pp. 107–122. Springer, Cham (2020). https://doi.org/10.1007/978-3-030-58621-8_7
5. Chen, L., Ai, H., Zhuang, Z., Shang, C.: Real-time multiple people tracking with deeply learned candidate selection and person re-identification. In: 2018 IEEE International Conference on Multimedia and Expo (ICME), pp. 1–6. IEEE (2018)
6. Bewley, A., Ge, Z., Ott, L., Ramos, F., Upcroft, B.: Simple online and realtime tracking. In: ICIP, pp. 3464–3468. IEEE (2016)

7. Redmon, J., Farhadi, A.: Yolov3: An incremental improvement. arXiv preprint arXiv:1804. 02767 (2018)

8. Kalman, R.E.: A new approach to linear filtering and prediction problems. J. Fluids Eng. **82**(1), 35–45 (1960)

9. Liang, C., Zhang, Z., Zhou, X., Zhou, Li, B., Lu, Y., Hu, W.: One more check: Making "fake background" be tracked again. arXiv preprint arXiv:2104.09441 (2021)

10. Carion, N., Massa, F., Synnaeve, G., Usunier, N., Kirillov, A., Zagoruyko, S.: End-to-end object detection with transformers. In: European Conference on Computer Vision, pp. 213–229. Springer (2020)

11. Zhang, Y., Sun, P., Jiang, Y., Yu, D., Weng, F., Yuan, Z.: ByteTrack: Multi-Object Tracking by Associating Every Detection Box. arXiv preprint arXiv:2110.06864 (2021)

12. Vaswani, A., Shazeer, N., Parmar, N., Uszkoreit, J., Jones, L., Gomez, A. N., Kaiser, L., Polosukhin, I.: Attention is all you need. In Advances in neural information processing systems, pp. 5998–6008 (2017)

13. Huang, G., Sun, Y., Liu, Z., Sedra, D., Weinberger, K.: Deep networks with stochastic depth. In: European conference on computer vision. Springer, Cham (2016)

14. Müller, R., Kornblith, S., Hinton, G.: When does label smoothing help? arXiv preprint arXiv: 1906.02629 (2019)

Embedding with Bounding Box Contracting for Multi-object Tracking

Like Zhang®, Wenjing Kang$^{(\boxtimes)}$ ®, and Guangdong Zhang®

School of Information Science and Engineering, Harbin Institute of Technology, Weihai 264209, Shandong , China
kwjqq@hit.edu.cn

Abstract. The development of 5G/6G network can achieve high data transmission speed, which promotes the wide application of remote video monitoring. Multi-object tracking (MOT) aims at detecting and tracking all the objects of interesting categories in videos. Appearance and motion information of each object are significant clues utilized for finding associations between detections and tracks. Many approaches model each object appearance through bounding box region, which is vulnerable to background noise and motion deformation. In this paper, we alleviate this problem, via embedding with object bounding box contracting. We also integrate an online tracking by detection model, comprehensive use of appearance and motion information for data association. Object bounding box contracting is introduced to relieve the impact of interference and obtain high-quality re-ID embeddings. Experimental results based on the MOT17 benchmark show that the integrated tracker with bounding box contracting for embedding achieves 80.6 MOTA, 79.4 IDF1 and 64.4 HOTA.

Keywords: Multi-Object Tracking · Object Detecting · Embedding Methods

1 Introduction

Multi-object tracking (MOT), which aims to detect and estimate trajectories of multiple target objects in a video, is widely used in autonomous driving, video surveillance and more [1].

Advanced online multi-object tracking algorithms follow two main paradigms: tracking by detection and joint detection and tracking [2]. The tracker belongs to tracking by detection (TBD) paradigm, divides the detection and tracking into two independent tasks. It usually adopts off-the-shelf high-performance object detection algorithm and focuses on the research of data association algorithms. Algorithms that follow the joint detection and tracking paradigm (JDT) perform detection and tracking simultaneously. It reuses the feature extracted by the backbone, which greatly reduces the amount of computation and speeds up the inference speed of the algorithm.

Although the joint detection and tracking algorithm has a faster inference speed, its accuracy often lags behind the detection-based tracking algorithm. Especially in

© ICST Institute for Computer Sciences, Social Informatics and Telecommunications Engineering 2023
Published by Springer Nature Switzerland AG 2023. All Rights Reserved
A. Li et al. (Eds.): 6GN 2022, LNICST 504, pp. 65–76, 2023.
https://doi.org/10.1007/978-3-031-36011-4_6

complex scenes such as occlusion, the feature embeddings extracted by the tracking algorithm of the joint detection and tracking paradigm are insufficient to distinguish the target, resulting in target identity switching [3]. The detection-based tracking algorithm is slow, but each part of it can be independently optimized in blocks, and often has high tracking accuracy. Therefore, the tracking by detection paradigm is still the current mainstream research direction.

Algorithms that follow the tracking by detection paradigm can be divided into SORT [4] like algorithms and Deep SORT [5] like algorithms. SORT like algorithms only use motion information for data association, while Deep SORT like algorithms use target motion information and appearance information for data association. Compared with SORT like algorithms, Deep SORT like algorithms have the ability to re-identify lost targets due to the introduction of appearance information.

The Deep SORT like algorithms focus on improving the utilization of object appearance information and motion information, and have achieved high tracking performances after years of development. For the feature information modeling of the object, most tracking by detection algorithms first scale the area where the target bounding box is located to the same size, and then extract feature through an independent convolutional neural network. Although Deep SORT like algorithms have made great progress, past algorithms focused on using re-ID convolutional neural networks with stronger feature extraction capabilities [6, 7] or increasing the number of appearance feature [8, 9]. However, these algorithms neglect the interference of bounding box area itself, such as the bounding box predicted by the detection algorithm contains a large amount of background caused by motion deformation.

In this paper, we alleviate the interference of background noise through contract the bounding boxes in the re-ID embedding stage, so that the re-ID model pays more attention to the target. Through this simple operation, most of the background noise can be eliminated, and the influence of motion deformation on re-ID embedding can be avoided at the same time.

We integrate a new tracker, follows the Deep SORT like paradigm. We adopt a recent high-performance detector YOLOX [10] to obtain the detection bounding boxes and associate them using appearance and motion information. To evaluate our algorithm, experiments are performed on the MOT17 [11] test sets. Our method achieves 80.6 MOTA, 79.4 IDF1 and 64.4 HOTA.

The main contributions of our work are summarized as follows:

- We propose a simple and effective method to alleviate the influence of background noise and motion deformation during re-ID embedding, and verify its effectiveness on the Deep SORT algorithm.
- We integrate a new tracker, follows the Deep SORT like paradigm. Evaluate the tracker's performance on the MOT17 test sets.

2 Related Work

Algorithms following the tracking by detection paradigm can be divided into two separate tasks: object detection and data association. Object detection estimates the bounding boxes and data association obtains the identities.

2.1 Object Detection

Object detection is one of the hot research directions in the field of computer vision and it is the pre-task of multi-object tracking. The MOT17 dataset [11] provides detection results obtained by object detector such as DPM [12], Faster R-CNN [13] and SDP [14]. Many tracking methods based on these published detection results and focus on research on data association algorithms.

With the development of convolutional neural networks, object detection algorithms have made great progress. Existing object detection algorithms can be divided into two-stage detection algorithms and one-stage detection algorithms. The two-stage object detection algorithms need to generate candidate boxes through the region proposal network at first stage. And perform object classification and bounding box regression in the subsequent network. For example, R-CNN [15], Fast R-CNN [16] and Faster R-CNN [13]. The one-stage object detection algorithms don't need to generate candidate boxes, and directly regard the object location as a regression task. The representative algorithm has the YOLO series [17, 18], SSD [19], etc.

Compared with the one-stage object detection algorithm, two-stage object detection algorithm often has higher detection accuracy and slower speed in the past. With the continuous development of object detection algorithms, the detection accuracy of the one-stage object detection algorithm has been greatly improved. YOLOX [10] is a one-stage object detection algorithm, which is also an anchor-free detector. Benefited from its decoupled object detection head design, the detection accuracy is greatly improved. This detector is widely used in the state-of-the-art tracking algorithms.

2.2 Multi-object Tracking

Tracking by detection paradigm still dominate the field of multi-object tracking. Algorithms that follow the detection-based tracking paradigm decouple detection and data association tasks, and can flexibly use high-performance object detectors to improve tracking performance and make full use of the achievements in the field of object detection.

With the development of object detection algorithms, the performance of detectors has been continuously improved. More and more tracking by detection algorithms employ high-performance object detectors to estimate object bounding boxes for better tracking results. ByteTrack [20] adopts YOLOX [10] as the object detection algorithm, achieves high tracking performance only uses motion information for finding association. Alpha-Refine [21] corrects the object bounding box by predicting the object mask to further improve the prediction accuracy of the bounding box.

Appearance and motion feature are the main basis for data association. The motion feature of most multi-object tracking algorithms are modeled by the Kalman filter algorithm. The object appearance feature of detection-based tracking algorithms usually use independent feature extraction networks to extract feature. BoT-SORT [7] and StrongSORT [6] use stronger feature extractor BoT [22], to obtain feature vectors.

Some algorithms only use motion information for data association, such as: SORT [4] and ByteTrack [20]. Although these algorithms also achieve high-quality tracking results, they rely on the performance of object detectors too much. Besides, since the appearance feature is not used, the tracking algorithms have no ability to re-identify the lost target leading to the ID switching problem.

3 Proposed Method

We alleviate the interference of background during the re-ID embedding stage with bounding boxes contracting. Further integrate a multi-object tracking algorithm, follow the tracking by detection paradigm. Adopt YOLOX [10] as the object detector and comprehensively using the motion and appearance information for data association.

3.1 Embedding with Bounding Box Contracting

Existing multi-object tracking algorithms neglect the interference caused by the background noise contained in the bounding boxes region output by the detector, as shown in the Fig. 1.

Fig. 1. Bounding boxes region contains background noise.

To alleviate this interference, we contract the bounding boxes horizontally during re-ID embedding. This simple but effective operation allows us to filter out a portion of the background noise in the bounding boxes. The coordinates of the object bounding boxes after contracting are calculated by the following:

$$x_i' = x_i + w_i \times perc \tag{1}$$

$$y_i' = y_i \tag{2}$$

$$w_i' = w_i(1 - 2 \times perc) \tag{3}$$

$$h_i' = h_i \tag{4}$$

where (x_i, y_i, w_i, h_i) is the i-th coordinate predicted by the object detector, (x, y) is the upper left corner coordinate, (w, h) is the width and height of the object bounding box. And (x_i', y_i', w_i', h_i') is the coordinate of the object bounding boxes after contracting. *Perc* is the contracting ratio, set to 5%.

By contracting $w_i \times perc$ width on the left and right sides of the object bounding box, effectively alleviate a large amount of background noise caused by motion deformation and other reasons in the output object bounding box of the detector. Therefore, the proportion of the human body in the bounding box is increased, the identity embedding network pays more attention to the main body of the target. The background interference and posture changes of the human body caused by motion, such as hands, feet, etc., are reduced. As shown in Fig. 2.

Fig. 2. Contracted bounding boxes for re-ID embedding.

3.2 Integrated Tracker

We utilize the advantages of existing multi-object tracking algorithms and the method proposed earlier in this paper to integrate a new multi-object tracker. Comprehensive use of object appearance and motion feature for data association, so that the algorithm has the ability to re-identify lost targets. Camera motion compensation and trajectory interpolation is employed to further improve tracking performance.

Kalman Filter. Pedestrian motion modeling using Kalman filter algorithm, propagate the track position from the previous frame to the current frame. We adopt the Kalman filter implementation form in the BoT-SORT [7] algorithm, and the variables are as follows:

$$x_k = \left[x_c(k), y_c(k), w(k), h(k), \dot{x}_c(k), \dot{y}_c(k), \dot{w}(k), \dot{h}(k) \right]^{\mathrm{T}} \tag{5}$$

$$z_k = \left[z_{x_c}(k), z_{y_c}(k), z_w(k), z_h(k) \right]^{\mathrm{T}} \tag{6}$$

$$\begin{aligned}
Q_k = diag((\sigma_p \hat{w}_{k-1|k-1})^2, (\sigma_p \hat{h}_{k-1|k-1})^2, \\
(\sigma_p \hat{w}_{k-1|k-1})^2, (\sigma_p \hat{h}_{k-1|k-1})^2, \\
(\sigma_y \hat{w}_{k-1|k-1})^2, (\sigma_y \hat{h}_{k-1|k-1})^2, \\
(\sigma_y \hat{w}_{k-1|k-1})^2, (\sigma_y \hat{h}_{k-1|k-1})^2)
\end{aligned} \tag{7}$$

$$\begin{aligned}
R_k = diag((\sigma_m z_w(k))^2, (\sigma_m z_h(k))^2, \\
(\sigma_m z_w(k))^2, (\sigma_m z_h(k))^2)
\end{aligned} \tag{8}$$

where x_k is the state vector of the k-th frame, z_k is the observation vector, Q_k is the process noise covariance and R_k is measurement noise covariance. Choose the noise factors to be $\sigma_p = 0.05$, $\sigma_y = 0.00625$ and $\sigma_m = 0.05$.

Re-ID Embedding. We utilize the method proposed in Sect. 3.1 to mitigate the influence of disturbances during re-ID embedding. Extract object appearance feature vector using OSNet [23] network. The objects area is scaled to the same size and sent to the convolutional neural network to extract feature, and finally obtain a 512-dimensional feature vector for each object.

Camera Motion Compensation. Motion feature matching heavily relies on the IoU distance between the tracklets and the detected objects bounding boxes. The camera movement will bring about a large target displacement, which will offset the trajectory position predicted by the Kalman filter. Although the camera position is kept unchanged in some scenes, factors such as vibration still cause the video picture to shake. We adopt the camera motion compensation model in BoT-SORT, to reduce ID switching and mismatches caused by camera motion.

The affine matrix $A_{k-1}^k \in \mathbb{R}^{2\times3}$ is solved by RANSAC, and the camera motion correction step can be performed by the following equations:

$$A_{k-1}^k = \left[M_{2\times2} | T_{2\times1} \right] = \begin{bmatrix} a_{11} & a_{12} & a_{13} \\ a_{21} & a_{22} & a_{23} \end{bmatrix} \tag{9}$$

$$\tilde{M}_{k-1}^k = \begin{bmatrix} M & 0 & 0 & 0 \\ 0 & M & 0 & 0 \\ 0 & 0 & M & 0 \\ 0 & 0 & 0 & M \end{bmatrix} \tilde{T}_{k-1}^k = \begin{bmatrix} a_{13} \\ a_{23} \\ 0 \\ \vdots \\ 0 \end{bmatrix}, \tag{10}$$

$$\hat{x}'_{k|k-1} = \tilde{M}_{k-1}^k \hat{x}_{k|k-1} + \tilde{T}_{k-1}^k \tag{11}$$

$$P'_{k|k-1} = \tilde{M}_{k-1}^k P_{k|k-1} \tilde{M}_{k-1}^k \tag{12}$$

where $\hat{x}_{k|k-1}, \hat{x}'_{k|k-1}$ is the Kalman Filter's predicted state vector of time k before and after compensation of the camera motion respectively. $P_{k|k-1}, P'_{k|k-1}$ is the Kalman Filter's predicated covariance matrix before and after correction respectively.

Data Association. The data association process is shown in Algorithm 1. We found that there are serious occlusions in low score detection boxes, and most of the extracted feature belong to another object, as shown in Fig. 3. Therefore, we only perform appearance feature matching on high score detections. It can not only avoid false matching, but also reduce the number of feature extraction to speed up network interference.

Detections that unmatched with tracklets and sub high score detections will be matched with motion feature. For low score detections motion feature matching also performed. In fact, the motion feature matching process is adopted from ByteTrack [20].

Fig. 3. Low score detections with serious occlusion.

Interpolation. Interpolation is widely used in trajectories' post processing, to further improve the tracking performance. Linear interpolation is high popular due to its simplicity, however its accuracy is limited. We adopt the GSI model in StrongSORT [6] for trajectories' post processing, which is a lightweight interpolation algorithm that employs Gaussian process regression to model nonlinear motion.

The GSI model is formulated by follows:

$$p_k = f^{(i)}(k) + \varepsilon \tag{13}$$

where $k \in F$ is the frame, $p_k \in P$ is the position coordinate variate at frame k and $\varepsilon \sim N(0, \sigma^2)$ is Gaussian noise. $S^{(i)} = \{k^{(i)}, p_k^{(i)}\}_{t=1}^L$ is the trajectories after linear interpolation with length L. The nonlinear motion processing is to fit the function $f^{(i)}$. StrongSORT assumes it obeys a Gaussian process.

Algorithm 1: Pseudo-code of integrated tracker.

Input: A video sequence V ; object detector Det ; Kalman Filter KF ; feature
extraction score threshold τ_f ; detection score threshold τ_{high} , τ_{low} ; tracking
score threshold ε ; camera motion compensation CMC

Output: Tracks T of the video

1 Initialization: $T \leftarrow \varnothing$
2 **for** $frame f_k$ in V **do**
3      $D_k \leftarrow Det(f_k)$
4      $D_f \leftarrow \varnothing$
5      $D_{high} \leftarrow \varnothing$
6      $D_{low} \leftarrow \varnothing$
7   **for** d in D_k **do**
8   **if** $d.score > \tau_f$ **then**
9              $D_f \leftarrow D_f \cup \{d\}$
10   **end**
11   **else if** $d.score < \tau_f$ and $d.score > \tau_{high}$ **then**
12             $D_{high} \leftarrow D_{high} \cup \{d\}$
13   **end**
14   **else if** $d.score < \tau_{high}$ and $d.score > \tau_{low}$ **then**
15             $D_{low} \leftarrow D_{low} \cup \{d\}$
16   **end**
17   **end**
18   **for** t in T **do**
19         $t \leftarrow KF(t)$
20         $t \leftarrow CMC(t)$
21   **end**
22   Association T and D_f using cosine distance
23     $D_{f-re} \leftarrow$ remaining object boxes from D_f
24     $T_{f-re} \leftarrow$ remaining tracks from T
25   Association T_{f-re} and $D_{high} \cup D_{f-re}$ using IoU distance
26     $D_{remain} \leftarrow$ remaining object boxes from $D_{high} \cup D_{f-re}$
27     $T_{remain} \leftarrow$ remaining tracks from T_{f-re}
28   Association T_{remain} and D_{low} using IoU distance
29     $T_{re-remain} \leftarrow$ remaining tracks from T_{remain}
30     $T \leftarrow T \setminus T_{re-remain}$ # delete unmatched tracks
31   **for** d in D_{remain} **do**
32   **if** $d.score > \varepsilon$ **then**
33             $T \leftarrow T \cup \{d\}$
34   **end**
35   **end**
36 **end**

4 Experiments

4.1 Setting

We evaluate the integrated tracker on MOT17 [11] datasets under the "private detection" protocol. Both datasets contain training sets and test sets. For ablation studies, we use the last half of each video in the training set of MOT17, same to the ByteTrack [20]. We also use the pretrain weight of YOLOX-X provided by ByteTrack, and the weight of OSNet [23] provided by Torchreid [24]. All the experiments are implemented on a NVIDIA GTX 1080 GPU, using Pytorch.

The feature extraction threshold τ_f is set to 0.85 and matching threshold is 0.13, other parameters is same to ByteTrack.

4.2 Ablation Study

Our ablation study aims to verify the effectiveness of the bounding box contracting during re-ID embedding. We use the MOT17 validation set, i.e. the last half of each video in the training set. First use the Deep SORT [5] for test, and also adopt YOLOX-X as the object detector. Table 1 shows the comparison results, budget is the number of embedding features for each object and percentage is the ratio of bounding box contracting. It can be seen that MOTA is significantly improved by contracting the bounding box during re-ID embedding. Experiments on our integrated method also prove this, as shown in Table 2.

Table 1. Comparison of difference contracting percentage using Deep SORT.

Tracker	Budget	Percentage(%)	MOTA↑	IDF1↑	IDs↓
Deep SORT	5	0	75.3	76.5	249
Deep SORT	10	0	75.3	76.7	250
Deep SORT	5	5	**75.4**	**76.8**	**247**

Table 2. Comparison of difference contracting percentage using our integrated tracker.

Tracker	Budget	Percentage(%)	MOTA↑	IDF1↑	IDs↓
Ours	1	0	76.8	80.6	121
Ours	1	5	**76.9**	80.6	**119**

4.3 MOT Challenge Results

We compare the integrated tracker with state-of-the-art trackers on the test set of MOT17. The evaluate results are shown in Table 3. Our tracker achieves state-of-the-art performance under the "private detector" protocol. We get 80.6 MOTA, 79.4 IDF1 and 64.4

HOTA. Moreover, the number of ID switches and fragments rank first in MOT17 "private detector" protocol due to precise appearance feature matching. We show some visualization results of difficult cases in Fig. 4.

Fig. 4. Visualization results of difficult cases.

Table 3. Comparison of the state-of-the-art methods under the "private detector" protocol.

Tracker	MOTA↑	HOTA↑	IDF1↑	FP↓	FN↓	IDs↓	Frag↓
ReMOT [25]	77.0	59.7	72.0	33204	93612	2853	5304
OCSORT [26]	78.0	63.2	77.5	**15129**	107055	1950	2040
MAA [27]	79.4	62.0	75.9	37320	**77661**	1452	2202
StrongSORT [6]	79.6	64.4	79.5	27876	86205	1194	1866
ByteTrack [20]	80.3	63.1	77.3	25491	83721	2196	2277
BoT-SORT [7]	80.5	**65.0**	**80.2**	22521	86037	1212	1803
Ours	**80.6**	64.4	79.4	22179	86379	**1062**	**1572**

5   Conclusion

In this paper, we present a simple, effective and generic method to alleviate the background noise and motion deformation interference during re-ID embedding. This method can easily be integrated into other tracking by detection trackers. We also integrate a new tracker, which follows the tracking by detection paradigm. The experimental results show that the tracker achieves 80.6 MOTA, 64.4 HOTA, 79.4 IDF1, and the number of ID switches and fragments rank first in MOT17 "private detector" protocol respectively.

Acknowledgement. This work was supported partially by National Natural Science Foundation of China (Grant Nos. 61971156, 61801144), Shandong Provincial Natural Science Foundation (Grant Nos. ZR2019QF003, ZR2019MF035, ZR2020MF141), the Fundamental Research

Funds for the Central Universities, China (Grant No. HIT.NSRIF.2019081) and the Scientific Research Innovation Foundation in Harbin Institute of Technology at Weihai (Grant No. 2019KYCXJJYB06).

References

1. Zheng, L., Tang, M., Chen, Y., Zhu, G., Wang, J., Lu, H.: Improving multiple object tracking with single object tracking. In: 2021 IEEE/CVF Conference on Computer Vision and Pattern Recognition, pp. 2453–2462 (2021)
2. Wu, J., Cao, J., Song, L., Wang, Y., Yang, M., Yuan, J.: Track to detect and segment: an online multi-object tracker. In: 2021 IEEE/CVF Conference on Computer Vision and Pattern Recognition, pp. 12347–12356 (2021)
3. Saleh, F., Aliakbarian, S., Rezatofighi, H., Salzmann, M., Gould, S.: Probabilistic tracklet scoring and inpainting for multiple object tracking. In: 2021 IEEE/CVF Conference on Computer Vision and Pattern Recognition, pp. 14324–14334 (2021)
4. Bewley, A., Ge, Z., Ott, L., Ramos, F., Upcroft, B.: Simple online and realtime tracking. In: 2016 IEEE International Conference on Image Processing, pp. 3464–3468 (2016)
5. Wojke, N., Bewley, A., Paulus, D.: Simple online and realtime tracking with a deep association metric. In: 2017 IEEE International Conference on Image Processing, pp. 3645–3649 (2017)
6. Du, Y., Song, Y., Yang, B., Zhao, Y.: StrongSORT: make DeepSORT great again. arXiv preprint arXiv: 2202.13514 (2022)
7. Aharon, N., Orfaig, R., Bobrovsky, B.: BoT-SORT: robust associations multi-pedestrian tracking. arXiv preprint arXiv: 2206.14651 (2022)
8. Kim, C., Fuxin, L., Alotaibi, M., Rehg, J.M.: Discriminative appearance modeling with multi-track pooling for real-time multi-object tracking. In: 2021 IEEE/CVF Conference on Computer Vision and Pattern Recognition, pp. 9548–9557 (2021)
9. Pang, J., Qiu, L., Li, X., et al.: Quasi-Dense similarity learning for multiple object tracking. In: 2021 IEEE/CVF Conference on Computer Vision and Pattern Recognition, pp. 164–173 (2021)
10. Ge, Z., Liu, S., Wang, F., Li, Z., Sun, J.: YOLOX: exceeding YOLO series in 2021. arXiv preprint arXiv: 2107.08430 (2021)
11. Milan, A., Leal-Taixe, L., Reid, L., Roth, S., Schindler, K.: MOT16: a benchmark for multi-object tracking. arXiv preprint arXiv: 1603.00831 (2016)
12. Felzenszwalb, P., Mcallester, D., Ramanan, D.: A discriminatively trained, multiscale, deformable part model. In: 2008 IEEE Conference on Computer Vision and Pattern Recognition, pp. 1–8 (2008)
13. Ren, S., He, K., Girshick, R., Sun, J.: Faster R-CNN: towards real-time object detection with region proposal networks. IEEE Trans. Pattern Anal. Mach. Intell. **39**(6), 1137–1149 (2017)
14. Wang, F., Choi, W., Lin, Y.: Exploit all the layers: fast and accurate CNN object detector with scale dependent pooling and cascaded rejection classifiers. In: 2016 IEEE Conference on Computer Vision and Pattern Recognition, pp. 2129–2137 (2016)
15. Girshick, R., Donahue, J., Darrell, T., Malik, J.: Rich feature hierarchies for accurate object detection and semantic segmentation. In: 2014 IEEE Conference on Computer Vision and Pattern Recognition, pp. 580–587 (2014)
16. Girshick, R.: Fast R-CNN. In: 2015 IEEE International Conference on Computer Vision, pp. 1440–1448 (2015)
17. Redmon, J., Farhadi, A.: YOLOv3: an incremental improvement. arXiv preprint arXiv: 1804.02767 (2018)

18. Bochkovskiy, A., Wang, C., Liao, H.M.: YOLOv4: optimal speed and accuracy of object detection. arXiv preprint arXiv: 2004.10934 (2020)
19. Wei, L., Dragomir, A., Dumitru, E., et al.: SSD: single shot multibox detector. In: 14th European Conference on Computer Vision, pp. 21–37 (2016)
20. Zhang, Y., Sun, P., Jiang, Y., et al.: ByteTrack: multi-object tracking by associating every detection box. arXiv preprint arXiv: 2110.06864 (2021)
21. Yan, B., Zhang, X., Wang, D., Lu, H., Yang, X.: Alpha-Refine: boosting tracking performance by precise bounding box estimation. In: 2021 IEEE/CVF Conference on Computer Vision and Pattern Recognition, pp. 5285–5294 (2021)
22. Luo, H., Jiang, W., Gu, Y., et al.: A strong baseline and batch normalization neck for deep person re-identification. IEEE Trans. Multimed. **22**(10), 2597–2609 (2019)
23. Zhou, K., Yang, Y., Cavallaro, A., Xiang, T.: Omni-scale feature learning for person re-identification. In: 2019 IEEE/CVF International Conference on Computer Vision, pp. 3701–3711 (2019)
24. Zhou, K., Xiang, T.: Torchreid: a library for deep learning person re-identification in pytorch. arXiv preprint arXiv: 1910.10093 (2019)
25. Yang, F., Chang, X., Sakti, S., Wu, Y., Nakamura, S.: ReMOT: a model-agnostic refinement for multiple object tracking. Image Vision Comput. **106**, 104091 (2021)
26. Cao, J., Weng, X., Khirodkar, R., Pang, J., Kitani, K.: Observation-Centric SORT: rethinking SORT for robust multi-object tracking. arXiv preprint arXiv: 2203.14360 (2022)
27. Stadler, D., Beyerer, J.: Modelling ambiguous assignments for multi-person tracking in crowds. In: 2022 IEEE/CVF Winter Conference on Applications of Computer Vision Workshops, pp. 133–142 (2022)

Cross-Stage Fusion Network Based Multi-modal Hyperspectral Image Classification

Yuegong Sun[1(✉)], Zhening Wang[1], Ao Li[1], and Hailong Jiang[2]

[1] School of Computer Science and Technology, Harbin University of Science and Technology,
Harbin, China
sunyuegong96@163.com
[2] Department of Computer Science, Kent State University, Kent, USA

Abstract. With the development of satellite technology and airborne platforms, there are more and more methods to acquire remote sensing data. The remote sensing data acquired by multiple methods contain different information and internal structures. Nowadays, single-mode hyperspectral image (HSI) data are no longer satisfactory for researchers' needs. How to apply and process the information of multimodal data poses a great challenge to researchers. In this paper, we propose a deep learning-based network framework for multimodal remote sensing data classification, where we construct an advanced cross-stage fusion strategy using a fully connected network as the backbone, called CSF. Like the name implies, CSF incorporated two separate stages of fusion strategies for moreeffective fusion of multimodal data: fusion at the pre-structure and fusion at the tail of the network. This strategy prevents the preservation of excessive redundant information in the pre-fusion and the details of information lost due to late fusion. Moreover, a plug-and-play cross-fusion module for CSF is implemented. On the Houston 2013 dataset, our model strategy outperformed the fusion strategy of each stage and the single-modal strategy, which also demonstrated that multimodal feature fusion has promising performance.

Keywords: Multi-modal · Feature Fusion · Hyperspectral Image Classification · Remote Sensing

1 Introduction

Compared with common RGB images, remote sensing data contains more information. However, the more information the more troublesome it is to process. Hyperspectral image is a kind of remote sensing data with a large number of spectral bands, which is characterized by rich information and high resolution, so it is widely used in objective detection [1], environmental exploration [2], mineral exploration [3], agricultural resource survey [4] and ocean research [5]. Since it contains a large amount of band information and the feature resemblance between adjacent bands is strong, it largely increases the computational complexity of hyperspectral image classification. Therefore, feature learning is needed for hyperspectral images to remove redundant

© ICST Institute for Computer Sciences, Social Informatics and Telecommunications Engineering 2023
Published by Springer Nature Switzerland AG 2023. All Rights Reserved
A. Li et al. (Eds.): 6GN 2022, LNICST 504, pp. 77–88, 2023.
https://doi.org/10.1007/978-3-031-36011-4_7

information, reduce data dimensionality, and improve classification accuracy. However, hyperspectral images are distorted by clouds and atmosphere, which causes significant problems for researchers, who have to allocate a considerable amount of effort to work on removing clouds and noise for the data, but the results are still unsatisfactory. However, Light Detection and Ranging (LiDAR) images are not affected by cloud cover and have image features that hyperspectral images lack, for example, the height and shape of land-covered objects. The image classification improves the classification accuracy after fusing the features of hyperspectral images and LiDAR images.

The technology in the field of hyperspectral image classification is gradually maturing. Traditionally, the main approach is feature dimensionality reduction and feature selection for hyperspectral images. Learning the potential subspaces of hyperspectral images or their intrinsic flow structures, and finding the information-rich bands of hyperspectral images among the redundant bands [6]. In the domain of deep learning, descending and feature extraction can be performed by modules such as fully connected networks, convolutional networks and attention mechanisms, and finally image classification by logistic regression [7]. The multimodal data classification of hyperspectral images and LiDAR images can be borrowed from the classification method of hyperspectral images, which is mainly studied in how to fuse the two features. This paper focuses on the performance impact of both features on the fusion stage in a fully connected network. Specifically, the contributions of this paper are summarized as follows.

1. Multi-modal data image classification framework dominated by fully connected networks with advanced cross-stage fusion strategy modules is designed.
2. A plug-and-play cross-stage fusion strategy module enables more effective reduction of redundant information while enhancing detailed information during processing of data fusion.

The rest of this paper is presented below. In Sect. 2, related work is presented. Section 3, presents the structure of our proposed model. Section 4, demonstrates the experimental results and provides an analysis. Section 5, discusses the limitations of the model and future work.

2   Related Work

2.1   Single-Modal Feature Learning

Compared with multi-modal, single-modal feature learning just requires model design considering the characteristics of its own data. For HSI, different ground objects may appear with the same spectral profile features; there may also be the same ground objects with different spectral profile features. One way is to pre-process the pixel points by extracting spatial texture information as well as morphological features to complete the task of feature extraction, and then input the extracted information into the classifier for classification. For example, the proposed Local binary pattern (LBP) algorithm [8] and the LBP improved feature extraction method [9] enable such local texture methods to be widely used. In another way, the pixel points to be classified and their neighborhood pixel points are directly input to the classification machine, which is performed by designing a high-quality and efficient classifier. An example is the support vector machine

(SVM) [10] classifier. Jia et al. [11] proposed a super pixel-level unsupervised linear discriminant analysis framework based on gabber to extract the most informative and the most discriminative features. These traditional methods mentioned above use manual feature extraction to obtain image features, while spectral images are often difficult to obtain features with high discriminative power due to interference from factors such as cloud noise. In recent years, deep learning has become the focus of image classification and has been widely used in the field of image classification. Hu et al. [12] argued that the core building block of convolutional neural networks is the convolutional kernel, which is usually viewed as an information aggregator that aggregates information on space and information on channels over local sensory fields, so that in addition to spatial information, channel information cannot be neglected as well. However, the low-level features in the early stage of the neural network in [13] are rich in spatial information but lack semantic information, while the high-level features in the later stage are rich in semantic information but lack spatial information, but the two are isolated from each other and difficult to fully utilize.

2.2 Multi-modal Feature Learning

In the literature [14], a three-layer point-to-point mapping was designed, while a point-to-point convolutional network was designed as a hidden layer in order to merge multi-scale features between two different sources and extract deeply fused features to obtain an accurate representation of hyperspectral image data. You et al. [15] proposed a multi-view common component discriminant analysis to jointly deal with view differences, discriminability and nonlinearity, mainly addressing the problem of nonlinear manifold subspaces leading to degraded classification performance by adding supervised information and local geometric information to the common component extraction process to learn to obtain discriminative common subspaces and to be able to deal with the nonlinear structure in the obtained multi-view data. A pixel-level decision fusion method fusing HSI and Lidar is proposed in [16]. The data are first processed using kernel principal component analysis. Then Gabor filter is used to obtain the amplitude and phase information, which is composed of three sets of data with the original data. Finally, inter-pixel information is obtained by super-pixel segmentation, with which the three sets of data are then fused for classification. In [17], a deep learning-based multimodal classification framework is proposed, in which convolutional neural networks (CNNs) are used as the backbone of a cross-channel reconstruction module. The cross-modal reconstruction strategy learns more compact fused representations of different data sources that can exchange information with each other more efficiently. In [18], provides a baseline solution for the simultaneous processing and analysis of multimodal data by developing a generic multimodal deep learning framework. In [19], CNN net is used to learn the spectral spatial features and the elevation information of the Lidar data. Using a composition of three convolutional layers, where the feature fusion is performed in the last two layers of the convolutional network. According to the sequence of feature fusion, these methods can be categorized as early fusion, intermediate fusion, and late fusion. An intuitive early fusion technique is to superimpose data from multiple modalities in the channel direction and input them to the network as 4- or 6-channel data. Marcos et al. [20] simply combined NIR, red-green spectra, and digital surface models (DSM) as inputs to the network. This image-level fusion approach, by not taking full advantage of the relationships between heterogeneous information, can introduce redundant features in the training. The medium-term fusion approach, also known as hierarchical fusion, combines feature mapping from different levels of multimodal specific encoders and uses a single decoder to up-sample the fused features. Marmanis et al. [21] design parallel branching networks to extract DSM data features and perform modal feature interactions in the middle layer, but this massive structure has a large number of parameters, is hardware demanding, and can be time consuming in the training and inference phases. Post-fusion approaches usually design identical networks that are first trained individually in a specific modality and then use cascade or element-level summation to fuse feature mappings to the end of the network, typically represented by V-FuseNet [22], which uses two convolutional neural networks for spectral and DSM data, respectively, and element summation fusion is performed.

3 The Proposed Method

3.1 Different Stages of Feature Fusion

In multi-modal data processing, data fusion strategy is a major problem, and different stages of fusing features have different effects. The unprocessed HSI and LiDAR are connected according to the spectral band dimension and input to the network for feature extraction for processing, called early fusion.

Let $X_1 \in \mathbb{R}^{d_1 \times N}$ and $X_2 \in \mathbb{R}^{d_2 \times N}$ denote multimodal data with d_1 and d_2 dimensions, N denote the number of samples, where $x_{1,i}$ denotes the i-th sample in the X_1 modal data. Let $Y \in \mathbb{R}^{C \times N}$ denote the same label information shared by multimodal data, with C categories and N samples, which is the one-hot code label matrix. With the definition as above, the input for early fusion can be expressed as $x_i = [x_{1,i}, x_{2,i}]$, $i = 1, ..., N$. The fused features are input to the fully connected network for processing, and the output of the l-th layer can be denoted as

$$z_i^{(l)} = \begin{cases} h_{W^{(l)}, b^{(l)}}(x_i) & l = 1, \\ h_{W^{(l)}, b^{(l)}}(z_i^{(l-1)}) & l = 2, ..., p \end{cases} \tag{1}$$

where l indicates the number of network layers. $h(\cdot)$ denotes the linear regression equation, where $W^{(l)}$ and $b^{(l)}$ denote the weights and biases that can be learned in layer l. ... We introduce batch normalization (BN) layers to speed up convergence and training, as well as control the gradient to prevent gradient explosion and training overfitting, which is added to the output $z_i^{(l)}$

$$z_{BNi}^{(l)} = \alpha \hat{z}_i^{(l)} + \beta \tag{2}$$

where $\hat{z}_i^{(l)}$ is the $z - score$ result of $z_i^{(l)}$, α and β denote the network parameters to be learned by the BN layer. In order to make sense of the deep fully connected network, a nonlinear activation ReLU operation is performed on the output of each layer with the following equation

$$a_i^{(l)} = ReLU(z_{BNi}^{(l)}) \tag{3}$$

Different from the earlier fusion, the mid-stage fusion first delivers the multimodal data to different fully connected layer networks for feature extraction separately. Then, the features are merged and sent to the fully connected layer network again for further feature fusion. Finally, the output results are used for classification. The connection of the two data after feature extraction is called later fusion, where the connected data are directly put into logistic regression for classification.

3.2   Cross-Stage Feature Fusion

Our proposed cross-stage feature fusion strategy is able to preserve the details of image data and remove the redundancy of image data. The reason is that the cross-stage feature fusion strategy combines the advantages of early fusion and later fusion by constructing pre-processing and post-processing modules. Pre-processing is used to retain the details lost in removing redundant information, whereas post-processing is used to boldly remove redundant information. The structure diagram is shown in Fig. 1.

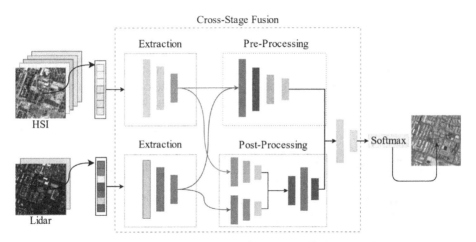

Fig. 1. Architecture diagram of cross-stage fusion method

CSF method mainly contains two parts: feature extraction and feature fusion. First, the samples are selected from the dataset for feature extraction through fully-connected (FC) network. Then, feature fusion is performed. Feature fusion is divided into a pre-processing of merging the two parts of data for deep fusion and a post-processing of continuing feature extraction to the end of the network to be merged and fused further, where the structure of the FC network is shown in Fig. 2.

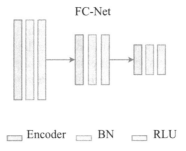

FC-Net

🔲 Encoder   🔲 BN   🔲 RLU

Fig. 2. Architecture diagram of FC-Net

The network structure is a fully connected network with internal blocks consisting of FC blocks as shown in Fig. 1. The purpose of the cross-stage fusion strategy is to minimize the mean squared error of the true value and the predicted value, and its loss function is as follows

$$L = \frac{-1}{N} \sum_{i=1}^{N} \left[y_i \log \hat{y}_i + (1 - y_i) \log(1 - \hat{y}_i) \right] \tag{4}$$

where y_i and $\hat{y}_i$ are the true value and predicted value of N samples, respectively. In order to prevent overfitting in the training process and reduce the complexity of the model, additional constraints are imposed on the network parameters, and the loss function can be written as

$$L = \frac{-1}{N} \sum_{i=1}^{N} \left[y_i \log \hat{y}_i + (1 - y_i) \log(1 - \hat{y}_i) \right] + \lambda \frac{1}{l} \sum_{i=1}^{l} \left\| W^{(l)} \right\|_2^2 \tag{5}$$

where λ is the parameter controlling the complexity, increasing the value of λ will reduce the complexity.

4   Experiments

4.1   Dataset

For the experiments, we used two datasets to test the effectiveness of our method, HSI-LiDAR Houston2013 Dataset and HSI-SAR Berlin Dataset [23], respectively.

HSI-LiDAR Houston2013 Dataset is grouped into two parts, HSI with 144 bands and Lidar with only 1 band, with a total of 349*1905 pixels, of which the number of training samples is 2832, and the number of testing samples is 12197, with the total number of categories being 15. Table 1 shows the number of training and testing samples for each category of the data set, respectively.

Table 1. Name, training set and test set of each category included in the Houston2013 data

Class	Class Name	Train Set	Test Set
Class 1	Healthy Grass	198	1053
Class 2	Stressed Grass	190	1064
Class 3	Synthetic Grass	192	505
Class 4	Tree	188	1056
Class 5	Soil	186	1056
Class 6	Water	182	143
Class 7	Residential	196	1072
Class 8	Commercial	191	1053
Class 9	Road	193	1059
Class 10	Highway	191	1036
Class 11	Railway	181	1054
Class 12	Parking Lot1	192	1041
Class 13	Parking Lot2	184	285
Class 14	Tennis Court	181	247
Class 15	Running Track	187	473
Total		2832	12197

HSI-SAR Berlin Dataset is composed of HSI with 244 bands and SAR with 4 bands, having 1723*476 pixels points, in which there are 2820 training samples and 461851 testing samples, totally 8 of classes. The number of training samples and the number of testing samples for each class of the dataset are shown in Table 2, accordingly.

Table 2. Name, training set and test set of each category included in the Berlin data

Class	Class Name	Train Set	Test Set
Class 1	Forest	443	54511
Class 2	Residential Area	423	268219
Class 3	Industrial Area	499	19067
Class 4	Low Plants	376	58906
Class 5	Soil	331	17095
Class 6	Allotment	280	13025
Class 7	Commercial Area	298	24526
Class 8	Water	170	6502
Total		2820	461851

Both datasets have similar numbers of total and training samples, whereas Berlin data has four times more test samples than Houston2013 data, but the number of categories is double that of the other.

4.2 Result Analysis

There are three metrics to judge the classification results of multimodal data, namely overall accuracy (OA), average accuracy (AA) and kappa coefficient (Kappa). Their equations are shown as follows

$$OA = \frac{N_p}{N_t} \tag{6}$$

$$AA = \frac{1}{C} \sum_{i=1}^{C} \frac{N_p^i}{N_t^i} \tag{7}$$

$$Kappa = \frac{OA - P_e}{1 - P_e} \tag{8}$$

where N_t and N_p denote the number of classified samples and the number of correct predictions, respectively. N_t^i and N_p^i denote the sample number for each class corresponding to N_t and N_p. P_e can be expressed as

$$P_e = \frac{N_p^1 \times N_t^1 + \cdots + N_p^i \times N_t^i + \cdots + N_p^C \times N_t^C}{N_t \times N_t} \tag{9}$$

In order to verify the effectiveness of our proposed method CSF-Net, it is compared with the single-modal methods HIS-FC and Lidar-FC, which validates the effectiveness of the multimodal method, separately, in addition to the Early-Net, Mid-Net and Later-Net multimodal methods, which validates the efficiency of our proposed fusion strategy. It is also compared with other recent multimodal hyperspectral classification methods, such as LeMA, CapsNet and CoCNN. Our experiments use the Tensorflow framework. The optimizer used is Adam optimization. The initial learning rate is set to 0.001. The network parameters are regularized with $l_2 - norm$ to prevent overfitting.

As shown in Fig. 3, there is a clear gap between the single-modal method and the multi-modal method, therefore, complementary information exists in both modalities which can be fused and utilized. Among the single-modal methods, there is a huge gap between the Lidar-Net method and the HSI-Net method, which shows that the HSI contains much more information than the Lidar. Our proposed method has the highest accuracy which proves that the cross-fusion strategy is a successful method.

As can be seen from Table 3, our method is the best in all three-evaluation metrics. Details of the classification of each category in the Houston2013 dataset are presented. Categories C3 and C14 are basically all predicted correctly, as synthetic grass and tennis courts, respectively, have distinct characteristics and regional invariance.

As shown in Table 4, our method is the best among the two-evaluation metrics. In the demonstration of the classification of each category, category C7 has a low correct prediction rate because of the chaotic features and regional irregularities of the commercial area. The overall evaluation metrics of Berlin dataset are low, indicating that this dataset has complex potential features and belongs to a relatively new and complex dataset. The next work will investigate this dataset more to increase the classification accuracy.

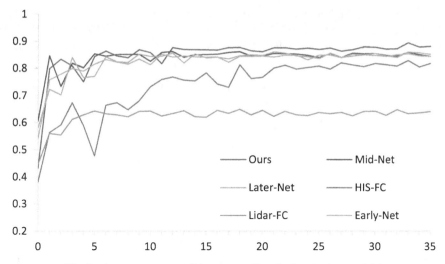

Fig. 3. Accuracy curves of the proposed method and other methods

Table 3. Experimental results for the Houston2013 dataset

Methods	HSIFC	EarlyNet	MidNet	LaterNet	LeMA	CapsNet	CoCNN	**Ours**
C1	82.91	82.15	82.81	8272	81.86	81.10	**83.10**	82.72
C2	83.74	83.74	82.33	83.83	83.80	81.02	**84.87**	82.24
C3	100	100	100	100	100	96.44	99.80	**100**
C4	91.57	92.52	93.18	93.18	**94.79**	88.35	92.42	92.52
C5	97.63	**99.62**	98.86	99.24	99.34	100	99.24	98.67
C6	95.10	83.92	95.80	95.10	**99.30**	95.80	95.80	95.10
C7	86.57	81.81	81.34	84.42	88.99	86.37	**95.20**	80.97
C8	45.30	81.58	79.58	78.73	74.26	90.10	81.86	81.67
C9	71.67	71.96	79.69	74.98	73.84	82.53	85.08	**86.87**
C10	**86.85**	79.63	70.85	70.27	72.20	72.78	61.10	79.63
C11	80.07	76.19	83.25	80.93	82.26	82.99	83.09	**83.30**
C12	86.84	81.56	90.20	**90.39**	90.30	83.09	91.26	88.95
C13	74.74	83.16	80.70	75.09	67.37	76.14	86.77	**87.37**
C14	100	100	100	99.60	100	93.93	91.09	**100**
C15	98.73	98.10	98.73	98.52	98.10	97.46	98.73	**99.52**
OA(%)	82.84	85.45	86.19	86.07	85.42	86.52	87.23	**89.42**
AA(%)	83.45	86.39	87.89	87.13	87.05	87.54	88.22	**89.24**
Kappa(%)	81.37	84.20	85.01	84.87	84.17	85.41	86.19	**88.51**

Table 4. Experimental results for the Berlin dataset

Methods	HSIFC	EarlyNet	MidNet	LaterNet	LeMA	CapsNet	CoCNN	Ours
C1	75.62	65.95	75.66	76.29	64.18	**84.96**	84.09	64.18
C2	51.78	57.68	63.04	62.50	64.11	65.22	**68.48**	64.11
C3	51.19	53.55	53.01	49.79	56.62	48.42	49.09	**56.62**
C4	76.32	**84.65**	80.45	77.58	70.28	80.8	79.43	70.28
C5	78.29	**82.37**	71.44	80.00	76.00	69.18	81.25	76.00
C6	66.97	64.48	63.87	61.73	70.10	55.08	50.68	**70.20**
C7	30.95	30.00	27.86	35.56	30.11	26.12	26.16	**36.11**
C8	**68.99**	64.30	63.99	64.27	59.77	59.69	59.52	59.77
OA (%)	64.42	67.33	71.07	70.27	66.71	66.55	68.51	**71.68**
AA (%)	63.01	63.58	62.42	63.47	62.35	61.18	62.34	**63.69**
Kappa (%)	43.13	47.78	53.75	52.48	53.12	52.77	54.76	**54.79**

5 Conclusion

In this paper, we propose a multi-modal feature fusion strategy based on FC-Net, we mainly explore the effect of multi-modal fusion strategy and the effect of different fusion strategies. Based on different period fusion strategies, the most discriminative features of the two stage methods are fused, finally extracting the more robust and easily distinguishable features. Experiments prove that our proposed method is the best. The output of pre-processing and post-processing is fused to obtain features that eliminate redundant information and retain detailed information, which improves the classification results. Although the method has promising results, however, hyperspectral image region invariance is not exploited. Next, we will prepare to explore the deep network model for multi-modal data with a combination of spatial and spectral information.

Acknowledgement. This work was supported in part by the National Natural Science Foundation of China under Grant 62071157, National Key Research and Development Programme 2022YFD2000500 and Natural Science Foundation of Heilongjiang Province under Grant YQ2019F011.

References

1. Liang, J., Zhou, J., Tong, L., Bai, X., Wang, B.: Material based salient object detection from hyperspectral images. Pattern Recognit. **76**, 476–490 (2018). https://doi.org/10.1016/j.patcog.2017.11.024
2. Gao, B., et al.: Additional sampling layout optimization method for environmental quality grade classifications of farmland soil. IEEE J. Sel. Top. Appl. Earth Obs. Remote Sens. **10**, 5350–5358 (2017). https://doi.org/10.1109/JSTARS.2017.2753467

3. Zadeh, M.H., Tangestani, M.H., Roldan, F.V., Yusta, I.: Mineral exploration and alteration zone mapping using mixture tuned matched filtering approach on ASTER Data at the Central Part of Dehaj-Sarduiyeh Copper Belt, SE Iran. IEEE J. Sel. Top. Appl. Earth Obs. Remote Sens. **7**, 284–289 (2014). https://doi.org/10.1109/JSTARS.2013.2261800

4. Lu, B., Dao, P., Liu, J., He, Y., Shang, J.: Recent advances of hyperspectral imaging technology and applications in agriculture. Remote Sens. **12**, 2659 (2020). https://doi.org/10.3390/rs1216 2659

5. Kobryn, H.T., Wouters, K., Beckley, L.E., Heege, T.: Ningaloo reef: shallow marine habitats mapped using a hyperspectral sensor. PLoS ONE **8**, e70105 (2013). https://doi.org/10.1371/journal.pone.0070105

6. Tang, C., Liu, X., Zhu, E., Wang, L., Zomaya, A.: Hyperspectral band selection via spatial-spectral weighted region-wise multiple graph fusion-based spectral clustering. In: Proceedings of the Thirtieth International Joint Conference on Artificial Intelligence, pp. 3038–3044. International Joint Conferences on Artificial Intelligence Organization, Montreal, Canada (2021). https://doi.org/10.24963/ijcai.2021/418

7. Chakraborty, T., Trehan, U.: SpectralNET: Exploring Spatial-Spectral WaveletCNN for Hyperspectral Image Classification. http://arxiv.org/abs/2104.00341 (2021)

8. Guo, Z., Zhang, L., Zhang, D.: A completed modeling of local binary pattern operator for texture classification. IEEE Trans. Image Process. **19**, 1657–1663 (2010). https://doi.org/10.1109/TIP.2010.2044957

9. Liu, L., Lao, S., Fieguth, P.W., Guo, Y., Wang, X., Pietikäinen, M.: Median robust extended local binary pattern for texture classification. IEEE Trans. Image Process. **25**, 1368–1381 (2016). https://doi.org/10.1109/TIP.2016.2522378

10. Camps-Valls, G., Bruzzone, L.: Kernel-based methods for hyperspectral image classification. IEEE Trans. Geosci. Remote Sens. **43**, 1351–1362 (2005). https://doi.org/10.1109/TGRS.2005.846154

11. Jia, S., et al.: Flexible gabor-based superpixel-level unsupervised LDA for hyperspectral image classification. IEEE Trans. Geosci. Remote Sens. **59**, 10394–10409 (2021). https://doi.org/10.1109/TGRS.2020.3048994

12. Hu, J., Shen, L., Sun, G.: Squeeze-and-excitation networks. In: 2018 IEEE/CVF Conference on Computer Vision and Pattern Recognition, pp. 7132–7141. IEEE, Salt Lake City, UT (2018). https://doi.org/10.1109/CVPR.2018.00745

13. Zhang, N., Li, J., Li, Y., Du, Y.: Global attention pyramid network for semantic segmentation. In: 2019 Chinese Control Conference (CCC), pp. 8728–8732 (2019). https://doi.org/10.23919/ChiCC.2019.8865946

14. Zhang, M., Li, W., Du, Q., Gao, L., Zhang, B.: Feature extraction for classification of hyperspectral and LiDAR data using patch-to-patch CNN. IEEE Trans. Cybern. **50**, 100–111 (2020). https://doi.org/10.1109/TCYB.2018.2864670

15. You, X., Xu, J., Yuan, W., Jing, X.-Y., Tao, D., Zhang, T.: Multi-view common component discriminant analysis for cross-view classification. Pattern Recognit. **92**, 37–51 (2019). https://doi.org/10.1016/j.patcog.2019.03.008

16. Jia, S., et al.: Multiple feature-based superpixel-level decision fusion for hyperspectral and LiDAR data classification. IEEE Trans. Geosci. Remote Sens. **59**, 1437–1452 (2021). https://doi.org/10.1109/TGRS.2020.2996599

17. Wu, X., Hong, D., Chanussot, J.: Convolutional neural networks for multimodal remote sensing data classification. IEEE Trans. Geosci. Remote Sens. **60**, 1 (2022). https://doi.org/10.1109/TGRS.2021.3124913

18. Hong, D., et al.: More diverse means better: multimodal deep learning meets remote-sensing imagery classification. IEEE Trans. Geosci. Remote Sens. **59**, 4340–4354 (2021). https://doi.org/10.1109/TGRS.2020.3016820

19. Hang, R., Li, Z., Ghamisi, P., Hong, D., Xia, G., Liu, Q.: Classification of hyperspectral and LiDAR data using coupled CNNs. IEEE Trans. Geosci. Remote Sens. **58**, 4939–4950 (2020). https://doi.org/10.1109/TGRS.2020.2969024

20. Marcos, D., Volpi, M., Kellenberger, B., Tuia, D.: Land cover mapping at very high resolution with rotation equivariant CNNs: towards small yet accurate models. ISPRS J. Photogramm. Remote Sens. **145**, 96–107 (2018). https://doi.org/10.1016/j.isprsjprs.2018.01.021

21. Marmanis, D., Wegner, J.D., Galliani, S., Schindler, K., Datcu, M., Stilla, U.: Semantic Segmentation of Aerial Images with an Ensemble of CNNS. In: ISPRS Annals of the Photogrammetry, Remote Sensing and Spatial Information Sciences, pp. 473–480. Copernicus GmbH (2016). https://doi.org/10.5194/isprs-annals-III-3-473-2016

22. Audebert, N., Le Saux, B., Lefèvre, S.: Beyond RGB: very high resolution urban remote sensing with multimodal deep networks. ISPRS J. Photogramm. Remote Sens. **140**, 20–32 (2018). https://doi.org/10.1016/j.isprsjprs.2017.11.011

23. Hong, D., Hu, J., Yao, J., Chanussot, J., Zhu, X.X.: Multimodal remote sensing benchmark datasets for land cover classification with a shared and specific feature learning model. ISPRS J. Photogramm. Remote Sens. **178**, 68–80 (2021). https://doi.org/10.1016/j.isprsjprs.2021.05.011

Higher Accuracy Yolov5 Based Safety Helmet Detection

Zizhen Wang$^{(\boxtimes)}$, Yuegong Sun, Zhening Wang, and Ao Li

School of Computer Science and Technology, Harbin University of Science and Technology, Harbin, China
wangjackson2022@163.com

Abstract. For the construction site with high-risk possibility, object detection based on safety helmet and reflective clothing will greatly reduce the risk of workers. At present, the algorithm based on deep learning is the mainstream algorithm of object detection. Among them, the YOLO algorithm is fast and widely used in real-time safety helmet detection. However, for the problems of small objects such as safety helmets and relatively dense detection scene objects, the detection effect is not ideal. For these problems, this paper proposes an improvement of the safety helmet detection algorithm based on YOLOv5s. The DenseBlock module is used in the improved algorithm to replace the Focus structure in the backbone network, which has an improved feature extraction capability for the network; secondly, Soft-NMS is used to retain more category frames when removing redundant frames. After the experiments, it is shown that the accuracy is improved on the homemade safety helmet dataset, which indicates the effectiveness of the improved algorithm.

Keywords: Deep Learning · Object Detection · YOLOv5

1 Introduction

On the construction site, safety helmet can be regarded as a necessary product for workers to protect their lives, which for the fall of objects from height to produce a certain buffer effect, can reduce the damage caused by the accident. Traditional safety helmet detection on construction sites adopt the manual supervision, but this approach is likely to fail to monitor all workers at the construction site, which can easily cause errors, and also cannot monitor the staff at all times.

To solve these problems, the algorithm based on deep learning have become the mainstream approach. Such detection algorithms, which can be deployed to mobile terminal is convenient and accurate, significantly reducing costs and being more efficient than manual monitoring, and it is also more important to develop highly accurate and high-performance detection models [1].

There are usually two types of object detection. One of the algorithms usually includes R-CNN, Fast R-CNN, etc. These algorithms first generate candidate frames

A. Li et al. (Eds.): 6GN 2022, LNICST 504, pp. 89–99, 2023.
https://doi.org/10.1007/978-3-031-36011-4_8

through a specialized module and then further classify them through the generated candidate frames. R-CNN [2], the earliest of this series of algorithms, also reveals many problems. Fast R-CNN [3] was proposed to address these problems, which reduces the large amount of redundancy in feature extraction, speeds up the algorithm, and the end of the grid uses different fully connected layers to achieve better results that output classification results and window regression results simultaneously, enabling end-to-end multi-task training and eliminating the need for additional storage. The RPN candidate frame extraction module of the generation network further improves the speed of the algorithm.

YOLO [5] was proposed as a classical single-stage detection algorithm by Redmon J et al. The most important feature of YOLOv1 is that it uses only one convolutional neural network to implement object detection end-to-end, and its algorithm is to divide the image into multiple grids and predict two bounding boxes for each grid, which differs from R-CNN to avoid the operation of completing the detection task in two steps and improves the detection speed. Later, YOLOv2 [6] was proposed, which introduced anchor frames based on YOLOv1, increasing the number of grids and prediction frames each grid is responsible for. YOLOv3 [7] uses a prediction head that produces three scales of output, with high scale predicting small objects and low scale predicting large objects, alleviating the loss of small, medium and large objects in YOLOv1 and YOLOv2. YOLOv4 [8] uses a large number of tuning techniques based on YOLOv3 to make the model more accurate, however, YOLOv4 has a large model size and slower inference speed. YOLOv5 uses a backbone network with adjustable model size to enable the algorithm to achieve better detection results while maintaining detection speed [9].

At present, many scholars have carried out relevant research on helmet detection, most of which adopt the method of deep learning. For example, Sun et al. added a self-attention layer to the two-stage object detection algorithm Faster R-CNN to extract multi-scale global information of the object and enhanced the training of small objects by improving the anchor frame. The final improved algorithm has better robustness for helmet detection in various general scenarios. Kai Xu et al. improved the detection of small objects by adding feature maps to the single-stage object detection algorithm YOLOv3, and then used K-means clustering to select suitable anchor frames, after which GIOU Loss was used instead of IOU Loss to calculate the border loss, and Focal Loss was added to balance the positive and negative samples. Cheng Rao et al. Used the depth separable convolution and residual (SR) module to replace the original convolution layer of yolov3 tiny algorithm, reducing the amount of parameters and calculation, and improved the spatial pyramid pooling (SPP) module that extract more features, and finally introduce CIOULoss as the border loss function to improve the regression accuracy. Improved the regression accuracy and significantly improved all metrics [10]. Zhang Jin et al. Added a multispectral attention module in the neck of yolov5 network, which improved the generalization ability of the model. Xu Chuanyun et al. proposed a scene enhancement-based data augmentation algorithm based on the YOLOv4 algorithm to improve the performance of the model in detecting small objects.

In this paper, two types of object, whether the construction workers wear safety helmets or not, are taken as detection tasks, and more than 6000 pictures are collected from the open-source safety helmet data set for preprocessing, and the data set of this experiment is constructed. In this paper, yolov5s model is selected for training, and an improved method is proposed for the detection of safety helmet based on yolov5s. Firstly, using the DenseBlock module to improve the Focus structure in the backbone network to be able to extract features better, and secondly, improving YOLOv5s algorithm for removing redundant frames and using Soft-NMS to solve the problem that the NMS algorithm retains only the highest confidence prediction frames of its kind when objects overlap in height The accuracy of safety helmet detection is further improved by fusing the two improvements. The experimental results show that the mAP (Mean Average Precision) of the improved YOLOv5 algorithm is significantly improved and can meet the requirements of detection in construction scenarios.

2   Related Work

2.1   YOLOv5s

Yolov5 provides four object detection networks, including yolov5s, yolov5m, yolov5l and yolov5x. Among these networks, yolov5s network has the smallest depth and the smallest width of the feature map. The other three types are continuously deepened and widened on this basis.The network structure of YOLOv5s is shown in Fig. 1.

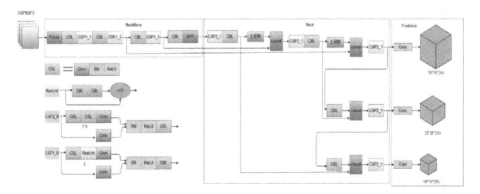

Fig. 1. Network structure of YOLOv5s

YOLOv5s network mainly consists of Backbone, Neck, and Head. Yolov5s uses mosaic data enhancement at the input end, which is the same as YOLOv4, adaptive anchor frame calculation, and self-use picture scaling; Focus structure and CSP (Cross Stage Partial network) are used at Backbone, which was not available in the previous generations of YOLOv5; The neck is a feature fusion network with a combined top-down and bottom-up feature fusion approach, which better fuses multi-scale features [11]. The current neck of YOLOv5 adopts the FPN + PAN structure as in yolov4. However, when yolov5 first came out, only the FPN structure was used, and the PAN structure was added later. In the post-processing of object detection, NMS operation is required for the screening of object frames. In yolov5s, weighted NMS is adopted, which has some improvements for some occluded overlapping objects. Compared with yolov4, the focus structure is added in the backbone network of yolov5, which is mainly used for slicing.

For feature extraction, Yolov5 will have a size of $3 \times 608 \times 608$ general image input network, converted to a feature map of size $12 \times 304 \times 304$ by a Focus slicing operation, and then converted to a feature map of size $32 \times 304 \times 304$ by a normal convolution operation with 32 convolution kernels. YOLOv5 algorithm designs two new CSP structures, which are different from yolov4, which only uses CSP structure in the backbone network. As can be seen from the yolov5s network structure above, the backbone network adopts CSP1_1 structure and CSP1_3 structure, CSP2_1 for neck structure to strengthen the feature fusion between networks.

3   The Proposed Method

3.1   DenseBlock

DenseBlock is an important part of the DenseNet network [12], and its main idea is that for each layer, the feature mappings of all the previous layers are used as the input of the current layer, while their own feature mappings are the input of the subsequent layers, forming a full mutual link. The feature mappings extracted from each layer are available for the subsequent layers. The advantages are that it can enhance the feature propagation, alleviate gradient disappearance and reduce the number of parameters. The structure diagram shown in Fig. 2.

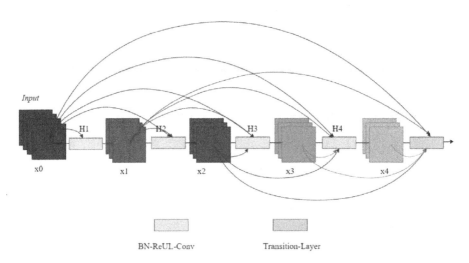

Fig. 2. Structure diagram of Densenet

Many deep learning networks choose to use ResNet, but DenseNet's dense connection mechanism is more prominent: as can be seen from the above structural diagram, each layer will have the input of all the previous layers, that is, the layers are connected and used as the input of the next layer. Assuming that there is an L-layer network,

DenseNet contains $L(L + 1)/2$ connections, which will form a more dense connection. The DenseNet network is a strategy of outputting feature maps for stitching before performing nonlinear transformations, i.e., doing stacking between channels, rather than summing pairs of values [13, 14], moreover, DenseNet directly connects feature maps from different layers, which allows features to be reused and improves efficiency. This feature is DenseNet's greatest advantage over ResNet.

This network has fewer parameters than traditional convolutional networks, due to the fact that the network does not have to relearn redundant feature maps. The DenseNet architecture makes a clear distinction between information added to the network and information saved. The DenseNet layers are very narrow, only a small group of feature maps are added to the network, and the remaining feature maps are kept unchanged. The final classifier makes decisions based on all feature maps in the network.

For DenseNet, in addition to better parameter efficiency, its advantage is its improved information flow and gradient in the network, which will be easier to train. The gradients of the loss function and the original input signal are directly available for each layer, leading to an implicit deep level of supervision. This helps to train deeper network architectures.The output of the traditional network at l layer is shown in (1):

$$x_l = H_l(x_{l-1}) \tag{1}$$

While for ResNet, the identity function from the input of the previous layer is shown in (2):

$$x_l = H_l(x_{l-1}) + x_{l-1} \tag{2}$$

In DenseNet, all previous layers are connected as inputs is shown in (3):

$$x_l = H_l([x_0, x_1, \cdots, x_l]) \tag{3}$$

The first layer of the original YOLOv5s backbone network is the Focus structure. In this structure, slicing is critical. The input image of 640×640 size with 3 channels is passed into the slicing structure and then convolved into a feature map of $320 \times 320 \times 2$ by a convolution operation of 11 size with 32 channels, which reduces the dimensionality and computation. This reduces the dimensionality and computation, as shown in Fig. 3.

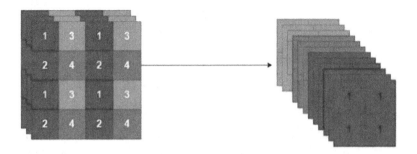

Fig. 3. Focus structure diagram operation diagram

In this paper, we propose to replace the Focus structure by DenseBlock, which can accomplish twice the downsampling to extract feature information at more scales and because this unique connection does not require learning a large amount of useless feature map information, it can improve the gradient information of the network to avoid gradient explosion, which may reduce the appearance of overfitting phenomenon. While increasing the number of finite parameters and computational effort, it improves the feature extraction capability of the network and enables the network to enhance the training of small object feature information. Furthermore, since the final output incorporates the feature outputs of all previous layers, it can retain the feature information of small objects as much as possible during the downsampling process and reduce the loss of their information [15], so that the subsequent convolution operation can extract more information of small objects. Thus, it is beneficial to enhance the training of the model for small objects and improve the performance of the model in detecting small objects.

3.2 Soft-NMS

The idea of NMS algorithm is to search the local maximum and suppress the maximum. NMS algorithm can be specific in different applications. Although its implementation methods are different, they are all the same idea. Non maximum suppression is widely used and plays an important role in edge detection, face detection and other object detection tasks. It removes the redundant frames by multiple iterations, selects the frame with the highest confidence in each iteration, then calculates the intersection ratio (IOU) between the highest confidence preselected frames and the remaining frames, removes the frames with IOU greater than the intersection ratio threshold, obtains the remaining highest confidence preselected frames, and repeats the above process.

The main drawback of non-extreme value suppression is that when objects are highly overlapping, only the prediction boxes with the highest confidence of the same kind are retained, which leads to the possibility that similar but different objects may be mistakenly deleted. Soft-NMS does not directly delete the remaining boxes that generate high intersection ratio with the highest confidence box [16], but reduces the confidence of the remaining boxes and retains more prediction boxes to avoid the mistaken deletion of overlapping objects from occurring in the extreme value suppression. The original NMS algorithm can be expressed as the following (4):

$$s_i = \begin{cases} s_i, & iou(M, b_i) < N_t \\ 0, & iou(M, b_i) \geq N_t \end{cases} \tag{4}$$

Soft-NMS algorithm is shown in (5):

$$s_i = \begin{cases} s_i, & iou(M, b_i) < N_t \\ s_i(1 - iou(M, b_i)), & iou(M, b_i) \geq N_t \end{cases} \tag{5}$$

where N_t is the threshold value, s_i is the new confidence generated by the currently selected object box and the highest confidence box, and $IOU(M, b_i)$ is the intersection ratio of the current highest confidence prediction box M and the remaining i-th prediction box bi. The image and the enhanced image are fed into the model at the same time, and all the prediction frames obtained by Soft-NMS often contain some useful information, so that when the highest confidence frame is not accurate enough, the information of the remaining frames can be used to correct the prediction frames.When the highest confidence preselected box is not accurate enough, the information of the remaining boxes can be used to correct the preselected boxes.

4 Experiments

4.1 Dataset

In order to carry out experiments related to deep learning object detection, there must be sufficient data sets. The only open source helmet dataset available is SHWD (SafetyHelmetWearing-Dataset), where the SCUT-HEAD dataset is a surveillance image or a photo taken by students in a classroom scene, therefore, the data set is not a picture in the scene of the construction site, and cannot meet the requirements under the background of safety helmet detection. In order to solve this problem, this paper makes a self-made data set that meets the requirements of helmet detection in a construction site.

The data set of this experiment has 6057 pictures about safety helmets, of which 4845 pictures are the training set and 1212 pictures are the validation set. The dataset was downloaded from the web, and the annotation tool was used to mark the object type as well as the coordinates of each photo, and the dataset was divided into two categories, one for the unwearing safety helmet marked as 0, and one for the safety helmet marked as 1. The objects for the unwearing safety helmet included the face as well as the head, and the safety helmet objects were the face and the safety helmet as a whole. The size of the overall dataset photos varies.

4.2 Metrics

Precision (P), recall (R) and mean accuracy (mAP) are used as the relevant metrics for model performance evaluation. The precision rate is used to measure the accuracy of model detection, i.e., the accuracy rate. Recall rate is used to assess the comprehensiveness of model detection, i.e., the check-all rate [17]. The single-category accuracy (AP) is calculated using the integration method to calculate the accuracy and recall curves as well as the area enclosed by the coordinate axes. By summing the single-category AP values and then dividing them by the number of categories, the mAP value can be obtained. mAP values are generally calculated when IOU = 0.5, i.e., mAP@0.5, where IOU is the intersection ratio and is an important function for calculating mAP [9], as shown in the following equation.

$$IOU = \frac{A \cap B}{A \cup B} \tag{6}$$

$$P = \frac{TP}{TP + FP} \tag{7}$$

$$R = \frac{TP}{TP + FN} \tag{8}$$

$$AP = \int_0^1 P(r)dr \tag{9}$$

$$mAP = \frac{\sum_{i=1}^C APi}{C} \tag{10}$$

where A and B are the prediction frame and the true frame, respectively, the denominator is the intersection of the two frames, and the numerator is the concatenation of the two frames. TP is true positive; predicting positive object as positive; false positive TP; incorrectly predicting negative object as positive; false negative FN; incorrectly predicting positive object as negative. $P(r)$ is the smoothed accuracy and recall curve, for which the integration operation is to find the area occupied by the smoothed curve. C is the number of categories, and APi denotes the accuracy rate of the i th category, where i is the ordinal number, and the number of categories in this paper is 2.

4.3 Process and Results

The yolov5 improved algorithm experiment proposed in this paper is based on the code provided by the official. The original $3 \times 608 \times 608$ image input Focus structure in the original YOLOv5s, using a slicing operation, first becomes a $12 \times 304 \times 304$ feature map, and after convolution, it finally becomes a $32 \times 304 \times 304$ feature map. For the method proposed in this paper, firstly, the DenseBlock module is used to replace the first layer of Focus structure at the input side, which can pass more information and reduce the gradient between networks by using its dense connection and unique feature map information transfer, thus effectively reducing the loss of small object information in the process of downsampling at the input side. Next, the NMS model is improved and the prediction frame is enhanced using the Soft-NMS algorithm.

Experiments will record the unimproved model parameters, as well as the MAP indices using the two improved methods and after fusing the two methods, respectively.

Since the dataset images vary in size, the trained images are resized to 640 size. The model is trained for 100 rounds, and the learning rate is set to 0.02. Finally, the last trained model and the best one are obtained, and the obtained model is tested to get the results of the unimproved model trained by mAP, and the results of the unimproved model are shown in Table 1.

Table 1. Results of the original model

	P%	R%	mAP@ 0.5%	mAP@ 0.5: 0. 95%
All	92.2	84.0	89.1	55.4
Person	93.6	88.0	92.7	46.6
Hat	90.7	80.0	85.4	64.1

In order to compare the results of different models more intuitively, the model with DenseBlock is denoted as DN-YOLOv5s, the model with Soft-NMS algorithm is denoted as S-YOLOv5s, and the method incorporating both algorithms is denoted as DNS-YOLOv5s. The parameters such as the number of training rounds are not changed and the comparison of the improved model after the safety helmet set is shown in Table 2.

Table 2. Results of the improved model on the dataset

	P%	R%	mAP@ 0.5%	mAP@ 0.5: 0. 95%
YOLOv5s	92.2	84.0	89.1	55.4
DN-YOLOv5s	92.7	86.0	90.4	57.1
S-YOLOv5s	93.0	87.3	91.6	58.6
DNS-YOLOv5s	93.2	87.5	92.2	59.8

In order to further measure the performance of the algorithm for helmet detection in this paper, Table 3 was drawn with reference to the model data of other papers for safety helmet detection, which can be more intuitive to compare the data obtained from the experiments done in this paper. After the comparison, the feasibility of the improved model is again verified.

Table 3. Performance of other object detection algorithms

	mAP@ 0.5%	mAP@ 0.5: 0. 95%	Fps/(frame)
YOLOv3	74.39	44.67	17.36
YOLOv3-tiny	72.87	43.12	21.48
YOLOv3-spp	75.78	47.15	16.58
YOLOv4	84.16	53.92	16.03
YOLOv5s	81.37	52.26	24.01
YOLOv5m	84.93	54.42	19.94
YOLOv5l	86.58	56.31	17.87
YOLOv5x	87.12	56.96	16.07
YOLOX-L	86.89	57.17	17.23
PP-YOLOv2	86.73	57.03	17.12
Pre Model	89.1	55.4	23.12
Our Method	92.20	59.80	23.35

4.4 Result Analysis

After the results of this experiment, it is obvious that the improved model has some optimization. For the D-YOLOv5s model with the addition of the DenseBlock block, there is an increase of 1.3% points on mAP@ 0.5% and 1.7 percentage points on mAP@ 0.5: 0. 95% compared to the original model. The other method also increased by 2.5% and 3.2%, respectively, compared to the original model. The model after incorporating the two improved methods increased by 3.1% on mAP@ 0.5% and 4.4% on mAP@ 0.5: 0. 95% compared to the initial model. In summary, from the two results in Table 1 and Table 2, and compared with other object detection algorithms in Table 3, it is clear that the use of the two improved methods proposed in this paper does effectively increase the accuracy of the model detection, and there is a significant improvement from the data.

5 Conclusion

In this paper, we proposed an improved method of safety helmet detection based on YOLOv5s algorithm. Aiming at the problems such as small safety helmet targets and dense detection scene targets, we proposed to use denseblock module to replace the focus structure in the network in YOLOv5, which improved the feature extraction ability of the network. Secondly, we adopted soft NMS algorithm to retain the effective prediction frame. Then, the relevant experiments are designed. Compared with the original model, the results of the experiments show that our method has a certain improvement in the accuracy of helmet detection, and the data after the experiments also prove the effectiveness of the improved algorithm, so as to obtain a more accurate helmet detection model.

Acknowledgement. This work was supported in part by the National Natural Science Foundation of China under Grant 62071157, National Key Research and Development Programme 2022YFD2000500 and Natural Science Foundation of Heilongjiang Province under Grant YQ2019F011.

References

1. Yan, G., Sun, Q., Huang, J., et al.: Helmet detection based on deep learning and random forest on UAV for power construction safety. J. Adv. Comput. Intell. Intell. Inform. **25**(1), 40–49 (2021)
2. Girshick, R., Donahue, J., Darrell, T., et al.: Rich feature hierarchies for accurate object detection and semantic segmentation. In: Proceedings of the IEEE Conference on Computer Vision and Pattern Recognition, pp. 580–587 (2014)
3. Girshick, R.: Fast R-CNN. In: Proceedings of the IEEE International Conference on Computer Vision, pp. 1440–1448 (2015)
4. Ren, S., He, K., Girshick, R., et al.: Faster R-CNN: towards real-time object detection with region proposal networks. In: Advances in Neural Information Processing Systems, p. 28 (2015)

5. Redmon, J., Divvala, S., Girshick, R., et al.: You only look once: unified, real-time object detection. In: Proceedings of the IEEE Conference on Computer Vision and Pattern Recognition, pp. 779–788 (2016)
6. Redmon, J., Farhadi, A.: YOLO9000: better, faster, stronger. In: Proceedings of the IEEE Conference on Computer Vision and Pattern Recognition, pp. 7263–7271 (2017)
7. Redmon, J., Farhadi, A.: Yolov3: an incremental improvement. arXiv preprint arXiv:1804.02767 (2018)
8. Bochkovskiy, A., Wang, C.Y., Liao, H.Y.M.: Yolov4: optimal speed and accuracy of object detection. arXiv preprint arXiv:2004.10934 (2020)
9. Liu, Y., Lu, B.H., Peng, J., et al.: Research on the use of YOLOv5 object detection algorithm in mask wearing recognition. World Sci. Res. J. **6**(11), 276–284 (2020)
10. Cheng, R., He, X., Zheng, Z., et al.: Multi-scale safety helmet detection based on SAS-YOLOv3-tiny. Appl. Sci. **11**(8), 3652 (2021)
11. Zhu, L., Geng, X., Li, Z., et al.: Improving yolov5 with attention mechanism for detecting boulders from planetary images. Remote Sens. **13**(18), 3776 (2021)
12. Wang, Y., Hao, Z.Y., Zuo, F., et al.: A fabric defect detection system based improved YOLOv5 detector. J. Phys. Conf. Ser. **2010**(1), 125–134 (2021)
13. Li, G., Zhang, M., Li, J., et al.: Efficient densely connected convolutional neural networks. Pattern Recogn. **109**, 107610 (2021)
14. Albahli, S., Ayub, N., Shiraz, M.: Coronavirus disease (COVID-19) detection using X-ray images and enhanced DenseNet. Appl. Soft Comput. **110**, 107645 (2021)
15. Jung, E., Chikontwe, P., Zong, X., et al.: Enhancement of perivascular spaces using densely connected deep convolutional neural network. IEEE Access **7**, 18382–18391 (2019)
16. Bodla, N., Singh, B., Chellappa, R., et al.: Soft-NMS–improving object detection with one line of code. In: Proceedings of the IEEE International Conference on Computer Vision, pp. 5561–5569 (2017)
17. Hsu, W.Y., Lin, W.Y.: Adaptive fusion of multi-scale YOLO for pedestrian detection. IEEE Access **9**, 110063–110073 (2021)

Landslide Detection of 6G Satellite Images Using Multi-level Transformer Network

Dong He[1], Liang Xi[1(✉)], and Lu Liu[2(✉)]

[1] School of Computer Science and Technology, Harbin University of Science and Technology, Harbin 150080, China
xiliang@hrbust.edu.cn
[2] College of Biomedical Information and Engineering, Hainan Medical University, Haikou 571199, China
liulu@hainmc.edu.cn

Abstract. The 6G satellite system can help humans detect natural disasters and respond quickly through a low-altitude full-coverage network. Analyzing and identifying landslide images captured by satellites can help humans address the various hazards posed by landslides. Recently, deep learning models have been developed rapidly and demonstrated the effectiveness of landslide detection. Many models use convolutional neural networks (CNN) to extract the features of landslide images for landslide detection. However, CNN-based models cannot obtain global semantic information of images, resulting in low accuracy of landslide detection or some misjudgments. In this paper, we adopt a pre-training feature extraction network and an unsupervised multi-level transformer autoencoder for landslide detection. We first extract multi-scale features from the pre-training network, then reconstruct the image features using an autoencoder transformer network with a U-Net shape, which can better get global semantic information. We use the Bijie landslide dataset captured by satellites for experiments. The experimental results show that, compared with the original CNN model, our method can improve the detection accuracy and effectively distinguish landslide and non-landslide image data.

Keywords: 6G satellite image · landslide detection · autoencoder · vision transformer

1 Introduction

Landslide is a common geological disaster, which can bring unpredictable damage to the natural environment, public infrastructure, and human life [1, 2]. Recently, with the development of 6G satellite communication network and remote sensing technology, people can apply the high-resolution satellite images to disaster management, landslide detection and identification [3, 4]. There are various landslide features in the landslide images, how to comprehensively use them for accurate and effective landslide detection is extremely meaningful to reduce the economic risks and protect human life.

A. Li et al. (Eds.): 6GN 2022, LNICST 504, pp. 100–110, 2023.
https://doi.org/10.1007/978-3-031-36011-4_9

Traditional landslide detection methods usually use statistical features such as image texture and color, to detect landslide. Martha et al. [5] investigated landslide detection using spectral, shape, and contextual information from landslide images. In addition, some machine learning methods, such as support vector machine [6], random forest [7], and genetic algorithm [8], combine statistical methods for landslide detection. However, machine learning methods do not have good feature extraction capability and cannot automatically detect.

Deep learning models have powerful representation learning capability, can automatically extract features and apply them to landslide detection. Specifically, the convolutional neural network (CNN) has surpassed traditional statistical feature extraction and machine learning methods in various image-based tasks [9]. Using optical data and terrain factors from the Rapid Eye satellite, Ghorbanzadeh et al. [10] analyzed the performances of different CNN-based models for landslide detection, and the experimental results showed that CNN-based deep learning methods can achieve better results. Ji S et al. [11] focus on landslide detection from satellite images using CNN-based methods based on the attention mechanism to enhance the CNN to extract more distinctive landslide feature representations. However, CNN focuses on extracting local image features, and it is difficult to learn the global context features of images [12].

Vision transformer (ViT) [13] is the first vision transformer. It proves that the NLP transformer [14] framework can be transferred to the image recognition and detection task [15, 16] with excellent performance. Compared with CNN, ViT can learn image contextual features through patch-level image and global attention mechanism [17]. To capture local and global information of image, we focus on combining transformers on multiple levels for better image detection and discrimination.

Hence, we propose an unsupervised deep learning model for landslide detection. The model mainly contains a feature extraction network and a multi-level transformer autoencoder framework. Firstly, we extract features from a pre-training network; Then the image features can be reconstructed using a multi-level transformer network. In this way, not only fine-grained features but also coarse-grained features can be extracted. At last, we fuse the two kinds of features of satellite images for the landslide detection tasks.

2 Related Work

2.1 6G Satellite Communication

6G satellite communication will play an important role in the global communication and monitoring. Through the integration of satellite communication and terrestrial network, the goal of mobile network coverage in the entire global area will be achieved, realizing user access at any time and business continuity. Satellite networks can provide various services to vast areas, and satellite services have been evolved from traditional voice and broadcast services to broadband Internet services [18], which can monitor the behaviors of mobile users, buildings, aircraft, ships, emergency base stations, and forecast of weather conditions and natural disasters [19]. By transmitting the detected statistical information or captured satellite images to the ground, combining with AI intelligent technology, we can effectively detect weather or geological disasters, such as landslide detection of satellite images.

2.2 Deep Learning Models

U-Net. The original intention of U-Net [20] is to perform medical image segmentation. The U-shaped network structure is used to obtain context information and position information. It is a simple and efficient deep learning network and easy to build and train.

Therefore, we employ U-Net to capture both shallow and deep features simultaneously. Because both low-level features and high-level semantic features are important in landslide detection of satellite image. The skip connection structure (feature splicing) of U-shaped structure is quite effective, which can help distinguish abnormal landslide images from normal non-landslide images. The framework of U-Net is shown in Fig. 1.

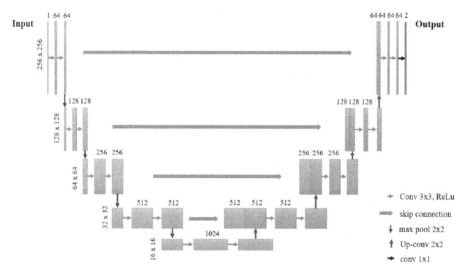

Fig. 1. The U-Net framework

Vision Transformer. ViT mainly processes images by splitting them into multiple patches; then the two-dimensional patches are converted into a one-dimensional vector. The class vector and position vector are also added as the model input. Due to the spatial connections between multiple patches, ViT achieves good performance in downstream tasks [21]. Our framework mainly involves the transformer encoder and decoder with the attention mechanism. The framework of the original vision transformer is shown in Fig. 2.

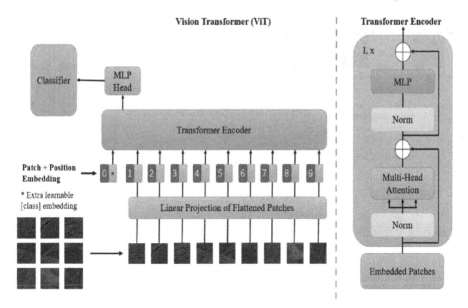

Fig. 2. The ViT framework

Considering the ability of the transformer to handle contextual semantics, we utilize transformers of different granularities to extract image features to provide multi-scale features for image reconstruction. In addition, due to the skip connection structure of U-Net that can reduce information loss, we apply multiple transformers with different granularities to U-Net to obtain a U-shaped transformer autoencoder, which can effectively extract the image features, and use the reconstruction error map to distinguish landslide and non-landslide images.

3 Methodology

We apply an unsupervised multi-level transformer encoder-decoder framework to landslide detection from satellite images, shown in Fig. 3. Our model contains a pre-training CNN network and a multi-level autoencoder with transformer structure. First, we introduce the structure of pre-training network to extract latent features from images; Next, we present the specific implementation details of the multi-level transformer autoencoder with U-Net to reconstruct the features; Finally, we give the loss function and the evaluation method of anomaly score.

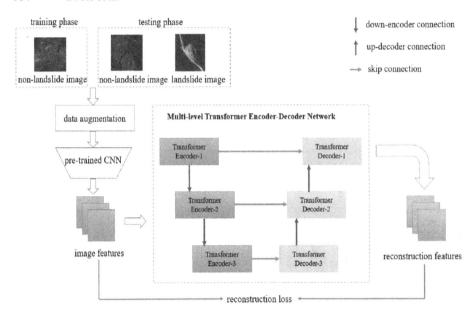

Fig. 3. Model framework

3.1 Pre-training Network

Due to the different distribution of landslide and non-landslide images in the feature space, we perform feature extraction through a pre-training network based on CNN, which can map the original images to the feature space.

We utilize the pre-training Resnet-18 [22] on ImageNet [23]. And the reason we use Resnet-18 as a pretrained network is because of its simplicity and effectiveness. We not only use the output features of the last layer, but also connect the features of the middle three layers along the channel to form feature representations of different levels. Then, the fused features are taken as the whole image features and put into the multi-level auto-encoder for reconstruction. The formula is as follows:

$$z = F_{Resnet18}(x) \tag{1}$$

3.2 Multi-level Transformer Network

Compared with the traditional convolutional neural network, the transformer has greater abilities of the extraction and reconstruction of image features due to its attention mechanism. To capture both coarse-grained and fine-grained image features, we use multiple scale transformer encoders and decoders. In addition, we combine the advantages of U-Net, the encoder and decoder in the same level use skip connections for information transfer. The compression or decompression information of the previous level is sequentially transferred between the encoders and decoders in different levels. The following is an introduction to the entire transformer encoder and decoder framework.

Multi-Level Transformer Encoder. Consistent with the traditional vision transformer processing, we convert the feature maps to patches, and add zero padding token and positional encoding as the input of the transformer encoder. We divide the feature map of the $H \times W$ landslide image into patches with a block size of $P_H \times P_W$, and such patches have a total of $N_H \times N_W$ blocks. The output of the level-1 encoder includes a latent head vector and a latent feature vector. The input of the level-2 encoder is the latent head vector of the level-1 encoder, and the latent feature vector is used as the input of the level-1 decoder for feature reconstruction. Similar to the level-1 encoder, the level-2 and level-3 encoders also follow this transfer process. The formula of the encoder of the level-i transformer is as follows,

$$E_0^{(n)}, \left(E_1^{(n)}, \ldots, E_{P_i \times P_i}^{(n)} \right) = F_{encoder} \left(z_0, z_1^{(n)}, \ldots, z_{P_i \times P_i}^{(n)} \right) \tag{2}$$

where $z_1^{(n)}, j = \{1, \ldots, P_i \times P_i\}$ are the feature vectors after pre-training. $E_0^{(n)}, E_j^{(n)}, j = \{0, \ldots, P_i \times P_i\}$ are the output of the level-i encoder. z_0 is the zero-padding token, i is the number of levels of the encoder, and n is the number of patches.

Multi-Level Transformer Decoder. The input of the decoder consists of two parts, one is the latent feature vector from the output of the same level encoder, and the other is the output of the previous level decoder, which is the latent head vector. In addition, the output of the decoder is the reconstruction feature for each patch, and they are all reconstructed into a feature map of $H \times W$ shape. The formula of the decoder of the level-i transformer is as follows,

$$\hat{z}_1^{(n)}, \ldots, \hat{z}_{P_i \times P_i}^{(n)} = F_{decoder} \left(E_0^{(n)}, E_1^{(n)}, \ldots, E_{P_i \times P_i}^{(n)} \right) \tag{3}$$

where $E_j^{(n)}, j = \{1, \ldots, P_i \times P_i\}$ are the outputs of the same level encoder using skip connections, and $E_0^{(n)}$ is the output from the previous level transformer decoder. $\hat{z}_j^{(n)}, j = \{0, \ldots, P_i \times P_i\}$ are the outputs of the current decoder.

Based on the image features extracted by pre-training, the feature map can be reconstructed by a symmetric multi-level U-shaped transformer to get the reconstruction error map $\hat{z}$:

$$\hat{z} = R(z) \tag{4}$$

where $R(z)$ represents the multi-level transformer autoencoder network. z is the image features extracted by the pre-training CNN network.

3.3 Loss Function

The reconstruction loss makes the output features reconstructed from the multi-level transformer similar to its input image features. Specifically, we calculate the $L2$ distance between z and the reconstructed, $\hat{z}$, which ensures that our model can reconstruct image features contextually similar to non-landslide images in the training phase. The reconstruction loss is shown below,

$$L_{rec} = \mathbb{E}\|z - \hat{z}\|_2 \tag{5}$$

3.4 Landslide Detection

Since the reconstruction error can reflect the differences between the landslide and non-landslide images, we can directly use the reconstruction error as the anomaly score. When the normalized anomaly score exceeds a predefined threshold, this image is classified as a landslide image.

$$S(z) = L_{rec}(z) \tag{6}$$

$$N(S(z)) = (S(z) - \min(S(z)))/(\max(S(z)) - \min(S(z))) \tag{7}$$

$S(z)$ represents the anomaly scores, and $N(S(z))$ represents the min-max normalization over the whole samples.

Algorithm 1 Multi-level Transformer Autoencoder for Landslide Detection

---

Input: image, $x = \{(x_i, y_i)\}_{i=1}^{N}$, Iterations, L, threshold, τ
Initialize l=0, $S = 0$

1. Get z by feeding x into the pre-training network
2. while $l<L$ do
3. Sample $\{(x_1, y_1), ..., (x_m, y_m)\}$ from non-landslide and landslide images
4. For $i = 1$ to 3 do
5.   Split the feature map, z, to patches, $P_i \times P_i$, and add position encoding, then fed into the level-i encoder
6.   The latent vectors, e_i, is calculated using Equation (2)
7. For $i = 3$ to 1 do
8.   Fed the latent feature vector into the level-i decoder
9.   The reconstructed feature map, z_i, is calculated using Equation (3)
10. The reconstruction loss is calculated using Equation (5)
11. Calculate the anomaly score, S, using Equations (6) and (7)
12. Classify each image as a landslide image if $S >\tau$, otherwise the non-landslide image.
13. End

---

4   Experiment

4.1   Datasets Description

Ji S et al. [12] created an open-source large landslide dataset named the Bijie landslide dataset. So, we use it to evaluate our model. The dataset consists of satellite optical images, shapefiles of landslides' boundaries and digital elevation models which contains 770 landslide images and 2003 non-landslide images. They were cropped from the TripleSat satellite images. Some image examples of the Bijie landslide dataset are shown in Fig. 4.

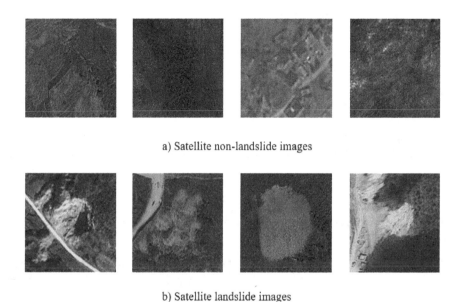

a) Satellite non-landslide images

b) Satellite landslide images

Fig. 4. The Bijie landslide dataset

We treat the experiment as a one-classification task to detect landslide images. The training phase uses only non-landslide images, and the test phase contains both landslide and non-landslide images. We divide 70% of the 2003 non-landslide images as normal training data, and the rest of the non-landslide images and landslide images are used as the test data. Our purpose is to identify landslide images from a wide variety of landslide and non-landslide images to verify the effectiveness of our method. Details of the datasets and corresponding data distributions used in our experiments are shown in Table 1.

4.2   Performance Metrics

We use five metrics to evaluate the model, including AUC, Accuracy, Precision, Recall, and F1-score. AUC is the area under the receiver operating characteristic curve. The other metrics are described and presented as follows.

Table 1. Details of Bijie dataset

Dataset	Training data	Testing data
Bijie [12]	1402 non-landslide images	601 non-landslide images and 770 landslide images

Accuracy indicates the ratio of correctly predicting landslide and non-landslide images in the overall images. The formula is shown as follows,

$$Accuracy = \frac{TP + TN}{TP + TN + FP + FN} \tag{8}$$

Precision indicates the ratio of correctly predicting landslide images in the overall images. The formula is shown as follows,

$$Precision = \frac{TP}{TP + FP} \tag{9}$$

Recall indicates the ratio of correctly predicting landslide images among all landslide images. The formula is shown as follows,

$$Recall = \frac{TP}{TP + FN} \tag{10}$$

F1-score is calculated by considering both precision and recall, and is the weighted average of both. The formula is shown as follows,

$$F1 - score = \frac{2 \times Precision \times Recall}{Precision + Recall} \tag{11}$$

where false negative (FN) indicates the number of non-landslide images that were falsely judged to be landslide images. The false positive (FP) represents the number of landslide images that were falsely identified as non-landslide images. The true positive (TP) represents the number of non-landslide images correctly identified as positive. The true negative (TN) is the number of landslide images correctly identified as negative.

4.3 Implementation Detail

Before training and testing, we randomly rotate the images by 10 degrees and crop them to the same size of 256 × 256. The entire network contains three transformer encoders and decoders, respectively. And the patch size is set as 4. Different from the original transformer structure, we set the attention layer dimension to 512 and the feedforward layer dimension to 1024. We used the Adam optimizer to train the multi-level transformer, and the learning rate is set to 0.0001. The model is trained by 200 epochs, and the batch size is 2. We use U-net as a comparison method, which adopts the conventional CNN network structure to reconstruct the pre-trained image features. We conduct our experiments on an NVIDIA RTX 3090 GPU on Pytorch 1.9.1.

5 Result and Discussion

Table 2 shows the results of one-class landslide detection on the Bijie dataset. Compared to CNN and U-Net as an autoencoder, our multi-level transformer autoencoder model has a significant improvement in AUC due to the multi-level feature extraction. In addition, our model has a slight improvement over the U-Net in accuracy, precision, recall, and F1-score. Especially, the recall can reach 92.5% on the basis of certain accuracy performance, which shows that our model can be effectively used for landslide detection.

Table 2. Landslide detection results

Method/Metric	AUC	Accuracy	Precision	Recall	F1-score
CNN	0.564	0.573	0.544	0.885	0.674
U-Net	0.597	0.602	0.589	0.907	0.726
Our model	**0.658**	**0.622**	**0.61**	**0.925**	**0.735**

6 Conclusion

We apply a feature extraction network and a multi-level transformer network to feature extraction and reconstruction of landslide images to perform landslide detection task. Based on the U-Net network structure, we built a U-shaped transformer autoencoder, which can extract and reconstruct image features from both local and global perspectives. Experiments show that compared with the U-Net model using the traditional convolutional neural network, our model has different degrees of improvement in indicators such as AUC and F1-score. In addition, our method can reach a higher recall result based on ensuring a certain precision, which is exceptionally suitable for natural hazard detection like landslides. This will be of great help in the identification of landslide images captured by 6G satellites.

Acknowledgment. This work was supported by Heilongjiang Province Natural Science Foundation under Grant LH2022F034.

References

1. Chen, W., et al.: Spatial prediction of landslide susceptibility using an adaptive neuro-fuzzy inference system combined with frequency ratio, generalized additive model, and support vector machine techniques. Geomorphology **297**, 69–85 (2017)
2. Cullen, C.A., Al-Suhili, R., Khanbilvardi, R.: Guidance index for shallow landslide hazard analysis. Remote Sens. **8**, 866 (2016)
3. Liu, Y., Gross, L., Li, Z., Li, X., Fan, X., Qi, W.: Automatic building extraction on high-resolution remote sensing imagery using deep convolutional encoder-decoder with spatial pyramid pooling. IEEE Access **7**, 128774–128786 (2019)

4. Liu, Y., Li, Z., Wei, B., Li, X., Fu, B.: Seismic vulnerability assessment at urban scale using data mining and GIScience technology: application to Urumqi (China). Geomat. Nat. Haz. Risk **10**(1), 958–985 (2019)

5. Martha, T.R., Kerle, N., Jetten, V., van Westen, C.J., Kumar, K.V.: Characterising spectral, spatial and morphometric properties of landslides for semi-automatic detection using object-oriented methods. Geomorphology **116**(1–2), 24–36 (2010)

6. Cortes, C., Vapnik, V.: Support-vector networks. Mach. Learn. **20**(3), 273–297 (1995)

7. Pradhan, B., Seeni, M.I., Nampak, H.: Integration of LiDAR and QuickBird data for automatic landslide detection using object-based analysis and random forests. In: Pradhan, B. (ed.) Laser Scanning Applications in Landslide Assessment, pp. 69–81. Springer, Heidelberg (2017). https://doi.org/10.1007/978-3-319-55342-9_4

8. Dou, J., et al.: Automatic case-based reasoning approach for landslide detection: integration of object-oriented image analysis and a genetic algorithm. Remote Sens. **7**(4), 4318–4342 (2015)

9. Huang, G., Liu, Z., Pleiss, G., et al.: Convolutional networks with dense connectivity. IEEE Trans. Pattern Anal. Mach. Intell. (2019)

10. Ghorbanzadeh, O., Blaschke, T., Gholamnia, K., Meena, S.R., Tiede, D., Aryal, J.: Evaluation of different machine learning methods and deep-learning convolutional neural networks for landslide detection. Remote Sens. **11**(2), 196 (2019)

11. Ji, S., Yu, D., Shen, C., et al.: Landslide detection from an open satellite imagery and digital elevation model dataset using attention boosted convolutional neural networks. Landslides **17**(6), 1337–1352 (2020)

12. Raghu, M., Unterthiner, T., Kornblith, S., et al.: Do vision transformers see like convolutional neural networks? Adv. Neural. Inf. Process. Syst. **34**, 12116–12128 (2021)

13. Dosovitskiy, A., Beyer, L., Kolesnikov, A., et al.: An image is worth 16x16 words: transformers for image recognition at scale. arXiv preprint arXiv:2010.11929 (2020)

14. Vaswani, A., Shazeer, N., Parmar, N., et al.: Attention is all you need. In: Advances in Neural Information Processing Systems, p. 30 (2017)

15. Yuan, L., Hou, Q., Jiang, Z., et al.: Volo: vision outlooker for visual recognition. arXiv preprint arXiv:2106.13112 (2021)

16. Wang, W., Xie, E., Li, X., et al.: Pvt v2: improved baselines with pyramid vision transformer. Comput. Vis. Media **8**(3), 415–424 (2022)

17. Lee, Y., Kang, P.: AnoViT: unsupervised anomaly detection and localization with vision transformer-based encoder-decoder. IEEE Access **10**, 46717–46724 (2022)

18. Botta, A., Pescapé, A.: On the performance of new generation satellite broadband internet services. IEEE Commun. Mag. **52**(6), 202–209 (2014)

19. Chini, P., Giambene, G., Kota, S.: A survey on mobile satellite systems. Int. J. Satell. Commun. Network. **28**(1), 29–57 (2010)

20. Ronneberger, O., Fischer, P., Brox, T.: U-net: convolutional networks for biomedical image segmentation. In: Navab, N., Hornegger, J., Wells, W.M., Frangi, A.F. (eds.) MICCAI 2015. LNCS, vol. 9351, pp. 234–241. Springer, Cham (2015). https://doi.org/10.1007/978-3-319-24574-4_28

21. Liu, Z., Lin, Y., Cao, Y., et al.: Swin transformer: hierarchical vision transformer using shifted windows. In: Proceedings of the IEEE/CVF International Conference on Computer Vision, pp. 10012–10022 (2021)

22. He, K., Zhang, X., Ren, S., et al.: Deep residual learning for image recognition. In: Proceedings of the IEEE Conference on Computer Vision and Pattern Recognition, pp. 770–778 (2016)

23. Deng, J., Dong, W., Socher, R., et al.: Imagenet: a large-scale image database. In: 2009 IEEE Conference on Computer Vision and Pattern Recognition, pp. 248–255. IEEE (2009)

Survey on Anti-jamming Technology of UAV Communication

Tong Liu[✉], Jiaqi Huang, Jianming Guo, and Yongzhi Shan

Norinco Group Air Ammunition Research Institute, Beijing, China
liutongsasa@hotmail.com

Abstract. Modern warfare is a five-in-one joint operation involving sea, land, air, air and electricity. Information weapons have become an important combat force. As the nerve center of UAV system, UAV data link is an information bridge connecting UAV with other information systems, command and control systems, weapon systems and so on. It is also a means to realize joint operations such as information communication and interoperation. In recent years, several military operations involving UAVs have shown that the UAVs data link can greatly shorten the time of reconnaissance, control, strike and evaluation, and has become an important means to improve combat effectiveness. At present, with the wide application of UAVs in military operations of various countries, unmanned systems are gradually developing from supporting combat equipment to main combat equipment, and countries are also developing anti-UAV means. UAV data links are faced with many challenges, such as shortage of spectrum resources, complex spectrum environment, serious environmental interference and human interference. Thus, higher requirements are put forward for its security, reliability and adaptability in complex environment.

Keywords: UAV · Data Links · Anti-jamming Technique

1 Introduction

Nowadays, the electromagnetic environment of battlefield is extremely complex, and the development of communication jamming equipment is rapid. For example, the EC2130 compass call communication electronic warfare aircraft jamming system operating frequency can reach 1GHz, power up to 5–10 kW, can suppress the enemy command and control network and air defense network; The Wolf pack system of the US Army mainly deals with frequencies-hop, low-power and networked communication systems. The working frequency band is 20 MHz–2.5 GHz. It uses small low-power and distributed equipment to destroy enemy communication networks through internal network interconnection technology. The distributed system which is close to and encircling the combat target is adopted to obtain the advantages of tactical power and detection sensitivity. Each distributed jamming point obtains the advantages of tactical radio frequency through internal networking. Therefore, in order to give full play to the role of data link, the anti-jamming ability of data link must be further improved.

© ICST Institute for Computer Sciences, Social Informatics and Telecommunications Engineering 2023
Published by Springer Nature Switzerland AG 2023. All Rights Reserved
A. Li et al. (Eds.): 6GN 2022, LNICST 504, pp. 111–121, 2023.
https://doi.org/10.1007/978-3-031-36011-4_10

Design of UAV data link more complicated than in other wireless communication system design, in terms of anti-interference of UAVs faces the challenge of the information transmission over a long distance caused the decline of the obstacles in the path loss, route of transmission, high-speed movement of unmanned aerial vehicle (UAV) doppler frequency shift and complex spectrum environment of interference and obstruction.

1.1 A Link Long Distance Path Loss

The most serious challenge of the UAV data link system is the long-distance transmission of information, which will bring the following challenges to the performance of the data link system:

(1) Power attenuation and spectral efficiency reduction. The wireless transmission link of IEEE802.11, also known as Wi-Fi, can only cover 100 m, while the later developed IEEE802.16, also known as WiMAX, can cover 3 km in rural areas and 1 km in urban areas. The above coverage range also applies to 3GPPLTE. General aviation data links require 360 km coverage, so the use of these traditional wireless communication links to implement long-distance measurement, control and transmission will cause serious power attenuation and extremely low spectral efficiency. Literature [8] shows that WiMAX network can achieve spectrum efficiency of 3 bps–5 bps/Hz in the range of 0.9 km. For long-distance transmission, the spectral efficiency will be even lower.

(2) Transmission delay. The long distance transmission of information will also cause serious delay of back and forth transmission time, which will greatly increase the communication protection time slot. Compared with the minimum delay of 17 μs for WiMAX networks over a range of 5 km, a one-way transmission of 360 km requires 1.2 ms.

(3) In addition, the long-distance transmission of information will increase the bit error rate of the system, reduce the signal to noise ratio of the receiver, and increase the probability of packet loss.

1.2 High Speed Movement of UAV Platform

The high speed movement of the UAV can bring Doppler frequency shift to the receiver, and the size of Doppler frequency shift is proportional to the speed of movement and inversely proportional to the wavelength. It can be calculated that the Doppler shift of L-DACS1 at 600 km/h and 1164 MHz is 1213 Hz, while the Doppler shift of WiMAX at 100 km/h and 2.5 GHz is 231.5 Hz. Because the frequency of electromagnetic wave is inversely proportional to the wavelength, the lower the working frequency band, the smaller the Doppler shift will be for the UAV moving at high speed. However, the spectrum resources in the low frequency band are very tight, so the Doppler shift brought by the high-speed movement of the UAV is a great challenge to the UAV data link.

1.3 Fading Caused by Obstacles in Link

The main frequency band of UAV data link application is microwave (300 MHz–3000 GHz), because microwave link has higher available bandwidth, but the microwave frequency is high, the wavelength is very short, and there is no diffraction function. This characteristic of links creates the following communication challenges:

(1) Shadow fading. The obstacles encountered in the communication process of UAV data link can partially or completely block the signal transmission and cause serious shadow fading.

(2) Multipath fading. On a smaller scale, the receiver receives different phases of different copies of the same signal from different paths due to the scattering and reflection of electromagnetic waves through obstacles, resulting in multipath fading of wireless signals. Because the UAV data link is changing dynamically, the phase difference between replicas is also changing dynamically, so it is impossible to eliminate multipath fading by adding a fading overhead in traditional static wireless communication.

(3) In addition, multipath fading will cause serious symbol interference.

1.4   Human Non-malicious Interference and Malicious Interference

Non-malicious interference refers to the interference caused by the radio signals of other devices in the spectrum environment to the UAV data link. Such interference is superimposed on the signals transmitted in the communication channel, which distorts the original signal and leads to information error or loss. For example, when a signal with the same or similar frequency is generated in a circuit with different frequencies, intermodulation interference will occur. The malicious interference mainly exists in the military field, mainly the partial pressure type interference and deception type interference.

(1) Suppression interference refers to a kind of artificial communication interference in which the interference signal power continuously transmitted by the jammer is greater than the signal power of the UAV data link, so that the communication nodes in the data link cannot receive the radio frequency signal correctly, leading to the interruption of the communication link. According to the form of interference signal, clamped interference can be divided into three types: single frequency interference, narrowband interference and wideband interference. Since the clamped interference power swamps the desired signal or blocks the RF front end, its modulation information is irrelevant.

(2) To cheat interference with UAV data link using signal structure similar signals as a cheat, so can not detect induced receiver tracking capture deception signals, thus achieve the purpose of reduce its anti-jamming ability, and can be used with data link signal approximation power, avoid the excessive power be detected and reduced costs. In practical applications, such as the military field, the receiver is often faced with high dynamic, weak signal, strong interference or signal occlusion and other complex and variable environment, then the receiver will lose the lock to capture the deception signal or the influence of the deception signal increases in the tracking, and the whole system will be affected.

1.5   Crowded Spectrum Environment

Due to the shortage of spectrum resources, it is inevitably threatened by external interference signals. Traditional UAV data link uses HF, VHF and SATCOM frequency bands, but SATCOM frequency band cannot guarantee that every data transmission stage can be used, and HF and VHF are becoming more and more crowded. In China, according to the frequency usage requirements of unmanned aerial vehicles issued by the Ministry of Industry and Information Technology, the frequency bands can be used: 840.5 MHz–845 MHz, 1430 MHz–1444 MHz and 2408 MHz–2440 MHz. Due to the shortage of spectrum resources, it is inevitably threatened by external interference signals. The modern UAV combat environment and combat mission are becoming more and more complex. The traditional anti-interference methods can no longer guarantee the high efficiency and reliability of the UAV data link communication. It is urgent to improve the anti-interference ability of the UAV data link in the complex electromagnetic environment under the limited spectrum resources.

To sum up, the use of unmanned aerial vehicle (UAV) to fight the implementation of the cluster, complex battlefield environment, bad data link communications facing enemy remote accurate fire fighting, electrical interference suppression and battlefield electromagnetic compatibility interacting multiple threats, such as to make the UAV can cluster anti-jamming communication under the complex battlefield environment, requires UAV data link system have the following abilities:

(1) Extensive spectrum management and allocation capabilities: available spectrum resources can be dynamically allocated to UAVs in any region and at any time;
(2) the ability to address large-scale power attenuation caused by long-distance transmission of information;
(3) the ability to avoid and avoid non-malicious interference;
(4) Ability to resist malicious interference: on the one hand, it is necessary to have strong anti-reconnaissance ability, which can reduce the probability of enemy reconnaissance system intercepting signals of UAV data link system through technical means such as concealing signal waveform, controlling transmission power and controlling transmission direction. On the other hand, in the process of system development, strong interference suppression, anti-interference modulation and adaptive filtering and other technologies should be fully adopted to improve the communication ability of strong resistance of UAV data link system under complex conditions, so as to effectively cope with various interference modes of targeting and arresting.
(5) Network survivability: Data link system should have good network topology and routing protocol design, as the key transmission network node paralysis of fire fighting or network attack, information network can according to the UAV flying position and the relationship between ground control site, automatically adjust the information communication nodes, to optimize the data link information transmission route, achieve against the dense deposit under the condition of communication;
(6) Capable of identifying friend or foe: in a complex confrontation environment, the enemy may take advantage of electromagnetic interference and suppression, and at the same time, use network intrusion, sending false instructions and other ways to remotely kidnap and control the UAV. Therefore, the identification function of friend or foe should be strengthened in the UAV data link system to prevent the false ground stations from pretending to be our ground control force to obtain the control authority of the UAV, or pretending to be our air formation combat force, so as to destroy and interfere with the scheduled combat plan of our formation.

2 Anti-jamming Technology (Mode and Principle)

In the future battlefield, the electromagnetic environment will be very bad, the situation of information warfare will be extremely complex. The difficulty of anti-interference ability lies in how to determine the interference spectrum and how to use the strategy to suppress it. In order to improve the anti-interference ability of UAV data link equipment, it is necessary to solve the interference caused by a variety of wireless signals, signal characteristics exposure, poor confidentiality and other problems. Multi-dimensional comprehensive anti-interference, anti-interception and anti-detection means are adopted to realize multi-dimensional anti-strong interference information transmission and distribution to cope with the future complex electromagnetic battlefield environment, and improve the reliability and persistence of UAV data link information transmission.

At present, the UAV data link USES a variety of anti-jamming technology, mainly including channel coding technology, spread spectrum technology, etc., and multiple input multiple output (MIMO) and orthogonal frequency division multiplexing (OFDM) technology, adaptive antenna technology and the emergence of cognitive radio (CR) technology, will also be the anti-interference ability of the UAV data link, provide strong technical support.

2.1 Channel Coding Technique

Due to interference or other reasons, there will be error codes during data transmission in the data link, so that the remote control instructions, telemetry parameters or images received by the receiver will be wrong. According to Shannon's channel coding theory, as long as the transmission rate of information is lower than the channel capacity, a channel coding method can always be found to make the error probability arbitrarily small. Therefore, the anti-interference ability of the data link can be improved by processing the data through channel coding.

The alternative channel coding methods mainly include convolutional code, BCH code, RS code, interleaved code and concatenated code. For example, the us army's Link16 data link adopts RS(31,16) coding in the information segment, and a 16bit supervision segment is added after every 15bit information segment, which can detect and correct 8 bit errors. When the Link16 data link is interfered with, the bit error rate of Link16 should be 0.45 at least, so that Link16 can not detect and correct the bit error and realize effective interference. According to the simulation results of Yang Guang et al., the modulation system with RS coding and interleaving has better anti-interference performance compared with the modulation system with RS coding and the modulation system without coding under the condition of partial frequency band interference, which can effectively ensure the reliability of datalinks message transmission [1]. The higher the complexity of channel coding, the longer the processing time of link equipment. Therefore, the channel coding of UAV data link should be designed by considering the requirements of transmission delay and anti-interference performance of UAV data link.

2.2 Spread Spectrum Technology

The basic principle of spread spectrum technology is that the transmitted signal is expanded to a very wide frequency band, which is much wider than the band width of the transmitted information. The signal is recovered to the information bandwidth through correlation reception at the receiver. The basic principle can be expressed as

$$C = B \log_2\left(1 + \frac{S}{N}\right) = B \log_2\left(1 + \frac{S}{n_0 B}\right) \tag{1}$$

where, N is the noise power; S is the average power of the signal; B is the signal bandwidth; C is the channel capacity; N0 is the power spectral density of white noise. To improve the channel capacity C, it can be achieved by increasing the signal-to-noise ratio S/N or increasing the signal bandwidth B. However, there is a pairwise ratio between the signal-to-noise ratio S/N and the channel capacity C, so increasing the signal bandwidth B is more effective.

Spread spectrum technology is a widely used anti-jamming technology in US military datalink. It can be divided into direct sequence spread spectrum technology (DSSS), frequency hopping technology (FHSS) and time hopping technology (THSS) according to different ways of spreading spectrum.

2.2.1   Direct Sequence Spread Spectrum Technology

The working principle of DSSS system is shown in Fig. 1. At the origin, the spread spectrum code sequence with high bit rate is used to expand the spectrum at the origin, which reduces the power spectral density of the data link signal, makes it difficult for the enemy to detect it, and improves the anti-interference ability. In the receiving end with the same spread spectrum code sequence, interference and noise signal after the spread code sequence modulation, spectrum broadening, power spectral density reduction, spread spectrum signal after demodulation into a narrowband signal, power spectral density improvement, the gain of the system has increased several times, also improve the anti-interference ability of the system.

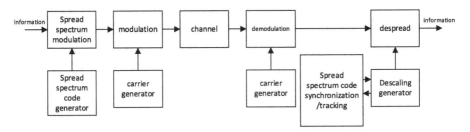

Fig. 1. Principle of direct sequence spread spectrum communication system

2.2.2   Frequency Hopping Technology

The working principle of the FHSS system is shown in Fig. 2. The spread spectrum code sequence signal is used for frequency shift keying modulation at the origin end to make the carrier frequency jump continuously, and the spread spectrum code sequence is used for signal recovery at the receiver end. In the time domain, the FH signal is a multi-frequency shift keying signal. In the frequency domain, the FH signal jumps in a wide frequency band at unequal intervals. Compared with fixed frequency signal, as long as the enemy is not clear about the law of carrier frequency hopping, it is difficult to intercept our communication content, even if some frequency points are interfered by the enemy, it can still carry out normal communication on other frequency points that have not been interfered, so as to have good anti-interference ability.

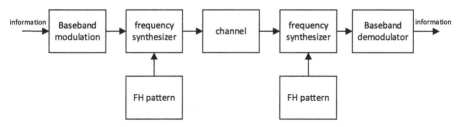

Fig. 2. Working principle of frequency hopping communication system

2.2.3 Time Hopping Technology

THSS is to make the transmitted signal jump on the time axis. The time axis can be divided into many time slices. Which time slice the transmitted signal in a frame is controlled by the spread spectrum sequence. Figure 3 is the basic block diagram of THSS system. The input data at the origin is stored first, and the on-off switch is controlled by the spread spectrum code sequence of the spread spectrum code generator. After two-phase or four-phase modulation, it is transmitted after RF modulation. At the receiving end, the IF signal output by the RF receiver is controlled by the locally generated spread spectrum code sequence which is the same as the origin, and then sent to the data memory and the output data after retiming through the two-phase or four-phase demodulator. As long as the receiving and receiving ends are strictly synchronized in time, the original data can be correctly recovered. Because the simple time-hopping method is not strong anti-interference, it is usually combined with other methods.

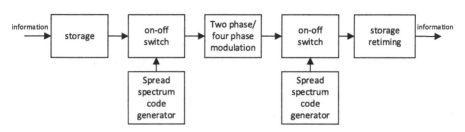

Fig. 3. Principle of time-hopping spread spectrum system

2.2.4   Combination Technology

Data link in the use of spread spectrum technology, usually adopt a combination of several spread spectrum methods. For example, American Link16 data link uses the combination technology of direct sequence spread spectrum, frequency hopping and time hopping, and CCSK code direct spread spectrum sequence with good autocorrelation performance. It hops 51 frequency points between 969 MHz and 1206 MHz at a rate of 77,000 times seconds, and each pulse symbol changes the carrier frequency once. However, the signal duration of each pulse is only the first 6.4 μs, and the hop time delay is up to 2.4585 ms [2]. This combination technique increases the difficulty of the synchronization technique. Both to complete the frequency hopping pattern synchronization. And to complete the spread spectrum sequence synchronization, and under the condition of know the characteristic of spread spectrum code sequence, by blocking interference with non-coherent PN code spread spectrum interference of modular interference, can effectively interference [3] to spread spectrum communication system, which leads to the defects of the current spread spectrum communication, therefore, it is necessary to develop a better spread spectrum sequence.

2.3   Multiple Input Multiple Output Technology

MIMO technology is an important communication technology emerging in recent years, which has attracted extensive attention. It refers to the wireless communication technology in which signals are transmitted through multiple antennas at the transmitter end and received by multiple antennas at the receiver end. MIMO technology, combined with OFDM and space-time coding, can achieve spatial diversity, time diversity and frequency diversity, and can achieve anti-interference in airspace, time domain and frequency domain. However, how to apply MIMO technology to anti-jamming technology of data link still needs to be studied on antenna configuration, power allocation and signal detection.

2.4   Orthogonal Frequency Division Multiplexing Technology

OFDM technology divides the channel into several orthogonal sub-channels, converts the high-speed data signals into parallel low-speed sub-data streams, and then modulates them to the sub-channels for transmission. Orthogonal signals can be separated by adopting correlation techniques at the receiver to reduce the mutual interference between sub-channels. The signal bandwidth on each subchannel is less than the correlation bandwidth of the signal, then each subchannel can be regarded as flat fading, so as to eliminate inter-symbol interference.

2.5   Adaptive Antenna Technology

At present, directional antenna technology is mostly used for anti-interference in UAV data link. Directional antenna means that the transmitted and received electromagnetic waves are particularly strong in one or several specific directions, while the received electromagnetic waves of the transmitter are 0 or minimal in other directions. The purpose of anti-interference can be achieved by suppressing the reception of interference signals. The narrower the antenna beam, the stronger the concealment and the stronger the anti-interference ability.

Adaptive antenna technology using the principle of phased array antenna, the beam space filtering from all directions, it through to the antenna array element excitation adjustment, optimize the antenna array pattern, using the digital signal processing technology of jamming signal processing and recognition, in the direction of interference sources to form a beam of zero, restrain direction outside the reception, reduces the interference, At the same time reduce electromagnetic environmental pollution. The combination of spread spectrum technology and adaptive antenna technology is the main means of anti-jamming in American military satellite communication system.

The disadvantage of the adaptive antenna is that it forms a blind area in the zero-point direction, which affects the normal use of users in this area.

2.6 Cognitive Radio Technology

J.M itola puts forward the concept of cognitive radio, he thought the cognitive radio is an intelligent wireless communication system, through the study of the perception of the radio environment and active learning, real-time change communication system working parameters, such as encoding and modulation mode, working frequency and transmission power, dynamic testing and the use of idle spectrum, Adapt to changes in the external radio environment.

UAV data link can make use of cognitive radio technology monitoring communication frequency interference, according to the features of the interference signal, the real-time change the way data link channel coding and spread spectrum code sequence and frequency hopping pattern, jump way, the parameters such as power configuration, antenna model, the use of wireless spectrum resources reasonably, improve the information transmission ability and anti-interference ability.

3 Anti-jamming Technology of UAV Data Link

The anti-jamming technologies applied to UAV data link are mainly divided into three categories: related technologies to improve system reliability and effectiveness, based on cooperative communication technology and anti-jamming technology based on cognitive radio.

3.1 Improve Communication Reliability and Effectiveness

These related technologies include performance evaluation of multiple-input multiple-output (MIMO) systems [4, 5], information transmission strategies [6, 7], and the use of cellular systems and other wireless communication systems [8, 9]. Technical research focuses on physical layer and link layer are as follows:

(1) Integration of low-power MIMO systems.
(2) Research and use of anti-interference technology represented by spread spectrum and frequency hopping technology.

(3) Physical layer and MAC layer protocols and policies with high throughput and high reliability under limited spectrum resources.

(4) Integration of UAV data link system, satellite communication system and other wireless communication systems.

3.2 Based on Cooperative Communication

Literature [10] puts forward a cooperative communication method under the condition of multiple sources, and simulation results show that this scheme reduces the bit error rate of the received signal. Under the condition of dynamic transmission rate, the transmission reliability of the scheme is higher. The research of multi-source cooperative communication points out the direction of multi-link cooperative information transmission of UAV data link. Literatures [10] and [11] proposed the method of asynchronous cooperative information transmission on the basis of cooperative communication, and enhanced the reliability of information transmission from the physical layer (to build asynchronous cooperative transmission mode in 3D space) and the link layer (through multi-link cooperative forwarding protocol) respectively. The former makes full use of three kinds of spatial diversity technology in the physical layer, improves the diversity gain, and greatly improves the anti-interference ability. The latter can eliminate the influence of short-time link variation by single transmit multiple receive and bootstrap response algorithm based on random synchronous competition window at the link layer, obtain better network arrival rate and energy efficiency, enhance transmission reliability, and improve anti-interference ability. Literature [12] puts forward a relay selection method for cooperative communication under the outdated channel state information generated when the receiver and transmitter move relative to each other or the environment changes rapidly. Selecting the optimal relay can resist the interference to the cooperative communication system to a certain extent. Reference [13] proposed a channel state information prediction technology based on MAP criterion to improve the anti-interference ability of cooperative communication systems.

3.3 Based on Cognitive Radio

In addition, in order to solve the problem of spectrum resource shortage and the increasing difficulty of spectrum management with the widespread use of UAVs, cognitive radio technology for spectrum sensing and system reconstruction of UAVs is studied. Literature [14] proposes a prediction and evaluation method combining support vector machine and power criterion for the interference degree of UAV data link in the complex environment composed of geographical environment, meteorological environment, electromagnetic environment, etc. The predicted results can be used for the reconstruction of UAV data link. On the basis of analyzing the current problems of UAV data link, literature [15] puts forward the concept and connotation of UAV intelligent data link based on cognitive radio, describes the working process, and gives the index system and function classification of UAV intelligent data link. Based on the function of UAV data link, the architecture of UAV intelligent data link is put forward. Literature [16] proposes a multi-parameter planning method for UAV data link based on state machine, which provides a feasible and effective idea for the reconstruction of UAV data link.

References

1. Yang, G., Zhou, J., Luo, P.: Performance analysis of JTIDS data link under partial frequency band interference. J. Natl. Univ. Defense Technol. **32**, 122–126 (2010)
2. Yin, L., Yan, J., Fan, Y.: Evaluation and simulation of anti-jamming performance of link-16 tactical data link. Fire Control Command Control **34**, 70–75 (2009)
3. Wang, P., Wang, Z., Sun, S.: Research on communication jamming for US Military joint tactical information distribution system. Ship Electron. Countermeas. **29**, 3–5 (2006)
4. Gans, M.J., et al.: Enhancing connectivity of unmanned vehicles through MIMO communications. IN: 2013 IEEE 78th Vehicular Technology Conference (VTC Fall), pp. 1–5 (2013). https://doi.org/10.1109/VTCFall.2013.6692190
5. Su, W., Matyjas, J.D., Gans, M.J., Batalama, S.: Maximum achievable capacity in airborne MIMO communications with arbitrary alignments of linear transceiver antenna arrays. IEEE Trans. Wirel. Commun. **12**(11), 5584–5593 (2013). https://doi.org/10.1109/TWC.2013.101 613.121746
6. Li, J., Zhou, Y., Lamont, L.: Communication architectures and protocols for networking unmanned aerial vehicles. In: 2013 IEEE Globecom Workshops (GC Wkshps), pp. 1415–1420 (2013). https://doi.org/10.1109/GLOCOMW.2013.6825193
7. Cheng, B.N., Charland, R., Christensen, P., Veytser, L., Wheeler, J.: Evaluation of a multihop airborne IP backbone with heterogeneous radio technologies. IEEE Trans. Mob. Comput. **13**(2), 299–310 (2014). https://doi.org/10.1109/TMC.2012.250
8. Gomez, K., Rasheed, T., Reynaud, L., Kandeepan, S.: On the performance of aerial LTE base-stations for public safety and emergency recovery. In: 2013 IEEE Globecom Workshops (GC Wkshps), pp. 1391–1396 (2013). https://doi.org/10.1109/GLOCOMW.2013.6825189
9. Yanmaz, E., Kuschnig, R., Bettstetter, C.: Channel measurements over 802.11a-based UAV-to-ground links. In: 2011 IEEE GLOBECOM Workshops (GC Wkshps), pp. 1280–1284 (2011). https://doi.org/10.1109/GLOCOMW.2011.6162389
10. Ribeiro, A., Wang, R., Giannakis, G.B.: Multi-source cooperation with full-diversity spectral-efficiency and controllable-complexity. In: 2006 IEEE 7th Workshop on Signal Processing Advances in Wireless Communications, pp. 1–5 (2006). https://doi.org/10.1109/SPAWC. 2006.346422
11. Ribeiro, A., Sidiropoulos, N.D., Giannakis, G.B., Yu, Y.: Achieving wireline random access throughput in wireless networking via user cooperation. IEEE Trans. Inf. Theory **53**(2), 732–758 (2007). https://doi.org/10.1109/TIT.2006.889718
12. Fer, L., Gao, Q., Zhang, J., et al.: Relay selection with outdated channel state information in cooperative communication systems. IET Commun. **7**, 1557–1565 (2013)
13. Fer, L., Zhang, J., Gao, Q., et al.: Outage-optimal relay strategy under outdated channel state information in decode-and-forward cooperative communication systems. IET Commun. **9**, 441–450 (2015)
14. Zhang, W., Ding, W., Liu, C.: Pre-test method for dry disturbance effect of data chain without human and machine in complex heterocyclic environment. Syst. Eng. Electr. Technol. **38**, 760–766 (2016)
15. Chen, Z., Tao, J., Fan, J.: Intelligent data link architecture of UAV. Wire-Free Electr. Eng. **39**, 4–6 (2009)
16. Wenqian, H., Wenrui, D., Chunhui, L.: Multi-parametric programming approach for data link of UAS based on state machine. In: 2015 International Conference on Industrial Informatics - Computing Technology, Intelligent Technology, Industrial Information Integration, pp. 156–159 (2015). https://doi.org/10.1109/ICIICII.2015.122

Research on Building Emergency Supply Chain Decision-Making Platform Using Big Data Mining Technology

Mai Ying[✉]

Guangzhou City Polytechnic, Guangzhou, People's Republic of China
1368256332@qq.com

Abstract. For public emergencies, building an emergency supply chain platform by using big data technology can quickly realize the supply of materials. Based on the analysis of the user needs of the emergency supply chain and the factors and constraints involved in resource scheduling, the emergency resources are uniformly allocated through intelligent scheduling and other methods with big data mining as the core, so as to achieve efficient operation and provide social support for public emergencies.

Keywords: Emergency Supply Chain · Decision-making Platform · Big Data Mining Technology

1 Introduction

Since the outbreak of the COVID-19 pandemic, President Xi Jinping has delivered many important speeches to emphasize that people's life safety and health shall always be taken as the top priority and that the pandemic prevention and control currently shall be the most crucial focus. Relevant government departments and some regions were busy transferring pandemic prevention materials to Wuhan through the central medical reserve and were also rapidly organizing enterprises to resume work and production. In accordance with the data released by the Ministry of Industry and Information Technology of the People's Republic of China (MIIT), 154,500 pieces of medical protective clothing, 133,600N95 facial masks, and 82 sets of full-automatic infrared detectors have been dispatched to Hubei Province from all over China by February 2, 2020. Fortunately, the pandemic prevention materials have changed from an emergency state to a "tight balance" and progressively stayed "stably balanced". This sudden pandemic, occurring in China, a state with a large population, along with the dense flow of people during the Spring Festival and the shortage of emergency supplies, has made it such a matter worthy of discussion and research as how to effectively protect people's lives and maintain the stability of the whole society.

Supported by Guangzhou Innovation Team Scientific Research Project: Innovation team of emergency materials collection and dispatching management under major emergencies (202032794); The innovation team project of Guangdong Province universitier: Collaborative Innovation Research Term of Guangdong Strategic Emerging Industry Group (2020WCXTD032)

A. Li et al. (Eds.): 6GN 2022, LNICST 504, pp. 122–129, 2023.
https://doi.org/10.1007/978-3-031-36011-4_11

As science and technology continuously develops in China, we have entered into an era of computer network and to this day, computer network technology is being applied in a host of fields, encompassing a key one, namely, emergency management. In the operation and management of enterprises or society, the occurrence of sudden emergencies may exert an adverse influence upon the stability and safety of enterprise and social operation. Nevertheless, the implementation of emergency management measures can greatly alleviate the harm engendered by emergency accidents. In this regard, it is vital to handle emergencies in a scientific and reasonable way. China is now facing some conspicuous challenges about the emergency resources, such as insufficient investment, low degree of resource integration, and inadequate management performance. To change the status quo, the supply chain management of emergency materials dispatch can be adopted to advance cities' capability of emergency resource guarantee.

Emergency supply chain decision-making is quite sophisticated, which is composed of a series of decisions and involves the balance of multiple parties' interests. Also, the decision-making entities are diversified, the decision-making behaviors are highly complex, and the structure of the problem is not clear enough. Therefore, scientific decision-making mechanisms and methods have to be established.

2 A Decision-Making Mechanism of Emergency Supply Chain and Data Mining Technology

2.1 A Decision-Making Mechanism of Emergency Supply Chain

The research idea of emergency supply chain management derives from "the research of airlines' emergency management system". The term of emergency management was initially proposed by Causen et al. and later, in the case of demand fluctuation spawned by emergencies, Qi X. (2019) probed into the situation of a certain linear demand function where the quantity discount contract was adopted in the supply chain to deal with these emergencies. Subsequently, Xu M. et al. (2020) made a similar study on the case of the nonlinear demand function. Lei Z. and Xu J. P. (2021) defined and classified emergencies in the supply chain, and further proposed the system, organization, and process of emergency management in supply chain emergencies.

Yu H., Chen J., and Yu G. (2020) conducted research on the impact of emergencies on the supply chain coordinated by quantity discount contracts, and proposed a quantity discount contract with the feature of emergency resistance. Veronneau S. and Roy J. (2021) studied the characteristics and major influencing factors of the supply chain of dynamic global cruises. It is fair to say that Case Based Reasoning (CBR) is a paramount reasoning method in the field of artificial intelligence.

2.2 Data Mining Technology Employed in Emergency Decision-Making

To date, the data mining technology adopted in emergency decision-making chiefly encompasses: an AI Agent system with autonomous reasoning and decision-making capability to simulate and optimize the operation of the control supply chain, which has already become one of the pivotal methods in the research of supply chain. Swam M. et al. applied the multi-agent method to model the supply chain; Kalakota et al. used the Multi-Agent Simulation Model for What-if analysis, and Nissen employed a general business model to elucidate the process between Buy-Seller with Agent. Case Based Reasoning (CBR) was first proposed by Professor Schank of Yale University in a monograph published in 1982. Since the late 1980s, scholars in foreign countries have systematically studied this theory, and made some practical achievements in the fields of general problem solving, legal case analysis, auxiliary planning and others. Fu Y. et al. introduced CBR into the risk estimation of the supply chain, and effectively solved the key problems of case description, storage organization, matching case retrieval.

Bayesian Network and Bayesian Inference: in terms of supply chain emergency risk management, Roshna et al. established a risk analysis model of NTT supply chain by adopting Bayesian Network, which can help analyze the risks in the production and distribution links. Hu X. X. et al. (2017) discussed the application of Bayesian Network in supply chain emergency management. And the Method of Support Vector Machine, a machine learning algorithm based upon statistical learning theory put forward by Vapnik et al. of Bell Laboratories in the 1990s, has been extensively employed in realms of pattern recognition, data mining, nonlinear system control, modeling, distribution forecasting, collaborative early warning of supply chain partners, and supply chain performance evaluation.

3   Overall Scheme Design of the Platform

3.1 Overall Structure of the Platform

To alleviate the shortage of emergency resources in case of any emergencies, this study combines big data technology to construct a platform integrating five central links, namely, intelligent reservation, intelligent order distribution, intelligent scheduling, intelligent distribution and intelligent after-sales. Furthermore, the platform is divided into eight subsystems pursuant to business function modules, including customer center, supplier management, intelligent distribution, trading platform, scheduling center, intelligent after-sales, statistical analysis and rights management (see Fig. 1).

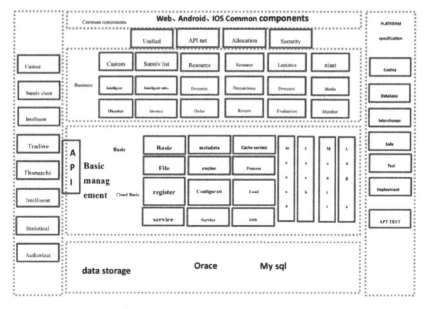

Fig. 1. Platform System Architecture

3.2 Platform Businesses

In case of sudden disasters, the platform provides intelligent scheduling, production and distribution services of emergency resources, and adopts big data to comprehensively carry out intelligent reservation; intelligent order distribution, intelligent scheduling, intelligent distribution, intelligent after-sales and evaluation services (see Fig. 2). The target users of the platform primarily involve enterprises and institutions, scientific research institutes, government departments, self-employed households, social individuals and others.

Whenever a major disaster occurs, the platform will release a corresponding special feature. Upon the release, it is necessary to distinguish the disaster type to which it belongs (meteorological disaster, marine disaster, flood disaster, geological disaster, earthquake disaster, forest-related disaster or pandemic disaster) [5]. Then, the corresponding emergency resources under different disaster types can be allocated through the classified management function of system rights management. For instance, the platform released the special feature of NCP in 2019 and the disaster type was classified into pandemic disaster, so that the system preset the following emergency supplies according to its type, such as facial masks, protective goggles, protective clothing, medical gloves and oxygen respirators. Additionally, when the supplier entered into the system, they were also required to select the disaster type in the first place and then set the emergency supplies to provide.

When a customer makes a reservation for emergency supplies, the system will conduct intelligent order distribution after the intelligent matching of the suppliers. If the reservation is made successfully, the customer will be required to pay the order successively; after this phase, the supplier can set about conducting material production and providing distribution services. In the phase of intelligent scheduling, the system provides the manual scheduling function based upon the relevant national strategic deployment requirements, and gives priority to the scheduling in the worst hit areas as well as the allocation of emergency supplies from suppliers. For example, in this NCP pandemic, the platform could conduct artificial intelligence (AI) scheduling for Wuhan and other cities in Hubei Province, gave priority to intelligent scheduling of emergency resource reservation orders in this region, and prioritized suppliers to provide emergency material production and distribution services.

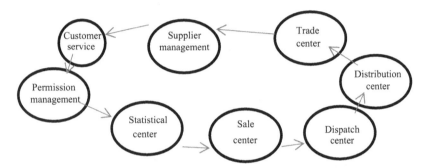

Fig. 2. The Business Process of Platform

When a major emergency disaster occurs, the platform will publish a feature about the disaster. In order to publish the feature, the platform user needs to confirm the type of disaster to which it belongs (e.g., meteorological disaster, marine, flood, geological disaster, earthquake, forest-related disaster, or epidemic disaster) and then set the emergency resources corresponding to the different pandemic types through the category management function of the system rights management. For example, if the platform releases the feature about the 2022 COVID-19 pandemic and chooses the disaster type as a pandemic disaster, the system will present the following emergency supplies, including masks, protective goggles, protective clothing, medical gloves, and ventilators. In addition, suppliers will also need to confirm the disaster type when entering the system and then set the emergency supplies to be provided.

When a customer makes a reservation for emergency supplies, the system will intelligently dispatch the order after matching the supplier in an intelligent way, and require the customer to pay for it if the reservation is successful; after the order is successfully paid, the supplier will produce the supplies and provide delivery services. In the intelligent dispatching link, the system provides an artificial dispatching function based on the requirements of the relevant national strategic plan, giving priority dispatching to the hardest hit areas and assigning suppliers to provide emergency supplies. For example, in the face of the COVID-19 pandemic, the platform can perform artificial intelligence

(AI) dispatching for Wuhan and other cities in Hubei Province, prioritizing the intelligent dispatching of emergency resource booking orders for these regions and assigning suppliers to provide emergency supplies production and delivery services.

3.3   The Specific Functional Design of the Platform

(1) Customer Centre. It includes several subsystem functions such as my appointment, shopping cart, order management, logistics management, invoice management, after-sales management, personal settings, security settings, and real-name authentication. The order management module supports the order payment function. After a successful booking of emergency supplies, the system interface will jump to the order payment page. Not only that, customers can choose to pay for their orders through the order management page. As the core module of the platform's financial business, the payment module has a relatively high-security demand required to use Hypertext Transfer Protocol Secure for transactions.

(2) Supplier Centre. It includes order management, production management, logistics management, invoice management, after-sales management, personal settings, security settings, real-name authentication, capacity settings, and other subsystem functions.

(3) Transaction Centre. It includes four subsystem function modules of order management, dispatch management, invoice management, and after-sales management.

(4) Distribution Centre. It includes four subsystem function modules: logistics distribution, air distribution, express distribution, and dedicated distribution. The distribution center is able to distribute emergency resources in an intelligent, orderly, and efficient way.

(5) Dispatch Centre. It includes six sub-system functional modules: requisitioning enterprise resources, dispatching enterprise receiving orders, dispatching enterprise distribution, dynamic monitoring of resources, dynamic monitoring of resource supply and demand, and dynamic monitoring of resource distribution. The dispatch center enables emergency resources to be allocated intelligently and rationally to solve the resource scarcity in a rapid way.

(6) After-sales center. It includes five sub-system function modules: cancellation of transactions, refund management, return management, complaint management, and AI customer service center. The after-sales center provides quality after-sales service, including 24-h online customer service, customer hotline, material reporting service, and AI customer service consulting services for products.

(7) Statistical analysis. It includes nine subsystem function modules: resource inventory statistics, resource capacity statistics, resource distribution statistics, resource shortage warning, customer statistics, supplier statistics, order statistics, appointment statistics, and dispatch statistics.

(8) Rights management. It includes seven subsystem function modules: classification management, business dictionary, system information, account management, role management, menu management, and AI database management.

4 The Expected Application of the Platform

According to the Urgent Notice by the General Office of the State Council of Effectively Organizing the Resumption of Operation and Production of Manufacturers and the Scheduling of Key Supplies for Epidemic Prevention and Control, a cohesive work mechanism should be established to ensure 24-h smooth liaison and deal with coordinated works, including the timely production, allocation, transportation and distribution of key medical emergency prevention and control materials. The platform is able to provide rapid supply and demand matching services for major disaster events. According to the nationwide production demand reflected centrally on the platform, the platform is able to dispatch orders to the corresponding suppliers through intelligent allocation; at the same time, this platform represents several sectors, such as intelligent reservation, intelligent order distribution, intelligent scheduling, and intelligent after-sales big data services to build an intelligent docking platform for customers and suppliers. Overall, the platform is able to efficiently dispatch global resources and global suppliers, seamlessly matching production and demand, reducing resource waste, and speeding up resource supply. Regional linkage of emergency resources is at the core of regional emergency linkage and establishing regional linkage of emergency resources is necessary to make up for the shortage of emergency resources, improve the efficiency of the use of emergency resources and effectively respond to major emergencies across administrative regions. In addition, under the influence of mass media and the benefits of the internet, the platform can rally social forces and provide huge social support for major disasters, and therefore serve as an intelligent demonstration platform for big data emergency resources.

5 Conclusion

The platform built in this research provides strategic emergency resources for major disasters through big data technology for intelligent reservation, intelligent order distribution, intelligent scheduling, and intelligent after-sales. This platform is able to achieve intelligent matching of supply and demand as well as dynamic monitoring by dispatching global suppliers in a fast and intelligent way, which can satisfy the demand for emergency resources under disaster situations, providing a third-party emergency resource service platform for the prevention and control of major domestic disasters as well as a powerful strategic emergency resource guarantee service platform for the prevention and control of natural disasters, natural pandemic and other major disasters in China. In addition, the platform provides a whole process support service from customer booking; order dispatching, payment, allocation, scheduling, production, distribution, and after-sales, providing an effective demonstration for solving the problem of resource shortage in the face of major disasters.

References

1. Xinhuanet. Take epidemic prevention and control as the most important work at present [EB/OL]. http://www.xinhuanet.com/politics/2020-01/27/c_1125506288.htm. Accessed 02 Feb 2020

2. Xinhuanet. Always put the people's life safety and health first: resolutely win the fight against epidemic prevention and control [EB/OL], 05 February 2020. http://www.xinhuanet.com/2020-02/05/c_1125535838.htm. Accessed 02 Feb 2020

3. Jiang, W.: Application of big data in emergency management. Electron. World (10), 79–80 (2019)

4. Chen, G., Duan, Y.: Suggestions for improvement of emergency resource management in China. Shanghai Manag. Sci. (4), 44–45 (2006)

5. Emergency management department. Natural disaster type [EB/OL], 02 February 2020. https://www.mem.gov.cn/kp/zrzh/qxzh/. Accessed 02 Feb 2020

6. Guo, H.: Analysis of advantages and disadvantages of HTTPS for website security. Comput. Netw. (5), 50–51 (2017)

7. Xinhua News Agency: The general office of the State Council issued the emergency notice on organizing and arranging the resumption of production and scheduling of key material production enterprises for epidemic prevention and control [EB/OL], 30 January 2020. http://www.gov.cn/xinwen/2020-01/30/content_5473212.htm. Accessed 02 Feb 2020

8. Xu, M., Qi, X., Yu, G.: The demand disruption management problem for a supply chain system with nonlinear demand functions. J. Syst. Sci. Syst. Eng. 12(1), 1–16 (2019)

9. Véronneau, S., Roy, J.: Global service supply chains: an empirical study of current practices and challenges of a cruise line corporation. Tour. Manag. 30(1), 128–139 (2019)

Security and Privacy for 6G Networks

Design and Implementation of Ad Hoc Communication Demonstration System

Jinpeng Wang[1], Shuo Shi[1(✉)], and Rui E[2]

[1] Harbin Institute of Technology, Harbin 150001, Heilongjiang, China
crcss@hit.edu.cn
[2] Heilongjiang Polytechnic, Harbin 150001, Heilongjiang, China

Abstract. In general, in production and life, network is required to convey all kinds of information, but in the situation of emergency and disaster relief where the terrain is complex and the battlefield or communication facilities are dam-aged and difficult to be repaired quickly, it is more common to rely on the base station to deploy the network facilities, but at this time, the troops in the battlefield or rescue and relief personnel are required to communicate and dispatch by the network. At this point, the Ad Hoc network can play a very important role. The focus of this paper is to build a ground demonstration system based on wireless self-organizing network through the raspberry pie development plat-form. Implement basic communication. Using Linux system in Raspberry Pi 4B, network layer routing protocol uses OLSR to form multi-node wireless ad hoc network and cellular network dual-mode communication, which ultimately enables message file transfer between nodes, location display and conducting initial video collection tests. With these work, a communication demonstration system using Ad Hoc network is initially built, which will lay the foundation for the application of wireless self-organizing network.

Keywords: Ad Hoc Network · OLSR · Socket Communication

1 Introduction

1.1 Background, Purpose and Significance of the Study

Wireless ad hoc network (Ad Hoc) is a temporary non-static network composed of multiple communication nodes, and each node can freely join or exit. Its emergence originated from the group wireless network established by the United States considering that it is difficult to maintain the normal communication in the complex battlefield war as described in [1]. Later, the IEEE organization named this type of network as ad hoc network, and the common name in China is wireless ad hoc network. The composition of this network does not depend on a special node as the core role in the network, but each node has the same status. They jointly establish the network and maintain routing information. When the node sending information and the node receiving information cannot communicate directly, some nodes in the network will help them forward data packets to maintain the normal operation of the network as described in [2] (Fig. 1).

© ICST Institute for Computer Sciences, Social Informatics and Telecommunications Engineering 2023
Published by Springer Nature Switzerland AG 2023. All Rights Reserved
A. Li et al. (Eds.): 6GN 2022, LNICST 504, pp. 133–145, 2023.
https://doi.org/10.1007/978-3-031-36011-4_12

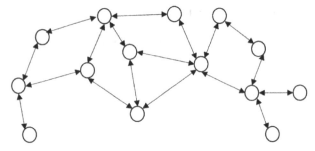

Fig. 1. Wireless Ad Hoc network system.

In the situation of rescue and disaster relief in the battlefield with complex terrain or the communication facilities are damaged to some extent, however, at this time, the troops in the battlefield or the rescue and disaster relief personnel need to communicate and dispatch through the network as described in [3]. At this time, the traditional communication facilities are more time-consuming and labor-consuming, and a more portable and faster way is needed to solve the communication problem. In general, radio or satellite communication may be used to realize actual communication. However, for radio, the number of channels transmitted is relatively limited as described in [4]. For example, during emergency rescue and disaster relief, a large number of disaster relief workers are prone to interference due to limited frequency when using radio communication, which seriously affects the transmission speed of important information, and it is not easy to share image information of different disaster relief sites in real time. However, satellite communication may not be able to respond at the fastest speed due to a certain delay in the transmission of its information, thus delaying the rescue or the best time in the battlefield, and also having a high use cost as described in [5]. In this situation, the ad hoc network shows its advantages. As long as everyone carries a small ad hoc network node, the nodes can organize the network by themselves. In addition, even if a node exits the network due to terrain or battery failure, it will not have a great impact on the whole network as described in [6]. Other nodes can still communicate normally, and the equipment of the node can join the whole network at any time after startup, It has a good effect on such temporary battlefield and real-time command in front of disasters. Therefore, it is valuable to build a ground ad hoc communication Demonstration System (terminal) to provide a solution for rescue and disaster relief scenarios as described in [7].

1.2 Main Research Contents

Raspberry Pi Platform

Raspberry pi is a very portable small processor, which can be used as a portable small personal computer after the system is installed. Raspberry PI foundation first developed it in Britain in order to popularize computer knowledge to students. Now it is often used as the motherboard of tracking cars and small intelligent robots.

Many kinds of hardware and software of raspberry pi are open source. The I/O pins and USB interfaces on it can be connected to various modules to realize personalized customization, and then use their own programs to achieve the desired functions. At present, the raspberry pi B product, which is widely used, only includes a core circuit board. If you want to use it normally, you need an SD card that has burned the system and a power supply. If you connect the display through HDMI, and the keyboard, mouse and graphical interface system connected with USB, the raspberry pi will have a feeling similar to that of an ordinary desktop computer.

Raspberry party has good compatibility and strong computing power with different systems. Therefore, based on the raspberry pi platform, the development of wireless ad hoc network system and rapid and stable networking will be well realized. Building a development environment and burning the Linux system into the development board is the basis for porting the OLSR protocol and building a network environment.

Linux System Installation and Environment Configuration

Linux is an operating system that opens the source code completely. It contains a lot of micro kernels, and each part can find the complete source code. Therefore, anyone can modify and tailor Linux according to their own needs to build their own functional system. At the same time, it also supports various network protocols and a set of very complete development tools, which is very conducive to program development and migration.

Generally speaking, a Linux system contains the following parts:

(1) A boot loader for loading the Linux kernel into the main memory of the computer.
(2) An initialization program, such as traditional sysvinit and updated systemd, openrc and upstart.
(3) A software library that contains code that can be used by running processes.
(4) A standard library for the normal operation of programs written by c voice. For example, the GNU C library is a common choice.
(5) A software package for using UNIX commands of the system. For example, GNU coreutils is the most commonly used.
(6) A library of various widgets for users to write graphical user interface program projects. Common projects such as Gnome project or QT project.
(7) A management system for installing, deleting, or configuring software packages, such as dpkg or rpm.
(8) A user-friendly interface program.

Install the required compiler and other programs in the Linux system to complete the required environment as described in [8].

OLSR Protocol

Optimized Link State Routing Protocol (OLSR) is a routing protocol commonly used in ad hoc networks, which was first found in the article RFC3626. Due to the characteristics of the self-organizing network, nodes in the network may exit at any time, or some nodes may suddenly temporarily join the network as described in [9]. Therefore, each node in the OLSR protocol group network will transmit the grouping information of this node to other nodes at regular intervals, thus realizing the information update of each node in the network, so that each node can update the link and the overall network state.

The routing table is modified according to the updated information. To meet the routing requirements of non-static network structure of Ad Hoc network as described in [10].

Socket Communication

Socket is a software program used to connect IP and port. The main purpose of its call is to send and receive TCP or UDP packets. The structure and properties of a socket are defined by the application programming interface used for the network architecture. Sockets are only used when they are created in a node and when the program is finished, socket communication stops.

Socket is gradually emerging in the standardization process of TCP/IP protocol during the development of Internet. Socket is recognized externally by other hosts through the address of the socket. The address of the socket is determined by three factors: routing protocol, IP address and port number.

QT Cross Platform Development Tool

QT is a framework that supports multiple compilers and provides multiple interface designs to facilitate program development. When the application developed by it runs across platforms, such as MacOS, Android windows, Linux or embedded systems, its code basically does not need to be changed to facilitate cross platform program development.

This project plans to use QT to complete the design of graphical user interface and message exchange.

Real Time Video Transmission

Write a program using the OPENCV library to obtain the camera video data in real time and display it locally, then use the UDP protocol to send and transmit the video stream, and carry out the transmission test of the multi-channel video reception.

Node Positioning and Map Display

In this paper, BDS and GPS dual-mode positioning are used. At present, GPS is the mainstream positioning system, and has a lot of application space in military and civil fields. Beidou Satellite Navigation System (BDS) is a system developed in 2012 in China. The main reason is that the communication frequency points are different from GPS, so dual-mode signal reception can be achieved by using hardware that supports multiple frequency points. Coordinate display uses offline Baidu map, which has a number of practical APIs to achieve good display results.

2 Design Scheme of Ad Hoc Network Demonstration System

2.1 Hardware Scheme

The main components of the single-point structure of the Ground Ad Hoc Network Demonstration Platform are industry-controlled embedded computer devices, wireless network communication devices, satellite positioning devices, human-computer interaction devices, video acquisition devices and energy management devices (Fig. 2).

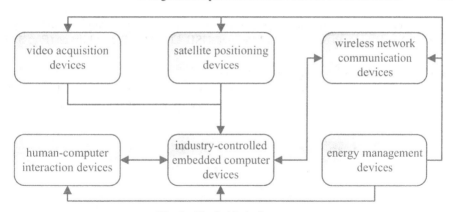

Fig. 2. Single Node Structure

The industrial control embedded computer equipment is mainly responsible for the overall planning and management of all equipment in the ground ad hoc network platform. The wireless network communication equipment is mainly responsible for data communication with other wireless ad hoc network nodes, and uses RJ45 network cable to connect with the industrial control embedded computer equipment. The satellite positioning equipment is mainly responsible for calculating the satellite signals from the Beidou satellite positioning system, and calculating and estimating the global latitude and longitude position information of the current equipment. Human-computer interaction equipment is mainly responsible for connecting with users, providing users with the operation entry and usage guidance of all functions of the ground ad hoc network platform. The video acquisition equipment is mainly responsible for the acquisition of video data, and transmits the data to the industrial control embedded computer equipment through the MIPI interface or the CSI interface. The energy management equipment is mainly responsible for providing power support for all electronic devices in the ground ad hoc network platform and supporting fast charging.

Industry-Controlled Embedded Computer Devices
Key features of the Raspberry Pi 4B include a high-performance 64-bit quad-core processor, support for dual displays with resolutions up to 4K via a pair of micro-HDMI ports,

Fig. 3. Raspberry Pi 4B development board

hardware video decoding up to 4Kp60, up to 4 GB of RAM, dual-band 2.4/ 5.0 GHz wireless LAN, Bluetooth 5.0, Gigabit Ethernet, USB 3.0 and PoE capabilities (Fig. 3).

Wireless Network Communication Devices
ST9800GB-SC is a portable product suitable for wireless ad hoc networks. It has high signal coverage and is more suitable for ad hoc network construction (Fig. 4).

Fig. 4. Schematic diagram of wireless ad hoc network card

In order to realize the connection of the cellular network, use the CAT4 LTE module, use the copper column and the thimble to connect the Raspberry Pi, and then you can connect to the Internet (Fig. 5).

Fig. 5. Schematic diagram of cellular network card

Energy Management Devices
The power supply module uses the Raspberry Pi UPS module of Micro Snow, 5V regulated output, up to 2.5A continuous output current, which can be directly connected to the Raspberry Pi motherboard, or can be powered externally through its own USB interface, which can be used for Raspberry Pi. Pie use 2–3 h (Fig. 6).

Fig. 6. Schematic diagram of power supply module

Video Acquisition Devices

The 720P 150-degree high-definition wide-angle camera of Lin Bo Shi HD908 model is selected. It has high compatibility and is suitable for Windows and Linux systems (Fig. 7).

Fig. 7. Schematic diagram of the camera

Satellite Positioning Devices

As a satellite positioning device in the ground ad hoc network platform, it is mainly responsible for computing satellite signals from the Beidou satellite positioning system, and computing and estimating the global latitude and longitude position information of the current device.

Satellite positioning equipment is required to maintain at least 10 effective satellites for positioning in an open and sunny field, and requires at least meter-level positioning accuracy. Based on the consideration of higher positioning accuracy and more complex application scenarios, satellite positioning equipment is required to be supported by at least inertial devices to realize multi-sensor information fusion integrated navigation system.

Considering the above requirements, Shenzhen Weite Intelligent's high-precision integrated navigation equipment is suitable for this solution (Fig. 8).

Fig. 8. Schematic diagram of positioning equipment

Human-Computer Interaction Devices

The touch screen uses a 7-in JETSON NANO brand IPS touch screen, using HDMI and USB as interfaces, HDMI is used for image data transmission, and USB is used for touch control (Fig. 9).

Fig. 9. Schematic diagram of touch screen

2.2 Software Scheme

Industrial Control Embedded Computer Equipment

The industrial control embedded computer equipment is selected as the Raspberry Pi 4B embedded computer, which completes the installation of the Linux kernel operating system, the installation of various routing protocols and the corresponding scheduling interface.

When in use, users only need to use the USB Type-C interface to provide power for it, or use the USB Type-A interface to provide power for the Raspberry Pi with the energy management device installed, and do not need to care about the software environment and dependencies of the Raspberry Pi relation.

Wireless Ad Hoc Communication System

The wireless ad hoc network communication system is designed based on the ST9800GB-SC wireless ad hoc network communication board. The basic control, information reading and other logic design of the interactive system for the communication board.

When using, the user needs to connect the communication board and the Raspberry Pi computer through the provided RJ45 Ethernet cable, and provide power for the communication board through the provided power cord.

Satellite Positioning System

The satellite positioning system is designed based on Shenzhen Weite intelligent integrated navigation equipment, completes the GPS + IMU integrated navigation position and attitude estimation system, completes the information exchange debugging between the Raspberry Pi computer and the integrated navigation equipment, and completes the satellite positioning information based on the human-computer interaction system. Read and display.

When using, the user needs to connect the combined navigation device and the Raspberry Pi computer through the provided USB Type-C interface.

Human-Computer Interaction System

The human-computer interaction system is designed based on the Raspberry Pi computer equipment and the adapted 7-in capacitive touch screen equipment, completes the design of the touch driver and display driver, completes the design of the graphical UI interface based on the touch screen, and completes the design of the following functions:

Read and display the relevant information of the current node device, including: added network label, address, communication delay, latitude and longitude coordinates, etc.

The user can select any one or more other nodes on the network topology display page, send the specified information or specified file to the specified node, or apply for the specified information to the specified node. The information content can be text, command words and video, and the user can configure the information content for each target node and source node after specifying the node.

The location can also be manually marked on the map, or graphics can be drawn to record the required information on the map.

Image Acquisition System

The image acquisition system is designed based on the Raspberry Pi computer equipment and various types of camera equipment with USB interfaces, completes the design of the camera device driver, completes the real-time acquisition of the video information of the Raspberry Pi camera, and completes the data provided for the human-computer interaction system. Upload interface.

When users use it, they only need to select different types of cameras according to their needs, and use a USB data cable to connect the camera to the Raspberry Pi.

Energy Management Equipment

The energy management equipment is designed based on the special power supply for Raspberry Pi computer equipment, completes the program design of power information acquisition, power management driver, etc., and completes the data extraction and control interaction between the special power supply for Raspberry Pi and the human-computer interaction system.

When using it, users only need to install the Raspberry Pi correctly on the dedicated power supply device. After installation, the Raspberry Pi computer and the power supply device only need to be charged through the copper column connection, and there is no need to separately power the Raspberry Pi.

3   Function Realization of Wireless Ad Hoc Network Demonstration Platform

3.1   Successful Realization of Ad Hoc Network Among Multiple Nodes

Connect the Raspberry Pi node to the networking device through an RJ45 network cable, then set an IPv4 address for the Raspberry Pi that is different from the networking device in the network settings, and then use the./olsrd command to enable the olsrd protocol through the terminal. It can be observed in the terminal that different ad hoc network nodes are successfully networked through olsrd. The local IP is 10.10.10.26, and the Ad Hoc network is successfully established with three devices whose IPs are 10.10.10.31, 10.10.10.88 and 10.10.10.44 (Fig. 10).

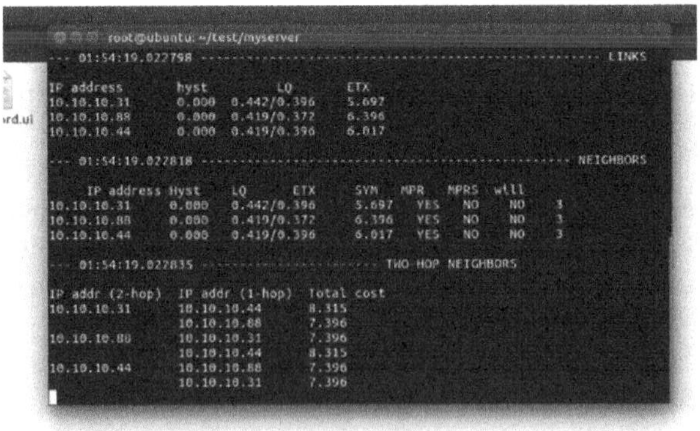

Fig. 10. Networking between devices through olsrd

3.2   Realization of Cellular Network Networking

After using the cellular network device to connect to the Internet, use the zerotier tool to configure the network, and then the device can be connected through the cellular network.

3.3   Implementation of Multi-node Positioning and Status Display

After the device is connected to the positioning device, the mobile test is performed outdoors, and the real-time location display can be realized on the offline map (Fig. 11).

Fig. 11. Single node positioning display

When multiple nodes are connected, the positions of all nodes can be displayed and shared on the map, and the dual-mode connection status of the ad hoc network and the cellular network can be displayed (Fig. 12).

Fig. 12. Multi-node positioning and status display

3.4   Implementation of File/message Transfer Function

Select the node on the map to communicate, enter the information in the message box and select send to send it, and select the TCP connection to establish a connection to perform file transfer (Figs. 13 and 14).

Fig. 13. Message send/receive display

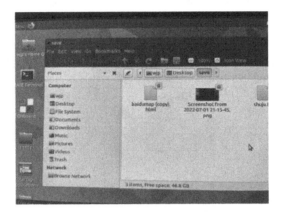

Fig. 14. File reception display

3.5 Preliminary Video Transmission Test

Using the ad hoc network and the cellular network respectively, the image information obtained by the cameras of the two nodes is pushed to another node, and received and displayed (Fig. 15).

Fig. 15. Dual-channel video reception display

4 Conclusion

This paper applies self-organizing network, socket and positioning related technologies. Firstly, the characteristics of wireless ad hoc network without central node and non-static network structure are expounded, and then the overall hardware and software scheme is proposed according to the research goal of this paper. Realized the construction of the ground ad hoc network demonstration system based on Raspberry Pi 4B, realized the operation of the OLSR protocol in the Raspberry Pi, and completed the connection of the cellular network based on the cellular network hardware, and displayed all network nodes on the offline map. Location, and on this basis, the transmission of messages and files, and the use of camera to acquire image data and conduct transmission tests, demonstrate the practicability of wireless ad hoc networks and this demonstration system.

Acknowledgement. This work was supported by the National Natural Science Foundation of China under Grant 62171158 and Research Fund Program of Guangdong Key Laboratory of Aerospace Communication and Networking Technology under Grant 2018B030322004.

References

1. Palazzi, C.E., Bujari, A., Marfia, G., Roccetti, M.: An overview of opportunistic ad hoc communication in urban scenarios. In: 2014 13th Annual Mediterranean Ad Hoc Networking Workshop (MED-HOC-NET), pp. 146–149 (2014)
2. Ren, B., Zhang, X., Gou, X.: System design of high speed ad hoc networking with directional antenna. In: 2016 12th International Conference on Mobile Ad-Hoc and Sensor Networks (MSN), pp. 429–433 (2016)
3. Kim, B., Kim, K., Roh, B., Choi, H.: Hierarchical routing for unmanned aerial vehicle relayed tactical ad hoc networks. In: 2018 IEEE 15th International Conference on Mobile Ad Hoc and Sensor Systems (MASS), pp. 153–154 (2018)
4. Jiang, L., Ke, S.Q., Zhang, L.: Research on key technologies of topology control in mobile predictive ad hoc networks. In: 2020 International Conference on Wireless Communications and Smart Grid (ICWCSG), pp. 190–194 (2020)
5. Grodi, R., Rawat, D.B., Bajracharya, C.: Performance evaluation of Unmanned Aerial Vehicle ad hoc networks. SoutheastCon 2015, pp. 1–4 (2015)
6. Yin, J., Wang, L., Han, C., Yang, Y.: NC-OLSR: A network coding based OLSR multipath transmission scheme for FANETs. In: 2017 4th International Conference on Systems and Informatics (ICSAI), pp. 1007–1012 (2017)
7. Ouacha, A., Lakki, N., El abbadi, J., Habbani, A., El koutbi, M.: OLSR protocol enhancement through mobility integration. In: 2013 10th IEEE International Conference on Networking, Sensing And Control (ICNSC), pp. 17-22 (2013)
8. Krug, S., Brychcy, A., Seitz, J.: A mobile embedded-Linux-based testbed for outdoor ad hoc network evaluation. In: 2016 IEEE International Conference on Wireless for Space and Extreme Environments (WiSEE), pp. 164–166 (2016)
9. Dong, S.Y.: Optimization of OLSR routing protocol in UAV ad HOC network. In: 2016 13th International Computer Conference on Wavelet Active Media Technology and Information Processing (ICCWAMTIP), pp. 90–94 (2016)
10. Prajapati, S., Patel, N., Patel, R.: Optimizing performance of OLSR protocol using energy based MPR selection in MANET. In: 2015 Fifth International Conference on Communication Systems and Network Technologies, pp. 268–272 (2015)

Design and Implementation of Dual Channel Speech Signal Transceiver System Based on FPGA

Tongbai Yang[1]([✉]) and Shuo Shi[1,2]

[1] School of Electronic and Information Engineering, Harbin Institute of Technology, Harbin 150001, Heilongjiang, China
yangtongbai2000@163.com, crcss@hit.edu.cn
[2] Peng Cheng Laboratory, Network Communication Research Centre, Shenzhen 518052, Guangdong, China

Abstract. Real-time speech information has always been the main way of information transmission, but there are still problems in transmission. Firstly, while speech signals are easy to transmit information, they also bring information leakage and malicious tampering. Secondly, speech signals are more or less affected by noise, interference and transmission effects in the transmission process, which will make the recovery of speech signals more complicated. Based on the above, the wireless transmission of speech signals is taken as the background to realize the merging and separation of dual-channel speech signals. The problems of information leakage and distortion during the transmission of speech signals are studied. The encryption and decryption of speech signals are taken as the key points. Realize dual speech signal receiving and receiving based on Field Programmable Gate Array (FPGA). The frequency division multi-plexing method is used to transmit dual speech signals simultaneously, realize speech signal convolution on FPGA and extract two speech signals from the convolution signal. AES algorithm is realized the encryption and decryption of on FPGA. 2FSK modulation and demodulation in digital modulation is selected to complete the design and implementation of the whole system, and the research is completed through the final overall modulation and analysis.

Keywords: speech signal processing · FPGA · AES algorithm

1 Introduction

The rapid development of science and technology drives the progress of society, so does the field of communication. The diversified and multi-scene application of contemporary communication technology enables people to obtain relevant valuable and important information in a timely manner in multiple ways. Strong real-time speech information has always been the main way of human information transmission, but there are still problems in information transmission. First of all, while speech signals are

A. Li et al. (Eds.): 6GN 2022, LNICST 504, pp. 146–157, 2023.
https://doi.org/10.1007/978-3-031-36011-4_13

easy to transmit information, they also bring information leakage and malicious tampering. Secondly, speech signals are more or less affected by noise, interference and transmission effects in the transmission process, which makes it more difficult to separate and extract the source speech signals, that is, speech signals will reach the same receiver through multiple different channel conditions. The received signal will be a convolution mixture of multi-channel speech signals with attenuation, delay and phase effects. This kind of receiving signal is more complex, which makes the subsequent receiving and processing of speech signal more difficult. Against the above background, the background of this topic in wireless transmission of speech signal, two-way road and separation of speech signals as the key point, first of all, the speech signal distortion of information disclosure and transmission process, and then focus on modulation of two-way speech signal encryption and decryption algorithm, selecting the appropriate modulation demodulation method, based on the above research, FPGA based dual speech signal transceiver.

At present, the mainstream speech processing is designed on the basis of software platform, and it is still a minority to realize the speech processing with hardware devices. However, field programmable gate array (FPGA) is very suitable for processing speech signal with its advantages of high parallelism and high flexibility. There are some pre-validated IP cores for signal processing algorithms in FPGA. The design of these IP cores can achieve higher performance of some commonly used signal processing functions, which is very convenient to use in the development process and can greatly shorten the development time. Moreover, the effective integration of multiple signal processing algorithms can effectively reduce the actual cost and reduce the risk. With the development of FPGA technology, the realization of signal proc-essing algorithm in FPGA is becoming a new alternative because of its relatively low implementation cost and high parallel processing speed. By implementing the speech signal processing algorithm in FPGA, the traditional limitation separation between hardware and software design level is gradually overcome [1].

Speech encryption is to transform the information processing, so that in addition to the target receiver of the communication system, can not get the real speech information in the transmission signal. The method of speech signal transformation is speech encryption and decryption algorithm. The most common method is to transform speech signal by key control. Speech decryption is the process of restoring the encrypted signal to the original speech signal using the opposite processing operation. The research of speech encryption has been deepening at home and abroad [2, 3].

In addition to ensuring the security of speech communication, it is also necessary to ensure that the information in speech communication can be accurately and completely transmitted. Otherwise, speech encryption is meaningless when the information cannot be completely transmitted. For the problems that speech communication must face, the requirements of speech encryption generally include the following: with the increasing awareness of information security in modern people, people hope to be able to protect their personal information security through speech encryption; On the other hand, for the country and the enterprise, if the confidential information leakage will bring irreparable huge economic losses to the country and the enterprise, which more reflects the importance of speech encryption [4].

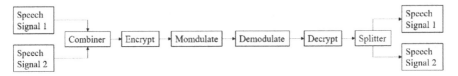

Fig. 1. System flow chart

Based on the overall process, the speech signal is input into the system in the form of digital signal in this study. The two-channel speech signal successively passes through the combination, encryption, modulation, demodulation, and decryption. After separating the complete system, the two-channel signal is extracted without distortion. Figure 1 shows the specific flow chart.

Therefore, it is mainly divided into three parts: speech signal routing and separation, speech signal encryption and decryption, and signal modulation and demodulation. In this study, frequency division multiplexing (FDM) is selected to combine and separate dual speech signals. Because of ensuring the integrity of the signal to the greatest extent, it is easy to operate, easy to implement, and does not occupy too many resources. The AES speech encryption algorithm can protect the two speech messages from being easily deciphered and meet the security requirements. 2FSK modulation and demodulation method is selected to complete and accurately demodulate the original modulated signal.

2   Speech Signal Combination and Separation

In order to reduce the communication cost, the current communication system pursues the high efficiency and low cost scheme of transmitting multiple signals in the same channel. Under the condition that the transmitted signals do not interfere with each other, multiple signals can be merged, so that they can be completely separated after transmission at the same time.

In the process of speech signal convolution transmission, because the two speech signals are simultaneously transmitted, it is difficult to recover the two speech signals from the convolution signal completely and without distortion in the time domain in the processing of the convolution signal transmitted through the same channel. Therefore, considering the time of signal processing and the degree of difficulty of implementation, the frequency division multiplexing processing method in frequency domain is adopted.

2.1   The Realization of Speech Signal Combination

Firstly, one speech signal 1 is processed, its spectrum is transformed to a higher frequency, and then it is transmitted with another speech signal 2 as a closed signal. The two do not affect each other, and the transformed speech signal 1 and speech signal 2 have no overlap in spectrum to complete the closed path.

The realization of speech signal jointing mainly lies in the generation of fixed carrier for spectrum shifting and the multiplication of speech signal and carrier for frequency division multiplexing. The generation of the fixed carrier can be generated by the IP core of the DDS (Direct Digital Synthesis) built into Vivado.

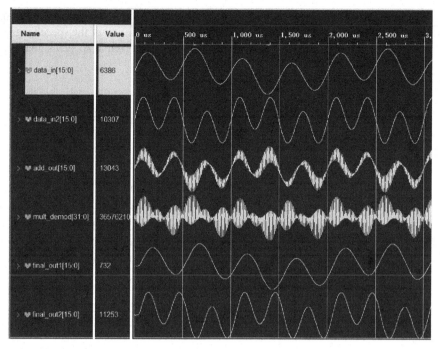

Fig. 2. Results of speech signal combination and separation

Because the carrier with a fixed frequency needs to be generated, it is not necessary to write a frequency control word to change the frequency of the output waveform, but only need to fix the phase increment to generate a single frequency wave with a fixed frequency. A fixed phase increment is selected, which does not change during operation, and a sinusoidal waveform with a fixed frequency is generated. The output frequency of the IP core of DDS is controlled by the frequency control word, clock frequency and Phase Width. The output frequency is:

$$f_{out} = (f_{clk} \cdot f_{word})/2^{PhaseWidth} \qquad (1)$$

Subsequent operations only need to connect the input speech signal 1 and DDS output carrier signal to the multiplier, and connect the output of the multiplier and another speech signal 2 to the adder, and the output of the adder is the signal to complete the circuit closing.

2.2 The Realization of Speech Signal Separation

Considering the spectrum characteristics of the two channels of speech signal after processing, the two channels of speech signal can be obtained only by two different processing of the combined channel signal. The first processing is to directly low-pass filter the received combined channel signal to get the original speech signal 1. Of the second processing the received signal to bandpass filter, bandpass filter center frequency is a way to deal with the carrier frequency, bandwidth of 2 times the signal bandwidth, and after the road processing carrier multiplication, the modulation of the speech signal after 2 spectrum move back to its original position, then the original speech signal 2 is obtained by low pass filter.

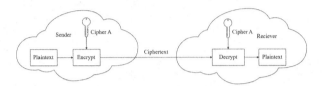

Fig. 3. Symmetric Encryption Algorithm

Using the IP core of the Vivado FIR Compiler. The IP core can be designed according to the Filter Designer in Matlab to generate the required Filter. This greatly simplifies the difficulty of filter design, so the parameters can be directly designed and selected according to the characteristics of speech signals.

In order to facilitate the analysis, data_in and data_in2 are the input two-way speech signals, add_out is the join-way signal, and final_out1 and final_out2 are the separated two-way speech signals. The realization results of speech signal combining and separating FPGA are shown in Fig. 2:

According to the results, the two signals are separated without distortion. It verifies the correctness of the dual speech signal merging and separating module implemented by FPGA.

3   The Implementation of AES Algorithm

3.1   Principle of AES Algorithm

Because the inverse function of the decryption algorithm of the AES algorithm is itself, the encryption and decryption algorithm of the AES algorithm [5] has symmetry. In the algorithm, the same key is used, and both the sender and the receiver process the data with the same key. As shown in Fig. 3:

The AES algorithm mainly has four different stages, which are SubByte layer, Shift Rows layer, Mix Column layer and Add Round Key. The subsequent 128bit key is selected for 10 rounds of processing, and the length of the plaintext and the key are both 128bit.

Most of the processing of AES algorithm is byte processing, so according to the regulations, the data should be arranged by byte, the input order is arranged by column from left to right into 4·4 array. Similarly, the encrypted ciphertext is read in the same order, and the array is changed into the original 128bit form. In the same decryption, the data is also processed in a 4·4 array byte arrangement and read in the same order.

(1) Round key addition: 128bit plaintext and key are processed in round key addition.
In the finite field used in round key addition, each element can be represented as:

$$A(x) = a_7 x^7 + a_6 x^6 + \ldots + a_1 x + a_0 \qquad (2)$$

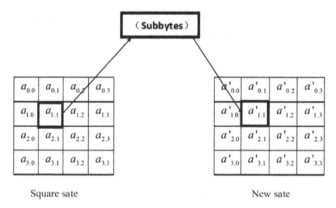

Fig. 4. S-box Processing

The addition and subtraction of two elements give the same result because it is equivalent to an XOR gate in a digital circuit. The object of the operation is the round transformation result of each round except the round key plus itself and the specific generated round key. The final processing result obtained by XOR operation is the output result of this layer.

(2) byte substitution layer: byte substitution layer to the processing of data of the main is to make the input data through the S-box table finish from a byte changes into another completely different, the conversion operation is the input data of each byte by S-box table to find the corresponding new byte as output bytes, S-box table lookup method is: The input of a former four bytes of data value as the table to find S-box, and after the bytes of the value of the four as a table column value to find S box, by the number value and the value of the column to identify the S-box in the table the transformation output of new bytes address, find the corresponding new byte as complete through the address byte substitution transformation output, Fig. 4 abstracts this transformation.

There are 256 8bit long elements in the S-box table, which can be defined as a two-dimensional number table. The method of reading the data in the S-box is to take the first 4 bits of each byte in the input data to represent the row value in the table, and the last 4 bits to represent the column value in the table. Because the corresponding processing can be carried out in FPGA, the S-box is regarded as a two-dimensional number table for subsequent processing and research. The inverse S-box has the same principle as the S-box, which is applied to the data processing of byte replacement during decryption.

(3) Row displacement: Row displacement operation is very easy compared with other processing stages. It is used to process the 16-byte input data of this layer as the state matrix, the input bytes as the units of the state matrix, and then the position of the unit rows in this state matrix is changed. The operation of row shift is to change the position of a single byte to affect other byte positions and thus affect the entire state matrix. Row displacement is the data processing operation only between the rows of

the state matrix, without changing the position of the cell column in the matrix. In the state matrix, for the data with four units in each row, the first row of the state matrix is guaranteed to remain unchanged during processing. The second row is moved to the left by 1 unit, the third row is moved to the left by 2 units, and the fourth row is moved to the left by 3 units. According to the symmetry feature, in decryption and encryption operation opposite, the retrograde displacement processing is still keeping the first row unchanged, the second row to the right one unit, the third row to the right two units, the fourth row to the right three units.

(4) Column confusion: The data processing in the column confusion stage is the most complex in this algorithm. Column obfuscation operation shuffles each column of the input state matrix, so that any byte of the input data will affect the four bytes of the result, which is the most important diffusion element in this algorithm. The operations performed by column obfuscation include matrix multiplication, finite field addition and finite field multiplication. For encryption, column obfuscation right-multiplies a particular matrix by the input state matrix.

(5) AES key generation: Sub-key generation is to process the columns in the key matrix, not the rows. A column contains 4 bytes, and the four columns together constitute the sub-key. Because the first key addition layer also uses sub-keys for XOR addition, the number of generated sub-keys is one more than the round number of AES algorithm, that is, 11. The sub-key data is all in the extension. However, if the column generated by the operation is the first column of the sub-key, the processing transformation of G function should be carried out on the data in the column of the operation.

The G function is to first invert the four bytes of the input column, then replace each byte through the S-box table, and finally XOR calculate the round coefficient with the first byte after replacement. The round coefficient contains 10 data, each of which is 8bit in length. Clearing the symmetry of AES and improving the nonlinearity of the key arrangement process are the reasons for the existence of G function. With these two features, the probability of password cracking attacks is greatly reduced.

AES decryption process and encryption stream operation process relative comparison can find the symmetry of the symmetric encryption and decryption algorithm process, the content of the data processing process is similar, the difference is only that the decryption is the inverse process of encryption, and the use of the same key, so no longer related to the specific introduction.

3.2 AES Algorithm Implements the Results on FPGA

The setup of the pin is described first. Input pin: clock is the clock signal, the clock frequency is 100 MHz, resetn is the reset signal, the low level is effective; Enc_dec is the choice of encryption and decryption algorithm, low level means encryption, high level means decryption; Start is to start the operation of the encryption and decryption algorithm (valid when key_val is 1). The rising edge is triggered, and the next clock starts the operation. Key_in indicates the input value of the 128-bit key value. Text_in indicates the input value of 128-bit plaintext or encrypted data value. Key_val is a module enabled interface. The module can be executed only when the value is 1. Output pin: text_val changes to high level, indicating that the encryption and decryption operation has been completed; Busy indicates that the module is performing operations. Text_out represents the calculated output of 128-bit encrypted or decrypted data [6].

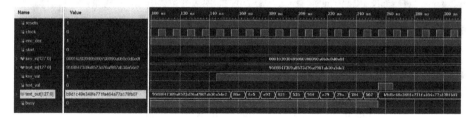

Fig. 5. AES Decryption Result

The AES encryption algorithm is running, where the input value is B9D1C48E348FE771FA464A77A178FB07 (in hexadecimal format, and the subsequent data is also displayed in hexadecimal format). The key input is 000102030405060708090A0B0C0D0E0F, and the final output is 95F8847369A8573D 76AF987AB30A5DE2.

As shown in Fig. 5, AES decryption algorithm is carried out, and the input encrypted data is the output value of the above encryption algorithm, namely 95F8847369A8573D76AF987AB30A5DE2, The key is also 0001020 30405060708090 0A0B0C0D0E0F, and it can be found that the decrypted output is B9D1C48E348FE771FA464A77A178FB07. It can be clearly found that although the corresponding data generated by each round of encryption and decryption is different, the final output result is correct.

4 2FSK Modulation and Demodulation Implementation

2FSK can use the IP core of DDS to complete the generation of carrier on FPGA. Only two different frequency control words are needed to complete the modulation of 2FSK. The keying of frequency control words can be completed by the value of the input digital signal. Then, different frequencies are generated for the IP core control of the DDS that generates the modulation signal to complete the modulation of 2FSK.

Demodulation using a relatively simple non-coherent demodulation, that is, envelope detection. The central frequencies of the passband frequencies of the two bandpass filters are respectively those of the two frequencies generated by keying. The power of the corresponding frequency signal in the received signal can be output by bandpass filtering, rectification and low-pass filtering. The output of two low-pass filters is subtracted to find the difference between the two frequency components. When the difference is large enough, the decision can be considered to receive a signal of "0" or "1" [7].

Bpf1_m_data_out is a signal that passes through a bandpass filter, where BPF1_abs is the output after rectification of one of the channels, and rectification is completed by taking the inverse. Bpf1_m_data_valid indicates that the output of the bandpass filter is enabled. If there is data output, set this parameter to 1. The results of 2FSK demodulation on FPGA are shown in Fig. 6:

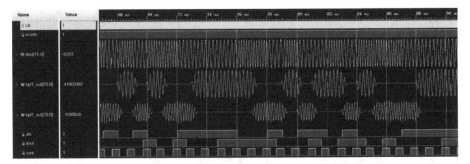

Fig. 6. 2FSK Demodulation Is Implemented on FPGA

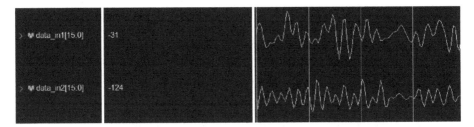

Fig. 7. FPGA Speech Signal Input

In the figure, bpf1_out and bpf2_out are respectively the outputs of two bandpass filters. Approximately, it can be seen that there are outputs only when the sequence signal value is the center frequency corresponding to the filter, dout is the final output sequence, sync is the positioning signal, and the length of a cycle is the length of a symbol, which is used for positioning and output signals. By comparing the input sequence din with the output sequence dout, it is found that only the time is changed, and the information carried by the sequence signal is not changed, which proves the accuracy of 2FSK demodulation [8].

5   System Testing and Analysis

After all the main modules of the system are built, the system is coordinated to correspond to the quantized data of FPGA input, as shown in Fig. 7. In the figure, data_in1 represents the input speech signal 1, and data_in2 represents the input speech signal 2. Ensure that the information of the speech signal is input into the system for subsequent processing [9].

The output of the whole system is shown in Fig. 8: Final_out1 and final_out2 are 16-bit signed speech signals 1 and 2 output by the system. The reason why the waveforms become "smooth" is that the low-pass filter is used to process the signals when separating the speech signals. By comparing the signals in the time domain, it is obvious that the final output is almost the same as the original speech signals. The reason for the error is the quantization error caused by quantization, which is unavoidable. In order to more

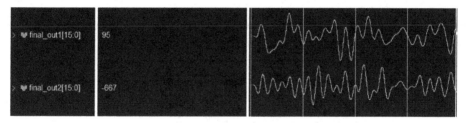

Fig. 8. FPGA System Output

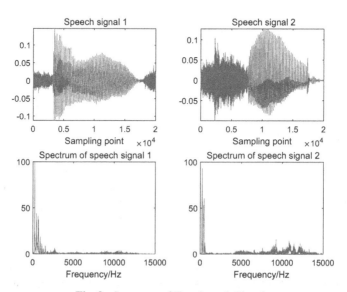

Fig. 9. Spectrum of Two Speech Signals

accurately determine whether to achieve distortion-free demodulation signal, the system output is sampled according to the sampling rate of the original speech signal, and then converted into floating point numbers for the convenience of subsequent operations.

Fourier transform is applied to the original speech signal to obtain the spectrum of two speech signals [10], as shown in Fig. 9. Then Fourier transform is applied to the two signals output by the system to obtain the spectrum of speech signals, as shown in Fig. 10.

The original speech signal and the system output speech signal spectrum is compared, found that the output of the speech signal of high frequency component has been filter, this is because the shunt processing used by low pass filter, is the low pass filter is not only completed the separation effect of signal, and to filter out the noise of the original speech signal.

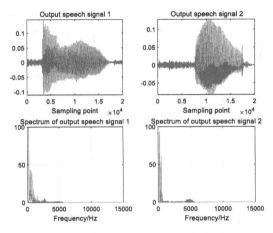

Fig. 10. Spectrum of System Outputs

6   Conclusion

This paper first explains the background and significance, and then introduces and analyzes the current situation.In this paper, the wireless transmission of speech signals as the background, the realization of dual speech signal convolution and separation, first of all, the study of information leakage and distortion in the process of speech signal transmission, AES algorithm, the selection of 2FSK modulation and demodulation method, based on the above research, the realization of dual speech signal transceiver based on FPGA. In the final process of the system, through the analysis of the results, it is found that the whole system can achieve distortion free separation of two speeech signals, which verifies the correctness of the system. On the basis of ensuring the integrity of the signal to the greatest extent, it is easy to operate, easy to implement, does not occupy too many resources, and can be correctly implemented in FPGA.

Acknowledgement. This work is supported by the National Natural Science Foundation of China under Grant 62171158 and Research Fund Program of Guangdong Key Laboratory of Aerospace Communication and Networking Technology under Grant 2018B030322004.

References

1. Kajur Renuka, V., Prasadm K,: Design and analysis of optimized CORDIC based GMSK system on FPGA platform. Int. J. Electric. Comput. Eng. **10**(5) (2020)
2. Renza, D., Ballesteros, D.M., Martinez, E.: Spreading-based voice encryption by means of OVSF codes. Appl. Sci. **10**(1), 112 (2019). https://doi.org/10.3390/app10010112
3. Sathiyamurthi, P., Ramakrishnan, S.: Speech encryption using chaotic shift keying for secured speech communication. EURASIP J. Audio Speech Music Process. **2017**(1), 1–11 (2017). https://doi.org/10.1186/s13636-017-0118-0
4. Bagwe, G.R., Apsingekar, D.S., Gandhare, S., Pawar, S.: Voice encryption and decryption in telecommunication. In: 2016 International Conference on Communication and Signal Processing, pp. 1790–1793 (2016)

5. Noorbasha, F., Divya, Y., Poojitha, M.: Koteswara Rao,K Hari Kishore. FPGA design and implementation of modified AES based encryption and decryption algorithm. Int. J. Innov. Technol. Explor. Eng. **8** (2019)
6. Strachacki, M., Szczepański, S.: Power equalization of AES FPGA implementation. Bull. Polish Acad. Sci. Techn. Sci. **58**(1) (2010). https://doi.org/10.2478/v10175-010-0013-7
7. Guo, F., Xi, L., Xing, G.: Design of low-power 2FSK demodulation circuit. MATEC Web Conf. **232**, 04069 (2018). https://doi.org/10.1051/matecconf/201823204069
8. Xie, L., Tang, M., Li, H.: Joint design of physical-layer network coding and LDPC code modulated by 2FSK. J. Phys. Conf. Ser. **1792**(1) (2021)
9. He, Z., Liu, Y., Ye, X.: A new method of image encryption/decryption via voice features. In: 2009 2nd International Congress on Image and Signal Processing, pp. 1–4. Tianjin, China (2009)
10. Malakooti, M.V., Dobuneh, M.R.N.: A lossless digital encryption system for multimedia using orthogonal transforms. In: 2012 Second International Conference on Digital Information and Communication Technology and It's Applications, pp. 240–244. Bangkok, Thailand. (2012)

Network Coding Based Efficient Topology Construction and Flow Allocation Method for Satellite Networks

Ruisong Wang[1] , Wenjing Kang[1] , Shengliang Fang[2], and Ruofei Ma[1](✉)

[1] School of Information Science and Engineering, Harbin Institute of Technology,
Weihai 264209, China
{kwjqq,maruofei}@hit.edu.cn
[2] School of Space Information, Space Engineering University, Beijing 101416, China

Abstract. As a key component of the sixth generation (6G) communication network, satellite network has attracted extensive attention due to its advantages of wide coverage and high capacity. However, the current limited resources are difficult to meet the growing data requirements. Therefore, this paper considers a multicast satellite network and uses network coding technology to improve the resource utilization of inter satellite links. Furthermore, we are committed to optimizing network topology and coding flow allocation to improve network capacity. The proposed optimization problem is formulated as an integer linear programming problem, which is difficult to solve. In order to improve computing efficiency, we propose a heuristic topology construction and flow allocation method. The flow allocation problem is equivalent to the maximum flow problem of multiple source-to-destination pairs for a given network topology. Based on this, the topology construction method is given by iteratively deleting the links that have the least impact on the overall performance. Finally, the simulation results indicate that the proposed method can significantly improve the network capacity compared with the traditional methods.

Keywords: Network Coding · Topology Construction · Flow Allocation Method · Satellite networks

1 Introduction

In the sixth generation (6G) communication network, global seamless coverage is expected to realize with the data transmission assisted by satellite network. Especially in some remote areas, it is more necessary to use satellite networks

This work was supported partially by National Natural Science Foundation of China (Grant Nos. 61971156, 61801144), Shandong Provincial Natural Science Foundation, China (Grant Nos. ZR2019QF003, ZR2019MF035, ZR2020MF141), the Fundamental Research Funds for the Central Universities, China (Grant No. HIT.NSRIF.2019081).

A. Li et al. (Eds.): 6GN 2022, LNICST 504, pp. 158–170, 2023.
https://doi.org/10.1007/978-3-031-36011-4_14

to access backbone networks because of the contradiction between the growing demand and the expensive ground network deployment. However, due to limited satellite network resources, traditional data transmission methods are difficult to meet the needs of large-scale user access. Combined with satellite multicast technology, linear network coding technology may provide a solution for large-scale data transmission on satellite networks. The transmitted data will be compressed after being encoded, so the occupation of satellite link resources and storage resources can be reduced. By using multicast technology, multiple satellites can receive the same coded packet in only one transmission, and the destination satellite can successfully decode when enough coded packets are received. The failure probability of random linear network coding (RLNC) has been analyzed in [1] and the results indicates that the partial network topology information may be beneficial for the failure probability of RLNC. The authors in [2] proposed to use RLNC to improve the security of data transmission. The author in [3] considered the design problem of linear network coding from the perspective of cost and provided two distributed algorithms to solve them efficiently. Similarly, the authors in [4] aimed to maximize the secure multicast rate and proposed a topology construction method based on Lagrangian relaxation method.

Although network coding technology can improve network capacity, the upper bound of capacity is closely related to network topology. However, the satellite network topology is time-varying due to the periodic motion of satellites, which brings difficulties to topology optimization. In order to reveal the temporal and spatial relationship of satellite networks, some characterization methods have been proposed, such as time expanded graph and time aggregation graph. In [5,6], the authors applied time expanded graph to characterize the inter satellite storage resources, communication resources, and the dynamic changes of satellites in a period of time. The authors in [7,8] proposed a more efficient time aggregation graph, in which the graph size does not change with time, so it is suitable for networks with large time scales.

Inspired by the above analysis, this paper aims to apply time expanded graph to characterize the dynamic changes of satellite network and the connection between network resources. Moreover, a multicast satellite network is taken into account that sends the same content to multiple destination satellites. On the one hand, the main idea is to apply network coding technology to reduce the occupation of communication resources and storage resources during data transmission. On other hand, the main idea is to further improve the network coding capacity through topology optimization and flow allocation methods. According to the simulation results, the network capacity is significantly increased when using network coding technology and the proposed optimization scheme.

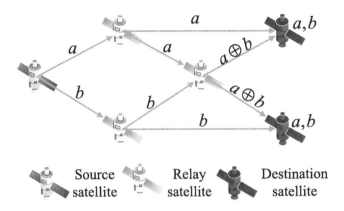

Fig. 1. System model of multicast satellite network with network coding.

2 System Model and Problem Formulation

2.1 System Model

As shown in Fig. 1, we consider a multicast satellite network, including a source satellite, some relay satellites, and multiple destination satellites. The source satellite stores some content of interest to the destination satellites and tries to deliver the content to the required destination satellites. The original information of the source satellite is first encoded and transmitted to the destination satellites through the relay satellites. After receiving the coded packets, the relay satellites will further encode these packets and forward them. Finally, after receiving enough coded packets, the destination satellites can successfully decode all the required information. In addition, due to the periodic motion of satellites, the network topology is time-varying and predictable. In order to describe the dynamics of satellite networks, we assume that the network is time-varying for a period of time, but the network can be reasonably considered as static when the time change is small. Therefore, the duration of information transmission T is divided into N time slots, in which the length of each time slot is $\tau = T/N$. The length of time slot is considered to be small enough that the change of network topology can be ignored. Let's denote the set of all satellites as $\mathcal{S} = \{s\} \cup \mathcal{R} \cup \mathcal{D}$ where s represents the source satellite, $\mathcal{R}$ denotes the relay satellites, and $\mathcal{D}$ is the set of destination satellites. Moreover, let's denotes the set of time slot as $\mathcal{N}$. Based on the above definition, the satellite network topology can be represented by a time expanded graph $\mathcal{G} = (\mathcal{V}, \mathcal{E})$. Specifically, $\mathcal{V} = \{v_i^{(t)} | v_i^{(t)} \in \mathcal{S}, t \in \mathcal{N}\}$ is the set of vertices and $v_i^{(t)}$ represents i-th satellite in the t-th time slot. The set of edges consists of two components, i.e., $\mathcal{E} = \mathcal{E}^{com} \cup \mathcal{E}^{sto}$ where $\mathcal{E}^{com} = \{e(v_i^{(t)}, v_j^{(t)}) | v_i^{(t)}, v_j^{(t)} \in \mathcal{S}, t \in \mathcal{N}\}$ is denoted as all communication edges and $\mathcal{E}^{com} = \{e(v_i^{(t)}, v_i^{(t+1)}) | v_i^{(t)}, v_i^{(t+1)} \in \mathcal{S}, t \in \mathcal{N}\}$

represents the storage edges. For each destination satellite, as long as all encoded data packets are collected within a given time, the data packet transmission is successful without losing timeliness. In fact, the vertices in graph $\mathcal{G}$ corresponding to the destination satellite in different time slots can be considered as one vertex. Therefore, we need to add some virtual vertices in the graph $\mathcal{G}$ according to this idea by letting $\mathcal{V} = \mathcal{V} \cup \widetilde{\mathcal{D}}$ where $\tilde{d} \in \widetilde{\mathcal{D}}$ corresponds to the destination satellite $d^{(t)}$ in different time slots. After adding the virtual vertices, corresponding edges must be added to ensure the integrity of the graph. Let's denote the set of virtual edges as $\mathcal{E}^{vir} = \{e(v_i^{(t)}, v_j)|v_i^{(t)} \in \mathcal{S}, v_j \in \widetilde{\mathcal{D}}\}$ and add it to the edge set of graph $\mathcal{G}$ by setting $\mathcal{E} = \mathcal{E} \cup \mathcal{E}^{vir}$. Then, the multicast transmission problem from source satellite to destination satellites is equivalent to flow assignment problem of time expanded graph $\mathcal{G}$ between source vertex $s^{(1)}$ and destination vertex set $\widetilde{\mathcal{D}}$. Before formulating the proposed problem, we need to define the capacity of different types of edges in the graph. For the communication edges, the edge capacity should be defined as the throughput of the inter satellite link (ISL) between two satellites. Specifically, the capacity of edge $e(v_i^{(t)}, v_i^{(t+1)})$ is expressed as

$$C_{i,j}^{(t)} = \tau B \log(1 + p_{i,j}^{(t)} h_{i,j}^{(t)}) \tag{1}$$

where B is the ISL bandwidth, $p_{i,j}^{(t)}$ is the transmission power of i-th satellite in t-th time slot, $h_{i,j}^{(t)}$ is the gain-to-noise ratio (GNR) in t-th time slot. The GNR $h_{i,j}^{(t)}$ can be calculated as

$$h_{i,j}^{(t)} = \frac{\lambda^2 G^{tr} G^{re}}{(4\pi l_{i,j}^{(t)})^2 \kappa B \Gamma} \tag{2}$$

where λ is the wavelength, G^{tr} and G^{re} represent transmission gain and receiving gain respectively, $l_{i,j}^{(t)}$ is the distance between two satellites, κ is the Boltzmann's constant, and Γ is the noise temperature.

For the edge $e(v_i^{(t)}, v_i^{(t+1)})$, the edge's capacity is equivalent to i-th satellite's storage capacity ST_i. For the virtual edge $e(v_i^{(t)}, v_j)$, the edge's capacity is infinite because two vertices represent the same satellite.

2.2   Problem Formulation

It can be noted that the actual information flow has been compressed due to the encoding operation at each satellite. At this time, the inflow and outflow of each node are not necessarily equal. However, the amount of encoded flow to be sent to given destination satellite will follow the flow balance constraint at each node. Hence, we define $x(v_i^{(t)}, v_j^{(t)}, \tilde{d})$ as the amount of encoded flow of which the destination satellite is $\tilde{d}$ through the ISL $e(v_i^{(t)}, v_j^{(t)})$. Then, the flow balance constraint is expressed as

$$\sum_{v_j^{(t)} \in \mathcal{S}} x(v_i^{(t)}, v_j^{(t)}, \tilde{d}) = R_{\tilde{d}}, v_i^{(t)} = s, t = 1 \tag{3}$$

$$\sum_{v_j^{(t)} \in \mathcal{S}} x(v_i^{(t)}, v_j^{(t)}, \tilde{d}) + x(v_i^{(t)}, v_i^{(t+1)}, \tilde{d})$$

$$= \sum_{v_j^{(t)} \in \mathcal{S}} x(v_j^{(t)}, v_i^{(t)}, \tilde{d}) + x(v_i^{(t-1)}, v_i^{(t)}, \tilde{d}), v_i^{(t)} \neq s, t \in \mathcal{N} \tag{4}$$

$$\sum_{v_j^{(t)} \in \mathcal{D}} x(v_j^{(t)}, v_i, \tilde{d}) = R_{\tilde{d}}, v_i = \tilde{d} \tag{5}$$

where the constraint (3) indicates that the outflow of the source satellite is equal to the total amount of data it will send, the constraint (4) means that the inflow and outflow of each node are equal, and the constraint (5) indicates that the coded data packets collected by the target satellite in a given time are sufficient.

Although satellites may be visible to multiple satellites, each satellite can only establish a limited number of ISLs due to the limited number of antennas. Hence, we define a binary variable $a(v_i^{(t)}, v_j^{(t)})$ where $a(v_i^{(t)}, v_j^{(t)}) = 1$ indicates that the ISL $e(v_i^{(t)}, v_j^{(t)})$ has been established and otherwise $a(v_i^{(t)}, v_j^{(t)}) = 0$. Then, we have

$$\sum_{v_j^{(t)} \in \mathcal{S}} a(v_i^{(t)}, v_j^{(t)}) \leq A_{out} \tag{6}$$

$$\sum_{v_j^{(t)} \in \mathcal{S}} a(v_j^{(t)}, v_i^{(t)}) \leq A_{in} \tag{7}$$

For a given ISL $e(v_i^{(t)}, v_j^{(t)})$, the actual amount of data passing through is equal to the maximum amount of all encoded packets. Because the throughput of the ISL is limited, the actual data throughput cannot exceed the ISL throughput. Hence, we have

$$\max_{\tilde{d} \in \tilde{\mathcal{D}}} x(v_i^{(t)}, v_j^{(t)}, \tilde{d}) \leq a(v_i^{(t)}, v_j^{(t)}) C_{i,j}^{(t)} \tag{8}$$

Similarly, if the code packet cannot be transmitted to other satellites in time, it can be temporarily stored in the current satellite, but the storage amount cannot exceed the maximum storage capacity. Hence, we have the following constraint.

$$\max_{\tilde{d} \in \tilde{\mathcal{D}}} x(v_i^{(t)}, v_i^{(t+1)}, \tilde{d}) \leq ST_i \tag{9}$$

The purpose of this paper is to maximize the coding capacity by optimizing the establishment of ISLs $\mathbf{a} = \{a(v_i^{(t)}, v_j^{(t)})\}$, the flow allocation $\mathbf{x} = \{x(v_i^{(t)}, v_j^{(t)})\}$, and the coding capacity $\mathbf{R} = \{R_{\tilde{d}}\}$. According to the linear network coding theory, the coding capacity of satellite networks is equal to the minimum amount of the flow to different destinations. Overall, the optimization problem is given as follows.

$$\max_{\mathbf{a,x,R}} \min_{\tilde{d} \in \tilde{\mathcal{D}}} R_{\tilde{d}}$$

$$s.t. \ (3) - (9) \tag{10}$$

$$a(v_i^{(t)}, v_j^{(t)}) \in \{0,1\}$$

The proposed optimization problem obviously belongs to integer linear programming, so there is usually no efficient method to obtain the optimal solution. Therefore, this paper focuses on designing an efficient algorithm to obtain suboptimal solutions. Once the variable $\mathbf{a}$ is given, the optimization problem is transformed into a linear programming so that it is easy to solve. So we are committed to an efficient topology construction method to optimize variable $\mathbf{a}$.

3   Heuristic Topology Construction Method

In this section, we propose a topology construction method that starts with a completed network topology and continues to delete the ISLs until a feasible network topology is obtained. The main idea of topology construction method is to delete the ISL that has the least effect on the overall performance. In order to evaluate the importance of different ISLs, we propose a weighting method by considering the characteristics of the encoded fow.

The proposed algorithm consists of three steps. The first step is to build a complete network topology, the second step is to define the weight of each ISL, and the third step is to iteratively delete redundant ISLs.

1) Complete network topology construction: It is assumed that the ISL can be established as long as two satellites are visible, which indicates that the variable $\mathbf{a}$ has been given. Then, the original optimization problem can be decomposed into several parallel subproblems.

$$\max_{\mathbf{x,R}} R_{\tilde{d}} \tag{11}$$

$$s.t. \ \sum_{v_j^{(t)} \in \mathcal{S}} x(v_i^{(t)}, v_j^{(t)}, \tilde{d}) = R_{\tilde{d}}, v_i^{(t)} = s, t = 1 \tag{11a}$$

$$\sum_{v_j^{(t)} \in \mathcal{S}} x(v_i^{(t)}, v_j^{(t)}, \tilde{d}) + x(v_i^{(t)}, v_i^{(t+1)}, \tilde{d}) \tag{11b}$$

$$= \sum_{v_j^{(t)} \in \mathcal{S}} x(v_j^{(t)}, v_i^{(t)}, \tilde{d}) + x(v_i^{(t-1)}, v_i^{(t)}, \tilde{d}), v_i^{(t)} \neq s, t \in \mathcal{N} \tag{11c}$$

$$\sum_{v_j^{(t)} \in \mathcal{D}} x(v_j^{(t)}, v_i, \tilde{d}) = R_{\tilde{d}}, v_i = \tilde{d} \tag{11d}$$

$$x(v_i^{(t)}, v_j^{(t)}, \tilde{d}) \leq a(v_i^{(t)}, v_j^{(t)}) C_{i,j}^{(t)} \tag{11e}$$

$$x(v_i^{(t)}, v_i^{(t+1)}, \tilde{d}) \leq ST_i \tag{11f}$$

It can be seen that the optimization problem (11) is equivalent to the max-imum flow problem from the source satellite s to the destination satellite $\tilde{d}$, so it can be solved well with the current method. Then, aiming at the pairs $\langle s, \tilde{d} \rangle$ of different source satellite and destination satellite, we can get the amount of maximum flow $R_{\tilde{d}}$ and corresponding coding flow allocation $\mathbf{f}$ through different ISLs.

2) *Weight design method*: When a ISL is deleted, the amount of maximum coding flow corresponding source-destination pair will be reduced. Specifically, for the source-destination pair $\langle s, \tilde{d} \rangle$, the amount of maximum coding flow will be decreased to $R_{\tilde{d}} - f(v_i^{(t)}, v_j^{(t)}, \tilde{d})$. Then, according to linear coding theory, the actual network throughput is expressed as $\min_{\tilde{d} \in \tilde{\mathcal{D}}} \{ R_{\tilde{d}} - f(v_i^{(t)}, v_j^{(t)}, \tilde{d}) \}$ after deleting the ISL $e(v_i^{(t)}, v_j^{(t)})$. In addition, the original network throughput is $\min_{\tilde{d} \in \tilde{\mathcal{D}}} \{ R_{\tilde{d}} \}$ before deleting the ISL $e(v_i^{(t)}, v_j^{(t)})$. Moreover, the weight of ISL $e(v_i^{(t)}, v_j^{(t)})$ can be defined as the difference between the original throughput and the modified throughput. Hence, we have

$$
w_{i,j}^{(t)} = \begin{cases} \min_{\tilde{d} \in \tilde{\mathcal{D}}} \{R_{\tilde{d}}\} - \min_{\tilde{d} \in \tilde{\mathcal{D}}} \{R_{\tilde{d}} - f(v_i^{(t)}, v_j^{(t)}, \tilde{d})\}, & \text{constraints (6) and (7) are met;} \\ \infty, & \text{otherwise.} \end{cases}
$$

$$(12)$$

In fact, the proposed weight design method actually shows the decreasing degree of the overall performance when the link is deleted. It is worth noting that the storage edge and virtual edge are not deleted in the time expanded graph because the satellite storage resource always exists, while the virtual edge does not exist in the actual satellite network.

3) *Iterative ISL deletion process*: According to the weight design method, it is obvious that $w_{i,j}^{(t)} \geq 0$. In particular, $w_{i,j}^{(t)} = 0$ indicates that the ISL $e(v_i^{(t)}, v_j^{(t)})$ has no effect on the overall network performance and hence can be removed.

The coding flow balance constraint is no longer valid due to deleting a ISL. To ensure that the flow balance constraint is still satisfied, we need to update the flow allocation results of the existing ISLs. We define $\Phi(v_i^{(t)}) = \{v_j^{(t)} | a(v_j^{(t)}, v_i^{(t)}) = 1, v_j^{(t)} \in \mathcal{S}\}$ to represent the satellites corresponding to incoming edges of i-th satellite in the t-th time slot. Similarly, we denote $\Psi(v_j^{(t)}) = \{v_i^{(t)} | a(v_j^{(t)}, v_i^{(t)}) = 1, v_i^{(t)} \in \mathcal{S}\}$ as the satellites corresponding to outgoing edges of j-th satellite in the t-th time slot. Furthermore, we define a matrix $\mathbf{z} = \{z(v_i^{(t)}, v_j^{(t)}, \tilde{d})\}$ to represent the degree of coding flow reduction on each ISL. Naturally, we know $z(v_i^{(t)}, v_j^{(t)}, \tilde{d}) = f(v_i^{(t)}, v_j^{(t)}, \tilde{d})$ if the ISL $e(v_i^{(t)}, v_j^{(t)})$ is deleted. Then, the amount of flow on different ISLs that should be reduced is calculated as follows.

$$
z(v_k^{(t)}, v_i^{(t)}, \tilde{d}) = \frac{f(v_k^{(t)}, v_i^{(t)}, \tilde{d})}{\sum\limits_{v_k^{(t)} \in \Phi(v_i^{(t)})} f(v_k^{(t)}, v_i^{(t)}, \tilde{d})} z(v_i^{(t)}, v_j^{(t)}, \tilde{d}), v_k^{(t)} \in \Phi(v_i^{(t)})
$$

$$(13)$$

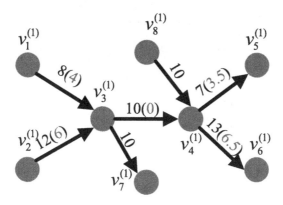

Fig. 2. Example of coding flow update method.

$$z(v_j^{(t)}, v_k^{(t)}, \tilde{d}) = \frac{f(v_j^{(t)}, v_k^{(t)}, \tilde{d})}{\sum\limits_{v_k^{(t)} \in \Psi(v_j^{(t)})} f(v_j^{(t)}, v_k^{(t)}, \tilde{d})} z(v_j^{(t)}, v_k^{(t)}, \tilde{d}), v_k^{(t)} \in \Psi(v_j^{(t)}) \quad (14)$$

Then, for the satellites $v_k^{(t)} \in \Phi(v_i^{(t)})$ and $v_k^{(t)} \in \Psi(v_j^{(t)})$, we can reconstruct their incoming set Φ and outgoing set Ψ and then recalculate the decrement according to formula (13). Finally, each ISL needs to update the flow allocation result. Hence, we have

$$f(v_i^{(t)}, v_j^{(t)}, \tilde{d}) = f(v_i^{(t)}, v_j^{(t)}, \tilde{d}) - z(v_i^{(t)}, v_j^{(t)}, \tilde{d}) \quad (15)$$

To better understand the proposed flow update method, an example is given to show the process in Fig. 2 where the black number represents the amount of the original coding flow and the red number represents the amount of the updated coding flow. Suppose that the ISL $e(v_3^{(1)}, v_4^{(1)})$ is deleted and corresponding amount of coding flow on this ISL is $f(v_3^{(1)}, v_4^{(1)}, \tilde{d}) = 10$. By the definition of $\Phi(v_3^{(1)})$ and $\Psi(v_4^{(1)})$, we can know that $\Phi(v_3^{(1)}) = \{v_1^{(1)}, v_2^{(1)}\}$ and $\Psi(v_4^{(1)}) = \{v_5^{(1)}, v_6^{(1)}\}$. Then, based on two formulas (13) and (14), the decreasing amount of coding flow is calculated as follows.

$$\begin{aligned}
z(v_1^{(1)}, v_3^{(1)}, \tilde{d}) &= \frac{8}{8+12} * 10 = 4 \\
z(v_2^{(1)}, v_3^{(1)}, \tilde{d}) &= \frac{12}{8+12} * 10 = 6 \\
z(v_4^{(1)}, v_5^{(1)}, \tilde{d}) &= \frac{7}{7+13} * 10 = 3.5 \\
z(v_4^{(1)}, v_6^{(1)}, \tilde{d}) &= \frac{13}{7+13} * 10 = 6.5
\end{aligned} \quad (16)$$

Then, the flow allocation can be updated by using the formula (15).

$$f(v_1^{(1)}, v_3^{(1)}, \tilde{d}) = 8 - 4 = 4$$
$$f(v_2^{(1)}, v_3^{(1)}, \tilde{d}) = 12 - 6 = 6$$
$$f(v_4^{(1)}, v_5^{(1)}, \tilde{d}) = 7 - 3.5 = 3.5 \qquad (17)$$
$$f(v_4^{(1)}, v_6^{(1)}, \tilde{d}) = 13 - 6.5 = 6.5$$
$$f(v_3^{(1)}, v_4^{(1)}, \tilde{d}) = 10 - 10 = 0$$

Now, we have completed the whole algorithm design and summarized this process in Algorithm 1.

Algorithm 1. The Proposed Topology Construction Algorithm

Input: The visual relationship between satellites within a given time and the ISL throughput.
Output: The topology construction result **a**.
1: Solve optimization problems (11) in parallel to obtain the coding flow allocation **f** and coding capacity **R**.
2: Define the weight of each ISL according to the formula (12).
3: **while** $w_{i,j}^{(t)} == 0$ **do**
4:    Delete the ISL $e(v_i^{(t)}, v_j^{(t)})$ by letting $a(v_i^{(t)}, v_j^{(t)}) = 0$.
5: **end while**
6: **while** $\min\limits_{i,j,t} w_{i,j}^{(t)} \neq \infty$ **do**
7:    $(i^*, j^*, t^*) = \arg\min\limits_{i,j,t} w_{i,j}^{(t)}$.
8:    Delete the ISL $e(v_{i*}^{(t^*)}, v_{j*}^{(t^*)})$ by letting $a(v_{i*}^{(t^*)}, v_{j*}^{(t^*)}) = 0$.
9:    Calculate the decreasing amount of coding flow on each ISL by using formulas (13) and (14).
10:   Update the flow allocation result by using formula (15).
11:   Update the weight of each ISL by using formula (12).
12: **end while**

---

4   Simulation Results and Discussions

In this section, we provide simulation results to evaluate the effectiveness of the proposed topology construction method. We have established a LEO satellite network consisting of 3 orbits and 45 LEO satellites, of which the constellation is delta type Walker constellation and each orbit contains 15 LEO satellites. The source and destination satellites are randomly selected from 45 LEO satellites. All the simulations are the average results after 300 iterations. The parameters involved in the paper are listed in the Table 1 if there is no special description.

The proposed method is evaluated by comparing it with existing fair contact plan (FCP) methods and the case without network coding. The performance

Table 1. Parameters in Simulation.

Parameters	Value
Channel bandwidth B	20 MHz
Wavelength λ	0.125 m
Duration of time slot ΔT	30 s
The noise temperature Γ	354.81 K
Transmission antenna gain G^{tr}	10 dB
Receiving antenna gain G^{re}	10 dB
Maximum number of transmission antennas A_{out}	2
Maximum number of receiving antennas A_{in}	2
Altitude of satellite orbit	1400 km
Inclination of satellite orbit	60°

evaluation includes two aspects: one is that the network coding capacity is equal to the objective function value of the original optimization problem (10), and the other is that the total network capacity is equal to the sum of the throughput of all destination satellites, i.e., $|\widetilde{\mathcal{D}}| \min_{\tilde{d} \in \widetilde{\mathcal{D}}} R_{\tilde{d}}$. Specifically, for the case without network coding, the network coding capacity refers to the minimum amount of data received by each destination satellite, and total network capacity refers to the sum of data received by all destination satellites.

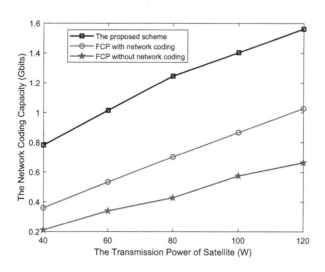

Fig. 3. Network coding capacity versus transmission power of satellite.

Figure 3 has shown the performance of network coding capacity with respect to the transmission power of satellite. It can be seen that the network coding capacity is improved with the increase of satellite transmission power. The reason is that increasing the satellite transmission power will increase the throughput of the ISLs, so more encoded packets can be passed in each time slot. Compared with the two benchmarks, the proposed topology construction algorithm has obvious advantages on improving network coding capacity. By taking the satellite transmission power of 100 W as an example, the network coding capacity with our proposed scheme is improved by 62.8% than FCP with network coding and improved by 145.6% compared with FCP without network coding.

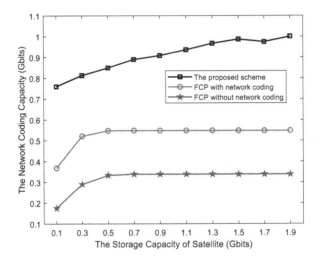

Fig. 4. Network coding capacity versus the storage capacity of satellite.

In Fig. 4, the effect of storage capacity on the performance of network coding capacity is given. It is obvious that the network coding capacity also increases when the storage capacity of satellites increases. The reason is that the storage capacity of the satellite is increased so that more data packets not transmitted are stored in the satellite to wait for a better time slot to transmit. From the perspective of time expanded graph, increasing the capacity of storage edge can increase the connectivity of network topology between different time slots, so it is possible to avoid some link bottlenecks and thus increase the network capacity. In addition, increasing storage capacity can not increase network coding capacity indefinitely. The reason is that network coding capacity is related to storage capacity and link throughput. When the storage capacity is particularly large, the link throughput becomes the limit of the network coding capacity. In terms of performance improvement, the proposed topology construction algorithm is superior to FCP with network coding and FCP without network coding.

Figure 5 has shown the change trend of network coding capacity with respect to the number of destination satellites. It can be seen that the network coding capacity decreases when the number of destination satellites increases. According to the linear network coding theory, the network coding capacity depends on

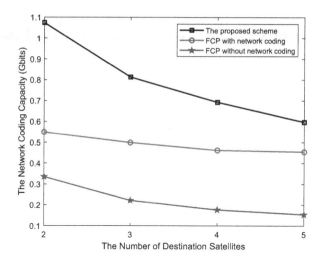

Fig. 5. Network coding capacity versus the number of destination satellites.

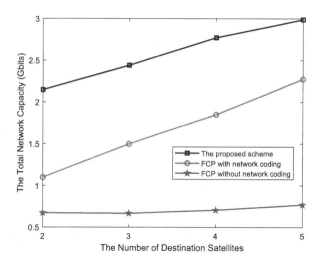

Fig. 6. Total network capacity versus the number of destination satellites.

the minimum capacity between multiple source-to-destination pairs. If the number of destination satellites is added, there is a greater possibility of encountering a link bottleneck, which will lead to the reduction of network coding capacity.

In Fig. 6, the relationship between the total network capacity and the number of destination satellites is given. It can be seen that the total network capacity increases by increasing the number of destination satellites for the case of applying network coding. The reason is that network resources are fully utilized through network coding technology, and the higher the number of destination satellites, the higher the resource utilization. However, when network coding is not used, the total network coding capacity is almost unchanged because the utilization rate of network resources is fixed, so the total network throughput is also fixed.

5 Conclusions

This paper studies the application of network coding technology in satellite multicast networks to improve network capacity. By performing the encoding operation, multiple data flows can be compressed on the satellite, thus reducing the occupation of communication resources and storage resources. Moreover, we propose a heuristic topology construction method and flow allocation method in order to improve the efficiency of network coding. From the simulation results, the network capacity is significantly improved after the network coding technology is adopted. In addition, the proposed optimization method is more effective than the traditional optimization method.

References

1. Li, D., Guang, X., Zhou, Z., Li, C., Tan, C.: Hierarchical performance analysis on random linear network coding. IEEE Trans. Commun. **66**(5), 2009–2021 (2018)
2. Wu, R., Ma, J., Tang, Z., Li, X., Choo, K.K.R.: A generic secure transmission scheme based on random linear network coding. IEEE-ACM Trans. Netw. **30**(2), 855–866 (2021)
3. Cui, Y., Medard, M., Yeh, E., Leith, D., Duffy, K.R.: Optimization-based linear network coding for general connections of continuous flows. IEEE-ACM Trans. Netw. **26**(5), 2033–2047 (2018)
4. Zhao, R., Wang, J., Lu, K., Chang, X., Jia, J., Zhang, S.: Optimal transmission topology construction and secure linear network coding design for virtual-source multicast with integral link rates. IEEE Trans. Multimedia **20**(11), 3069–3083 (2018)
5. Zhou, D., Sheng, M., Wang, X., Xu, C., Liu, R., Li, J.: Mission aware contact plan design in resource-limited small satellite networks. IEEE Trans. Commun. **65**(6), 2451–2466 (2017)
6. Zhou, D., Sheng, M., Liu, R., Wang, Y., Li, J.: Channel-aware mission scheduling in broadband data relay satellite networks. IEEE J. Sel. Areas Commun. **36**(5), 1052–1064 (2018)
7. Zhang, T., Li, H., Li, J., Zhang, S., Shen, H.: A dynamic combined flow algorithm for the two-commodity max-flow problem over delay-tolerant networks. IEEE Trans. Wirel. Commun. **17**(12), 7879–7893 (2018)
8. Zhang, T., Li, H., Zhang, S., Li, J., Shen, H.: Stag-based QoS support routing strategy for multiple missions over the satellite networks. IEEE Trans. Commun. **67**(10), 6912–6924 (2019)

Critical Separation Hashing for Cross-Modal Retrieval

Zening Wang[1]([✉]), Yungong Sun[1], Liang Liu[2], and Ao Li[1]

[1] School of Computer Science and Technology, Harbin University of Science and Technology,
Harbin, China
1335028185@qq.com
[2] School of Electrical Engineering and Computer Science, Pennsylvania State University,
New York, USA

Abstract. With the development of Internet technology, unimodal retrieval techniques are no longer suitable for the current environment, and mutual retrieval between multiple modalities is needed to obtain more complete information. Deep hashing has clearly become a simpler and faster method in cross-modal hashing. In recent years, unsupervised cross-modal hashing has received increasing attention. However, existing methods fail to exploit the common information across modalities, thus resulting in information wastage. In this paper, we propose a new critical separation cross-modal hashing (CSCH) for unsupervised cross-modal retrieval, which explores the similarity information across modalities by highlighting the similarity between instances to help the network learn the hash function, and we carefully design the loss function by introducing the likelihood loss commonly used in supervised learning into the loss function. Extensive experiments on two cross-modal retrieval datasets show that CSCH has better performance.

Keywords: Unsupervised · Cross-modal · Smilarity Matrix

1 Introduction

Along with the rapid development of the Internet and the popularity of smart devices and social networks, multimodal data has exploded on the Internet [1]. Multimodal data is simply a representation of the same thing in different modalities. How to follow one modality to retrieve other modalities becomes the key to searching information, which makes cross-modal retrieval emerge. General cross-modal retrieval methods use generic real values from different modalities to retrieve each other, but drawbacks such as high computational complexity and storage inefficiencies limit their use.

Cross-modal hashing methods have gained increasing interest due to the efficiency of storing binary hash codes and the simplicity of calculating Hamming distances [2], which map modal features to the same Hamming space for retrieval. In general, unsupervised methods using only information from the input image-text pair to mine out potential relationships and supervised methods using semantic labels to reduce the modal gap, which in turn aids hash code learning and obtains better performance. However, in most

© ICST Institute for Computer Sciences, Social Informatics and Telecommunications Engineering 2023
Published by Springer Nature Switzerland AG 2023. All Rights Reserved
A. Li et al. (Eds.): 6GN 2022, LNICST 504, pp. 171–179, 2023.
https://doi.org/10.1007/978-3-031-36011-4_15

cases, the data obtained does not have labels to work with, so unsupervised methods are more convenient [3].

The emergence of deep neural networks has facilitated the development of cross-modal hashing, and deep neural networks have a stronger semantic representation capability, which helps in the learning of further hash codes. There are still problems to be solved in unsupervised cross-modal hashing. The creation of similarity matrices requires uniform calculation of pairwise distances between different features, such as Hamming distance. In the method of constructing similarity matrices from features extracted by pre-training networks, the similarity matrix is constructed only by the direct relationship of features or by offsetting certain similar values, which is not ideal for subsequent use as a supervised matrix to learn hash codes. To solve the above problem, we propose a Critical Separation Cross-Modal Hashing method to assist in the construction of the similarity matrix, enhance or weaken the connection between features depending on the degree of similarity between instances to guide the learning of hash codes. The contributions of this paper are as follows:

- We designed a new similarity matrix, called Critical Separation Cross-Modal Hashing (CSCH), for unsupervised cross-modal retrieval. Supervised learning of hash functions using more accurate similarity matrices.
- Experimental results on two widely used retrieval datasets show that CSCH consistently outperforms other advanced techniques.

2 Related Work

2.1 Supervised Cross-Modal Hashing

Supervised cross-modal hashing methods have made some progress in cross-modal retrieval by using label information to learn how to generate hash codes. Through continuous development, benchmarks for supervised cross-modal retrieval have been improved somewhat. DCMH integrates feature learning and hash code learning into the same framework with deep neural networks [4]. THN learns cross-modal correlations jointly from auxiliary datasets, employing RNN networks and aligning the data distribution of the auxiliary dataset with the data distribution of the query or database domain to generate compact transfer hash codes for efficient cross-modal retrieval [5]. SSAH incorporates adversarial learning into cross one of the early attempts at cross-modal hashing uses adversarial networks to maximise the semantic relevance [6]. DLFH is based on a discrete latent factor model approach that allows direct learning of binary hash codes for cross-modal hashing and is suitable for cross-modal similarity search [7]. GCH learns modally uniform binary codes via affinity graphs and graph convolutional networks are used to explore inherent similarity between data points structure [8].

2.2 Unsupervised Cross-Modal Hashing

Unsupervised cross-modal hashing has no labelling information to work with and can only be learned from the data. There are two broad approaches to learning, one is shallow cross-modal hashing; the other is using deep neural networks to learn from the data. The shallow cross-modal hashing framework, CVH extends spectral hashing to multi-modal scenarios, maintaining semantic consistency of modalities in the same space [9]. LSSH extracts the intrinsic features under different modes by sparse coding and matrix decomposition [10]. CMFH goes a step further from both by learning a unified hash code through collective matrix decomposition and latent factor model, and at the same time, multiple information sources can be integrated to improve the retrieval accuracy during retrieval [11]. The above methods are not very effective in retrieval due to the shortcomings of containing insufficient information and the time-consuming and laborious extraction process, as all the features are produced manually.

With the further development of neural networks, it compensates for the inability of shallow structures to fully exploit the non-linear relationships between different modalities. UGACH uses the unsupervised representation learning capability of GAN to exploit the underlying streaming structure to maintain similarity between data [12]. DJSRH proposes a new joint semantic affinity matrix that integrates raw neighborhoods from different modal information to capture the potential connections of the input different modal instances [13]. DSAH makes full use of co-occurring image-text pairs and designs semantic alignment loss functions to maintain consistency between the input features and the hash codes output by the network [14]. JDSH refines the joint modal similarity matrix in a weighted manner based on the original feature distribution [15]. However, the unsupervised method proposed above still suffers from the problem of inaccurate similarity, thus obtaining only sub-optimal retrieval of the Hamming space (Fig. 1).

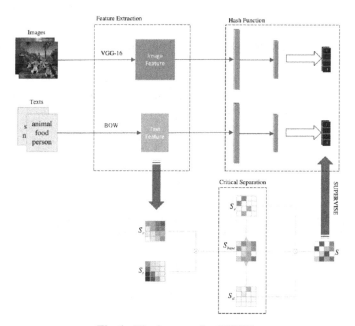

Fig. 1. The framework of CSCH.

3 The Proposed Method

3.1 Problem Definition

We assume that in the training set, $v_i \in \mathbb{R}^{d_v}$ and $t_i \in \mathbb{R}^{d_t}$ are the image and text features of the i_th instance. We use $V = \{v_i\}_{i=1}^N$ represent the initial image and $T = \{t_i\}_{i=1}^N$ represent the initial text features, respectively. The goal of this method is to learn the hash function $f_v(v; \theta_v)$ and $f_t(t; \theta_t)$, where θ_v, θ_t for parameters of ImgNet and TextNet. We discard Hamming similarity and use cosine values to measure the degree of similarity between instances, defined as:

$$\cos(x, y) = \frac{x \cdot y}{\|x\| \cdot \|y\|}, \tag{1}$$

where $\| \cdot \|$ denotes the l_2 norm of the vector and the Frobenius norm of the matrix.

3.2 Separation of Similarity Matrix

Since there is no labelling information available, it is not possible to directly construct pairwise similarity matrices to represent the relationships between instances. We can use a pre-trained deep neural network to extract features, and a deep perceptron to extract useful semantic information to construct the similarity matrix. We use $V = \{v_i\}_{i=1}^N$ to construct a similarity matrix between images $S_v = \left\{ s_{ij}^v \right\}_{i,j=1}^N$, where s_{ij}^v is $\cos(v_i, v_j) = \frac{v_i \cdot v_j^T}{\|v_i\| \cdot \|v_j\|}$, representing cosine similarity between image features $v_i, v_j \in \mathbb{R}^{d_v}$, and $T = \{t_i\}_{i=1}^N$ to construct a cosine similarity matrix between images $S_t = \left\{ s_{ij}^t \right\}_{i,j=1}^N$, where s_{ij}^t is $\cos(t_i, t_j) = \frac{t_i \cdot t_j^T}{\|t_i\| \cdot \|t_j\|}$, representing cosine similarity between text features, $t_i, t_j \in \mathbb{R}^{d_t}$.

First, we weight the fusion of S_v and S_t, which represent the degree of similarity between images and text, and use them as the initial similarity matrix

$$S_{base} = \frac{1}{2}(S_v + S_t), \tag{2}$$

where $S_{base} = \{s_{ij}\}_{i,j=1}^N$, $s_{ij} \in [0, 1]$, which maintains the cosine features of the image-text pairs, relates the relationship between the different feature pairs, we believe that the two modalities should have the same effect on the initial similarity matrix.

In the similarity critical separation section, we start by presenting several cases of values in S_{base}:

$$S_{base} \begin{cases} Strong & s_{ij} \in [1 - \sigma, 1) \\ Normal & s_{ij} \in (0 + \sigma, 1 - \sigma), \\ Weak & s_{ij} \in (0, 0 + \sigma] \end{cases} \tag{3}$$

where σ is the range parameter, controling the critical range to be divided in the similarity matrix. When Normal, this part of the instances is generally similar and does not favour either side, and we do not treat it. When it is Strong, it is called Strong similarity, this part of the instances are strongly similar to each other and can be easily distinguished at optimisation time, we choose to enhance this part to improve the accuracy at retrieval time, when it is Weak, we call it No similarity, this part of the instances are almost unrelated to each other and have little impact on optimisation, we want to further weaken the impact of this part on retrieval. The above three definitions of similarity are helpful for us to further investigate the similarity relationship between instances. In order to better generate distinguished hash codes, we need to further process the matrix S_{base} further.

First, we need to remove the extraneous parts of S_{base}:

$$S_e = S_{base} + S_{base}(Strong), \tag{4}$$

$$S_d = S_{base} - S_{base}(Weak), \tag{5}$$

where S_e is the part we need to enhance in S_{base} and S_d is the part we need to weaken in S_{base}. After normalization, we combine it with S_{base} to obtain the final similarity matrix S:

$$S = (1 - \alpha)S_{base} + \alpha S_e - \beta S_d, \tag{6}$$

where α, β indicates the weighting of the parts, and in order to map S to $[-1, 1]$, we simply pass $S = 2S - 1$.

3.3 Objective Functions

This paper proposes comprehensive similarity preservation loss and separation loss by helping neural networks learn hash functions in three ways: distance similarity preservation, intra- and inter-modal consistency preservation, and likelihood similarity preservation.

We define, $Z_v = f_v(v; \theta_v), Z_t = f_t(t; \theta_t), Z_v, Z_t$ as the real-valued eigenmatrices, then the similarity matrix for the same modality as $S_c(Z_v, Z_v), S_c(Z_t, Z_t)$, the similarity matrix for different modalities as $S_c(Z_v, Z_t), S_c(Z_t, Z_v)$, the distance similarity preservation loss as L_{dis}, and the intra- and inter-modal consistency loss as L_{in}, respectively.

$$L_{dis} = \sum_{p,q} \left\| S_c(Z_p, Z_q) - S \right\|_F, \tag{7}$$

$$L_{in} = \sum_{p,q,p_1,q_1} \left\| S_c(Z_p, Z_q) - S_c(Z_p, Z_q) \right\|_F, \tag{8}$$

where $p, q, p_1, q_1 \in \{v, t\}$. S is the similarity matrix computed from (6). $\| \cdot \|_F$ is the Frobenius parametrization. The likelihood similarity loss L_l is defined as:

$$L_l = - \sum_{i,j=1}^{N} \left(S_{ij}\Theta_{ij} - \log(1 + e^{\Theta_{ij}}) \right), \tag{9}$$

where $\Theta = {}^1\!/_2\mathbf{Z}_v\mathbf{Z}_t^T$.

From the definition of the likelihood function, it is clear that when the value is large, two instances should have a high probability of being similar, and vice versa. Also, quantifying the similarity between instances can be turned into the problem of calculating the size of the inner product of the original features of the instances. The critical separation matrix reflects whether there is similarity between two instances and is used as supervisory information in L_{dis} instead of labels.

For maintaining intra- and inter-pattern consistency, data from different patterns of the same instance should have strong similarity, regardless of the pattern in which the data are in, as an inherent data relationship within and between patterns. Therefore, we expect intra- and inter-modal consistency to mitigate the errors arising from critical separation for some instances.

In summary, the loss function L is defined as:

$$L = L_{dis} + L_{in} + \eta L_l, \tag{10}$$

where η is the parameter used to adjust the importance of the likelihood similarity loss.

4 Experiments

4.1 Datasets

We use two public datasets. NUS-WIDE [16] and MIRFlickr-25K [17], where 10 classes commonly used in the NUS-WIDE dataset are used as our original dataset, with a total of 186,577 image text pairs. We select 2000 data pairs from them as our query set. Then we select 5000 from the remaining 166,577 data pairs as our training set. In addition, to reduce the retrieval time, we select 10,000 from the remaining data pairs as our retrieval set.

MIRFlickr-25K has 20,015 image text pairs left after removing the problematic data. We select 2000 to form the query set. The rest are used as the retrieval set, from which 5000 are selected as the training set.

For the image features, the original image is preprocessed (e.g., scaled, cropped, flipped, etc.) and fed with the trained VGG_16, keeping the features of the last fully connected layer as the input to ImageNet. The text is represented by the features of 1000-dimensional BoW and 1386-dimensional BoW, respectively.

4.2 Evaluation Metrics

We use the common mAP to measure the retrieval ability of the method. The average precision AP is defined as:

$$AP = \frac{\sum_{q=1}^{R} P(q)rel(q)}{\sum_{q=1}^{R} rel(q)}, \tag{11}$$

where $rel(q) = 1$ if the item at rank q is relevant, $rel(q) = 0$ otherwise. $P(q)$ denotes the precision of the result ranked at q. When querying, we take the average of all AP to get mAP. The experimental results are shown in Fig. 2.

Table 1. Performance comparison of ten UCMH methods on two public datasets.

Task	Method	MIRFlickr-25K				NUS-WIDE			
		8-bit	16-bit	32-bit	64-bit	8-bit	16-bit	32-bit	64-bit
I2T	CVH	0.573	0.580	0.579	0.579	0.371	0.379	0.378	0.377
	FSH	0.581	0.590	0.597	0.597	0.391	0.400	0.414	0.424
	CMFH	0.574	0.588	0.592	0.594	0.479	0.483	0.488	0.486
	LSSH	0.627	0.630	0.634	0.631	0.463	0.475	0.484	0.474
	UGACH	0.674	0.686	0.695	0.702	0.532	0.548	0.563	0.567
	DJSRH	0.646	0.666	0.678	0.699	0.496	0.513	0.535	0.566
	UKD-SS	0.693	0.700	0.706	0.709	0.554	0.564	0.557	0.561
	DSAH	0.690	0.701	0.712	0.722	0.560	0.569	0.576	0.583
	JDSH	0.651	0.669	0.683	0.698	0.548	0.554	0.561	0.582
	CSCH	**0.721**	**0.735**	**0.747**	**0.752**	**0.572**	**0.591**	**0.600**	**0.611**
T2I	CVH	0.572	0.580	0.579	0.580	0.369	0.378	0.378	0.379
	FSH	0.571	0.589	0.595	0.595	0.390	0.395	0.408	0.417
	CMFH	0.588	0.590	0.595	0.598	0.483	0.487	0.488	0.493
	LSSH	0.612	0.621	0.628	0.626	0.462	0.476	0.481	0.477
	UGACH	0.689	0.692	0.698	0.699	0.543	0.557	0.562	0.580
	DJSRH	0.672	0.683	0.694	0.717	0.532	0.546	0.561	0.583
	UKD-SS	0.694	0.704	0.705	0.714	0.580	0.587	0.583	0.583
	DSAH	0.697	0.707	0.713	0.728	0.577	0.589	0.601	0.609
	JDSH	0.682	0.686	0.699	0.716	0.567	0.572	0.586	0.605
	CSCH	**0.720**	**0.733**	**0.745**	**0.750**	**0.588**	**0.604**	**0.612**	**0.621**

4.3 Implementation Details

For image and text features, we use two fully connected layers each as sub-networks to learn the representation of hash codes. Only the relevant parameters of the sub-networks are updated during training. For critical hyperparameters, first, we set α from 0.1 to 0.9 at an increment of 0.1 per step and set β from 1 to 0.001 with 10 times increments per step. For simplicity, we change the range we set k from 2500 to 4900 at an increment of 500. Finally, we determine the values of the parameters of the negative log-likelihood function η, we set η from 1 to 0.0001 with 10 times increments per step. We use the mAP results of the query set to determine the final parameters, which are: $\alpha = 0.3, \beta = 0.01, k = 4900, \lambda = 4000, \eta = 0.001$.

4.4 Results Analysis

Table 1 shows the mAP results on our proposed CSCH and other baseline methods. We can find that the best results are obtained for CSCH with different number of bits of hash codes. Our conclusions are as follows:

(1) Among all the methods on this dataset, CSCH achieves the best results on both the image query text task(I2T) and the text query image(T2I) task. This indicates that our CSCH improves accuracy by optimising the similarity matrix.

(2) As can be seen in Table 1, CSCH obtained the most recent results on this dataset. For I2T and T2I, CSCH outperformed the previous best model (DSDH) on 8, 16, 32 and 64 bits on both datasets by 4.5%, 4.9%, 4.9%, 4.1% and 3.3%, 3.7%, 4.5%, 3.0% on MIRFlickr, respectively, and on NUS-WIDE by were 2.1%, 3.9%, 4.2%, 4.8% and 1.9%, 2.5%, 1.8%, 2.0%.

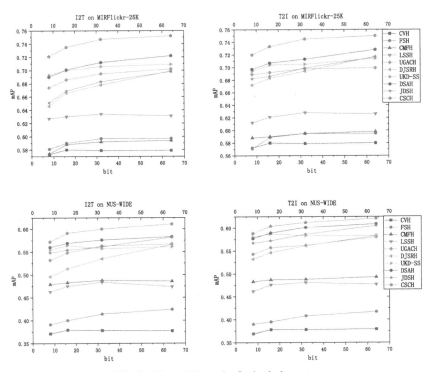

Fig. 2. The mAP results for both datasets.

5   Conclusion

In this paper, we have proposed a new unsupervised cross-modal retrieval method. Specifically, CSCH proposes 1) constructing a similarity matrix by critical separation to supervise the learning of hash functions; 2) using three complementary loss functions to aid the learning of hash functions, and specifically, invoking the likelihood loss commonly used in supervised learning to achieve stability in maintaining similarity learning. 3) A comparison with other superior techniques on two publicly available large cross-modal retrieval datasets shows that CSCH is superior and proves its superiority.

Acknowledgement. This work was supported in part by the National Natural Science Foundation of China under Grant 62071157, National Key Research and Development Programme

2022YFD2000500 and Natural Science Foundation of Heilongjiang Province under Grant YQ2019F011.

References

1. Lin, Z., Ding, G., Hu, M., Wang, J.: Semantics preserving hashing for cross-view retrieval. In: CVPR, pp. 3864–3872 (2015)
2. Zhou, J., Ding, G., Guo, Y.: Latent semantic sparse hashing for cross-modal similarity search. In: Proceedings of the 37th international ACM SIGIR Conference on Research and Development in Information Retrieval, pp. 415–424. ACM, 2014
3. Gu, W., Gu, X., Gu, J., Li, B., Xiong, Z., Wang, W.: Adversary guided asymmetric hashing for cross-modal retrieval. In: ICMR, pp. 159–167. ACM (2019)
4. Jiang, Q.Y., Li, W.J.: Deep cross-modal hashing. In: IEEE CVPR, pp. 3232–3240 (2017)
5. Cao, Z., Long, M., Yang, Q.: Transitive hashing network for heterogeneous multimedia retrieval. CoRR,2016,abs/1608.04307
6. Li, C., Deng, C., Li, N., Liu, W., Gao, X., Tao, D.: Self-supervised adversarial hashing networks for cross-modal retrieval. In: Proceedings of IEEE CVPR, pp. 4242–4251 (2018)
7. Jiang, Q., Li, W.: Discrete latent factor model for cross-modal hashing. In: IEEE Transactions on Image Processing, pp. 3490–3501 (2019)
8. Zhou, X., et al.: Graph convolutional network hashing. IEEE Trans. Cybern. 1460–1472 (2020)
9. Kumar, S., Udupa, R.: Learning hash functions for cross-view similarity search. In: Twenty-Second International Joint Conference on Artificial Intelligence (2011)
10. Zhou, J., Ding, G., Guo, Y.: Latent semantic sparse hashing for cross-modal similarity search. In: Proceedings of the 37th International ACM SIGIR Conference on Research Development in Information Retrieval, pp. 415–424 (2014)
11. Ding, G., Guo, Y., Zhou, J.: Collective matrix factorization hashing for multimodal data. In: Proceedings of the IEEE Conference on Computer Vision And Pattern Recognition, pp. 2075–2082 (2014)
12. Zhang, J., Peng, Y., Yuan, M.: Unsupervised generative adversarial cross-modal hashing. In: Proceedings of the AAAI Conference on Artificial Intelligence, vol. 32 (2018)
13. Su, S., Zhong, Z., Zhang, C.: Deep joint-semantics reconstructing hashing for large-scale unsupervised cross-modal retrieval. In: Proceedings of the IEEE International Conference on Computer Vision, pp. 3027–3035 (2019)
14. Yang, D., Wu, D., Zhang, W., Zhang, H., Li, B., Wang, W.: Deep semantic-alignment hashing for unsupervised cross-modal retrieval. In: Proceedings of the 2020 International Conference on Multimedia Retrieval, pp. 44–52 (2020)
15. Liu, S., Qian, S., Guan, Y., Zhan, J., Ying, L.: Joint-modal distribution-based similarity hashing for large-scale unsupervised deep cross-modal retrieval. In: Proceedings of the 43rd International ACM SIGIR Conference on Research and Development in Information Retrieval, pp. 1379–1388 (2020)
16. Chua, T.-S., Tang, J., Hong, R., Li, H., Luo, Z., Zheng, Y.: NUS-WIDE: a real-world web image database from National University of Singapore. In: Proceedings of the ACM International Conference on Image and Video Retrieval, pp. 1–9 (2009)
17. Huiskes, M.J., Lew, M.J.: The MIR flickr retrieval evaluation. In: Multimedia Information Retrieval. ACM, pp. 39–43 (2008)

An Improved DBSCAN Algorithm to Analyze Taxi Pick-Up Hotspots

Wu Zheng[1], Yuan Cheng[1], Nan Li[2], Zizhen Wang[1(✉)], and Ao Li[1]

[1] College of Computer Science and Technology, Harbin University of Science and Technology, Harbin 150080, China
2589377022@qq.com
[2] Information Center of State Administration of Science, Technology and Industry for National Defense, Harbin, China

Abstract. The DBSCAN algorithm is improved to analyze taxi pick-up hotspots. The time is divided into multiple time periods, and the load threshold and neighborhood radius are automatically extract. The accuracy of the DBSCAN algorithm for analyzing passenger areas is improved.

Keywords: Clustering · DBSCAN Algorithm · Pick-up Hotspots

1 Introduction

As the population grows, there is an increasing demand for taxis for residents to travel. However, there are many situations in which drivers are looking for passengers and passengers are waiting for drivers. Through the analysis of taxi passenger data, the hotspots in the city can be obtained. Therefore the efficiency of driver's pulling passengers can be improved that is a great significance for the urban traffic planning. In the past, the questionnaire survey method was mostly used in the investigation of hotspot areas [1]. This is not applicable to current large-area cities with large populations. At present, the unsupervised clustering method is used to cluster and analyze taxi trajectory data, which can extract hotspots more efficiently and accurately [3–5]. There are three main methods for clustering taxi trajectory data: the first is a clustering algorithm based on a grid, the second is a density-based clustering algorithm and the third is a partition-based clustering algorithm. Jiang H J [6] proposed an improved DBSCAN algorithm that takes into account the constraints of the road network and adds road topology relationships and road length information as constraints on the original basis. Xu [7] proposed a combination of the HIST algorithm and the K-means algorithm to calculate the traffic flow value in the region to extract passenger hotspots. Han Y. [8] optimized the parameters of the traditional DBSCAN algorithm. Zheng L.J. proposed a grid density-based GScan algorithm. Bao G.W. [9] used the A* path finding algorithm to select the passenger-carrying points in the neighborhood, which improved the speed of the DBSCAN algorithm. Liu P.P [10] added the R parameter to the FDBSCAN algorithm to limit the range of clusters.

© ICST Institute for Computer Sciences, Social Informatics and Telecommunications Engineering 2023
Published by Springer Nature Switzerland AG 2023. All Rights Reserved
A. Li et al. (Eds.): 6GN 2022, LNICST 504, pp. 180–195, 2023.
https://doi.org/10.1007/978-3-031-36011-4_16

Sun J. [11] obtained taxi hotspots through road feature information. Chakraborty S [12] proposed an incremental DBSCAN algorithm to dynamically cluster new data on the basis of the original clusters, which can better discover new clusters. Chen M et al. [13] proposed the P-DBSCAN algorithm which divides the data into regions and clusters each region separately and combines the results. Huang Z F [14] proposed an algorithm based on FGP-DBSCAN and improved it based on the P-DBSCAN algorithm which transforms the hard boundary problem of grid division into fuzzy grid partition.

Most of the existing passenger hotspot analysis algorithms have improved the accuracy and performance of the algorithm. However, the existing algorithms lack the analysis and processing of different time situations. A direct analysis of the data for the whole day does not provide a precise indication of the hot passenger pick-up areas at each time period. The DBSCAN algorithm is more suitable for processing taxi passenger data [15]. Because the algorithm can find clusters of arbitrary shapes and noise points are also regarded as unpopular areas for urban planning, the existing DBSCAN algorithm needs to adjust the input parameters. The problem of dividing the time is very complicated to manually adjust parameters for multiple time periods. This paper proposes an optimized DBSCAN algorithm (Auto-DBSCAN, A-DBSCAN for short). By dividing the time of the day every hour as a time period, more accurate hotspots at different times can be obtained. After extracting the passenger load situation in each time period, the driver's passenger load situation and the passenger's search situation are analyzed. The flow of people at different times is different. This results in different driving speeds of drivers and different times to find customers. The distance of seeking customers is determined by analyzing the time and speed of customer-seeking in each period. Thereby, the Eps parameter of DBSCAN is determined. The MinPts parameter of DBSCAN is determined by the average number of passengers carried in this period and the automatic processing of parameters is realized. This paper uses taxi trajectory data from New York City to optimize the processing results of the original DBSCAN algorithm with insufficient accuracy and difficult parameter adjustment. Analyzing the passenger loading situation in different time periods and performing a more accurate analysis of travel hotspots are helpful for urban construction planning.

2 Optimization of the DBSCAN Algorithm Through the Division of Time

2.1 Parameter Automation for Passenger-Carrying Analysis and Passenger-Seeking Analysis

DBSCAN is one of the most classic algorithms for density-based clustering. Eps is the neighborhood radius that defines the density and MinPts is the threshold that defines the core point [16]. An object is a core point if it contains more than MinPts' number of points within its radius Eps. An object is a boundary point if the number of points within its radius Eps is less than MinPts. However, when an object falls within the neighborhood of the core point, the object is ta boundary point. An object is a noise point if it is neither a core point nor a boundary point. Core points and boundary points can be regarded as hotspots, and noise points can be regarded as sparsely populated areas. Through the distribution of these points, urban planning can be better carried out. It is helpful for drivers to carry passengers.

Passenger data need to be processed at different times; otherwise, it is difficult to obtain accurate results. The problem brought by the division of time is that different data are clustered many times and the input adjustment of parameters is difficult. It is important to consider the relationship between the Eps parameter and the MinPts parameter and the actual driver-passenger relationship. If the driver spends too much time looking for passengers, it will lead to unnecessary economic losses and environmental pollution. Such areas do not qualify as hotspots. In contrast, the driver can find the next passenger after driving the appropriate distance, which is the most beneficial result for both the passenger and the driver. Therefore, it is also in line with the actual customer-seeking situation by calculating the average customer-seeking distance of drivers during this period as the minimum radius of the neighborhood. The average search distance for a certain period is equal to the product of the average search time and the average travel speed for the period. The average customer-seeking distance during this period is shown in Formula 1:

$$Eps = avgVelocity * avgPickupTime \qquad (1)$$

In the formula, avgVelocity is the average driving speed during the period, and avgVelocity is the average customer-seeking time during the period.

At the same time, the average number of passengers carried by drivers in this period is used as the threshold, which is also in line with the relationship between the flow of people and the number of passengers carried by drivers in this period. The threshold formula for this period is:

$$MinPts = len(data)/carCount \qquad (2)$$

where carCount is the number of drivers for this period.

2.2 A-DBCSAN Algorithm Flow

Based on the above analysis, the algorithm will analyze and process the parameters according to the passenger load situation of each time period. In addition it realizes the automation of parameters. The specific algorithm flow is as follows:

Algorithm 1: This is the main algorithm of the A-DBSCAN algorithm. Time division is first performed on the incoming and outgoing passenger data. The passenger loading conditions at different times are recorded. The number of drivers is calculated, and then the threshold and neighborhood radius are determined to achieve automatic parameter extraction. Iteration is conducted over each point at that moment.

Input: D - Passenger Data.
1. time=[]
2. for i in range (24):
3. time.append(D[D['pickup_datetime'].dt.hour.isin(np.arange(i,i+1))])
4. data=time[i]
5. carCount=set(len(D['medallion']))
6. MinPts = len(data) / carCount
7. Eps = avgVelocity * avgPickupTime /
8. for each point P in dataset time[i]:
9.   if P is visited
10.   continue next point
11.   mark P as visited
12.   NeighborPts = regionQuery (P, eps)
13.   if sizeof (NeighborPts) < MinPts
14.   mark P as NOISE
15.   else
16.   C = next cluster
17.   expandCluster (P, NeighborPts, C, Eps, MinPts)

Algorithm 2: The expandCluster function merges adjacent clusters. The extended category core points are added first. The points in the core point neighborhood are traversed. If the point is a core point, the class is augmented.

Inputs: P—passenger points, NeighborPts—set of neighboring passenger points for a point P, C—new clustered passenger dataset.
1. add P to cluster C
2. for each point P' in NeighborPts
3.   if P' is not visited
4.   mark P' as visited
5.   NeighborPts'= regionQuery(P', eps)
6.   if sizeof(NeighborPts') >= MinPts
7.   NeighborPts = NeighborPts joined with NeighborPts'
8.   if P' is not yet a member of any cluster
9.   add P' to cluster C
Algorithm 3: The regionQuery function calculates the neighborhood.
Input: P—passenger point, Eps—neighborhood radius.
Return all points within P's Eps-neighborhood.

3   Experimental Analysis

3.1   Data Analysis and Processing

The application of GPS enables the record keeping of a taxi's itinerary [17]. This paper uses taxi passenger data from February 1, 2010, to February 3, 2010, in New York City. A total of 11711 taxis were obtained from the taxi license plate number (hack_license), and a total of 601821 pieces of data were generated during the period. First, the date format of the data is converted, and then unreasonably wrong data are cleaned and canceled. The taxi data trajectory points are shown in Table 1.

Table 1. Taxi data parameters.

Parameter	Value
hack_license	2010000001
pickup_datetime	2010-01-01 00:00:00
dropoff_datetime	2010-01-01 00:34:00
trip_time_in_secs	34.00
trip_distance	14.05
pickup_longitude	−73.948418
pickup_latitude	40.724590

3.2 Passenger Data Distribution

First, the passenger data from February 1, 2010 to February 3, 2010 are extracted, and there are 11,711 taxis carrying 601,821 passenger data. The three-day travel time distribution is shown (in Fig. 1):

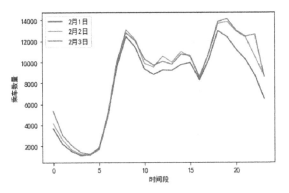

Fig. 1. Passenger time distribution.

The number of rides gradually decreases between 0:00 and 5:00. Then, it climbs quickly from 5:00 to 8:00. It drops slightly from 8:00 to 10:00 and flattens out until 16:00. After that, it climbs rapidly until 19:00. Finally, it drops rapidly until 24 o'clock. This is in line with the daily travel situation of most residents. The dataset covers the geographic space with a longitude range of [−74°03', −73°77'] and a dimensional range of [40°63', 40°85']. The map is shown. (in Fig. 1) (Fig. 2):

Fig. 2. Passenger area.

4 Comparison of Experimental Results

4.1 Division of Time and Parameter Automation

The original DBSCAN algorithm cannot divide the time and can only obtain the data results of the whole day. Without time division, the repeatability of data is too high. As a result, the distribution of ride points in some areas is too dense. The obtained clustering results combine the areas with a large amount of data and high repetition into a whole block. It is not possible to identify passenger hotspots at different times. Figure 3 shows the analysis of the total ride points without time division and some areas are too dense.

Fig. 3. Ride distribution without time division.

The results obtained by clustering are shown in Fig. 4 below. Regardless of how the parameters are adjusted, multiple time periods are mixed together. The clustering results of areas with high traffic and high repetition are not good. It is also difficult to pinpoint when drivers should pick up passengers in hotspots. Such a result cannot provide more detailed assistance for the driver to carry passengers.

Fig. 4. Clustering results without time division.

Due to the huge passenger capacity of taxis, the time interval is divided into one-hour intervals. The passenger load situation is analyzed at 0:00-1:00 on February 1, 2010. At 0:00–1:00, the number of people and drivers is relatively small. The passenger load situation is shown in Table 2 below.

Table 2. Passengers at 0:00–1:00.

Parameter	Value
Number of taxis	2055
Number of passengers	3603
Average seeking distance	6.833 km
Average search time	19.5 min
Average number of pull loads	2
Time period selected	0:00–1:00

The distribution of passenger load points at 0:00–1:00 is shown in the figure below (Fig. 5).

Fig. 5. Ride distribution at 0:00–1:00.

The clustering results of the A-DBSCAN algorithm are shown in the following figure (Fig. 6).

Fig. 6. A-DBSCAN clustering results at 0:00–1:00.

From 7–8 o'clock on the 1st is the peak travel time with the largest number of people and drivers. The passenger load situation is shown in Table 3 below. During peak travel times, the increase in foot traffic allows drivers to carry more passengers. Compared with the time when there is less traffic, the time to find customers is shorter. The distance to find customers is also shorter. This reflects the versatility of the A-DBSCAN algorithm for different times.

Table 3. Passenger load at 7–8 o'clock.

Parameter	Value
Number of taxis	9428
Number of passengers	3399
Average seeking distance	3.72 km
Average search time	14.1 min
Average number of pull loads	3
Time period selected	7:00–8:00

Table 4. Running time comparison

Algorithm	Running time
DBSCAN	0.5501
RL-DBSCAN	0.5366
P-DBSCAN	1.1928
A-DBSCAN	0.4463

Table 5. Davies–Bouldin index comparison

Algorithm	Davies–Bouldin Value
DBSCAN	0.9964
RL-DBSCAN	0.9962
P-DBSCAN	0.9987
A-DBSCAN	0.9988

The distribution of bus rides at 7:00–8:00 on the 1st is shown in the figure below (Fig. 7):

The clustering results of the A-DBSCAN algorithm are shown in the following figure (Fig. 8).

Through the above A-DBSCAN clustering results, it can be observed that the algorithm can obtain better clustering results in periods of high traffic and low traffic. This reflects the versatility of the A-DBSCAN algorithm and the realization of automation and conforms to the real passenger situation.

Fig. 7. A-DBSCAN clustering results at 7:00–8:00.

Fig. 8. A-DBSCAN clustering results at 7:00–8:00.

4.2 Comparison of Multiple Clustering Algorithms

Taking JFK International Airport as an example, a total of 1,103 drivers carried 1,829 passengers on the 1st. The distribution of rides is shown in the figure below (Fig. 9):

As seen from the above figure, some data repetitions are too high. The clustering results of the DBSCABN algorithm are shown in the following figure. Due to the high degree of data repetition without time division, the effect of clustering is not accurate. The average number of passengers picked up per driver is doubled here. The clustering results show many duplicate data as hotspots (Fig. 10).

Fig. 9. JFK International Airport passenger distribution.

Fig. 10. DBSCAN algorithm clustering results.

The figure below shows the clustering results of the RL-DBSCAN algorithm for JFK Airport on the 1st. Although the RL-DBSCAN algorithm adds road topology constraints, the clustering results are better and fewer clusters are formed. Although the index is improved, it still does not meet the actual passenger load. The parameters also need to be debugged. Additionally, the time constraints are not considered. A large amount of data leads to the formation of dense travel hotspots. It does not correspond to the real situation which the actual average number of passengers carried is doubled (Fig. 11).

Fig. 11. RL-DBSCAN algorithm clustering results.

The figure below shows the clustering results of JFK Airport by the P-DBSCAN algorithm. The division of the region is more detailed than the results obtained by the original DBSCAN algorithm. However, the time is also not divided, which results in data that are too dense. The results obtained do not correspond to the actual passenger load situation. The P-DBSCAN algorithm will divide multiple regions and make the adjustment of parameters more complicated (Fig. 12).

Fig. 12. P-DBSCAN algorithm clustering results.

Using the A-DBSCAN algorithm to divide the time, the passenger distribution of JFK Airport from 7:00 to 8:00 is shown in the figure below (Fig. 13):

Fig. 13. Bus distribution at JFK International Airport from 7:00–8:00.

The clustering results of the airport between 7:00 and 8:00 by the A-DBSCAN algorithm are shown in the following figure. Through time division, a large number of data-intensive situations are avoided. The hotspot areas are also more accurate than those obtained from the traditional DBSCAN algorithms and RL-DBSCAN algorithms. These areas are in line with the driver's real passenger situation. At the same time, it also solves the difficult situation of manual parameter adjustment (Fig. 14).

Fig. 14. A-DBSCAN algorithm clustering results.

4.3 Clustering Algorithm Performance Comparison

After the A-DBSCAN algorithm conducts time division, the data-intensive situation is reduced. The performance is also improved. The following table compares the running time of the A-DBSCAN algorithm and other algorithms for JFK Airport clustering. The running time of the A-DBSCAN algorithm is less than that of the DBSCAN, RL-DBSCAN and P-DBSCAN algorithms (Table 4).

Davies–Bouldin [18] and Silhoette [19] introduced an internal evaluation index of clustering algorithms. Different clustering algorithms are used to test the airport data. The Davies–Bouldin index is calculated by dividing the sum of the average distances within the class of any two categories and dividing the distance between the two cluster centers to find the maximum value. The smaller the index is, the better the clustering effect. The table below shows the comparison between the A-DBSCAN algorithm and other algorithms in terms of the Davies–Bouldin index (Table 5).

Comparing the above experimental results, the A-DBSCAN algorithm consumes less time. The Davies–Bouldin index results are better than those of the other algorithms. The results of several clustering algorithms in terms of the Silhoette index results are similar. The accuracy and performance of the A-DBSCAN algorithm are improved.

5 Conclusions

This paper uses New York City taxi trajectory data for analysis and processing. The traditional DBSCAN algorithm lacks time analysis and processing. This results in a large amount of data being too dense. The obtained clustering results cannot determine the passenger hotspots well. The traditional DBSCAN algorithm requires parameter adjustment that is very time-consuming and difficult in the case of multiple sets of experiments. In view of the above problems, this paper uses time division based on the DBSCAN algorithm to solve a large number of data-intensive problems and improve the accuracy of the experimental results. It analyzes the relationship between the distance of the driver to find passengers and the relationship between passengers to achieve parameter automation to solve the difficult problem of parameter input adjustment. First, the data format is dealt with. Then, duplicate data and unreasonable data are deleted. The distribution of residents' rides on multiple days is analyzed, and the results obtained reflect the regularity of travel. Then, the time is divided, and the passenger-carrying and passenger-seeking situations are analyzed at each time. The number of drivers, the passenger-seeking time, the passenger-seeking distance, and the average number of passengers carried by the drivers are extracted as the parameters of MinPts and Eps. The extracted parameters are in line with the real driver's passenger-seeking situation, and the algorithm can automatically extract the parameters. It solves the problem that multiple sets of data need a large number of input parameters to adjust parameters. The passenger loading situation is analyzed in different time periods. Through the experimental comparison and analysis, the versatility of the parameters extracted by the A-DBSCAN algorithm for different time periods is verified. Then, JFK Airport is analyzed in detail, and the results of various clustering algorithms are compared. The results show that the A-DBSCAN algorithm is more accurate and more in line with the real passenger situation. Finally, the A-DBSCAN algorithm is compared with other algorithms in terms of time and clustering internal indicators, and both achieve better results, proving that the performance is also improved.

Acknowledgement. This work was supported in part by the National Natural Science Foundation of China under Grant 62071157, National Key Research and Development Programme 2022YFD2000500 and Natural Science Foundation of Heilongjiang Province under Grant YQ2019F011.

References

1. Shi, F., et al.: Sampling methods of resident trip investigation. J. Traffic Transport. Eng. **4**(4), 72–75 (2004)
2. Wang, L., et al.: Mining frequent trajectory pattern based on vague space partition. Knowledge-Based Systems 50. Complete, 100–111 (2013)
3. Yu, et al.: Urban computing: concepts, methodologies, and applications. ACM Trans. Intell. Syst. Technol. Spec. (2014)
4. Tang, J., et al.: Uncovering urban human mobility from large scale taxi GPS data. Phys. A **438**, 140–153 (2015)
5. Yuan, J., et al.: Discovering regions of different functions in a city using human mobility and POIs. ACM 186 (2012)
6. Cai, Y.W., Yang, B.R.: Improved DBSCAN algorithm for public bus station cluster. Comput. Eng. **34**(10), 190–192 (2008)
7. Xu, C., Zhang, A., Chen, Y.: Traffic congestion forecasting in shanghai based on multi-period hotspot clustering. IEEE Access (99), 1–1 (2020)
8. Han, Y., et al.: Exploring the temporal and spatial distribution of passengers based on taxi trajectory data. Periodical of Ocean University of China (2019)
9. Zheng, L., et al.: Mining urban attractive areas using taxi trajectory data. Computer Applications and Software (2018)
10. Bao, G.: Research and system implementation of taxi passenger hotspot recommendation method. North China University of Technology (2019)
11. Liu, P.: Research on hotspots mining of taxi passengers based on spatial clustering and Weka platform. Jilin University (2014)
12. Sun, J., Guan, C., Jinhong, M.: Exploiting optimization mechanism for pick-up points recommendations. In: International Conference on Computer Systems, Electronics and Control
13. Chakraborty, S.: Analysis and study of incremental DBSCAN clustering algorithm. Eprint Arxiv **1**(2), 2011 (2014)
14. Chen, M., Gao, X.D., Li, H.F.: Parallel DBSCAN with Priority R-tree. In: 2010 The 2nd IEEE International Conference on IEEE Information Management and Engineering (ICIME) (2010)
15. Huang, Z.: Mining and recommendation of customer-seeking areas based on taxi trajectories. Hangzhou Dianzi University (2020)
16. Yi, L.I., et al.: A weighted centroid localization algorithm based on DBSCAN clustering point density. J. Henan Univ. Sci. Technol. (Natl. Sci.) (2018)
17. Ester, M., et al.: A Density-Based Algorithm for Discovering Clusters in Large Spatial Databases with Noise. AAAI Press (1996)

18. Murakami, E., Wagner, D.: Can using global positioning system (GPS) improve trip reporting? Transport. Res. Part C Emerg. Technol. **7**(2–3), 149–165 (1999)
19. Rousseeuw, Peter J.: Silhouettes: a graphical aid to the interpretation and validation of cluster analysis. J. Comput. Appl. Math. **20**, 53–65 (1987). https://doi.org/10.1016/0377-042 7(87)90125-7

Classification of Deforestation Factors in 6G Satellite Forest Images

Yuhai Li[1(✉)], Yuxin Sun[1(✉)], Xianglong Meng[2], and Liang Xi[2]

[1] Science and Technology on Electro-Optical Information Security Control Laboratory,
Tianjin 300300, China
liyuhai.cn@qq.com, sunyuxin@tju.edu.cn
[2] School of Computer Science and Technology, Harbin University of Science and Technology,
Harbin 150080, China

Abstract. The terrestrial satellite network will play an essential role in 6G. Through the satellite system, people can obtain a lot of ground image information to process tasks and feedback. Forest resource is an essential resource. Determining the causes of deforestation is crucial for the development and implementation of forest protection plans. In this article, we propose a novel deep neural network model for distinguishing drivers of deforestation events from satellite forest images. To solve the problems of image rotation caused by satellite angle rotation and image blurring caused by extreme weather occlusion during satellite image acquisition, we add data enhancement and a self-supervised rotation loss to the model to improve the robustness and adaptability. We use deforestation maps generated from Landsat 8 satellite imagery as a dataset and demonstrate that our approach achieves better results than the baselines.

Keywords: 6G network · deforestation factor classification · deep learning

1 Introduction

Radio communication technology has developed rapidly. The fifth-generation mobile information system (5G) is combined with the Internet of things. Radio communication technology can meet more and more application needs, and communication speed is getting faster and faster. Now, we has begun to move towards the sixth generation mobile information system (6G).

On the basis of 5G technologies, The 6G network will be fully connected communication network with global coverage, combining terrestrial communication network and space satellite communication network. So, in 6G, terrestrial-satellite networks (TSN) will become the critical leverage to explore airspace resources for communications [1]. Through the integration of satellite signals, global seamless signal coverage, the global positioning satellite system, image satellite system and 6G ground network, the 6G network can help people quickly explore the ground information.

In modern times, protecting forest resources can prevent species extinction, create clean air and water, and detect climate change [2]. For some reason, forest loss in the

A. Li et al. (Eds.): 6GN 2022, LNICST 504, pp. 196–207, 2023.
https://doi.org/10.1007/978-3-031-36011-4_17

tropics results in about 10% of the world's annual greenhouse gas emissions [3], which should be reduced to decrease the potential for climate tipping points [4]. The direct factors or specific activities leading to the deforestation of tropical rainforests include natural events (such as fire and flood), manufactured land occupation (such as industrial and agricultural development), and human activities [5]. Accurately identifying these factors is crucial for implementing targeted policies and actions to protect forests. In terms of the rate of rainforest loss, Indonesia ranks among the highest in the world, so analyzing the causes of forest loss in Indonesia can help us to classify forest loss factors globally.

Through the 6G ground-satellite network interconnection system, we can obtain high-resolution forest satellite images to analyze the direct causes of forest loss and provide essential information for conservation work. With the development of interconnectivity between satellites and terrestrial networks, and the advances in various deep learning methods, it possible to obtain and analyze terrestrial geographic information automatically. Compared with the previous machine learning methods, such as decision trees, random forest classifiers, etc. [6–9], Convolutional neural network (CNN) is the most effective method for extracting data features [10–13]. However, these CNN-based methods usually only use clear and standard data for model training, the performance becomes unstable once the data changes, such as image angle changes due to satellite rotation or image blurring due to cloud or fog interference.

In this paper, considering the increasing the data diversity, we present a new model based on the CNN network to classify deforestation images. We used an encoder, a classification header, and an angle prediction header. Through data fuzzy and rotation processing, the model can by trained more deeply by the combined data and predict the factors of forest loss more efficiently and accurately. We used the satellite forest image dataset of Indonesia processed and made by Irvin et al. [14] to conduct the experiments. The results show that our model has high robustness and classification accuracy.

2 Related Work

2.1 6G Network

In the era of the 5G networks, it is expected that more than 80% of land areas and more than 95% of sea areas could not be covered by satellite signals. Moreover, as the signal range of the 5G network is concentrated within 10km above the ground, the actual "global Omni-sphere" and "Internet of Things' cannot be truly realized. To this end, 6G will be further upgraded based on 5G, featuring complete coverage and application.

For the global signal coverage, 6G satellite communication will play an important role. By integrating the satellite networks with the ground networks, 6G can achieve the goal of global mobile network coverage, and People all over the world can use it anytime, anywhere.

6G satellite network has been able to provide complementary satellite services in many areas, and satellite services have evolved from traditional voice and broadcast services to broadband Internet services [15]. It can detect the movements of ground users, ground information, vehicles, emergency base stations, and other satellites [16], and predict weather conditions. By transmitting detected statistics or captured satellite images to the ground, combined with models trained through artificial intelligence technology, it can effectively respond to current geographic information or weather disasters.

Therefore, we use the 6G satellite image dataset of Indonesia's rainforests to analysis why they are being cut down. The used 6G ground-space satellite network framework is shown in Fig. 1.

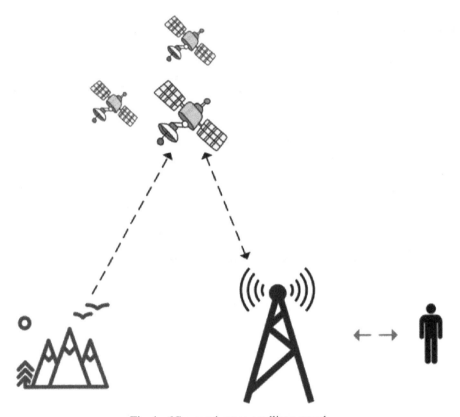

Fig. 1. 6G ground-space satellite network

2.2 Resnet Network

With the increase of layers of neural networks, the problem of vanishing/exploding gradients would appear [17, 18]. In the early, this problem was solved to some extent by normalized initialization [18–20], which used stochastic gradient descent and backpropagation [21], but it also exposed another problem: as the number of layers of the neural network increases, the network accuracy peaks and then drops off at a high-speed rate.

In view of the above problems, Kaiming He [22] proposes the Resnet network framework. Resnet network is mainly composed of two/three-layer residual blocks. In the [22], five network frameworks are proposed: 18-layer, 34-layer, 50-layer, 101-layer, and 152-layer. The network framework of Resnet18 is adopted in this paper, and its framework parameters are shown in Table 1. From the parameter table, we can know the image information is constantly changing through each network layer. The network framework is shown in Fig. 2. There are four residual blocks are used in Resnet18, each consisting of two basic blocks, the details are shown in Fig. 3. In Resnet18, each basic block is a double-layer foundation block consisting of two convolutions and a short circuit connection. Figure 4 shows the detailed structure of the basic block.

Because Resnet18 network framework has the advantages of no gradient disappearance/gradient explosion and network degradation compared with the convolutional network, we choose it as our encoder to extract image features.

Table 1. Resnet18 Network framework

Layer name	Output size	18-layer
Conv1	112×112	7×7, 64, stride 2
Residual block_1	56×56	3×3 max pool, stride 2
		$\begin{bmatrix} 3 \times 3 \ 64 \\ 3 \times 3 \ 64 \end{bmatrix} \times 2$
Residual block_2	28×28	$\begin{bmatrix} 3 \times 3 \ 128 \\ 3 \times 3 \ 128 \end{bmatrix} \times 2$
Residual block_3	14×14	$\begin{bmatrix} 3 \times 3 \ 256 \\ 3 \times 3 \ 256 \end{bmatrix} \times 2$
Residual block_4	7×7	$\begin{bmatrix} 3 \times 3 \ 512 \\ 3 \times 3 \ 512 \end{bmatrix} \times 2$
	1×1	Average pool, 512-d fc, SoftMax
FLOPs		1.8×10^9

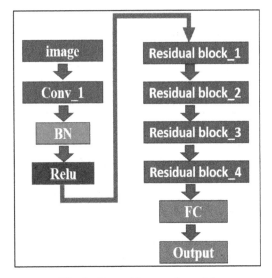

Fig. 2. Resnet18 network model   **Fig. 3.** Residual block

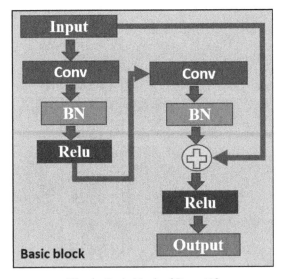

Fig. 4. Basic block of Resnet18

3 Method

We change the image size from 332×332 to 160×160. The input data are defined as $x = \{(x_i, y_i)\}_{i=1}^{N}$, Where N is the number of data. $y_i \in \{1 \ldots \ldots C\}$ is the labels of x_i, C represents the number of classes. This method carries out fuzzy and rotation processing on the original data, x, and get the processed sample, defined as $x^g = \{(x_i^g)\}_{i=1}^{N}$ and $x^r = \{(x_i^r, y_i^r)\}_{i=1}^{N}$, where x^g represents the data of x after rotation and fuzzy enhancement. x^r

represents the data augmented by rotation only, and the rotation label, $y_i^r \in \{0, 1, 2, 3\}$ is generated by its rotation angle, respectively representing rotation $0°$, $90°$, $180°$, $270°$ (Fig. 5).

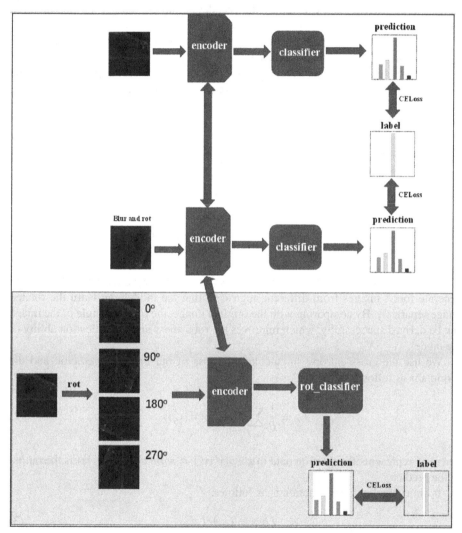

Fig. 5. Model framework: The standard supervised learning module is shown on the white background, and the rotating self-supervised learning model is shown on the gray background.

Our model defines the encoder as $E: X \rightarrow F$, where F is the extracted picture feature vector. Then we represent a rotation Angle predictor $f_r: F \rightarrow p^r$ and a classifier $f_c: F \rightarrow p^c$ for data classification and rotation Angle prediction. The details are mainly in five parts.

(1) Our encoder structure uses the model framework of Resnet18 proposed by Kaiming He et al. [11]. It consists of 17 convolutional layers and one fully connected layer.

(2) The classifier and the rotation angle predictor use three linear layers to reduce the dimension of the features extracted by the encoder and finally output the classification and angle prediction.

(3) We use encoders and predictors with the same framework as classification prediction and share the weight of the encoder.

(4) Moreover, by data enhancement with fuzzy and rotation, the model can avoid unclear satellite images caused by extreme weather, such as fog, typhoons, and shape changes of areas due to satellite rotation, which can lead to the inaccurate identification of deforestation factors.

We use the cross-entropy to calculate the loss of our encoder and classifier, and our actual loss function is shown below:

$$L_c = \frac{1}{2B} \sum_{b=1}^{2B} H(y_b, p(y|x_b)) \tag{1}$$

where B represents the size of batch size, x_b represents the labeled data, x and x^g, $p(y|x_b) = softmax(f(E(x_b)))$ is classification prediction. H is the cross-entropy between y_b and $p(y|x_b)$.

(5) For the prediction of rotation angle, we randomly rotate the original image to generate forest images from different angles, so that the model can learn the rotated image separately. By comparing with the original image, the rotation angle of the image can be derived successfully, which improves the robustness and identification ability of the model.

We use the cross-entropy to calculate the loss of our encoder-predictor, and the formula is as follows:

$$L_r = \frac{1}{B} \sum_{b=1}^{B} H(y_b^r, p(y^r|x_b^r)) \tag{2}$$

where x_b^r represents the rotation data in x^r, $p(y^r|x_b^r) = softmax(f(E(x_b^r)))$ is the output of the predictor.

In short, the final loss function is as follows:

$$Loss = L_r + L_c \tag{3}$$

L_r is the rotation loss, and L_c is the supervision loss.

The details of our model are shown in Algorithm 1.

Algorithm 1 Forest loss classification

Input: Labeled data, $x = \{(x_i, y_i)\}_{i=1}^N$; fuzzy data, $x^g = \{(x_i^g)\}_{i=1}^N$; Batch size, b; Epoch number, e

1.   while $e < epoch$ do
2.   for i=1 to b do
3. $x_i^r = rotate(x_i)$
4. $y_b = f_c(E(x))$
5. $y_b^g = f_c(E(x^g))$
6. $y_b^r = f_r(E(x^r))$
7.   The loss is calculated by the Formula (1), (2), (3)
8.   End for
9.   End while

---

4 Experiment

4.1 The Dataset

In this work, we use the same dataset as Irvin et al. [14], where annotations on deforestation events are curated by Austin et al. [23]. These images of natural forest loss are from the global forest change (GFC) map with 30 million resolution published from 2001 to 2016. The GFC map contains satellite forest images with various types and resolutions. The missing images were classified and annotated by Austin et al. [23]. The main reasons and classifications of deforestation are shown in Table 2. Figure 6 provides some examples of each class. Table 3 shows the details of each group. We use the relationship between deforestation factors and classification factors and the partition method of training/validation/test set given by Irvin et al. [14].

Table 2. The reasons and classifications of deforestation details of the dataset.

Deforestation Category	Classification
Oil palm plantation Timber plantation Other large-scale plantations	Plantation
Grassland/shrubland	Grassland/shrubland
Small-scale agriculture Small-scale mixed plantation Small-scale oil palm plantation	Smallholder agriculture
Mining Fishpond Logging road Secondary forest Other	Other

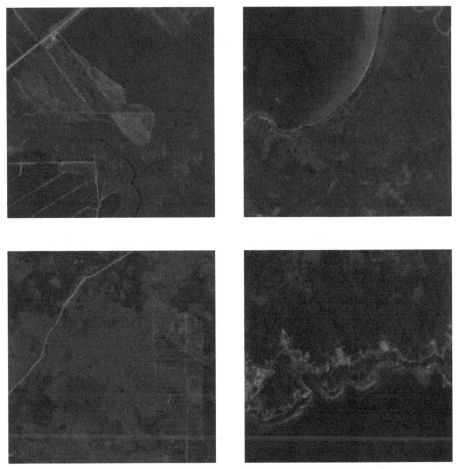

Fig. 6. Data instances from left to right and top to bottom are Plantation, Smallholder agriculture, Grassland/shrubland, etc.

Table 3. The details of dataset according to [11].

Classification	Training	Validation	Test
Plantation	686	219	265
Grassland/shrubland	556	138	207
Smallholder agriculture	143	47	85
Other	231	70	112
Overall	1616	474	669

4.2 Experimental Settings

In this experiment, we perform the experiments on a Server with NVIDIA GeForce RTX 3090, and the framework is PyTorch. The learning rate of the model was set to 0.001, and the Adam algorithm was used to optimize the neural network. The model was trained by 300 epochs, and the batch size was set to 16.

4.3 Results and Analysis

We test the performance of our proposed model on a dataset of Indonesian deforestation factors [14] and compare it with a supervised approach that only applies the Resnet18 as an encoder. According to the results in Table 4, we can see that the performances of our model on the training set, validation set, and test set are better than that of the comparative method. Specially, on the test set, our model achieves an accuracy of 66.42%, which is 7% higher than the comparative method's 59.03%. The experimental results directly verify that our model can accurately classify deforestation data images. In addition, through experimental tests, the experimental resources occupied by the self-supervised module and the supervised learning module are almost the same, which proves the availability of our model.

Table 4. Experimental results of our model and the baseline

Model	Train	Validation	Test
Resnet18-Supervised	99.56	67.64	59.03
Resnet18-Our	99.75	72.8	66.42

5 Conclusion

We propose a new deep learning model for deforestation factor classification in 6G satellite forest images. The model's performance can not be disturbed even in the face of clouds or extreme weather. In addition, the classification prediction of the model can be stable even by applying the data rotation and self-supervised method. Compared with traditional deep learning methods, the classification accuracy of our model is improved by 7%. The results show that our approach has a more substantial effect than other methods. In the future, with the continuous development of the 6G technology, how to better connect the 6G satellite network with the model and improve the operation efficiency will be our next project.

Acknowledgments. This work was supported by Heilongjiang Province Natural Science Foundation under Grant LH2022F034.

References

1. Fu, S., Gao, J., Zhao, L.: Integrated resource management for terrestrial-satellite systems. IEEE Trans. Veh. Technol. **69**(3), 3256–3266 (2020)
2. Foley, J.A., et al.: Global consequences of land use. Science **309**(5734), 570–574 (2005)
3. Arneth, A., et al.: "Ipcc special report on climate change". Desertification, Land Degradation, Sustainable Land Management, Food Security, and Greenhouse Gas Fluxes in Terrestrial Ecosystems (2019)
4. Lenton, T.M., et al.: Climate tipping points — too risky to bet against. Nature **575**(7784), 592–595 (2019). https://doi.org/10.1038/d41586-019-03595-0
5. Hosonuma, N., et al.: An assessment of deforestation and forest degradation drivers in developing countries. Environ. Res. Lett. **7**(4), 044009 (2012)
6. Phiri, D., Morgenroth, J., Cong, X.: Long-Term land cover change in Zambia: an assessment of driving factors. Sci. Total Environ. **697**, 134206 (2019)
7. Descals, A., Szantoi, Z., Meijaard, E., Sutikno, H., Rindanata, G., Wich, S.: Oil palm (Elaeis Guineensis) mapping with details: smallholder versus industrial plantations and their extent in Riau, Sumatra. Remote Sens. **11**(21), 2590 (2019)
8. Poortinga, A., et al.: Mapping plantations in Myanmar by fusing landsat-8, sentinel-2 and sentinel-1 data along with systematic error quantification. Remote Sens. **11**(7), 831 (2019)
9. Hethcoat, M.G., Edwards, D.P., Carreiras, J.M.B., Bryant, R.G., França, F.M., Quegan, S.: A machine learning approach to map tropical selective logging. Remote Sens. Environ. **221**, 569–582 (2019)
10. Sohn, K., Berthelot, D., Carlini, N., et al.: Fixmatch: simplifying semi-supervised learning with consistency and confidence. Adv. Neural. Inf. Process. Syst. **33**, 596–608 (2020)
11. Berthelot, D., Carlini, N., Cubuk, E.D., et al.: ReMixMatch: semi-supervised learning with distribution alignment and augmentation anchoring. arXiv preprint arXiv:1911.09785 (2019)
12. Hu, Z., Yang, Z., Hu, X., Nevatia, R.: SimPLE: similar pseudo label exploitation for semisupervised classification. In: Proceedings of the IEEE/CVF Conference on Computer Vision and Pattern Recognition, pp. 15099–15108. IEEE, Nashville (2021)
13. Mitton, J., Murray-Smith, R.: Rotation Equivariant deforestation segmentation and driver classification. arXiv preprint arXiv:2110.13097 (2021)
14. Irvin, J., Sheng, H., Ramachandran, N., Johnson-Yu, S., Zhou, S., Story, K., et al.: ForestNet: classifying drivers of deforestation in Indonesia using deep learning on satellite imagery. arXiv preprint arXiv:2011.05479 (2020)
15. Botta, A., Pescape, A.: On the performance of new generation satellite broadband Internet services. IEEE Commun. Mag. **52**(6), 202–209 (2014)
16. Chini, P., Giambene, G., Kota, S.: A survey on mobile satellite systems. Int. J. Sat. Commun. **28**(1), 29–57 (2010)
17. Bengio, Y., Simard, P., Frasconi, P.: Learning long-term dependencies with gradient descent is difficult. IEEE Trans. Neural Networks **5**(2), 157–166 (1994)
18. Glorot, X., Bengio, Y.: Understanding the difficulty of training deep feedforward neural networks. In: AISTATS (2010)
19. LeCun, Y., Bottou, L., Orr, G.B., Müller, K.-R.: Efficient backprop. In: Orr, G.B., Müller, K.-R. (eds.) Neural Networks: Tricks of the Trade. Lecture Notes in Computer Science, vol. 1524, pp. 9–50. Springer, Heidelberg (1998). https://doi.org/10.1007/3-540-49430-8_2
20. He, K., Zhang, X., Ren, S., Sun, J.: Delving deep into rectifiers: surpassing human-level performance on ImageNet classification. In: ICCV (2015)
21. LeCun, Y., et al.: Backpropagation applied to handwritten zip code recognition. Neural Comput. **1**(4), 541–551 (1989)

22. He, K., Zhang, X., Ren, S., Sun, J.: Deep residual learning for image recognition. In: Proceedings of the IEEE Conference on Computer Vision and Pattern Recognition, pp. 770–778. IEEE, Las Vegas (2016)
23. Austin, K.G., Schwantes, A., Yaofeng, G., Kasibhatla, P.S.: What causes deforestation in Indonesia? Environ. Res. Lett. **14**(2), 024007 (2019)

6G Network Traffic Intrusion Detection Using Multiresolution Auto-encoder and Feature Matching Discriminator

Yuhai Li[1(✉)], Yuxin Sun[1(✉)], Dong He[2], and Liang Xi[2]

[1] Science and Technology on Electro-Optical Information Security Control Laboratory,
Tianjin 300300, China
liyuhai.cn@qq.com, sunyuxin@tju.edu.cn
[2] School of Computer Science and Technology, Harbin University of Science and Technology,
Harbin 150080, China

Abstract. With the development of 6G technology, security and privacy have become extremely important in the face of larger network traffic bandwidth. An effective intrusion detection system can deal with the network attacks. Deep learning has been developed in the field of intrusion detection, which can identify normal and abnormal traffic. However, existing methods cannot guarantee good performance in accuracy and efficiency. In this paper, based on the autoencoder and generative adversarial network, the multiresolution autoencoder is adopted in the network traffic feature extraction, which can obtain different encoding lengths and guarantee better data reconstruction. In addition, we add an extra feature matching loss to encourage the discriminator to get more discriminative information from the reconstructed samples. Our experimental results on the CIC-IDS2018 dataset indicates that compared with autoencoder and generative adversarial network, our model can effectively improve the detection accuracy and can be applied to 6G network traffic security detection.

Keywords: 6G · intrusion detection · autoencoder · generative adversarial network

1 Introduction

6G will bring network software and cloudification into network intelligence, revolutionizing wireless networks from connected things to "connected intelligence" [1, 2]. Hence, artificial intelligence (AI) technology plays an irreplaceable role in the whole network, especially for network security. With the rapid improvement of data transmission rate and coverage, people are seriously worried that the security and privacy of 6G may be worse than those of previous generations. For example, if the safety of the communication devices is not guaranteed, the probability of personal information leakage will be increased. Network attacks may cause irreparable losses and bring severe threats to private property, personal reputation, and even life. In addition, many criminals may use the excellent AI technologies for network attacks and network monitoring [3]. Therefore, how to ensure its security and privacy will be the key to 6G.

© ICST Institute for Computer Sciences, Social Informatics and Telecommunications Engineering 2023
Published by Springer Nature Switzerland AG 2023. All Rights Reserved
A. Li et al. (Eds.): 6GN 2022, LNICST 504, pp. 208–218, 2023.
https://doi.org/10.1007/978-3-031-36011-4_18

Artificial intelligence technology can detect and identify network intrusions. AI algorithms can be used to learn and extract network intrusion features based on the traffic behavioral characteristics, and identify attacks such as distributed denial of service (DDoS) [4]. An Intrusion Detection System (IDS) system is a network security device that contains multiple methods and mechanisms for identifying network intrusions. Traditional machine learning methods [5] have been proven to be effective in identifying important features and patterns in network traffic and identify network attacks skillfully. These methods can be used in IDS. However, machine learning methods fail to deal with huge datasets, and it has been demonstrated that the performance of machine learning does not perform well in detecting intrusions and network attacks when network nodes are extremely dispersed [6]. In recent years, deep learning has been one of the most popular data mining techniques. Many deep learning methods continue to emerge for intrusion detection. They can automatically extract data features to identify traffic types, and handle intrusions and network attacks well [7]. Compared with traditional machine learning methods, deep learning methods can further improve the accuracy of intrusion detection, making the IDS applications more flexible and efficient.

The autoencoder is shown in Fig. 1. Autoencoder mainly compresses the input data, x, into the latent representation space and reconstruct it. Its purpose is to ensure the data consistency between the output, $\hat{x}$, and the input, x. There are many autoencoder-based anomaly detection methods. For example, Sakurada M et al. [8] use an autoencoder with nonlinear dimension reduction in the anomaly detection task.

In addition, as shown in Fig. 2, GAN (Generative Adversarial Network) was proposed by Goodfellow I et al. [9]. GAN mainly trains both a generator, G, and a discriminator, D. The purpose of G is to learn the data distribution, while D is to distinguish between real data and fake data generated by G. G and D can reach Nash equilibrium through continuous iterations. The network can be combined with an autoencoder and applied to traffic attack detection to increase identification accuracy. Therefore, we proposes unsupervised intrusion detection using the autoencoder and GAN by improving the diversity of data and the output structure of the discriminator.

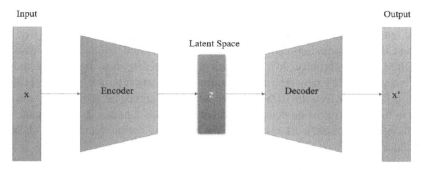

Fig. 1. The autoencoder framework

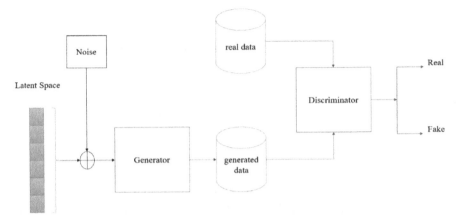

Fig. 2. The generative adversarial network framework

2 Related Work

2.1 Security and Privacy in 6G Networks

5G networks have already coped with many business application scenarios, which can facilitate the connection of more devices and provide services for various devices at the same time. The supported devices include smartphones, IoT devices, etc. However, the network security problems remain the biggest obstacles and will continue to exist in 6G.

Existing researches on 6G security and privacy include 6G wireless network [10], IoT [11] (such as wireless sensor network [12], Vehicle Networks [13, 14]), cellular networks [15], etc. With the development of machine learning and deep learning technologies, many related methods have been able to achieve adequate protection and monitoring [16].

2.2 6G IoT Intrusion Detection

A large amount of IoT traffics are transmitted and communicated between IoT devices [17], and these information-carrying devices and communications are vulnerable to cyberattacks to compromise IoT communications. Therefore, to protect the security and privacy in 6G IoT network, network intrusion detection is indispensable [18]. An Intrusion Detection System (IDS) is a technology designed to monitor the network events in time. The intrusion detection system constructs a normal behavior pattern. If the behavior of some network event does not match the normal pattern, it is classified as an attack.

Machine Learning Methods. Machine learning (ML) techniques are effective at extracting important information from network traffic to identify cyberattacks. To prevent the exposures of information and control flow, Yang et al. [19] proposed an effective KNN classification algorithm, which supports large-scale data classification on distributed servers. Ravi et al. [20] proposed a machine learning method to detect network attacks by combining the k-means algorithm with the repeated random sampling technique of data clustering. In addition, Ravi et al. [21] proposed a new mechanism called learning-driven detection mitigation, which can detect and mitigate DDoS [22, 23]. However, when the amount of data increases, ML cannot process large amounts of data. ML also faces the shortcomings, such as inaccurate identification of attack types.

Deep Learning Methods. In recent years, deep learning (DL) technology has been continuously applied to intrusion detection systems. Facing the complexity and diversity of network traffic, DL can work well on intrusion detection tasks, identify various types of network attacks promptly. Gao et al. [24] improve IDS performance by combining feed-forward neural networks and LSTM. Gamage et al. [25] conduct experimental research on intrusion detection using deep learning methods, such as autoencoder, deep belief network, and feed-forward neural network. In addition, Wu et al. [26] conduct unsupervised anomaly detection with training data only containing normal data. They propose a fault-attention generative probability adversarial autoencoder, which can find low-dimensional manifolds in high-dimensional space. Due to the advantages of the autoencoder, the information loss in the feature extraction process is reduced. Afterward, the abnormal data can be identified by the reconstruction errors and probability distribution of low-dimensional features.

In the above-mentioned network traffic intrusion detection methods using deep learning, however, for supervised scenarios, because a large number of labels need to be manually labeled, a lot of time and resource consumption are required, and the real operation is difficult. Although semi-supervised methods use some labeled data, there is still a large amount of unlabeled traffic data, which are still not possible to fully utilize these data for detection of network attacks. Therefore, to be more in line with the real 6G IoT network scenarios, the unsupervised methods for intrusion detection is worthiest attention. Because they do not require any traffic labels, the cost is greatly reduced compared to supervised and semi-supervised methods. Meanwhile, the inherent features in IoT traffic samples can be used to distinguish different network traffic types.

In this article, we present an unsupervised deep learning method based on reconstruction, which can reduce the cost of manual labeling and more closely to the real network traffic scenarios. Given the incompleteness of the compressed data of the original autoencoder and the inaccurate identification of the discriminator in the GAN, a multiresolution encoder and a discriminator with feature match loss are proposed, respectively. The multiresolution encoder can obtain multiple latent representations with different scales. Combining all the latent representations as a whole can get better reconstructed data. In addition, feature match loss can constrain the discriminator in the GAN to discriminate between real and fake data. At the same time, we combine the improved autoencoder with the GAN, and replace the entire autoencoder with the generator in the GAN network. The output is used as the fake reconstruction data. In the next stage, the discriminator makes inferences between fake data and real input data to determine whether it is real data or reconstructed fake data by the autoencoder. Through such repeated training, the generator and discriminator will eventually reach some balance. Finally, we can perform the 6G network traffic detection tasks.

3   Methodology

In this section, we describe the component details of our intrusion detection framework, which contains multiresolution autoencoder and feature matching discriminator. First, we introduce the multiresolution encoder to be the generator to perform the feature extraction and fusion; Next, we add a discriminator after the generator for adversarial training. The discriminator helps identify anomalies by comparing the features of the input network traffic data and the reconstructed data; Finally, we design the loss function and the evaluation method of anomaly score. The framework of our model is shown in Fig. 3.

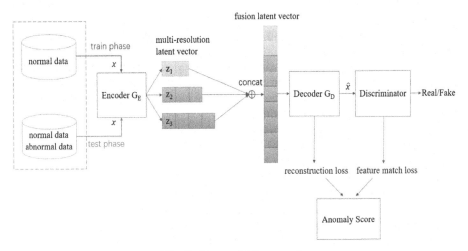

Fig. 3. The model framework.

3.1   Network Framework

Multiresolution Encoder. Our multiresolution autoencoder and discriminator network adopts an encoder, G_E, with three different scales channel and a decoder, G_D. The encoder network converts an input, x, into three latent representation vectors z_i, $i = 1, 2, 3$. After that, we concatenate these three representation vectors along the channel direction to obtain a fusion vector, z. Being asymmetric to G_E, the decoder G_D reconstructs the latent representation vector, z, back to a vector with the same size as the input, denoted as $\hat{x}$.

$$z_i = G_E(x), i = 1, 2, 3 \tag{1}$$

$$z = z_1 \oplus z_2 \oplus z_3 \tag{2}$$

$$\hat{x} = G_D(z) \tag{3}$$

where $\oplus$ is the concatenation operation.

Adversarial Training. In the face of the complexity of high-dimensional data, only the reconstruction loss calculated by the Euclidean distance is used as the anomaly score is easily affected by the training data, resulting in overfitting and cumulative error. Therefore, in order to better training and learning data features [27], we connect a discriminator after the autoencoder. Specifically, the multiresolution encoder and decoder network are treated as a generator, G, and a discriminator, D is appended after the decoder. As shown in Fig. 3, the discriminator, D, predicts whether the label is true or fake for a given input data.

During the training phase, D tries to distinguish real data, x, from the fake one, $\hat{x}$, generated by G. On the other hand, the objective of G is to fool the discriminator by minimizing the distance between the normal traffic data and the reconstructed data.

During the testing phase, D is utilized as a feature extractor to obtain features of the input, x, and the reconstructed $\hat{x}$. In addition to using the reconstruction error as the anomaly score, the feature match error is added to the abnormal score to enlarge the gap between the normal traffic data and abnormal intrusion traffic data, which can make the model more robust when it obtains poor reconstruction.

3.2 Loss Function

Reconstruction Loss. The goal of reconstruction loss is to make the reconstructed traffic data by generator similar to the real traffic data. Further, we compute the distance between the input, x, and the reconstructed output, $\hat{x}$, which ensures the generator learns enough latent feature representations from normal traffic data. The reconstruction loss is shown as follows:

$$\mathcal{L}_{rec} = \mathbb{E}\|x - \hat{x}\|_2 \tag{4}$$

Adversarial Loss. As shown in Eq. (5), we utilize the traditional adversarial loss function proposed in [9] to train the generator and discriminator. The generator tries to generate the real reconstructed data, $\hat{x}$, as much as possible, and the discriminator strives to distinguish the real input data and the fake reconstruction data. The adversarial loss, L_{adv}, is shown as follows,

$$\mathcal{L}_{adv} = \mathbb{E}_{x \sim p(data)}\left[log D(x)\right] + \mathbb{E}_{\hat{x} \sim g(data)}\left[log(1 - D(G(\hat{x})))\right] \tag{5}$$

Feature Match Loss. The purpose of feature match loss is to force the distribution of feature representations to be consistent with the reconstructed $\hat{x}$ and the input x. By feeding x and $\hat{x}$ to the discriminator, D, we can obtain the high-dimensional features at each layer of D. The corresponding features of x and $\hat{x}$ are denoted as $H_D(x)$ and $H_D(\hat{x})$, respectively. Therefore, the feature match loss is defined as follows:

$$\mathcal{L}_{fm} = \mathbb{E}\|H_D(x) - H_D(\hat{x})\|_2 \tag{6}$$

The final loss function can be expressed as follows,

$$\mathcal{L} = \lambda_{rec}\mathcal{L}_{rec} + \lambda_{adv}\mathcal{L}_{adv} + \lambda_{fm}\mathcal{L}_{fm} \tag{7}$$

3.3 Intrusion Detection

During the testing phase, anomaly traffic data are detected by fusing the reconstruction error and the feature match error. For the input traffic data, x, we define the anomaly score as follows:

$$S = \eta R(x) + (1 - \eta)M(x) \tag{8}$$

$R(x)$ is the reconstruction score calculated by the distance between the input data and the reconstructed data based on Eq. (4). $M(x)$ is the feature match score calculated by the distance between the feature representations of the input and the reconstructed data based on Eq. (6). η is a hyperparameter used to adjust the ratio of $R(x)$ and $M(x)$. In addition, we normalized $R(x)$ and $M(x)$ before calculating the whole anomaly score to perform the network traffic detection tasks.

Algorithm 1 shows the process in detail.

Algorithm 1 Network Traffic Detection

Input: traffic data, $x = \{(x_i, y_i)\}_{i=1}^{N}$; Iterations, L; threshold, τ; Initialize l=0, S = 0

1. while l<L do
2. Sample $\{(x_1, y_1), ..., (x_m, y_m)\}$ from normal and abnormal data
3. Generate $\{(\hat{x}_1, y_1), ..., (\hat{x}_m, y_m)\}$ by multiresolution Encoder, G_E, and Decoder, G_D
4. The reconstruction loss is calculated using Equation (4)
5. Distinguish the input data and reconstruct data by the discriminator, D
6. The adversarial loss and feature match loss are calculated using Equations (5) and (6)
7. Calculate the anomaly score, S, using Equation (8) by reconstruction loss and feature match loss
8. Classify each traffic data as an anomaly data if S >τ, otherwise normal data
9. End

---

4   Experiment

4.1 Dataset Description

We select the CIC-IDS2018 [28] dataset to evaluate the performance of the network traffic detection. CIC-IDS2018 is a well-known real-world heterogeneous intrusion detection dataset containing various attack types, missing values, and irrelevant features. It includes millions of IoT traffic samples collected from the network traffic for 10 days. The dataset contains 79-dimensional data features and one-dimensional label features. The data labeled Benign represent normal data, and the rest ones represent abnormal data. Details of the dataset and corresponding data distributions used in our experiments are shown in Table 1.

Table 1. Details of CIC-IDS2018 Datasets and Data Distributions

Dataset	Number of data	Number of attack types	Normal type	Data attributes	Attack ratio
CIC-IDS2018 [28]	16233002	DDOS, attack-HOIC, DDoS attacks-LOIC-HTTP, DoS attacks-Hulk, Bot, FTP-BruteForce, SSH-Bruteforce, Infilteration, DoS attacks-SlowHTTPTest, DoS attacks-GoldenEye, DoS attacks-Slowloris, DDOS attack-LOIC-UDP, Brute Force-Web, Brute Force-XSS, SQL Injection	Benign	79	17%

4.2 Performance Metrics

We use five metrics to evaluate the model, including AUC, Accuracy, Precision, Recall, and F1-score. AUC is the area under the receiver operating characteristic curve. The other metrics are described and presented as follows.

Accuracy indicates the ratio of correctly predicting traffic samples in the overall sample. The formula is shown as follows,

$$Accuracy = \frac{TP + TN}{TP + TN + FP + FN} \tag{9}$$

Precision indicates the ratio of correctly predicting normal traffic samples in the overall sample. The formula is shown as follows,

$$Precision = \frac{TP}{TP + FP} \tag{10}$$

Recall indicates the ratio of correctly predicting normal traffic samples among all normal samples. The formula is shown as follows,

$$Recall = \frac{TP}{TP + FN} \tag{11}$$

F1 is calculated by considering both precision and recall, and is the weighted average of both. We use the threshold that maximizes the F1-score as the optimal threshold to calculate the corresponding indicators. The formula is shown as follows,

$$F1 - score = \frac{2TP}{2TP + FN + FP} \tag{12}$$

where false negative (FN) indicates the number of normal traffic samples that were falsely judged to be abnormal traffic samples. The false positive (FP) represents the number of abnormal traffic samples that were falsely identified as normal traffic samples. The true positive (TP) represents the number of normal traffic samples correctly identified as positive. The true negative (TN) is the number of abnormal traffic samples correctly identified as negative.

4.3 Implementation Detail

We treat the experiment as a one-classification problem, with 14 attack types of samples as anomalies and the samples with Benign label as normal values. Only normal data are used for unsupervised training in the training phase, and normal and abnormal data are used for anomaly detection in the testing phase.

Specifically, we eliminated three useless features (i.e., Dst Port, Protocol, Timestamp). The whole data was normalized by column.The Benign label was set to 0 and the others arer set to 1. We utilize 80% of the Benign data for training data, and the rest 20% and all abnormal data for testing data.

The number of multiresolution encoders is set as 3. We use the Adam optimizer to train generators and discriminators, and the learning rate is set to 0.001. In addition, the weight decay is 5e-7. The model is trained by 200 epochs and the batch size is 512. We conduct our experiments on an NVIDIA RTX 3090ti GPU on Pytorch 1.9.1.

4.4 Result and Discussion

Table 2 shows the detection results on the CICIDS-2018 dataset. We can conclude that the AUC of our model can reach 97.6%, and the Accuracy, Precision, Recall, and F1 can be achieved 97.1%, 94%, 99.7%, and 96.8%, respectively. Compared with auto-encoder and GAN, our model extracts data features from multiple resolutions and obtains more comprehensive feature information, which is beneficial to reconstruct information closer to the real data in the decoding stage. Additionally, our feature match loss distinguishes between normal and abnormal data more clearly than merely using the reconstruction error, to further improve the model performance.

Table 2. Intrusion detection in terms of several metrics on CICIDS-2018 Dataset

Method/Metric	AUC	Accuracy	Precision	Recall	F1-score
AE	0.756	0.734	0.625	0.951	0.754
GAN	0.906	0.924	0.845	0.995	0.919
Our model	**0.976**	**0.971**	**0.94**	**0.997**	**0.968**

5 Conclusion

This paper proposes an unsupervised deep learning model to detect network attacks from network traffic. We extract features using a multiresolution encoder from traffic data, and then the decoder reconstructs the fused features. Furthermore, we compute anomaly scores based on three errors. The experimental results highlight that our model outperforms the original auto-encoder and generative adversarial network by more than 20% and 7% on AUC, respectively. This can be applied to future 6G network traffic intrusion detection systems. In the future, we will improve the components of the model to accommodate more complex data characteristics, and practice the model on more 6G application scenarios and improve its usability and robustness.

Acknowledgment. This work was supported by Heilongjiang Province Natural Science Foundation under Grant LH2022F034.

References

1. Saad, W., Bennis, M., Chen, M.: A vision of 6G wireless systems: applications, trends, technologies, and open research problems. IEEE Network **34**(3), 134–142 (2019)
2. De Alwis, C., Kalla, A., Pham, Q.V., et al.: Survey on 6G frontiers: trends, applications, requirements, technologies and future research. IEEE Open J. Commun. Soc. **2**, 836–886 (2021)
3. Sun, Y., Liu, J., Wang, J., et al.: When machine learning meets privacy in 6G: a survey. IEEE Commun. Surv. Tutorials **22**(4), 2694–2724 (2020)
4. Mitrokotsa, A., Komninos, N., Douligeris, C.: Intrusion detection with neural networks and watermarking techniques for MANET. In: IEEE International Conference on Pervasive Services. IEEE, pp. 118–127 (2007)
5. Shafiq, M., Tian, Z., Bashir, A.K., et al.: CorrAUC: a malicious bot-IoT traffic detection method in IoT network using machine-learning techniques. IEEE Internet Things J. **8**(5), 3242–3254 (2020)
6. Li, L., Yan, J., Wang, H., et al.: Anomaly detection of time series with smoothness-inducing sequential variational auto-encoder. IEEE Trans. Neural Networks Learn. Syst. **32**(3), 1177–1191 (2020)
7. Wang, X., Han, Y., Leung, V.C.M., et al.: Convergence of edge computing and deep learning: a comprehensive survey. IEEE Commun. Surveys Tutorials **22**(2), 869–904 (2020)
8. Sakurada, M., Yairi, T.: Anomaly detection using autoencoders with nonlinear dimensionality reduction. In: Proceedings of the MLSDA 2014 2nd Workshop on Machine Learning for Sensory Data Analysis, pp. 4–11 (2014)

9. Goodfellow, I., Pouget-Abadie, J., Mirza, M., et al.: Generative adversarial nets. Advances in Neural Information Processing Systems 27, Curran Associates, Inc. (2014)

10. Alsharif, M.H., Kelechi, A.H., Albreem, M.A., et al.: Sixth generation (6G) wireless networks: vision, research activities, challenges and potential solutions. Symmetry 12(4), 676 (2020)

11. Ferrag, M.A., Maglaras, L., Derhab, A.: Authentication and authorization for mobile IoT devices using biofeatures: recent advances and future trends. Secur. Commun. Networks 2019, 1–20 (2019)

12. Majid, M., et al.: Applications of wireless sensor networks and internet of things frameworks in the industry revolution 4.0: a systematic literature review. Sensors 22(6), 2087 (2022)

13. Tang, F., Kawamoto, Y., Kato, N., et al.: Future intelligent and secure vehicular network toward 6G: machine-learning approaches. Proc. IEEE 108(2), 292–307 (2019)

14. Zhang, Z., Cao, Y., Cui, Z., et al.: A many-objective optimization based intelligent intrusion detection algorithm for enhancing security of vehicular networks in 6G. IEEE Trans. Veh. Technol. 70(6), 5234–5243 (2021)

15. Ahmad, I., Shahabuddin, S., Kumar, T., et al.: Security for 5G and beyond. IEEE Commun. Surveys Tutorials 21(4), 3682–3722 (2019)

16. S.A., et al.: 6G white paper on machine learning in wireless communication networks. https://arxiv.org/pdf/2004.13875.pdf. Accessed 10 Aug 2021

17. Anthi, E., Williams, L., Słowińska, M., et al.: A supervised intrusion detection system for smart home IoT devices. IEEE Internet Things J. 6(5), 9042–9053 (2019)

18. Pu, C.: Sybil attack in RPL-based internet of things: analysis and defenses. IEEE Internet Things J. 7(6), 4937–4949 (2020)

19. Yang, H., Liang, S., Ni, J., et al.: Secure and efficient k NN classification for industrial Internet of Things. IEEE Internet Things J. 7(11), 10945–10954 (2020)

20. Ravi, N., Shalinie, S.M.: Semisupervised-learning-based security to detect and mitigate intrusions in IoT network. IEEE Internet Things J. 7(11), 11041–11052 (2020)

21. Ravi, N., Shalinie, S.M.: Learning-driven detection and mitigation of DDoS attack in IoT via SDN-cloud architecture. IEEE Internet Things J. 7(4), 3559–3570 (2020)

22. Wang, J., Jiang, C., Zhang, H., et al.: Thirty years of machine learning: the road to Pareto-optimal wireless networks. IEEE Commun. Surveys Tutorials 22(3), 1472–1514 (2020)

23. Hussain, F., Hussain, R., Hassan, S.A., et al.: Machine learning in IoT security: current solutions and future challenges. IEEE Commun. Surveys Tutorials 22(3), 1686–1721 (2020)

24. Gao, J., Gan, L., Buschendorf, F., et al.: Omni SCADA intrusion detection using deep learning algorithms. IEEE Internet Things J. 8(2), 951–961 (2020)

25. Gamage, S., Samarabandu, J.: Deep learning methods in network intrusion detection: a survey and an objective comparison. J. Netw. Comput. Appl. 169, 102767 (2020)

26. Wu, J., Zhao, Z., Sun, C., et al.: Fault-attention generative probabilistic adversarial autoencoder for machine anomaly detection. IEEE Trans. Industr. Inf. 16(12), 7479–7488 (2020)

27. Grill, J.B., Strub, F., Altché, F., et al.: Bootstrap your own latent-a new approach to self-supervised learning. Adv. Neural Inf. Process. Syst. 33, 21271–21284 (2020)

28. CSE-CIC-IDS2018 Dataset, CIC, Fredericton, NB, Canada (2018). https://www.unb.ca/cic/datasets/ids-2018.html. Accessed 4 Oct 2020

A Design of Information Extraction Method on CNC Machine Tools Using C/S Structure

E. Rui$^{(\boxtimes)}$ and Shujie Yang

Heilongjiang Polytechnic, Harbin 150001, Heilongjiang, China
e_rui@163.com

Abstract. This paper studies the information extraction technology and thermal error compensation technology of CNC machine tools, and realizes the extraction, storage and display of the internal data parameters of CNC machine tools and the data information of external sensors. At the same time, the thermal error compensation control module is embedded in the system to form a set of CNC machine tool information. The integrated system of extraction and thermal error compensation makes up for the shortcomings and deficiencies of the traditional method of information extraction of CNC machine tools and thermal error compensation based on external embedded devices. It provides a way of thinking for the development of a large-scale CNC machine tool information extraction and thermal error compensation integrated system, and has important engineering application value.

Keywords: CNC machine tools · information extraction · Socket · multithread

1 Introduction

1.1 Background

Industrial manufacturing is the main body of the development of a country's economic system, a solid foundation for ensuring sustainable economic development and prosperity, and an important part of the country's implementation of the strategic plan for economic development. To this end, in order to seize market opportunities and win strategic high ground, countries around the world have successively put forward strategic plans for industrial manufacturing [1]. In 2013, Germany's "Industry 4.0" national strategic plan was put forward, which identified three major economic development themes for the manufacturing system: smart factory + smart production + smart logistics. Once put forward, it caused a huge sensation in governments, enterprises, scientific and academic circles around the world, and it was widely recognized that "Industry 4.0" represented the fourth industrial revolution in human history. In the same year, General Electric Company (GE) of the United States proposed and clarified the

© ICST Institute for Computer Sciences, Social Informatics and Telecommunications Engineering 2023
Published by Springer Nature Switzerland AG 2023. All Rights Reserved
A. Li et al. (Eds.): 6GN 2022, LNICST 504, pp. 219–229, 2023.
https://doi.org/10.1007/978-3-031-36011-4_19

concept of Industrial Internet. The development of industrialization involves a large number of machines, system networks, and on-site facilities, and the Industrial Internet uses sensors, control systems, and industrial software to connect these three factors together to promote green, energy-saving, and efficient industrial production. By integrating the advantages of informatization and network technology, the manufacturing industry will develop in the direction of digitization and intelligence [2]. In 2015, the Chinese government put forward the "Made in China 2025" national industrial strategic plan for the first time in the government work report in light of its own manufacturing development status. Three major goals are clarified: the transformation of Chinese manufacturing to Chinese creation, the transformation of Chinese speed to Chinese quality, and the transformation of Chinese products to Chinese brands. In addition, ten major fields are selected as breakthrough points, and the manufacturing level will enter the ranks of manufacturing powers by 2025. Among them, intelligent manufacturing technology represented by high-end CNC machine tools and robotics technology is also one of the major projects. The goal of intelligent manufacturing is to focus on key manufacturing links, integrate manufacturing equipment with new-generation information technology, and realize a complete closed-loop system capable of intelligent perception, control, execution, and decision-making. In the intelligent manufacturing process of modern manufacturing enterprises, CNC machine tools are widely used for cutting metal parts, but due to the wide variety of CNC machine tools and various structures, and the inability to automatically output internal information [3].

Therefore, the information extraction of CNC machine tools is the basic link to realize the intelligent manufacturing of modern manufacturing enterprises, and it is also an important prerequisite for building the Industrial Internet of Things and realizing the monitoring of the production process of all elements of products. Through the monitoring and management of CNC machine tool information extraction and interconnection, various abnormal states and potential problems of machine tool equipment can be discovered in time, which is of great significance to the stable, healthy and efficient operation of machine tool equipment. At the same time, the CNC machine tool information extraction technology is integrated with ERP (Enterprise Resource Planning), MES (Manufacturing Execution System, Manufacturing Execution System) systems, which can obtain a large number of real-time machine tools without the influence of human factors and other intermediate links. The operation data of the production process has guiding significance for the upper management of the enterprise to scientifically formulate the production plan and manage the process flow of the parts [4].

1.2 Related Works

In western countries, CNC machine tool information extraction and state monitoring operation and maintenance technology developed earlier, and in the development process, it was relatively mature, platform-based, and modular. A complete solution with remote control functions as one, creating great competitiveness for manufacturing enterprises. For example, the open Siemens.

MCIS (Motion Control Information System, motion control information system) information solution developed by Siemens, which integrates production data based on OPC interface and industrial Ethernet [5].

The MDC-Max machine tool data acquisition and monitoring system developed by CIMCO, a world-renowned DNC solution manufacturer, integrates equipment information extraction, network communication, Internet of Things and other technologies to accurately collect real-time data, understand machine tool performance and predict Potential alarm. The Extreme DNC information extraction software developed by American Ascend Technology Co., Ltd. can realize the functions of communication, information extraction, real-time monitoring and remote control of mainstream CNC machine tools in the market. The Massachusetts Institute of Technology in the United States has developed an integrated equipment for parts network processing and assembly based on the Industrial Internet. A research institution in Australia has developed a remote equipment status information extraction, monitoring and control system. Automatic acquisition and remote control platform [6]. The domestic research on CNC machine tool information extraction and state monitoring DNC platform started relatively late, and the technology is still immature. Dr. Fang Shuiliang from Nanjing University of Aeronautics and Astronautics proposed the concept of flexible DNC system, integrated development of two CNC wire cutting machine tools (WEDM) and one CNC milling machine (XK5040), and connected the machine tools into a hierarchical distributed management control flexible DNC system through Ethernet -FDNC system. Zhang Xumei, Liu Fei and others from Chongqing University put forward the concept of integrated DNC (IDNC) system. Based on communication and network technology, different types of manufacturing equipment are integrated with the central computer, so as to realize the integration of equipment and information in the machining workshop and functional integration [7].

1.3   Motivations and Contributions

The above mentioned numerical control machine tool information extraction and thermal error compensation research have made good progress in their respective aspects, but there are still some defects and deficiencies. It is difficult to integrate CNC machine tool information extraction and thermal error compensation because the thermal error compensation control in the traditional method is to develop the thermal error compensation function through hardware devices such as external embedded compensators based on ARM, DSP and other technologies to realize the output of compensation values and exchange data with the machine tool PLC to realize thermal error compensation control. But the compensator needs to communicate with the IO modules of the machine tool control cabinet (such as: the machine tool operation module of the FANUC system, the PP 72/48 module of the SIEMENS system, etc.), and a series of tedious operations such as hardware wiring, hardware configuration, and address assignment.

Meanwhile, if the thermal error compensation control of a large number of CNC machine tools is carried out, each machine tool needs to expand the IO module of the corresponding CNC system, and the cost is high. In addition, the external embedded compensator requires hardware development. Once the requirements change, the hardware compensator needs to be redeveloped to a large extent. The disadvantage is that the cycle is long and the cost is high. Nowadays, mainstream CNC devices have built-in network interfaces, and provide application development interface functions corresponding to CNC systems. Users can customize development according to their own needs, which provides the possibility for CNC machine tool information extraction and thermal error compensation control integration. Therefore, based on the respective application development interfaces of mainstream CNC systems, this paper proposes to use middleware technology to expand the information integration and thermal error compensation control integration of CNC machine tools. The data and thermal error compensation control are designed and realized by system integration.

To address this, in this paper, a set of information extraction and thermal error compensation control integration system for FANUC CNC machine tools is designed, and an interface is reserved for the information integration of other CNC systems. The integrated system can read the internal operating parameters of the numerical control system in real time, and output the compensation value in real time according to the thermal error prediction model established according to the thermal error measurement data to realize the thermal error compensation of the machine tool. The main contribution can be summerized as follows

- We first briefly expounds the subject source, research background and significance of this paper, introduces the research status of CNC machine tool information extraction technology and thermal error compensation technology, and expounds the research content of this paper.
- Then, we study the information extraction method of CNC machine tool. The hardware structure and function of each part of the numerical control machine tool are summarized. On this basis, the internal data signal and external data signal information transmission mechanism between CNC, PLC and the machine tool body in the working process of the numerical control system are analyzed, and the control process is realized. Four methods of information extraction of CNC machine tools are introduced, namely, information extraction methods based on PLC and electrical circuit, RS232 serial port combined with macro commands, FOCAS protocol and OPC UA protocol, and their advantages and disadvantages are described respectively.
- On the basis of the machine tool information extraction technology and the thermal error compensation technology in the network communication architecture of the integrated system is designed, and the middleware technology is introduced to expand the information integration of other CNC systems; the implementation of the integrated system is analyzed and discussed. Multi-threading mechanism and C/S communication principle based on Socket are introduced, and the design and implementation process of each functional module of the system is introduced in detail.

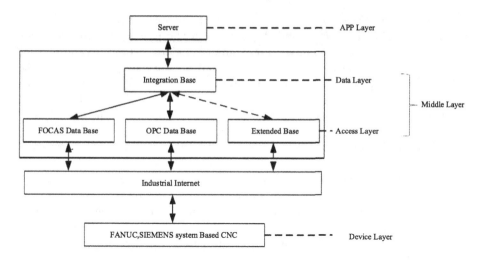

Fig. 1. An illustration of the communication principle of machine tool communication middleware technology

2   System Communication Architecture Design

In this paper, the LAN communication technology is used as the "medium" for information exchange between the host and the machine tool, that is, the industrial Ethernet communication based on the TCP/IP protocol. For the CNC machine tool of FANUC system, the FOCAS protocol class library is used as the interface for system communication and data access; for the CNC machine tool of the SIEMENS system, the OPC UA protocol class library is used as the interface for system communication and data access. However, CNC machine tools of various systems can only use their own communication libraries to communicate with machine tools and access data. In this regard, based on various communication libraries, in order to meet the needs of system expansion, this paper introduces a communication Middleware technology encapsulates the heterogeneous system subclass library, provides a unified data access interface, realizes the functions of heterogeneous system resource sharing, business coordination and allocation, and has the characteristics of flexibility and scalability. Figure 1 shows the communication principle of the machine tool communication middleware technology.

The communication middleware layer is located between the application layer (server program) and the machine tool equipment layer, and realizes the integrated design of the machine tool communication and data access class library, thereby encapsulating the general interface for integrated communication and data access. For better management and decoupling, the communication middleware layer is further divided into the data mezzanine layer (data acquisition adapter) of the communication integration class library and various subclass libraries (inherited from the corresponding parent class library, in order to pass the subclasses) Calling various methods, variables, enumerations, etc. defined in its parent class without changing the content in the parent class) data access layer two-layer logic layer. The data mezzanine provides instantiated objects for accessing various subclass libraries, and can call the data access methods of the objects, and encapsulates the communication connection and data access of various machine tools into a general interface method. Therefore, as long as the interface remains unchanged, changes to the logical content of the communication middleware layer will not affect the changes to the server program, and when new types of machine tools are added, only the data access layer of the communication middleware layer needs to be added. The new subclass library and the call to the subclass library in the communication integration class library, and the server program only needs to call the general interface method of the communication integration class library according to the system type, which reduces the difficulty of server program development and enhances the Extensibility, and realizes the decoupling between the server and machine tool interface access methods; and the data access layer stores various subclass libraries, this logic layer is mainly to access data sources, such as: database data The execution of commands such as add, delete, modify, query, etc., can also read and access some txt, ini and other text files and XML file information. The source of the underlying data in this article is mainly CNC machine tools And access is set in the data access layer, the main function is to encapsulate the communication connection method and data access method for various system machine tools.

3   System Network Architecture Design

The overall network architecture of the system designed in this paper is shown in Fig. 2. The system topology is divided into three layers, which are mainly composed of machine tool equipment layer, protocol layer and information extraction layer. The machine tool equipment layer is composed of CNC machine tools of FANUC system and SIEMENS system, as the carrier of CNC machine tool information extraction and thermal error compensation control. The protocol layer is mainly composed of serial communication protocol (RS232) and industrial Ethernet protocol (including FOCAS and OPC UA). Send commands to the temperature acquisition device (lower computer) regularly through USB to serial port. Once the temperature acquisition device receives the command sent by the host computer program in the interrupt service program, it will send the temperature value of the temperature sensor to the host computer through the serial communication channel. The program triggers the event function of the host computer, analyzes the temperature data in the event function, and brings the temperature value of the temperature-sensitive measuring point into the thermal error prediction model, and then outputs the compensation value. The industrial Ethernet protocol is mainly a channel for the transmission of the internal data information of the machine tool equipment layer and the data of the host computer program, and according to the difference of one-way or two-way transmission of data information, the data transmission through the

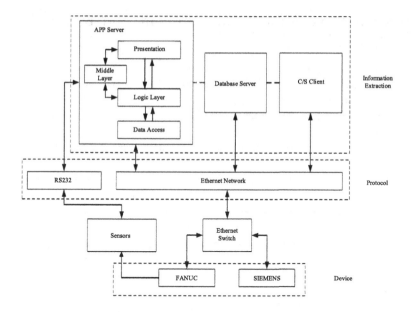

Fig. 2. An illustration of the network architecture of the proposed system.

industrial Ethernet is divided into real-time information extraction and thermal error compensation. Control two ways. The principle of the real-time information extraction control method is: the upper computer program sends the information extraction instruction, and transmits it to the machine tool equipment in real time through the industrial Ethernet. The machine tool also returns the sampled data information to the upper computer program through the industrial Ethernet, and the upper computer program obtains it. Once the data arrives, it can be further processed.

In this way, the data information transmission is bidirectional. The thermal error compensation control method is unidirectional for industrial Ethernet. The host computer program brings the temperature data sent by the external temperature acquisition device into the thermal error prediction model, outputs the compensation value, and transmits it to the numerical control system through the industrial Ethernet to achieve thermal error compensation control. The information extraction layer consists of application server, database server and C/S client. The main functions of the application server are human-computer interaction, outputting data to the database server or C/S client, and further processing the data information returned by industrial Ethernet or serial communication to realize data access, business logic processing and interface display functions; database server It is mainly used to store the real-time data extracted from the information for the client to access it; the main function of the C/S client is to query the database for interface display and the data information that the application server responds to through Socket communication.

4 System Development Environment and Key Technologies

In the designed system network architecture, for the CNC machine tool of the FANUC system, the FOCAS interface protocol is selected as the communication interface of the system; for the CNC machine tool of the SIEMENS system, the OPC UA interface protocol is selected as the communication interface of the system. From the research on the information extraction method of CNC machine tools, it can be seen that the FOCAS interface protocol and the SIEMENS interface protocol are encapsulated into a class library by the CNC system manufacturer, which supports the C.NET advanced application development language. The serial communication protocol is also encapsulated into a class library under the .NET platform, and developers can call it directly when using it. Therefore, this article is based on the above communication protocol and selects the C development language under the .NET platform to develop the host computer program of the CNC machine tool information extraction and thermal error compensation integrated system. Visual Studio 2019 is used as the integrated development environment, and the storage of data information is Sql Server database. In the field of computer communication, Socket is called "socket", which is the cornerstone of communication and the communication protocol between applications. Socket as a communication protocol has been widely used in many fields, such as: network communication, database management and so on. Through the agreement of Socket, a computer can also send data to other computers while receiving data.

The application server and client in this article communicate through Socket. Socket can be regarded as the endpoint of communication between two network applications. During communication, the data information to be transmitted by the client application is written into the Socket of the machine where it is located. Socket transmits the data information to the server application Socket of another machine through the network cable transmission medium, realizes the receiving and processing of the data information, and the server transmits the data to the client in the same way. In addition, when communicating, a Socket of a client application corresponds to a Socket of a server application one-to-one, that is, if there is a client Socket, there is a corresponding server Socket for data interaction with it. Socket is used in combination with IP address, port and transmission protocol. The IP address can be used to uniquely identify the host in the network program, and the transmission protocol and port can uniquely identify the application (process) in the host. There are two types of socket SOCK_STREAM and datagram socket SOCK_DGRAM. Stream socket SOCK_STREAM is based on the TCP (Transmission Control Protocol) of the transport layer, providing connection-oriented, reliable, sequential, byte stream data transmission services, while The datagram socket SOCK_DGRAM is based on the UDP (User Datagram Protocol) of the transport layer and provides connectionless data transmission services. It does not guarantee the reliability of data transmission, which may lead to data loss, duplication and confusion during transmission. The CNC machine tool information extraction and thermal

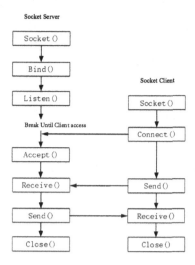

Fig. 3. An illustration of Socket Communication.

error compensation integrated system in this paper needs to meet the real-time, safe and reliable requirements of data information transmission. Combined with the analysis and comparison of the impact of the two transmission services on the data, it is decided to use the Socket communication based on the stream socket SOCK_STREAM protocol. Develop C/S applications. The principle of Socket communication is shown in Fig. 3.

5   Simulation Results

After the hardware experimental platform is built and the necessary preparations are completed, the test and verification of the integrated system can be carried out. The test and verification methods are as follows: Turn on the machine tool, turn on the power of the external acquisition equipment such as the temperature acquisition device and the eddy current sensor preprocessor device, run the server application program of the upper computer integrated system, configure the machine parameters in the program, and connect the machine tool, Start the server program, the Labview host computer program configures the serial port parameters and eddy current sensor channel related parameters, and connects the temperature acquisition device of the lower computer and the NI acquisition card.

Start the Labview host computer program, and measure the temperature acquisition device and displacement of the lower computer. The device sends a start measurement command, and the Labview host computer records the initial displacement data between each eddy current sensor and the standard test bar, and records the temperature data of the heat source sensitive parts of the machine tool at this moment. After the displacement and temperature

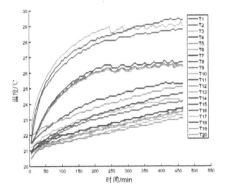

Fig. 4. An illustration of temperature v.s. time.

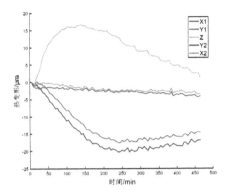

Fig. 5. An illustration of thermal deformation data curve.

data recording is completed, run the thermal error acquisition NC program on the machine tool side: the program controls the eddy current sensor on the machine tool table to slowly move away from the standard test bar clamped on the machine tool spindle from the initial measurement position, and reach a relatively safe After the interference position, control the feed axis and spindle of the machine tool to simulate the cyclic movement of the real processing scene. After continuous movement for about 5 min, stop the rotation of the spindle and make the eddy current sensor on the worktable return to the initial measurement position, and simultaneously record the displacement and temperature at this time data. Repeat the experiment for about 8 h until the temperature field of the machine tool is in a state of thermal equilibrium. At this point, the experiment of measuring the thermal error of the machine tool can be stopped.

It can be seen from Fig. 4 and Fig. 5 that the heat source sensitive parts and thermal deformation of the machine tool basically reach thermal equilibrium at about 450 mins after the start of the experiment, and the maximum thermal error in the X direction is 4.3 μm, the maximum thermal error in the Y direction is 20.3μm, and the maximum thermal error in the Z direction is 20.3 μm is 16.6μm, considering that the thermal error in the X direction of the Vcenter-55 CNC machining center, which is the object of this study, is small, and the thermal error in the Y and Z axes is large, so the thermal error compensation is performed on the Y and Z axes at the same time. The measured temperature data and thermal deformation data are used for the establishment of the thermal error prediction model. In the thermal error compensation experiment, the compensation value calculated in real time according to the prediction model is written into the numerical control system through the API interface protocol to realize reverse interpolation control.

6 Conclusion

Starting from the role of CNC machine tools in the digitalization process of modern manufacturing workshops and the practical significance of improving the accuracy and performance of machine tools, this paper designs an integrated system for information extraction and thermal error compensation for CNC machine tools with FANUC system. By integrating the two parts of the external sensor acquisition device and the internal information API function interface of the machine tool, and based on the .NET multi-threading mechanism, Socket communication and serial communication technologies, at the same time, considering the software design of "high cohesion and low coupling" Principles and the need to expand the information integration of other CNC systems, on this basis, a three-layer architecture model of "presentation layer, business logic layer, data access layer" combined with the system network architecture of "middleware layer" was proposed, and the system functions were designed and developed. Finally, based on the existing Taichung Seiki Vcenter-55 vertical CNC machining center in our laboratory, the integrated system is tested and verified. The experimental results show that the CNC machine tool information extraction and thermal error compensation integrated system developed in this paper is effective and efficient.

References

1. CIMCO. CIMCO MDC-Max 6 documentation[EB/OL]. http://www.cimco.com
2. Liang, Y., Su, H., Lu L., et al.: Thermal optimization of an ultra-precision machine tool by the thermal displacement decomposition and counteraction method. Int. J. Adv. Manuf. Technol. **76**(1–4), 635–645 (2015)
3. Seung, H.Y., Ki, H.K.: Measurement of spindle thermal errors in Machine tool using hemispherical ball bar test. Int. J. Mach. Tools Manuf. (44), 333–340 (2004)
4. Jin, C., Wu, B., Hu, Y.: Wavelet neural network based on NARMA-L2 model for prediction of thermal characteristics in a feed system. Chinese J. Mech. Eng. **24**(1), 33–41 (2011)
5. Miao, E.M., Niu, P.C., Fei, Y.T., et al.: Selecting temperature-sensitive points and modeling thermal errors of machine tools. J. Chinese Soc. Mech. Eng. **32**(6), 559–565 (2011)
6. Abdulshahed, A.M., Longstaff, A.P., Fletcher, S., et al.: Thermal error modelling of machine tools based on ANFIS with fuzzy c-means clustering using a thermal imaging camera. Appl. Math. Model. **39**(7), 1837–1852 (2015)
7. Mayr, J., Jedrzejewski, J., Uhlmann, E., et al.: Thermal issues in machine tools. CIRP Annals Manuf. Technol. **61**(2), 771–791 (2012)

Hierarchical System Architecture Design of UAV Cluster Based on Mission Requirements

Zhiqiang Xu, Tong Liu$^{(\boxtimes)}$, Hao Lv, and Yongzhi Shan

Norinco Group Air Ammunition Research Institute, Harbin, China
liutongsasa@hotmail.com

Abstract. Through the complexity analysis of UAV cluster, based on three modes of task, cluster management and control behavior, and information interaction behavior, the complex system element set, interaction relation set, complex criteria set, and complex feature set are summarized into the backbone architecture level of collaborative task subsystem, cluster management and control subsystem, and networking communication subsystem. And completed a variety of models, multiple levels and multiple types of sub member architecture level, comprehensive build a can not only the overall task oriented, and geared to the neseds of local task, to based on the global situation and based on the local situation, both can rapid response and can avoid conflict collaborative decision-making and execution of complex unmanned aerial vehicle (uav) cluster system architecture.

Keywords: UAV · Cluster of Drones · Layered Network

1 Introduction

Through the complexity analysis of UAV cluster, based on three modes of task, cluster management and control behavior, and information interaction behavior, the complex system element set, interaction relation set, complex criteria set, and complex feature set are summarized into the backbone architecture level of collaborative task subsystem, cluster management and control subsystem, and networking communication subsystem [1]. And completed a variety of models, multiple levels and multiple types of sub member architecture level, comprehensive build a can not only the overall task oriented, and geared to the needs of local task, to based on the global situation and based on the local situation, both can rapid response and can avoid conflict collaborative decision-making and execution of complex unmanned aerial vehicle (UAV) cluster system architecture [2].

Geared to the needs of different tasks, unmanned aerial vehicles (UAVs) based on hierarchical type cluster complex system architecture design, from the collaborative task, cluster control, network communication system analysis and design including three task oriented unmanned aerial vehicle clustering hierarchy type collaborative task architecture and behavior model [3], the hierarchical cluster model and the hierarchical control architecture and behavior type network communication architecture and behavior model [4].

© ICST Institute for Computer Sciences, Social Informatics and Telecommunications Engineering 2023
Published by Springer Nature Switzerland AG 2023. All Rights Reserved
A. Li et al. (Eds.): 6GN 2022, LNICST 504, pp. 230–239, 2023.
https://doi.org/10.1007/978-3-031-36011-4_20

2 Task-Oriented Hierarchical Collaborative Task Architecture Design of UAV Cluster

According to the characteristics of UAV cluster scale, rapid response to task and grasp situation change, a task-oriented hierarchical cooperative task architecture for UAV cluster is adopted [5].

According to the requirements of broad spectrum mission capability of UAV cluster, the characteristics of task styles are analyzed, which are divided into the distributed cooperative mode of single-task layer cooperative task, the centralized cooperative mode of single-task chain cooperative task, and the multi-level distributed cooperative mode of multi-task hybrid task.

For jamming, identity-strike, search-identity-strike, search-identity-relay and other single-mission chain closed-loop cooperative tasks, UAV cluster adopts centralized cooperative mode [6]. For single task collaborative tasks such as collaborative penetration, collaborative interference, collaborative search and collaborative identification, the UAV cluster adopts the distributed collaborative mode. For multi-missile cooperative jamming - multi-missile cooperative identification - multi-missile cooperative strike, multi-missile cooperative search - multi-missile cooperative identification - multi-missile cooperative strike, multi-missile cooperative search - multi-missile cooperative identification - multi-missile cooperative relay and other mission layer and mission chain hybrid cooperative missions, UAV cluster adopts multi-level distributed cooperative mode.

2.1 Distributed Collaborative Mode

For the single-task cooperative task styles such as collaborative penetration, collaborative interference, collaborative search and collaborative identification, the UAV cluster can be seen to be composed of various weapon units with consistent functions and equal roles, and there is no primary or secondary or functional serial among the clusters. Adopt the distributed collaborative mode, unmanned aerial vehicle within the cluster point-to-point communication, adopt the method of autonomy and cooperation to solve the problem of global control, to be able to see from the complex problems into a child of each node in the system to solve the problem, and then by each node calculation, give full play to the autonomous ability of each node cluster has the scalability, enhance the combat effectiveness.

2.2 Centralized Synergy Model

Aimed at "Jam-identity-strike, search-identity-strike, search-identity-relay" single task chain loop style of collaborative task, such as unmanned aerial vehicles by different functions and roles of each cluster weapons units, according to the function of serial cluster tasks, form the task chain relationship, centralized collaborative model are adopted to decrease the system complexity, reduce the communication cost produced by negotiation between nodes, improving system flexibility and rapidity.

2.3 Hierarchical Distributed Collaboration Model

Disturbance in play the synergy - play the synergy identification - more collaborative blow, play collaborative search - more collaborative recognition - play more cooperative combat, play collaborative search - more collaborative recognition - play play mixed relay tasks such as layer, task chain collaborative task style, unmanned aerial vehicle cluster by more units of different functions and roles of weapons, Same type unmanned aerial vehicle on a single mission collaborative task, and perform the task chain between different types of unmanned aerial vehicle closed loop task, using a multi-level distributed mode, all information through multiple master node for processing, and have more child nodes under each of the master node, the master node and use different frequencies for communication between child nodes, between the master node USES the distributed collaborative architecture, Centralized collaboration mode and distributed collaboration mode can be adopted in child nodes. This mode can realize the perception and decision from local situation to global situation according to the constraint information such as communication capability and node size, and improve the overall task efficiency of nodes. To achieve the large-scale, efficient and conflict-free execution and operation of the cluster, and improve the flexibility of UAV cluster tasks.

3 Task-Oriented Hierarchical Cluster Management and Control Architecture of UAV Cluster

In cluster management and control, the cluster management and control process is generally divided into four processes, namely, autonomous task decision, dynamic task allocation, cluster route planning and cooperative formation control. In order to realize the coordination of autonomous task decision, online dynamic task allocation, cooperative flight path planning, cooperative formation control and other functions of UAV cluster, a dynamic multi-level distributed cluster management and control architecture is designed.

Among them, in autonomous task decision-making, decision nodes are determined or polling decisions are made at the level of UAV cluster, task subgroup and machine cluster subgroup according to the situation, and cluster tasks are decided according to the battlefield situation.

In dynamic task allocation, the execution unit is determined according to the decision task situation, task execution subgroup size and cluster resource status, and the task allocation is completed.

In the cluster flight path planning, the cluster sub-group realizes the real-time flight path planning of each flight platform in the cluster sub-group according to the flight status of individuals in the group, the mission target position information or the patrol flight track point information.

In the formation cooperative control, the flight control quantity of the task execution individual and the formation is calculated, and the flight attitude of the weapon platform is adjusted in real time, so that each UAV platform can fly along the formation track planned by the flight path planning layer, and achieve the desired task of the top-level decision.

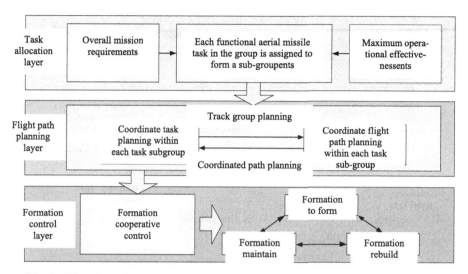

Fig. 1. Three-layer management mode under mission layer cooperation of UAV cluster

For UAV cluster tasks, the task requirements and cluster state information are analyzed, which are divided into task layer collaboration and task chain collaboration, and the corresponding cluster management and control mode is designed.

3.1 Task-Oriented Collaborative Three-Layer Cluster Management and Control Mode

From the analysis of cooperative task style in the task layer, UAV cluster is usually composed of UAVs with the same function and the individuals in the group complete the same task, or composed of UAVs with different functions but the function difference is not obvious or does not affect the task effect. In this regard, UAV clustering only involves allocation, planning and control in the cluster, not decision-making. The UAV cluster management and control architecture under the cooperation of the task layer is designed as a three-layer management mode, namely, the decision allocation layer, the flight path planning layer and the flight control layer. The specific architecture is shown in the Fig. 1.

Among them, the task allocation layer is at the top of the task cluster management architecture, which mainly completes the assignment of UAV cluster task groups, and determines the task subgroup scale, function configuration and execution unit according to the task type. The flight path planning layer is mainly carried out in each task subgroup. Through the calculation of one or several UAVs, the flight path planning of each UAVs in the task subgroup is completed, and the desired flight path of the formation is provided. The formation control layer is mainly carried out between each UAV and the UAV. By calculating the UAV flight control quantity, the cluster formation can be controlled to fly to the target point along the desired flight path obtained by the track planning.

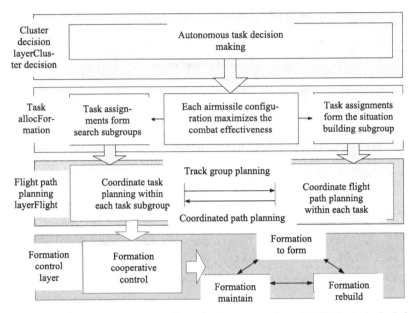

Fig. 2. Four-layer management mode under the cooperation of UAV cluster task chain

3.2 Task Chain-Oriented Cooperative 4-layer Cluster Management and Control Mode

The analysis of the cooperative task style of the task chain shows that the tasks are connected in the way of the task chain, which has a certain spatial and temporal cohesion. In terms of structure, the UAV cluster is composed of multiple functional UAVs in order to perform a variety of different tasks. However, the dynamic battlefield situation makes the UAV cluster can complete the task transformation according to the situation change at any time in the task process, that is, the UAV cluster needs to have the corresponding autonomous decision-making ability. After completing the task decision, it is necessary to have the task allocation and dynamic adjustment of each UAV in the cluster. In this regard, the UAV cluster under the cooperation of task chain involves the whole process of decision-making, allocation, planning and control in cluster management. Then, the UAV cluster management and control architecture under the cooperation of the task layer is designed as a four-layer management mode, namely, the cluster decision layer, the task allocation layer, the flight path planning layer and the formation control layer. The hierarchy of the architecture is shown in the figure below.

Among them, the cluster decision layer is mainly carried out at the top of UAV cluster, which completes the task decision function of UAV cluster, determines the macro type of tasks and the approximate scale of task subgroup. The task allocation layer is mainly carried out in each task subgroup. According to the task requirements and the status quo of cluster resources, the allocation of task execution units and the construction of cluster subgroups for task execution are completed according to the allocation principle of maximizing task efficiency. The flight path planning layer is mainly carried out in each cluster sub-group, which can be calculated by one or several UAVs in the group according to the scale of the sub-group, complete the planning of the cooperative flight path of each platform in the cluster sub-group, and provide the desired trajectory for the formation to execute the task. The formation control layer is also carried out in each cluster group. The flight control quantity of the platform is obtained by calculation, and the cluster formation is controlled to patrol along the corresponding desired flight track, and the formation formation is maintained.

The design of dynamic multi-level distributed cluster management and control architecture can effectively solve the complexity of large-scale cluster node cluster management and control. At the same time, it can make the UAV cluster quickly obtain global battlefield information, improve the management efficiency of UAV cluster for individual configuration tasks and behaviors, and has strong adaptability to battlefield changes.

4 Task-Oriented UAV Cluster Hierarchical Networking Communication Architecture

The task-oriented hierarchical network communication architecture of UAV cluster is adopted for the characteristics of UAV cluster network scale, fast change of network topology and big difference of node speed domain.

Network The communication system consists of a backbone network and subnets. Command centers/AWacs and relay weapons form the backbone network; The other weapons are divided into multiple clusters, each cluster as a subnet, the number of members in the cluster is not less than 8, each cluster based on the corresponding protocol to select the cluster head and sub-cluster head from the cluster members, sub-cluster head and cluster members have the same function, as the first alternative when the cluster head is off the network, accept the responsibility transfer of the cluster head at any time. Backbone nodes are responsible for relay information transmission, network maintenance, topology control, and information exchange and sharing between clusters. Cluster heads are mainly responsible for subnetwork maintenance and centralized processing of services within clusters.

For UAV cluster task, the network communication requirements and technical characteristics are analyzed, which are divided into four application modes: large-scale, high bandwidth, fast response and interference degradation.

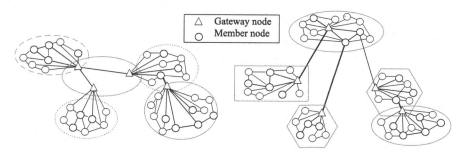

Fig. 3. Schematic diagram of large-scale network mode, time-sharing hierarchical topology (left), and frequency division hierarchical topology (right).

4.1 Large-Scale Network Model

For UAV cluster aerial assembly, dense penetration, formation recovery and other tasks, the network communication requirements are large number of network nodes, strong resistance to destruction, high connectivity between nodes, and relatively small end-to-end business volume.

The large-scale network mode adopts hierarchical clustering network architecture. According to the network scale, network topology change, node speed domain, space domain, function domain difference, the whole network is logically divided into multiple clusters, each cluster contains a number of nodes, one of which is the cluster head node, the rest are common member nodes. Compared with the centralized network, the hierarchical clustering network architecture can reduce the network maintenance scope to a single cluster and reduce the resource scheduling overhead. Compared with the fully distributed network, the pathfinding broadcast range is concentrated among cluster heads, which can reduce the pathfinding consumption and provide the possibility to increase the network scale requirements. According to the electromagnetic environment and specific task requirements, the hierarchical clustering network structure can be designed into time-sharing hierarchical topology and frequency hierarchical topology, as shown in the following figure. It is easy to realize the information interaction between clusters in the time-sharing and hierarchical topology design, and the end-to-end throughput is small. The frequency division topology achieves higher device cost in exchange for efficient information interaction between clusters and higher end-to-end throughput.

Hierarchical cluster network architecture uses cluster heads to manage the whole network in a hierarchical manner, reducing control signaling and enhancing the reliability of information transmission. The architecture can accommodate a large number of nodes, strong destruction resistance, high connectivity between nodes, and efficiently and reliably adapt to the network requirements of UAV cluster large-scale flying formation tasks such as air assembly, dense penetration, formation recovery, etc.

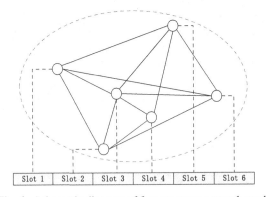

Fig. 4. Schematic diagram of fast response network mode

4.2 Quick Response Network Mode

For UAV cluster cooperative positioning and attack guidance tasks, the network requirements are high end-to-end interaction frequency and demanding delay, but the number of network nodes is small.

Fast response network adopts time-sharing and distributed architecture. In this architecture, all nodes are equal, and there is no need to set the center point of the network, so the network overhead is low. At the same time, time-sharing system ensures the network response speed and avoids data collision. Nodes and neighbors can apply for and authorize resources based on service types. The network architecture has a flexible topology, which enables elastic network extension, ensures local fast response performance optimization, improves communication frequency, and reduces network delay. The time-sharing and distributed architecture is shown in the Fig. 4.

In time-sharing and distributed architecture, communication resources of each node are allocated according to time slots, which minimizes information redundancy and collision and improves information response speed. The architecture has high interaction frequency between nodes, small end-to-end delay, and efficiently and reliably meets the network requirements of high-frequency interaction tasks of UAV clusters, such as collaborative positioning and guided strike.

4.3 High-Bandwidth Network Mode

For UAV cluster situation construction, wide area search, target recognition, evaluation and other tasks, the network requirements are large end-to-end communication bandwidth, but the number of network nodes is small, and the communication delay is not sensitive.

High bandwidth network adopts frequency division distributed architecture. This architecture does not require the network to set the center point, the network overhead is small, and the frequency division system ensures the network bandwidth is sufficient. The collision backoff algorithm is used to optimize the performance of local high bandwidth without affecting network services. It is suitable for reducing delay sensitivity and improving end-to-end throughput.

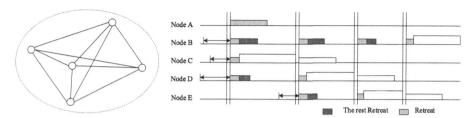

Fig. 5. Schematic diagram of high bandwidth network mode

In the frequency division distributed architecture, resources of each node are allocated according to demand, and the size of the competition window is adjusted by design to maximize the end-to-end throughput of the network. The architecture has large end-to-end communication bandwidth and is insensitive to communication delay. It can reliably meet the network requirements of UAV cluster image transmission tasks, such as situation construction, wide area search, target recognition, and evaluation.

4.4 Interference De-escalation Network Mode

When the UAV cluster communication environment changes and encounters enemy interference, the communication network switches to the interference degradation mode. In this mode, high-bandwidth and low-delay services are suspended, and adaptive sub-carrier deduction technology is adopted to ensure the highly reliable transmission of basic interactive information of weapon cluster.

According to the random fluctuation of channel response caused by frequency selective channel or certain interference, the communication frequency band is divided into multiple segments, and then whether to continue to use it is selected according to the quality of its transmitted data, so as to reduce the influence caused by channel and interference. Assuming that the random fluctuation of the channel has uneven influence on the transmitted signal frequency band, in the signal sender, the signal communication frequency band is divided into N equal parts before normal data transmission. According to the quality of each equal part recorded by the channel quality detection module, whether to use this frequency segment for the next data transmission is decided. If this frequency segment is used, the actual data delivered at the data link layer is transmitted on this frequency segment. If this frequency segment is not used, the populated data stored at the physical layer is transmitted on this frequency segment. In the signal receiver, the receiving node records the receiving quality of the transmitted data in each frequency segment, and then takes out the actual data from all frequency segments for demodulation and decoding according to the frequency band negotiated with the transmitter, discarding the filled data, so as to achieve the anti-interference effect in the frequency domain. The workflow of interference degradation mode is shown in the Fig. 6.

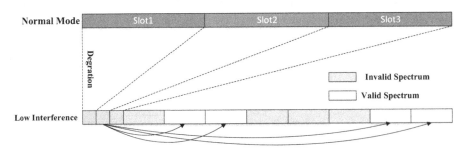

Fig. 6. Workflow of interference degraded working mode

5 Conclusion

Based on the unmanned aerial vehicle of the complexity of the cluster analysis, based on task, the cluster control behavior and information interaction model, the complex system elements, the interaction between the collection, complex rule set, complex feature set as a coordination task subsystem, cluster control subsystem, communication subsystem for the network architecture backbone architecture layers, And completed a variety of models, multi-level, multi-type sub member of the architectural layer, comprehensive build a can not only the overall task oriented, and can adapt to the need of the local task, can be based on the global and local based architecture, both can rapid response, and can avoid the complex unmanned aerial vehicle cluster system architecture of conflict collaborative decision-making and implementation.

According to different task requirements, unmanned aerial vehicles based on hierarchical cluster complex system architecture design, from the collaborative task, cluster control, network communication system analysis and design from three aspects including task oriented unmanned aerial vehicle hierarchical cluster collaborative task structure and behavior model, hierarchical cluster model and hierarchical control architecture and network communication behavior type structure and behavior model.

References

1. ur Rahman, S., Kim, G.-H., Cho, Y.-Z., Khan, A.: Positioning of UAVs for throughput maximization in software-defined disaster area UAV communication networks. J. Commun. Netw. **20**(5), 452–463 (2018). https://doi.org/10.1109/JCN.2018.000070
2. Pan, C., Yi, J., Yin, C., Yu, J., Li, X.: Joint 3D UAV placement and resource allocation in software-defined cellular networks with wireless Backhaul. IEEE Access **7**, 104279–104293 (2019). https://doi.org/10.1109/ACCESS.2019.2927521
3. Gupta, L., Jain, R., Vaszkun, G.: Survey of important issues in UAV communication networks. IEEE Commun. Surv. Tutor. **18**(2), 1123–1152 (2016). https://doi.org/10.1109/COMST.2015.2495297
4. Li, M., Tao, X., Li, N., Wu, H., Xu, J.: Secrecy energy efficiency maximization in UAV-enabled wireless sensor networks without Eavesdropper's CSI. IEEE Internet Things J. **9**(5), 3346–3358 (2022). https://doi.org/10.1109/JIOT.2021.3098049
5. Wang, Y., et al.: Joint resource allocation and UAV trajectory optimization for space–air–ground internet of remote things networks. IEEE Syst. J. **15**(4), 4745–4755 (2021). https://doi.org/10.1109/JSYST.2020.3019463
6. Baek, J., Han, S.I., Han, Y.: Energy-efficient UAV routing for wireless sensor networks. IEEE Trans. Veh. Technol. **69**(2), 1741–1750 (2020). https://doi.org/10.1109/TVT.2019.2959808

Reconstruction of Smart Phone Camera Effect Parameter Management Subsystem

Wanpeng Tang[1]([⊠]) [iD] and Guoming Rao[2]

[1] Guangzhou City Polytechnic, Guangzhou, Guangdong, China
46186518@qq.com
[2] Spreadtrum Communications (Shanghai Co. Ltd.), Shanghai, China

Abstract. For the camera effect parameter management and debugging of smart phone platform, customers have many complaints and dissatisfaction, the most important problems are: poor readability, poor separability, poor scalability, compilation free, there are a lot of redundant parameters. In this paper, a new system is constructed for parameter management, which is analyzed and reconstructed from the aspects of parameter structure, parameter search, parameter storage and parameter debugging, and the software system is redesigned to solve the above software problems completely from the system.

Keywords: process debugging parameters · Scenario · Mode Mode · block

1 The Research Status

With the concentration of smartphone customers to premium brand customers, the smartphone projects of premium brand customers have higher and higher requirements for camera effects, and the scene debugging requirements are more and more refined. At the same time, the company's chip camera module has expanded to more than 50, and the parameter scale of each module has also increased rapidly, Under the circumstance that the project period is determined, higher requirements are put forward in terms of commissioning scale and commissioning schedule. Meanwhile, brand mobile phone customers pursue the gene of product differentiation, requiring that the chip platform must be easy to integrate the post-processing algorithm of each camera [1]. To meet the above requirements, the camera effect parameter management of the current smartphone platform has many problems in the system, mainly in the following aspects: poor readability, poor separability, poor scalability, unable to completely achieve compile-free, poor debugging, and a large number of redundant parameters.

In view of the above problems, this study redesigns the current smart phone effect parameter management software subsystem, completely solves the above problems, and meets the needs of customers in the smart phone platform on the effect parameter debugging and integration.

© ICST Institute for Computer Sciences, Social Informatics and Telecommunications Engineering 2023
Published by Springer Nature Switzerland AG 2023. All Rights Reserved
A. Li et al. (Eds.): 6GN 2022, LNICST 504, pp. 240–250, 2023.
https://doi.org/10.1007/978-3-031-36011-4_21

2 Defects and Reconstruction Ideas of the Original Effect Parameter Management Subsystem

The current camera effect parameter management subsystem is still based on the system design of function machine era, which has the following design defects:

2.1 Poor Readability and Redundancy

The current parameter file is in C format, but there are a lot of incomprehensible hexadecimal data, and each module is intertwined and difficult to understand, there are great difficulties in dealing with multi-person debugging, and lack of corresponding annotations; After years of development of the whole debugging parameters, NR Block is bound with many denoising modules. If a single module is added, other NR modules need to be added synchronously, resulting in redundancy of parameters and low reuse of parameters. As a result, when multiple scene parameters are added to effect parameters, the parameter file is large, leading to large memory consumption.

2.2 Poor Divisibility and Scalability

Currently, parameter files are separated according to mode. For example, capture and preview are described in two files respectively, but each file contains the parameters of each module. Such parameters between different file can't reuse, and there are a lot of redundant parameters between different files.The debugger of different modules may modify the same parameter file. In addition, it is difficult to extend third-party algorithms and new modes. Coupling and compatibility should be considered. Due to customization requirements, customers often require different effect parameters for different application scenarios. At present, Mode Mode is difficult to meet integration requirements [2].

2.3 Compilation is not Exempt

The parameters of the current file is C description file, it is necessary to form parameter library files at compile time for running load, while debugging can also go directly to read C parameter file format, but there are two major drawbacks: first, crash will occur when the data size of the C file is inconsistent with that of the loaded SO-file; Second, you cannot update parameters locally; to update parameters, you must update them all.

Then, according to the above problems, consider the following points for system reconstruction design:

A) Considering the readability and convenience of THE XML file format, the parameter file format will be changed to XML format, and each parameter needs to be annotated in THE XML format to describe the default value, recommended value range, allowed value range, and debugging frequency of the parameter. Considering the performance of XML files when loading, the parameters of mass production products are bin files in binary format, which can be exchanged between XML and bin format. When defining XML, remove some of the old parameters that still exist in the parameter file and are not actually used; When multiple groups are configured, the maximum number of groups is not supported. Currently, the number of fixed groups is changed to a variable number for SMART and NR modules. The flexible number of Smart groups also requires that the Smart interpolation for each module should be distributed to each module.

B) Effect debugger debugging development trend is according to the algorithm module block or according to the module block field debugging, so the segmentation should be from the perspective of the module block. By storing parameters in different files according to the module block, the debugger of different modules will not have the problem of modifying the same parameter file. This design is especially beneficial for multi-user debugging. In addition, for third-party algorithms, their parameters often exist as independent files, which are stored as different parameter files in modules, and are also very friendly to the compatibility of third-party algorithms. Smart modules should also be scattered among modules. The original Mode Mode needs to be divided into more dimensions. The initial idea is to take Scenario as the outline, scene characteristics as the context, and algorithm module as the purpose to configure parameter architecture.

C) Use BIN files and XML files to solve the compile-free problem. Parameters themselves are only parameters and do not need to be compiled. Parameters are divided into independent small files according to the block module, and parameters of a certain module can be updated independently.

3   Parameter Storage Mode

3.1   Parameter File and Its Organizational Form

The parameter file adopts the format of BIN + XML. The parameter file of each module block is an independent bin file or an XML file. For example, the original Bayer NR module is independent of LM.BIN file or LM. XML file. The LM. BIN and LM. XML files can be converted to each other through tools. The debugger mainly uses XML files for debugging and parameter submission The LM. BIN and LM. XML files can be pushed to the phone, and the debugger and phone can parse these two formats respectively.

3.2   Organization Form of Parameter Files

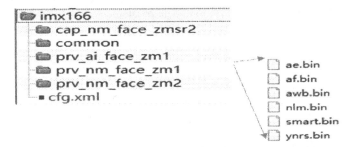

Fig. 1. Organization of a parameter file

For a module, the parameter file is divided into the module parameter root directory, Scenario subdirectory and module parameter file according to the hierarchical structure. There is also a unique cfg. XML file under the module parameter root directory, as shown in Fig. 1.

A Root Folder

For a module, the root directory of the parameters is named after the module, as before. Modules are usually referred to sensors, such as IMX166. If a project consists of multiple modules that use IMX166, you can use sensor_name + suffix, for example, IMX166_rear stands for rear and IMX166_front indicates forward photography.

B Subdirectories

Each subdirectory corresponds to a Scenario, which is the abbreviation of the scenario name. The shorthand rules can be spliced together according to each field of scenario. The mapping between Scenario ID and Scenario name (that is, subfolder) is described in cfg.xml.

C cfg.xml

The ID of scenario, name of Scenario and reuse relation of algorithm modules involved in scenario are described.

D Module Block Parameter File

The module block parameter is separated from each mode file and becomes an independent file: all algorithm modules used in Scenario should be separated. Not all module parameters in a scenario will exist. When the NLM parameters of Scenario #1 are recycled, the nlM.bin/NLM.xml file in the Scenario #2 folder will exist. The lm. Bin/lm. XML file will not exist in the scenario#1 folder. This reuse relationship is described in the cfg.xml file [3].

4   Design the Overall Parameter Framework Based on Scenario

4.1 Definition of Scenario

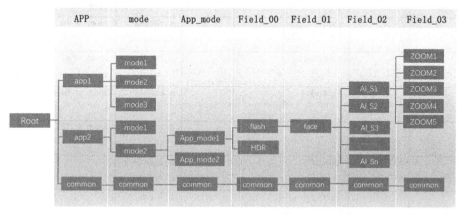

Fig. 2. Composing fields of Scenario

Scenario is defined based on the attributes of the applicable Scenario. Currently, it is defined from seven aspects: App, mode(related to image size), App_mode (related to App's level 1/level 2 menu), Field00–Field03 (describe scene feature from 4 levels), as shown in Fig. 2.

4.2 Field Instance List of Scenario

Table 1. Platform Scenario instantiation table

app	mode	app_mode	field_00	field_01	field_02	field_03	ID
common	common	common	Common	common	**common**	common	00
factory	preview_binning	**night**	**flash**	**face**	ai_sunriseset	**zoom_2x**	01
wechat	**preview_full**	panorama	hr		ai_firework	zoom_4x	02
tictok	capture_binning	Apture_bokeh			ai_food	zoom_8x	03
facebook	capture_full	portait			ai_foliage	zoom_16x	04
messager	video_preview_720p	pro			ai_document	zoom_32x	05
qq	video_preview_1080p	time_lapse			ai_pet	zoom_64x	06
snapchat	video_recording_720p	slow_motion			ai_flower	zoom_128x	07
whatapps	video_recording_1080p	moving_capture			ai_sky	zoom_sr_2x	08
	Video_call	capduringpreview			ai_snow	zoom_sr_4x	09
		qr			ai_overcast	zoom_sr_8x	0a
		sport			ai_chinese_building	zoom_sr_16x	0b
		landscape			ai_building	zoom_sr_32x	0c
		firework			ai_car	zoom_sr_64x	0d
		autumn			ai_bicycle	zoom_sr_128x	oe
		refocus			ai_autumn_leaf		0f
		filter			ai_beach		10
		fusion			ai_lake		11
		night_pr			ai_waterfall		12

Based on the above rules, the following Scenario list is instantiated, as shown in Table 1. All scenarios can be formed by free combination of each field. The actual Scenario supported by the platform is only a subset of all possible scenarios.

1) According to the ID column in Table 1, the Scenario ID of the current scenario is spliced from left to right in the above table. Scenario ID is defined as a 64-bit unsigned number with the highest bit complement 0x00. Such as red font marked fields in Table 1 (wechat/preview_full/night/flash/face/common/zoom_2x), the ID after stitching is 0 x00–02–02–01–02–02–01–01.

2) Match the ID level by level from left to right. If the ID exists, the field ID is the actual ID. If the field id does not match, the common ID is used.

3) Mode extension response: If the current conflict mode is no longer in the future, it can be extended by adding the items of this field to different fields. If HDR is first in field_00, then HDR takes precedence. If FLASH is first in field_00, then FLASH takes precedence.

4.3 Scenario-Block Map

The algorithm blocks involved in a Scenario are described by scenario-block Map. Generally, each platform should have a scenario-block Map table. The scenario-block Map table may change in different versions of the platform, and customers may even customize their own Map table according to their needs. Therefore, Scenario-block maps should be easy to configure and change, and should be consistent on the tool side and mobile side.

Table 2. Example of scenario-block Map

Scenario_id	Scenario_name																																																									
0x00000001	common	1	1	1	1	1	1	1	1	1	1	1	1	1	1	1	1	1	1	1	1	1	1	1	1	1	1	1	1	1	1	1	1	1	1	1	1	1	1	1	1	1	1	1	1	1	1	1	1	1	1	1	1	1	1	1	1	1
0x00010001	prv1_xx_xx_xx	1	1	1	1	1	1	1	1	1	1	1	1	1	1	1	1	1	1	1	1	1	1	1	1	1	1	1	1	1	1	1	1	1	1	1	1	1	1	1	1	1	1	1	1	1	1	1	1	1	1	1	1	1	0	0	0
0x00020001	prv2_xx_xx_xx	1	1	1	1	1	1	1	1	1	1	1	1	1	1	1	1	1	1	1	1	1	1	1	1	1	1	1	1	1	1	1	1	1	1	1	1	1	1	1	1	1	1	1	1	1	1	1	1	1	1	1	1	1	0	0	0
0x00050001	cap1_xx_xx_xx	1	1	1	1	1	1	1	1	1	1	1	1	1	1	1	1	1	1	1	1	1	1	1	1	1	1	1	1	1	1	1	1	1	1	1	1	1	1	1	1	1	1	1	0	0	1	1	1	1	1	1
0x00060001	cap2_xx_xx_xx	1	1	1	1	1	1	1	1	1	1	1	1	1	1	1	1	1	1	1	1	1	1	1	1	1	1	1	1	1	1	1	1	1	1	1	1	1	1	1	1	1	1	1	0	0	1	1	1	1	1	1

According to the example of scenario-block map in Table 2. Each row of the Map is a Scenario, and each column is an algorithm module (Block). Adding a Scenario means adding rows, and adding an algorithm module means adding columns.

The values in the table are defined as follows:

1: Scenario requires the parameters of the block.

0: Scenario does not require the parameters of the block.

Note that the scenario-block Map is sparse, and the Scenario IDS and column ids are not continuous. Corresponding rows or columns exist only when necessary. Scenario not described in the table, but if it may actually occur, it means that this Scenario will be replaced by Common if it occurs – that is, all scenarios not described are merged into Common [4].

4.4   Reuse Relationship of Blocks in Scenario

In order to reduce disk and memory usage, blocks of each Scenario should be allowed to reuse corresponding blocks of other Scenarios. A block with a reuse relationship will have only one memory entity; In principle, there should be only one bin or XML file entity. The following is a concrete example of reuse relationships, mechanisms, and implementations.

Table 3. Example table of scenario-block reuse relationship description

Scenario_name	"BLC"	"Y_AFL3"	"BCHS"
common	common	common	common
prv1_xx_xx_xx	common	common	common
prv2_xx_xx_xx	prv2_xx_xx_xx	prv2_xx_xx_xx	common
cap1_xx_xx_xx	common	common	common
cap2_xx_xx_xx	prv2_xx_xx_xx	prv2_xx_xx_xx	common

Table 3 is a tabular description of cfg. XML, which actually describes that Scenario prV1_XX_XX_XX BLC, Y_AFL3 and BCHS completely use Scenario common. Therefore, the prv1_XX_XX_XX folder will have no bin and XML files with three blocks. Prv2_xx_xx_xx BLC and Y_AFL3 do not reuse other Scenarios, so prV2_XX_XX_XX folder will have blc.bin and y_afl3.bin files, but PRV2_XX_xx_XX BCHS reuse common, Therefore, the bchs.bin file does not exist under prV2_xx_XX_xx. Similarly, cap2_xx_xx_XX BLC and Y_AFL3 are multiplexed from prV2_xx_xx_xx BLC. Bin and y_afl3.bin files. Cap2_xx_xx_xx does not have two BLCOK bin files. The Common directory contains bin or XML files for all blocks.

Table 3 Equivalent examples of cfg. XML are shown in Fig. 3. The equivalent data description of cfG. XML is shown in Table 4. Based on the data description table, the memory description for parameter loading can be further standardized.

```
<cfg>
    <sensor_name>imx586</sensor_name>
    <version_id>0x000c000f</version_id>
    <scenario_num>5</scenario_num>
    <scenario alia = "common">
        <id>0x00000001</id>
        <block_num>3</block_num>
        <block name = "blc">
            <block_id>0x4002</block_id>
            <param>common</param>
        </block>
        <block name = "Y_AFL3">
            <block_id>0x401A</block_id>
            <param>common</param>
        </block>
        <block name = "BCHS">
            <block_id>0x5065</block_id>
            <param>common</param>
        </block>
    </scenario>
    <scenario alia = "prv1 xx xx xx">
    <scenario alia = "prv2 xx xx xx">
    <scenario alia = "cap1 xx xx xx">
    <scenario alia = "cap2 xx xx xx">
</cfg>
```

Fig. 3. Example of the cfg. XML file

Table 4. Example table of datatization of scenario-block reuse relationship

Scenario_name	"BLC"	"Y_AFL3"	"BCHS"
0x00000001	0x00000001	0x00000001	0x00000001
0x00001001	0x00000001	0x00000001	0x00000001
0x00002001	0x00002001	0x00002001	0x00000001
0x00005001	0x00000001	0x00000001	0x00000001
0x00006001	0x00002001	0x00002001	0x00000001

4.5   Interface Design of Scenario Block Parameter Reuse Relationship in Debugging Tools

In order to facilitate the debugging personnel to configure the effect parameter multiplexing relationship, improve the efficiency of parameter multiplexing. Guide the debugger to take full advantage of parameter multiplexing to minimize memory and disk consumption, the debugging tool is designed as follows:

The Scenario List:

1) The Scenario List drop-down table should list all scenarios supported by the platform.
2) Select a Scenario and call out all non-0 blocks according to the configuration in the scenario-block map table to form a Block list to be debugged. Each Block can be a button as before. Click to call out the debugging interface of the module.

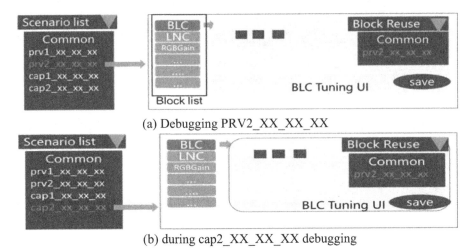

(a) Debugging PRV2_XX_XX_XX

(b) during cap2_XX_XX_XX debugging

Fig. 4. Shows the interface design of the BLC debugging tool

The operation and working mechanism are described, as shown in Fig. 4.

1) The Block reuse menu invokes all Scenario names of the Block data entity.
2) Select a Scenario and load the block data of the Scenario on the block debugging interface.
3) If the referenced block data is modified, the data of the block will be saved in the folder of the current Scenario (not the referenced Scenario) during save, and the reuse relation will point to the current Scenario.

For example, prV2_XX_XX_XX BLC has no data entity at the beginning. Prv2_xx_xx_xx starts debugging from Block.

Reuse Select Common from the drop - down list to reuse BLC data of Common. If the modification is performed on the BLC debugging interface, the data is saved to the blc.bin file in the prV2_XX_XX_XX folder, and cfg. XML is modified to indicate that PRV2_XX_XX_XX BLC uses prV2_XX_XX_XX_XX BLC parameters. Note that blc.bin in the common folder will not be modified at this time.

When debugging CAP2_XX_XX_XX, if both COMMON and PRV2_XX_XX_XX have BLC block entities,

Then the block reuse drop-down menu will list two Scenarios, common and PRV2_XX_XX_XX.

Assume that Scenario prV2_XX_XX_XX is selected, BLC data is not modified and click Save. Since BLC data is not modified, there is no need to save BLC. Bin to cap2_XX_XX_XX directory. Do not create cap2_xx_xx_xx if the cap2_xx_xx_xx directory does not already exist. However, the cfg. XML file needs to be modified to record that the BLC of CAP2_XX_XX_XX comes from the Scenario prV2_XX_XX_XX [5].

5   Commissioning and Conclusion

Through the reconstruction of camera effect parameter subsystem, the coupling pain point of parameter debugging for a long time was solved and the parameters were improved.The scalability of data improves the efficiency of fast integration of third-party algorithms. It used to take one month to integrate and stabilize a new algorithm, but now it only takes two weeks.

1) Parameter Storage Format and Advance Integration Ability

XML (xxx. XML + cfg. XML can be parsed and converted using tools). In cfg. XML, the relationship between Scenario and block parameters is configured. The implementation of XML format will allow algorithm and integration to get rid of the dependence of camera effect debugging tools, and advance the time point of integration to algorithm pre-research/simulation stage. Without tools, directly modify the content of XML file, effect simulation and debugging can be carried out.

2) Scenario Supported by the Current System

At present, a total of 121 scenarios are summarized before parameter reconstruction, which are described from 7 dimensions. Dimension classification and inclusion relations can be updated and expanded as required. Supporting 121 scenarios does not mean that you need to debug 121 scenarios. You need to make full use of the reuse relationship of parameters between scenarios, which gives the debugger great flexibility to implement different debugging strategies for different customers, different projects and different effect requirements.

3) Smart Function Outlook

The current SMART mechanism is relatively crude, and the new parameters will allow you to customize your SMART policy for each algorithm module. Although the current smart parameters are uniform, each block defines its own SMART parameters, which allows each block to have its own SMART policy. In other words, smart parameters can vary with different blocks.

In subsequent evolution, each block can allow the evolution of its own smooth and switch strategies, which require parameters determined by the module itself.

References

1. Vijayakumar, V.T.R., Subha, B.: Product quality and its relationship on customer satisfaction and brand loyalty of mobile phone users in Chennai city. ZENITH Int. J. Multi. Res. **3**(7), 264–270 (2013)
2. Khatri, F.I., Zogbi, G., Boroson, D.M.: Telescope divisibility limitations due to synchronization of array-based photon counting receivers in laser communications links. Physica A Stat. Mech. Appl. **6877**, 70–77 (2008)
3. China Academy of Telecommunications Technology, Researchers Submit Patent Application: Method and Device for Processing Quality of Service Parameter in Handover Scenario.USPTO 20190215735 (2019)

4. González-Portillo, L.F., Muñoz-Antón, J., Martínez-Val, J.M.: An analytical optimization of thermal energy storage for electricity cost reduction in solar thermal electric plants. Appl. Energy **185**, 531–546 (2017)
5. Wang, D., Chen, K., Wang, L.: Practical XML Course, Tsinghua University Press (2014)

Big Data Mining and Pattern Analysis Techniques for 6G Networks

An Empirical Analysis of the Tax Inspection and Law Enforcement Risk of Changchun Taxation Bureau in the Era of Big Data

Zhang Xinyue[✉]

Changchun University of Finance and Economics, JiLin 130000, China
zxy15546327003@163.com

Abstract. In this paper, we develop the static and dynamic non-cooperative game models based on the basic assumptions, and analyze them separately. It is concluded that the main factors affecting the overall benefit of the tax inspection department are the tax loss, the inspection cost and the fine of the inspection department. Combined with the specific situation of Jilin Province, it is the conclusion that the inspection ability of the tax inspection department of Changchun Taxation Bureau is increasing year by year, the inspection cost is lower than the national level, and the punishment for illegal behaviors is not enough.

Keywords: Big data Era · Tax inspection · Game theory

1 Application of the Game Model Between Tax Authorities and Taxpayers

The relationship between tax authorities and taxpayers is both opposite and unified, and using the game model can better analyze the relationship between tax authorities and taxpayers. In a narrow sense, the relationship between tax inspection and taxpayers is opposite and it is impossible to reach a binding agreement, that is, the interest relationship between them is also relative, and both parties pursue the goal of maximizing their own interests under the condition of mutual influence of interests. Therefore, the relationship between Changchun tax authorities and taxpayers is more applicable to the non-cooperative game theory model, and the contradiction between tax inspection and taxpayers mainly lies in the "check" part, so this model is established in the process of "check" [1].

1.1 Basic Assumptions of the Model

The establishment of a non-cooperative game model means that the relationship between tax inspectors and taxpayers is completely opposite, and there is no intermediate or cooperative relationship. In addition, since this game model cannot completely correspond to the actual situation of tax inspection in Changchun, it is necessary to assume some

A. Li et al. (Eds.): 6GN 2022, LNICST 504, pp. 253–261, 2023.
https://doi.org/10.1007/978-3-031-36011-4_22

premises based on the above reasons, and that the model should be established and further analyzed under these premises:

Firstly, the two parties participating in the game are tax inspection and law enforcement personnel and taxpayers respectively.

Secondly, both tax inspectors and taxpayers are economic rational people. In the game process, both players will pursue benefit maximization under the condition of considering risks. Generally speaking, the goal of tax inspectors is to maximize tax revenue, while the goal of taxpayers is to pay as little as much tax as possible.

Thirdly, tax inspectors only have two choices: "inspection" and "no inspection", while taxpayers only have two choices: "illegal" and "no illegal".

Forthly, tax inspectors can only find out that taxpayers are breaking the law through tax inspection.

Fifthly, tax inspectors shall not be affected by other factors in the inspection process [2].

Based on the above assumptions, non-cooperative game models of both sides can be established.

1.2 Model Construction

The tax payable by the taxpayer shall be TD (Tax Due); The actual tax paid by the taxpayer is TP (Tax Paid); The tax payable by a taxpayer is greater than or equal to the tax actually paid by the taxpayer, approach TD $\geq$ TP, The difference between the tax payable by the taxpayer and the actual tax actually paid by the taxpayer is the illegal amount or the amount of tax lost; The intensity of the fine imposed by tax inspectors on taxpayers for breaking the law is: $\alpha > 0$; The inspection cost of inspecting taxpayers by tax inspectors is IC (In s pection Co s t); The illegal co s t of the taxpayer is ic (illegal co s t); The probability of tax inspectors conducting tax inspections is p, The probability of tax inspectors not to carry out tax inspection is 1-p; The probability of a taxpayer breaking the law is q, The probability of taxpayers not breaking the law is 1-q; The probability of inspection seized by tax inspectors is r, The probability of not seized is 1-r.

Construction of the Static Non-cooperative Game Model. According to the above conditions, Table 1 is shown below.

Table 1. Table of the mutual selection results of the static non-cooperative game model.

Game subject		Tax inspectors	
		check (p)	No inspection (1-p)
taxpayer	break the law (q)	-TP -α *(TD -TP)-ic, TP + α * (TD -TP)-IC	-TP -ic, TP
	Non-illegal (1-q)	-TD, TD -IC	-TD, TD

The Construction of a Dynamic Non-Uncooperative Game Model. Because in the actual situation is the first taxpayer to break the law, and then the tax inspectors for tax inspection [3]. In the process of tax inspection, taxpayers do not know when they will be tax inspection, and tax inspectors do not know whether the taxpayer is illegal. According to the above conditions, it is shown in Table 2 below.

Table 2. Table of dynamic non-cooperative game model.

Game subject		Tax inspectors		
		check (p)		No inspection (1-p)
		hunt down and seize (r)	Not seized (1-r)	
taxpayer	break the law (q)	-TP -α * (TD -TP)-ic, TP + α * (TD -TP)-IC	-TP -ic, TP -IC	-TP -ic, TP
	Non-illegal (1-q)	-TD, TD -IC		-TD, TD

2 Model-Based Risk Analysis of Tax Inspection and Law Enforcement in Changchun City

According to the above static non-cooperative game model, the dual selection result table and the dynamic non-cooperative game model, the two models, the static game model and the dynamic game model, are analyzed.

2.1 Static Non-cooperative Game Analysis

According to the above conditions, if the probability that the tax inspector conducts a tax inspection is p, the expected income that the tax inspector chooses the inspection is:

$$p * [TP + \alpha * (TD - TP) - IC] + (1 - p) * (TD - IC) \tag{1}$$

The expected benefits of tax inspectors choosing not to inspect are:

$$p * TP + (1 - p) * (TD) \tag{2}$$

According to the Nash equilibrium theory, it can be concluded that when p * [TP + * (TD-TP) -IC] + (1-p) * (TD-IC) = p * TP + (1-p) * (TD):

$$P' = IC / (1 + \alpha) * (TD - TP) \tag{3}$$

If the probability that the taxpayer violates the law is q, the expected income that the taxpayer chooses the violation is:

$$q * [-TP - \alpha * (TD - TP) - ic] + (1 - q) * (-TD) \tag{4}$$

The expected income of taxpayers taxpayer chooses not to be illegal is:

$$p * (-TD) + (1 - p) * (-TD) \tag{5}$$

When q * [-TP- * (TD-TP) -ic] + (1-q) * (-TD) = p * (-TD) + (1-p) * (-TD):

$$q' = (TD - TP - ic)/(TD - TP) * (\alpha + 1) \tag{6}$$

Therefore, it can be concluded that the mixed Nash equilibrium of the static noncooperative game model is achieved when the probability of (TD-TP-ic)/(TD-TP) * (+ 1) and the tax inspectors conducts the tax audit with the probability of IC/(1 +) * (TD-TP).

When q < (TD-TP-ic)/(TD-TP-ic/(TD-TP) * (+ 1); when q > (TD-TP-ic)/(TD-TP) * (+ 1), and when q = (TD-TP-T P-i c)/(T D-T P) * (+ 1).

When p < IC/(1 +) * (TD-TP), the best choice for tax inspectors is not to audit; when p > IC/(1 +) * (TD-TP); when p = IC/(1 +) * (TD-TP).

Therefore, it can be concluded that the probability of taxpayers choosing to break the law or not is related to the inspection cost of tax inspectors, the illegal cost of taxpayer, the amount of tax paid by taxpayers and the fine intensity of tax inspection and law enforcement personnel to taxpayers breaking the law.

2.2 Analysis of Dynamic Non-cooperative Game

According to the above conditions, if it is assumed that the probability of the tax inspector inspecting and seizing it is r, then the taxpayer's selection scheme is Y1 = (Y11, Y12), among Y11That the taxpayer chooses illegal, Y12The taxpayer chooses not to be illegal. The choice scheme of the tax inspectors is Y2 = (Y21, Y22), among Y21It means that the tax inspectors choose the inspection, Y22Says that the tax inspectors chose not to check.TEiFor the taxpayer total expenditure (= -taxpayer total benefit), TBiFor the total benefit of the tax inspectors [4].

When the taxpayer chooses not to break the law and the tax inspector chooses not to inspect, the choice is (Y11, Y12) Down, the corresponding to (L1, E1) = (TD, TD).

When the taxpayer chooses not to break the law, and the tax inspector chooses to inspect, that is, the choice is (Y12, Y21) Down, the corresponding to (L2, E2) = (TD, TD -IC).

When the taxpayer chooses to break the law and the tax inspector chooses not to inspect, the choice is (Y11, Y22) Down, the corresponding to (L3, E3) = (TP + ic, TP).

When the taxpayer chooses to break the law, and the tax inspector chooses to inspect, the choice is (Y11, Y21) Next: If the tax inspector finds the taxpayer breaking the law, the corresponding (L4, E4) = [TP + * (TD-TP) + ic, TP + * (TD-TP) -IC]; if tax inspectors cannot detect taxpayer violations, the corresponding (L5, E5) = (TP + ic, TP -IC).

Then we can get non-cooperative game payments for taxpayer expectations of r * [TP + * (TD-TP) + ic] + (1-r) * (TP + ic) and tax inspectors' expectations of r * [TP + * (TD-TP) -IC] + (1-r) * (TP-IC) as shown in Table3.

According to the expected utility theory of non-cooperative game, we can know that when the taxpayer chooses the total illegal expenditure, the taxpayer will choose to be illegal; when the taxpayer chooses the total illegal expenditure, the taxpayer will choose not to be illegal. When the total benefit of the tax inspectors to choose the inspection is greater, the tax inspectors will choose not to inspect, and the tax inspectors will choose not to inspect. The Nash equilibria of the available game are as follows:

Table 3. Analysis table of Dynamic non-cooperative Game Model.

Game subject		Tax inspectors	
taxpayer	break the law (q)	check (p)	No inspection (1-p)
		r *[TP + α * (TD -TP) + ic] + (1-r) * (TP + ic), r *[TP + α * (TD -TP) -IC] + (1-r) * (TP -IC)	TP + ic,TP
	Non-illegal (1-q)	TD,TD -IC	TD,TD

When r * [TP + * (TD-TP) -IC] + (1-r) * (TP-IC) = TP, the solution is given:

$$IC = r * (1 + \alpha) * (TD - TP) \tag{7}$$

Therefore, when the audit cost of tax inspectors is IC > r * (1 +) * (TD-TP), r * [TP + * (TD-TP) -IC] + (1-r) * (TP-IC) > TP for taxpayers, and the T > T-IC; when the tax inspectors choose not to audit, TD > TP + ic, so the taxpayer should choose illegal, and there is a unique Nash equilibrium (Y11, Y22).

When the inspection cost of tax inspectors is IC < r * (1 +) * (TD-TP), there is no Nash equilibrium, and the mixed strategy equilibrium of both sides needs to be solved. For taxpayers, the aim is to minimize the total expenditure, namely, F (p, q, r) = (1-p) * [(1-q) * TD + q * TD] + p * {(1-q) * (TP + ic)) + q * {r * [TD + * (TD-TP) + ic] + (1-r) * (TP + ic)}} then F (p, q, r) Seek guidance, can get F (p, q, r) ' = -TD + TP + ic + q * r * (1 +) * (TD-TP) = 0, solved to:

$$q' = (TD - TP - ic)/r * (1 + \alpha) * (TD - TP) \tag{8}$$

That is, if the probability of tax inspectors choosing inspection is less than q ', then the taxpayer will choose to break the law, if the probability of tax inspectors choosing inspection is greater than q ', then the taxpayer will choose not to break the law, if the probability of tax inspectors choosing inspection is equal to q ', the taxpayer can choose whether to be illegal or not.

For tax inspectors, the purpose is to maximize the overall benefit, namely F (p, q, r) = (1-q) * [(1-p) * TD + p * TP] + q * {(1-p) * (TD-IC)) + p * {r * [TD + * (TD-TP) -IC] + (1-r) * (TP-IC)}} to obtain the minimum value of F (p, q, r) Seek guidance, can get F (p, q, r) ' = -IC + p * r * (1 +) * (TD-TP) = 0, solved to:

$$p' = IC/ r * (1 + \alpha) * (TD - TP) \tag{9}$$

That is, when the probability of the taxpayer choosing to break the law is less than the p ', the tax inspectors should choose to inspect; otherwise, the taxpayer should choose not to inspect. When the probability is equal to the p ', they can choose the inspection or not.

3   Analysis of the Basic Conclusion of the Model

As it is difficult to find the tax audit data for 2018–2020, so the text selects the data in the 2015–2018 tax audit Yearbook, namely the data of 2014–2017. Moreover, it is also difficult to find the inspection data of the tax inspection department of Changchun

Taxation Bureau. However, Changchun city is the provincial capital of Jilin Province, and its various indicators, such as tax revenue, the supplementary tax amount and the number of people set, account for a large and highly representative proportion. Therefore, according to the tax inspection data of Jilin Province in 2014–2017, the tax inspection data of Changchun city in 2014–2017 is estimated, so as to study the specific situation and risks of the tax inspection department of Changchun Tax Bureau. According to the analysis results of the above static non-cooperative game model and the dynamic non-cooperative game model and the relevant data of Jilin Province, the conclusions can be drawn.

3.1 The Inspection and Subsidy Capacity of Changchun Tax Department Has Been Improved year by year

The inspection and compensation ability of the tax department of Changchun has improved year by year, so the risk of tax inspection and law enforcement brought by the insufficient inspection ability is low. According to the above game model analysis, it can be learned that the total benefit of the tax inspection department is affected by the difference between the tax payable by the taxpayer and the amount actually paid by the taxpayer, namely TD-TP, also referred to as tax loss [5]. The greater the difference between the tax payable by the taxpayer and the amount actually paid by the taxpayer, the stronger the necessity for the tax inspection department to choose inspection; the smaller the difference between the tax payable by the taxpayer and the actual amount paid by the taxpayer, the weaker the necessity for the tax inspection department to choose inspection. Therefore, the inspection and compensation ability of the tax inspection department of Changchun city is increasing year by year, as shown in Table 4.

It can be seen that the tax revenue of the tax inspection department of Changchun Taxation Bureau from 2014 to 2017 was 32.03 billion yuan, 30.00 billion yuan, 30.99 billion yuan and 34.01 billion yuan respectively. There was no obvious rule in the tax revenue change in the four years, and the difference was less than 2 billion yuan. The total number of direct inspection and organization enterprise self-inspection and compensation income increased year by year from 2014 to 2016, and decreased in 2017. However, as the tax revenue of Changchun city in 2017 decreased compared with 2016, the decline in the total number and compensation income of direct inspection and organization enterprises can be explained. From 2014 to 2017, the difference between the inspection and subsidy income and the storage trend decreased year by year, and in 2016 and 2017, all the storage revenues were realized. It can be concluded that although the tax loss of Changchun city in increasing year by year, means that the Changchun city tax inspection department still can operate space, but the tax inspection department inspection ability is increasing, so Changchun city tax bureau tax inspection department face due to the lack of ability and risk is smaller, but also can't completely relax.

Table 4. Table of Changchun Tax Inspection Department

		a particular year							
		2014	2015	2016	2017	2014	2015	2016	2017
		Jilin Province				Changchun City			
Tax revenue (RMB 100 million)		884.40	867.10	872.95	853.95	320.30	300.00	309.90	340.10
						36.22%	34.60%	35.50%	39.83%
Tax inspection and compensation situation	Total number of direct inspection and organized enterprise self-inspection (households)	4044	6873	6959	5525	1465	2378	2470	2200
	Check the income (100 million)	29.20	38.43	44.85	36.58	10.58	13.30	15.92	14.57
	Warehousing (100 million yuan)	27.37	38.34	44.85	36.58	9.91	13.26	15.92	14.57
	The difference between checking income and warehousing (RMB 100 million)					0.67	0.04	0	0

Data source: China Tax Inspection Yearbook 2014–2017 data.

3.2 The Tax Inspection Cost of Changchun Taxation Bureau is Lower than the National Level

The tax inspection cost of Changchun Tax Bureau is lower than the national level, and the tax inspection risk brought by the inspection cost is relatively small. Based on the above analysis results of the above static non-cooperative game model and the dynamic non-cooperative game model, the inspection cost of the tax inspection department is obtained, that is, the IC is positively correlated with the probability of the taxpayer choosing the law. When the inspection cost of the tax inspection department increases, the higher the probability of breaking the law, the lower the probability of choosing against the tax inspection department, the lower the probability of the taxpayer choosing the law, and the higher the probability of choosing not breaking the law.

Therefore, the study of the specific situation of tax inspection of Changchun Tax Bureau in Jilin Province needs to study its inspection cost. Generally speaking, the inspection cost mainly includes two aspects. One is the fixed cost, and the other is the non-fixed cost. Fixed costs mainly include the expenses incurred by the tax inspection department of the tax bureau in its daily work, including the wages and salaries of the staff, the water and electricity charges generated in its daily work, and the necessary office supplies such as computers, paper and pens in their daily work. Fixed costs are generally not easily affected by other factors. Non-fixed costs include time cost, information cost, risk cost, etc. This paper mainly represents the time cost of the tax inspection department of Changchun Taxation Bureau, Jilin Province by the number of inspections per capita, so as to reflect its non-fixed cost, as shown in Table 5.

Table 5. The Comparison Table of Changchun City and the National Tax Inspection Situation

nationwide	a particular year			
	2014	2015	2016	2017
Direct inspection and organization of enterprise self-inspection total number (ten thousand households)	5.95	12.38	11.82	15.81
Number of personnel (person)	82334	80154	79239	79158
Number of inspections per capita (ten thousand households)	0.7	1.5	1.5	2.0
Jilin Province	a particular year			
	2014	2015	2016	2017
Total number of direct inspection and organized enterprise self-inspection(households)	1465	2378	2470	2200
Number of personnel (person)	814	705	776	848
Inspection quantity per capita (household)	1.8	3.4	3.2	2.6

It can be concluded that between 2014 and 2017, the per capita number of inspections in China was 7,000,15,000,15,000 and 20,000, respectively, and the per capita number of inspections in Jilin Province was 18,000,34,000,32,000 and 26,000, respectively. Both the national per capita inspections and the provincial per capita inspections were increasing year by year, with the per capita inspections in Jilin Province decreasing in 2017 and higher than the national levels in 2014–2017.

With the reform of the collection and management system and the merger of the national tax bureau and the local tax bureau, the fixed cost of the tax inspection department of the Changchun Tax Bureau in Jilin Province will also be reduced. Therefore, it can be concluded that the inspection cost of the tax inspection department of Changchun Taxation Bureau is lower and lower than the national level. Therefore, it can also be concluded that the tax inspection department of Changchun Taxation Bureau is faced with less law enforcement risk brought by the inspection cost, but it can not be ignored.

3.3 The Tax Inspection Department of Changchun Taxation Bureau Does not Punish Taxpayers Enough for Illegal Behaviours Enough

The tax inspection department of Changchun Taxation Bureau does not punish taxpayers enough for illegal acts, which brings risks to the tax inspection and law enforcement in Changchun. According to the above game model analysis, it can be known that the punishment intensity of the tax inspection department on taxpayers' illegal behavior is negatively related to the probability of taxpayers choosing illegal behavior. When the greater the fine of the tax inspection department, the lower the probability of taxpayers choosing not breaking the law, the higher the probability of choosing not breaking the law, the higher the probability, the lower the probability of choosing not breaking the law. Among the major illegal cases investigated and dealt with in Changchun in the first half of 2020, most of them received administrative penalties of 500,000 yuan, but the amount of money involved in these illegal and criminal cases is very different, which makes the tax inspection department of Changchun Taxation Bureau not punish enough for taxpayers who choose illegal cases to form a deterrent effect. Therefore, it is necessary to pay attention to the law enforcement risk risks caused by the insufficient punishment for illegal acts.

By establishing a game model between tax authorities and taxpayers, and analyzing the static non cooperative game and dynamic non cooperative game between Changchun tax authorities and taxpayers, it is concluded that the inspection subsidy capacity of Changchun tax authorities has been improved year by year, the tax inspection cost of Changchun tax bureau is lower than the national level, and the tax inspection department of Changchun tax bureau has not adequately punished taxpayers for illegal acts.

References

1. Olaoye, C.O., Ekundayo, A.T.: Effects of tax audit on tax compliance and remittance of tax revenue in ekiti state. Open J. Account. **8**(1) (2019)
2. Blaufus, K., Schndube, J., Wielenbergs, R.: Strategic interactions between tax and statutory auditors and different information regimes:Implications for tax audit efficiency. arqus Discussion Papers in Quantitative Tax Research (2020)
3. Battiston, P., Duncan, D., Gamba, S., Santoro, A.: Audit publicity and tax compliance:a natural experiment. The Scandinavian J. Econ. **122**(1) (2020)
4. Guangqiang, L., Yisihong, Z.: The internal mechanism and Countermeasures of big data driven Tax Governance. Tax Res. **2018**(04), 114–119 (2018)
5. Huan, H.: A feasible path to control tax inspection risks in the big data era. Econ. Res. Refer. **2018**(30), 26–27 (2018)

Research on the Challenges and Countermeasures of Tax Collection and Administration Under the Digital Economy

Zhang Xinyue[✉] and Jing Shuang

Changchun University of Finance and Economics, JiLin 130000, China
zxy15546327003@163.com

Abstract. With the rapid development of China's economy, as well as the rapid progress of cloud computing, big data, blockchain, 5G and other information technologies. These new technologies gradually applied in the work of enterprises and governments, which provides a good foundation for the rapid development of digital economy. As one of the important state organs, the taxation department has been gradually exploring the path of departmental reform under the digital economy, but in this context, it has to speed up the pace of exploration and keep up with the development of The Times. Tax collection and administration is the core work of the tax department. Exploring the challenges and optimization paths of tax collection and administration under the digital economy is conducive to the current and long-term development of the tax department.

Keyword: Digital economy · Tax collection and administration · Blockchain

1 The Logical Relationship Between Digital Economy and Tax Collection and Administration

1.1 The Logical Relationship Between Digital Economy and Tax Collection and Administration

The Digital Economy Forces a Change in Tax Collection and Administration. With the continuous development of the digital economy, its core technologies, such as big data, cloud computing, 5G, the Internet of Things and other information and communication technologies, have entered thousands of enterprises. Enterprises have made leapfrog progress with these emerging technologies, but also led some enterprises to use these technologies to hide and evade tax obligations, pay less or no taxes. Although tax authorities are also taking advantage of the digital economy to continuously promote their own technology and improve smart tax, their progress is far from enough, and not fundamentally get rid of the traditional tax pattern. So in such circumstances, the development of the digital economy forces tax collection and administration to change.

Tax Collection and Administration to Promote the Further Development of the Digital Economy. Tax collection administration, referred to as tax collection and administration, refers to the general term of the organization, management and inspection of the tax collection process by the state tax collection authorities in accordance with the provisions of the tax law and administration Law and other relevant laws and regulations. Generally speaking, there are three major links of tax collection and management, namely, collection, management and inspection. The promotion of tax collection and administration to the development of digital economy is also reflected in the three major links. From the perspective of collection, one of the most important principles of China's tax is "from the people and for the people" enrich the fiscal revenue through tax collection, so that it can have sufficient funds to build and maintain important information technology means to support the development of digital economy. From the perspective of management and inspection, as the "last mile" to ensure tax revenue into the national finance; on the other hand, tax management and inspection can crack down on tax-related laws and crimes, maintain the business environment under digital economy and provide a fair competition environment for taxpayers, so as to promote the healthy development of digital economy.

2 Challenges of Tax Collection and Management Under Digital Economy

2.1 The Traditional Tax System Structure Needs to be Optimized and Transformed

The New Profits are Difficult to Determined. With the emergence and development of new industries such as e-commerce, we-media and short video, the generation path of original profits has changed. The original profit is derived by the income of the enterprise minus the cost, whether the income or the cost, the tax authorities in addition to checking the accounting books of the enterprise, "tax control by ticket" is a powerful means of the tax authorities. Through the inspection of relevant bills, especially invoices, we can almost accurately check the cost and income of the enterprise, so as to accurately obtain its profits, and then calculate the tax basis of the enterprise. The new profits also generate more "user traffic", which is difficult to accurately verify the path. In this path, the most important force to provide and create value is network users. Since network users provide the number of views and clicks for related content, which indirectly create profits for related enterprises but do not directly participate in their transactions, this new type of profits, namely hidden profits, is difficult to be accurately verified. Therefore, it is very necessary for tax authorities to move forward from "tax control by ticket" and "information management tax" to "data management tax".

More Natural Person Businesses. The continuous development of digital economy has attracted many natural subjects to join the merchants. In addition to the natural persons who entered the online trading platform in the original form of e-commerce, more and more natural persons also become online transactions through live broadcast, live delivery, small video shopping cart, circle of friends and other ways. This leads to a series of problems. First of all, most of the natural persons in e-commerce do not have tax registration, so it is quite difficult for the tax authorities to manage and identify the tax payers. Secondly, the products provided by these natural persons are not all tangible products, and there are many intangible products, namely digital products and services, such as platform members, game equipment, game generation, etc. This makes the tax authorities are already difficult to manage the situation worse.

2.2 New Requirements for the Acquisition of Tax-Related Information

Information Sharing with Third-party Payment Platforms and Financial Institutions Needs to be Deepened. Digital economy mode of transaction is more convenient and hidden, the traditional cash payment and bank transfer is not most small and medium-sized operators such as individual industrial and commercial households and natural person mainstream payment method, and through the third-party payment platform payment method gradually become the primary choice, which makes it more difficult for the tax authorities to obtain tax subject tax-related information. Although a tax-related information sharing mechanism between tax authorities and third-party payment platforms and financial institutions has been gradually established, there are still many problems in practical operation. First, the tax authorities and third-party payment platforms share less and less information; second, when tax authorities need to obtain deeper tax-related information, they will miss the golden period of law enforcement, which may provide taxpayers with the opportunity to destroy evidence and even escape. Finally, third-party payment platforms and financial institutions to protect customers. The purpose of the tax authorities is to ensure that the tax can enter the fiscal revenue in time and in full. Therefore, due to the different purposes of the two sides, there will be third-party payment platforms and financial institutions not cooperating.

It is Difficult for "Control Tax by Votes" to Function in the Digital Economy. On the one hand, the traditional entity invoice is difficult to meet the actual needs of the business entities under the digital economy, and many enterprises also take the opportunity to avoid fulfilling tax obligations, so electronic invoices emerged at the historic moment. On the other hand, although the electronic invoice solved the part of the entity invoice, but due to the differences of electronic invoice technology and business standards, make the current electronic invoice actual application difference is bigger, regions cannot the electronic invoice collection analysis processing, thus affect the electronic invoice work, and affect the development of electronic invoice. In addition, there is no special platform to obtain taxpayers' transaction data and complete invoice issuance, which will undoubtedly make it difficult for tax authorities to play a role in "controlling tax by ticket" in the background of digital economy.

2.3 The Lack of Professional Talent

Few Tax Professionals. On the one hand, the educational structure of tax collectors in some areas is poor. Most of the tax collection and administration personnel are college graduates without relevant qualifications, while there are fewer tax collection and administration personnel with graduate degree or above or with qualification certificates [1]. Even some areas in the recruitment of tax personnel, only recruit undergraduate degree, and do not recruit graduate degree. This makes the basic professional quality of some tax authorities is not high, and their learning ability is also poor. On the other hand, due to the reform of China's tax structure and the constantly changing tax policies, tax collection and administration personnel have more learning content and greater learning pressure, and it is difficult to timely respond to new knowledge, new technology, new content and new situation.

Few Information and Data Application Talents. On the one hand, it is difficult for tax authorities in some regions to effectively recruit talents related to computer science and digital economy majors, most of whom are engaged in other industries, which fundamentally leads to very few talents among tax authorities who can be skilled in applying information and data and understand the digital economy. On the other hand, the age structure of tax collectors in some regions tends to be "aging". Generally speaking, these people have high professional quality and rich experience, but limited by age, it difficult for them to accept new things or slow to learn slowly, so it is difficult to meet the corresponding standards for the application of computer and data.

3 Optimization Path of Tax Collection and Administration Under Digital Economy

3.1 Optimize the Tax Structure and Improve the Tax System

mprove Laws and Regulations Related to Tax Collection and Administration of the Digital Economy. First, laws and regulations related to tax collection and administration of digital economy must be integrated and their legal level upgraded [2]. To improve the level of the legal basis of tax collection and administration of digital economy, it is necessary to accelerate the legislative process of digital economy and tax collection and administration. Generally speaking, we can start from the formulation of tax entity law and the promotion of tax procedure law. Secondly, the following contents should be clearly defined in the relevant laws and regulations. First, it is clear how to register and declare tax payers with natural persons as merchants, especially how tax authorities should supervise them. The second is to determine the boundary between tangible products and intangible products, clarify the tax calculation basis and applicable tax rate of intangible products, and determine the corresponding tax rate, tax calculation method and tax preferences according to the specific tax items. Third, it makes clear the basis and calculation method of the new profit. The new profit indirectly generated by user traffic, user browsing and user click is also taken as the basis for tax calculation. Because it is difficult to measure and calculate the new profit, what way to quantify it has become the top priority. Fourth, clarify the responsibilities of third-party payment platforms and financial institutions, including the withholding responsibility and the responsibility of providing tax-related information to tax authorities. It should be noted that the information provided by third-party payment platforms and financial institutions must be processed objective tax information and desensitization information, rather than original information.

Strengthen the Tax Collection and Administration of Natural Person. Individual income tax is a kind of direct tax closely related to the broad masses, which plays an important role in regulating the income gap of residents, reducing the gap between the rich and the poor and realizing common prosperity. Different from other taxes, personal income tax can be said to be a kind of tax closely related to most people, and it is also the most concerned by the public. At the end of 2018, China carried out the reform of the individual income tax system, and moved the classification collection to the "classification + comprehensive" collection method, which further realized the convenience, benefit and benefit of the people [3]. However, there are still problems in the structure of the individual income tax system, and it should continue to be improved. For example, under the background of the rapid development of digital economy, more and more natural persons have become businesses and taxpayers, but the matching tax collection and administration regulations are still missing. Both the income obtained by traditional natural persons and the income obtained by natural persons relying on information technology and other platforms under the digital economy are closely related to personal income tax. Therefore, the issues related to the tax collection and management of natural persons under the digital economy are undoubtedly the issues that should be paid attention to in the personal income tax reform.

3.2 Promote Digital Construction Process of Tax Collection and Administration

Establish a Digital Tax Bureau. First, the construction of the electronic tax bureau in each region should establish regional characteristics on the basis of the national unified construction and regulations. Different regions have different development conditions and different regional particularity, so the electronic tax bureau must "seek common ground while reserving differences". Second, the electronic tax bureau applies the latest digital technology to upgrade, so that it is highly intelligent. On the basis of signing the confidentiality agreement, we can cooperate with professional technicians or enterprises to enrich the electronic tax bureau with the latest information technology [4]. Third, the electronic tax bureau should share social and economic data to the greatest extent. Above mentioned to establish tax authorities and third-party payment platform and financial institutions information sharing mechanism, but in addition to the third-party payment platform and financial institutions, should also strengthen the tax authorities and, customs, public security organs, audit institutions, real estate management center, court and other third-party data platform of information sharing, only in this way can effectively data integration, data group, expand information sharing, improve information sharing speed, improve the utilization rate of data information. Fourth, the electronic tax bureau should have the most advanced technology but also have the network security management and quality management ability. On the one hand, the tax authorities, as the leader of the information sharing of the electronic tax bureau, should protect the relevant tax-related information. On the other hand, "the network is not outside the law", the electronic tax bureau should have the responsibility similar to the "Internet police", effectively supervise and manage the online transactions, and timely report to the police in case the relevant online activities are abnormal.

Define the Importance of Data. Although China has entered the mature stage of "information management tax", the main basis of —— information sharing of tax collection and management is still in the state of external sharing. This passive tax collection and management mode is difficult to adapt to the rapid development of digital economy, nor to adapt to the diverse and hidden tax evasion behaviors of taxpayers, and even more difficult to achieve the fair, efficient and comprehensive responsibilities of tax authorities. Therefore, in order to realize that to make data sharing play a role, tax authorities must break down departmental, industrial, regional and even national barriers, and form a huge tax database that is all-inclusive and incompatible. The formation of the huge tax database to rely on laws and regulations and the latest digital technology spending, can say the concept mentioned here is to optimize the structure of perfect tax system and promote the construction of tax collection and administration of preliminary ideas and logic, and optimize tax structure to improve the tax system and promote the construction of digital is the extension of clear "data tube tax" core [5].

3.3   Recruit and Train Digital Economy Professionals

Improve the Incentive Mechanism.   Effective and reasonable assessment, reward and punishment mechanism can stimulate the learning motivation of tax personnel, and it is an essential way to speed up the construction of talent team of tax authorities. The establishment of a reasonable assessment and incentive mechanism should be divided into the following parts: First, in order to improve the learning effect of tax personnel, the online and offline learning time and training times should be reasonably stipulated, and the learning time and training times of each tax personnel should be summarized every week. Online tests will be set up twice a week, and the ranking will be calculated directly after the test, so as to urge tax officials to constantly improve their professional ability. Set the minimum score limit, criticize the tax personnel who fail to meet the score standards, praise the top tax personnel and provide appropriate physical rewards, and then urge the tax personnel to strengthen the study of professional content. Secondly, the relevant professional certificates obtained by tax personnel are linked to their promotion and salary increase, especially the high-quality qualification certificates such as certified public accountants and tax accountants, which are closely related to tax professionals [6]. Finally, the incentive, reward and punishment mechanism should not only serve the tax professional knowledge, but also pay attention to the related skills of digital application, especially computer application, and encourage tax personnel to learn new technologies through the reward and punishment mechanism, so as to realize the promotion of the whole talent team of tax authorities and increase the number of tax talents related to digital economy.

Optimize the Training Methods.   The rapid development of digital economy further requires tax personnel to have a higher ability to use computers and network technology [7]. The age structure of tax collectors of tax authorities in some regions tends to be "aging". Generally speaking, these people have high professional quality and rich experience, but limited by age, it difficult for them to accept new things or slow to learn slowly, so it is difficult to meet the corresponding standards for the application of computer and data. Therefore, it is necessary to focus on improving the computer application ability and digital means application level of these tax personnel. Therefore, a mutual team can be formed by "bringing the old with the old and the old with the old", where young but less experienced tax personnel introduce the use of computers and Internet to older and solve difficult problems at any time; and older but more experienced tax personnel teach young but less experienced tax personnel.

From the perspective of tax collection and management of China's tax departments, the development of digital economy has promoted the reform of tax collection and management of China's tax departments, greatly improved the efficiency of tax collection and management, and thus improved the service quality of the tax departments. Due to the absence and imperfection of tax laws and regulations, the mismatch between data collection and development process, the low digital application means of tax authorities, and the lack of digital economy talent training channels, the tax authorities are faced with challenges such as the optimization and transformation of the traditional tax system structure, new requirements for tax related information acquisition, the single taxation mode and means of tax authorities, and the lack of digital economy related tax talents, It needs to be improved by optimizing the tax system structure, improving the tax system, promoting the digital construction process of tax collection and management, changing the focus of the traditional tax collection and management mode, and recruiting and cultivating digital economy professionals.

References

1. Lawrence, E., Garner, B.: Harmonizing global internet tax: a collaborative extranet model (1999)
2. Hungerford, T.L., Gravelle, J.G.: Business investment and employment tax incentives to stimulate the economy. Library of Congress: Congressional Research Service (2010)
3. Berdieva, U.: Digital technologies as a factor of increasing the efficiency of tax administration. Int. Financ. Account., 8 (2019)
4. Xiangju, L., Shuo, L., Qin, Y.: International experience and policy suggestions of tax collection and administration system under the background of digital economy. Econ. Syst. Reform, 156–163 (2020)
5. Jiaxi, Y., Hu, C.: On the positive interaction between domestic tax law and international tax law in the era of digital economy. Tax Res., 91–95 (2020)
6. Min, W., Minjiao, P.: Influence of digital economy development on the main behavior of tax collection and policy suggestions. Econ. Horizonta (08), 193–199 (2020)
7. Wang, L.: The opportunities and challenges of the digital transformation of tax collection and administration under the digital economy. Int. Taxation (12), 65–70 (2021)

Financial Pressure, Efficiency of Tax Collection and Administration and Regional Heterogeneity
Take the "2018 Consolidation of State and Local Taxes" as an Example

Cunhui Jia[✉]

Harbin University of Commerce, Harbin 150028, Heilongjiang, China
2316140887@qq.com

Abstract. Based on the quasi-natural experiment of "the combination of state and local taxes in 2018" and the generalized double difference model, this paper discusses whether there is regional heterogeneity in the impact of the policy of "the combination of state and local taxes" on the changes in the impact of tax collection efficiency on local financial pressure. The experimental results show that under the policy impact of "the combination of state and local taxes", the efficiency of tax collection and administration has a significant impact on local financial pressure, and education and science expenditure in livelihood expenditure has a significant effect on relieving financial pressure, while culture and health expenditure have no significant effect on relieving financial pressure. However, the effect of tax collection and administration efficiency on relieving financial pressure is not different in different regions with different levels of economic development. Therefore, in order to relieve the local financial pressure, the local government should, based on effectively improving the efficiency of tax collection and management, integrating the tax collection and management process, and perfecting the modern tax collection and management system, focus on broadening the channels of financial revenue, cultivating potential tax sources, and improving the efficiency of the use of financial funds.

Keywords: Financial Pressure · the Efficiency of Tax Collection and Administration · Fiscal Expenditure Structure

1 Introduction

In 2015, the State Council issued the "Plan for Deepening the Reform of Tax Collection and Administration System of State and Local Taxes", which proposed to build a modern tax collection and administration system, improve the efficiency of tax collection and administration, reduce collection costs, better serve taxpayers and ensure the effective exertion of tax functions. Compared with the 1994 tax-sharing reform to mobilize the enthusiasm of local taxation and safeguard the central government revenue, the combination of state and local taxes in 2018 is a collection of tax resources based on the

A. Li et al. (Eds.): 6GN 2022, LNICST 504, pp. 269–279, 2023.
https://doi.org/10.1007/978-3-031-36011-4_24

reform of modern tax collection and management system. The similarities lie in that they all serve the needs of the times. Although the direction of change is different, the ultimate goal of change is closely related to the overall economic development of the society. So how much impact will the combination of state and local taxes have on the efficiency of tax collection and management, and how much will the local fiscal pressure change? Will the financial pressure on local governments with different levels of economic development change after the merger of national and local taxes in combination with the changes in the intensity of tax collection and administration? This is the main issue to be discussed in this paper.

On the basis of introducing the policy background, based on the panel data of 31 provinces in China from 2007 to 2020, this paper uses the generalized double difference method to assess the impact of the changes in tax collection efficiency on fiscal pressure after the merger of national and local taxes, taking the "merger of national and local taxes" as a quasi-natural experiment, and discusses the impact in groups according to the different levels of economic development. The results show that the effect of tax collection efficiency on local financial pressure is significantly negative, that is, with the improvement of tax collection efficiency, financial pressure will be reduced to a certain extent. However, this effect is not obvious in regions with different levels of economic development.

This paper holds that after the merger of the State and Local Taxation Bureau, the relevant work of the Local Taxation Bureau will be brought into the overall management of the State Taxation Bureau. On the one hand, it may affect the efficiency of tax collection and management in different regions with different levels of economic development. On the other hand, as the non-tax revenue originally collected by local financial departments and other institutions after the merger of the State and Local Taxation Bureau will be collected and managed by the tax department, it may have a direct impact on local financial revenue and an indirect impact on local financial pressure.

Based on the above analysis, the following assumptions are proposed:

Hypothesis 1: The change in tax collection efficiency caused by the combination of state and local taxes has a significant impact on local financial pressure.

Hypothesis 2: The effect of tax collection efficiency on fiscal pressure will vary with different levels of economic development.

This paper has the following marginal contributions: First, it takes "the combination of national and local taxes" as a quasi-natural experiment to discuss the impact on the local government's financial pressure; Secondly, when discussing the effect of the efficiency of tax collection and administration on the financial pressure, the fiscal expenditure structure is taken as a consideration, trying to discuss the corresponding change of the financial pressure caused by the different fiscal expenditure structure; Third, different from domestic research on financial pressure and efficiency of tax collection and management, it tends to include corporate tax behavior for correlation analysis. This paper studies the relationship between efficiency of tax collection and management and local financial pressure from the perspective of the government.

The rest of this paper is structured as follows: The second part reviews the literature; The third part constructs the theoretical mechanism; The fourth part and the fifth part set up and test the model; The sixth part is the conclusion analysis. Due to the limitation of data availability, the model setting is somewhat inadequate in this paper, the experimental conclusions are limited, and the corresponding results need to be further improved.

2 Literature Review

In the study of the formation of financial pressure, it is generally believed that the formation of financial pressure is related to the level of economic development, the degree of national autonomy, the level of income collection and management technology, government functions and other factors. Tax efforts have strategic imitation competition among regions, and the transmission of fiscal pressure has strategic substitution with local tax efforts [1]. Promotion incentive has more obvious impact on the collection and management of large enterprises, non-state-owned enterprises and municipal enterprises [2]. Fiscal pressure will curb the fiscal absorptive capacity of local governments through effectiveness and standardization. And this kind of influence will be different because of the degree of decentralization and the influence of intergovernmental competition [3].

Most scholars believe that financial pressure has a certain positive effect on improving the efficiency of tax collection and management, and this effect will be transmitted through corporate tax avoidance behavior: Tax collection and management departments to improve the degree of tax collection efforts is the main reason to promote the growth of tax revenue [4]. The change of local government will improve the tax collection and administration of tax authorities [5], and local officials mainly influence the effective tax rate of enterprises by strengthening the tax inspection within their respective jurisdictions [6]. The greater the financial pressure, the lower the degree of tax avoidance, and mainly exists in private enterprises [7]. Financial pressure has a significant impact on the operating performance of micro-enterprises, and this impact is transmitted by influencing the financial pressure to urge the tax authorities to improve the degree of tax efforts, and enterprises will be more likely to evade taxes and reduce financing constraints [8]. In conclusion, from the financial pressure to the transmission mechanism of tax collection and management, most of them take corporate tax behavior as the intermediate research object and tax collection and management as the secondary effect research.

However, some scholars believe that improving the level of tax collection and administration can alleviate the local financial pressure. However, improving the level of tax collection and administration may not necessarily effectively alleviate the financial pressure: Local government will increase the actual tax burden on enterprises, thus transferring the financial pressure faced by some governments, but will lead to more tax evasion by enterprises, while the level of local tax collection and administration has not actually improved [9]. The improvement in the level of tax collection and administration will have a certain inhibitory effect on the illegal tax avoidance behavior of private enterprises with political status in the region, and thus will have a certain effect on alleviating the financial pressure [10]. The "multiplier effect" brought into play by tax collection and management will be transmitted to the regional economic development due to the difference in fiscal pressure among regions, which will further expand the difference in GDP per capita among regions [11].

In conclusion, when studying the interaction between the efficiency of tax collection and management and financial pressure, it is limited to the availability of data. Domestic research mostly focuses on the change of corporate tax burden under the influence of financial pressure, in which tax collection and management plays a conductive role. And think that the impact of financial pressure on the efficiency of tax collection and management is mostly considered to be a positive impact, that is, the greater the financial pressure faced by the local government, the corresponding tax department's tax collection and management efficiency will be improved to a certain extent, or the tax department's tax efforts will be relatively improved. There are few studies on the analysis of financial pressure and tax collection and management from the perspective of non-enterprise tax behavior.

3   Theoretical Mechanism

The procedures and means of tax collection and administration are directly affected by the central government. The procedures are consistent across the country and there is no regional heterogeneity. However, in terms of changes in financial pressure, provinces and cities have different problems that need to be solved urgently, and local financial departments have different priorities. In order to achieve the goals set by the higher authorities, the local government will significantly increase the overall financial pressure of the government by increasing the expenditure on education. However, different regions with different economic levels pay different costs if they fail to reach the policy objectives of their superiors [3]. Secondly, the focus of local government investment in related industries is different, which also affects the source of tax revenue of related industries. There is a lag effect in the use of fiscal expenditure funds. The change in the proportion of local finance expenditure in various fields will affect the development trend of this field in the next few years. When the government is under financial pressure, it will selectively contract and relax its spending on people's livelihood, and it will tighten its spending on technological innovation and the introduction of human capital [12]. Thirdly, each province has different areas of tax revenue growth under different situations of the subsequent development priorities of different provinces, and as the areas of financial capital tend to cultivate and stabilize new tax revenue growth points, that is, the local government's resource endowments will affect the local government's choice of livelihood expenditure areas for key arrangements. When local governments face financial pressure, the quality of public services will be significantly reduced, and this transmission relationship is achieved through the change in the structure of fiscal expenditures [13], which also confirms that the change in the structure of fiscal expenditures when local governments change the input of fiscal funds will lead to a series of effects in the development of public services and subsequent industrial development.

4   Sample Selection and Data Sources

4.1   Sample Selection

In this paper, the main data sources are the provincial databases and local statistical yearbooks. The relevant data of 31 provinces and cities in China from 2007 to 2020 are screened, the influencing factors of local financial pressure are screened, and indicators are selected to form a model.

4.2 Data Sources

This paper studies the effect of tax collection efficiency on local financial pressure, with tax collection efficiency as the main explanatory variable and other factors affecting local financial pressure as the control variable. As the local industrial structure and economic development foundation significantly affect the local fiscal revenue, indirectly affect the change of local fiscal pressure. Therefore, the control variables mainly select indicators that represent the fiscal expenditure structure and the level of economic development, effectively covering the local government's investment in improving people's livelihood and development priorities. The structure of fiscal expenditure is measured by the proportion of people's livelihood expenditure in fiscal expenditure, and the level of economic development is measured by GDP per capita.

The following generalized double difference model is constructed:

$$pressure_{i,t} = \beta_0 + \beta_1 \times TF_{i,t} \times post_{i,t} + \beta_2 TF_{i,t} + \beta_3 educate_{i,t} + \beta_4 technology_{i,t} + \beta_5 culture_{i,t} + \beta_6 health_{i,t} + \beta_7 personGDP_{i,t} + \gamma_i + \delta_t + \varepsilon_{i,t}$$

$pressure_{i,t}$ represents the dependent variable in this paper, i.e. the financial pressure of local government i and t represent provinces and time, γ_i, δ_t represent fixed effects of regions and time, and $\varepsilon_{i,t}$ are random error terms.

As mentioned above, the impact of the policy impact of the combination of state and local taxes on the efficiency of tax collection and management, and the change in the impact between the efficiency of tax collection and management and the local financial pressure, $TF_{i,t} \times post_{i,t}$ as a continuous variable of policy intensity, is used to measure the level of tax collection and management efficiency faced by various provinces and cities after the "combination of state and local taxes". $post_{i,t}$ Represents the province and time dummy variable, and the time dummy variable is 1 in 2018 and beyond; otherwise, it is 0; And set group regression. Referring to Chen. (2016) research [14], the efficiency of tax collection and administration (TF) is measured by the proportion of actual tax revenue and expected tax revenue in each region. In the regression analysis, $post$ and TF are interacted to examine the influence of different tax collection levels on the change of local financial pressure. And control the following variables: efficiency of tax collection and administration (TF), proportion of education expenditure to fiscal expenditure $(educate)$, proportion of science expenditure to fiscal expenditure $(technology)$, proportion of culture expenditure to fiscal expenditure $(culture)$, proportion of health expenditure to fiscal expenditure $(health)$, per capita GDP$(person\ GDP)$, etc.

4.3 Balance Inspection

In order to test the rationality of the index selection in this paper, the balance test is carried out. The results of balance test show that the control variables selected in this paper are significantly different between the treatment group and the experimental group after they are grouped according to the level of economic development. Before the variables are controlled, there are significant differences in the impact of tax collection efficiency on local financial pressure between regions with different levels of economic development, and the differences are no longer significant after the variables are controlled.

5   Regression Results and Testing

5.1   Descriptive Statistical Analysis

Table 1 reports the descriptive statistical results of the main variables, from which it can be found that the average value of the *pressure* variable is 1.6321, which indicates that the financial pressure of each province and city is generally large. While the minimum value of *pressure* is 0.0517. The maximum value is 14.6214, which indicates that the financial pressures of 31 provinces and cities in China are different. Combining with the performance of *Person GDP*, it also indirectly reflects the imbalance of regional economic development and fiscal revenue and expenditure. The average tax collection efficiency index is 0.0100, which needs to be improved as a whole. In the analysis of the fiscal expenditure structure that affects the local fiscal pressure, the average proportion of expenditure on science and technology and culture is about 0.02, and the expenditure on education accounts for a large part of the people's livelihood expenditure, which is 0.16. The average share of health expenditure was 0.07, which was higher than the share of science and culture expenditure.

Table 1. Summary Statistics

Variable	Mean	Std. Dev	Min	Max
pressure	1.6321	1.9627	0.0517	14.6241
TF	0.0100	0.0023	0.0038	0.0173
educate	0.1631	0.0263	0.0990	0.2222
technology	0.0207	0.0148	0.0030	0.0720
culture	0.0200	0.0070	0.0099	0.0580
health	0.0713	0.0161	0.0377	0.1208
person GDP	10.4749	0.6933	7.4082	12.0086

5.2   Analysis of Regression Results

Table 2 (1) and (2) show the regression results of the effect of "State-Local Tax Consolidation" on the relationship between tax collection efficiency and local financial pressure, which is the regression of the effect of "State-Local Tax Consolidation" on financial pressure, and the regression of the effect of "State-Local Tax Consolidation" on tax collection efficiency and local financial pressure. The results show that when the provinces and cities are not grouped according to the level of economic development, the regression coefficient of continuous variables of policy intensity is negative, and it is significant at 1%. This shows that after controlling other factors, the change in the efficiency of tax collection and administration caused by the "merger of state and local taxes" event slowed down the financial pressure of the local government. The regression results support the logic that the change in tax collection efficiency caused by the combination of national and local taxes has slowed down the local financial pressure to a certain extent. Hypothesis 1 has been verified. On the one hand, the combination of national and local taxes has made the tax collection and management process clear and the scope clear, and the tax collection and management process has been improved towards integration and standardization; On the other hand, the combination of the state and local taxes relieves the local government from having to bear the salaries of the former local tax bureau personnel and reduces the local financial expenditure accordingly, thus easing the financial pressure.

Among the regression results of other variables, the regression coefficients of *educate*, *technology* and *Person GDP* are significantly negative at the confidence level of 0.01, indicating that the greater the education expenditure/science expenditure/GDP per capita, the smaller the financial pressure, the greater the investment in education, the more scientific investment, and the more economic development, the greater the mitigation effect on the local financial pressure, which is consistent with the reality. Local governments pay attention to education expenditure, research and development of science and technology, and economic development, not only to meet the needs of public services, but also to nurture local development. Effectively adjusting the future local industrial structure and the internal driving force of the economy from the perspective of fiscal expenditure structure will help cultivate high-quality tax sources with strong growth. The regression coefficient of *culture* is significantly positive at the confidence level of 0.01, which indicates that the more cultural expenditure is for people's livelihood, the greater the financial pressure. Cultural expenditure focuses on improving the overall cultural literacy level of the people, mostly for public welfare projects, with less revenue and less effect on relieving financial pressure. Cultural expenditure is similar to "pure public goods", spending in order to meet public demand, which brings less revenue and has no significant effect on relieving financial pressure.

The level of economic development will also affect the local financial pressure. To a certain extent, the level of economic development determines the revenue side of financial pressure: tax revenue. Areas with good economic development have a strong foundation for tax sources and strong revenue growth. On the contrary, the tax sources dried up and the tax growth rate gradually declined.

In order to test the effect of the "combination of national and local taxes" on the efficiency of tax collection and administration and local financial pressure in different regions with different levels of economic development, the interaction term of *TF* and *post* is introduced to analyze the changes of local financial pressure. According to the economic development level of each province and city, the 31 provinces and cities in the country are divided into three levels: better, better and general. (3)(5) The central and eastern regions are the control group, while the central, western and northeastern regions are the experimental group, indicating better: good; (4)(6) The central and eastern regions are the control group, while the western and northeastern regions are divided into the experimental group, indicating good: average. The regression results in Table 2 show that the effect of "State-Local Tax Consolidation" on the relationship between tax collection efficiency and local fiscal pressure in regions with different levels of economic development is not significant, indicating that the change in fiscal pressure caused by the change in tax collection efficiency in regions with different levels of economic development is not obvious and there is no difference between different regions. Assumption 2 is not true. However, the regression coefficients of tax collection efficiency, education expenditure proportion and GDP per capita are significantly negative at the level of 0.01. The regression coefficient of health expenditure is significant at 0.05 level.

(5)(6) The regression results show that the regression coefficients of the proportion of education expenditure are quite different, while the regression coefficients of health expenditure and GDP per capita are relatively small. It shows that in regions with different levels of economic development, the impact of education expenditure on the efficiency of tax collection and management and financial pressure is stronger in regions with good economic development level than in regions with normal economic development level. That is, in areas with better economic development, the greater the expenditure on education, the more significant the trend that the financial pressure will be relieved by the impact of the efficiency of tax collection and administration.

However, the regression coefficient of tax collection efficiency is significantly negative, indicating that the change in tax collection intensity has a significant effect on relieving financial pressure. Modern tax collection and management technology can

Table 2. Regression table

Variables	(1)	(2)	(3)	(4)	(5)	(6)
TF × post		−83.76***	0.180	0.136	−15.75	−14.32
		(30.37)	(0.122)	(0.118)	(11.82)	(11.63)
TF		−205.1***			−220.9***	−220.5***
		(20.62)			(20.30)	(20.29)
educate	−30.93***	−7.387***	−6.084**	−6.334**	−7.120***	−6.884***
	(3.365)	(2.212)	(2.535)	(2.543)	(2.226)	(2.233)
technology	−53.78***	2.239	0.986	2.213	4.558	3.584
	(5.963)	(4.576)	(5.082)	(5.333)	(4.508)	(4.699)
culture	41.43***	−7.476	−19.22**	−19.15**	−9.299	−9.648
	(12.64)	(6.851)	(7.790)	(7.830)	(6.904)	(6.935)
health	7.356	8.487**	18.51***	18.53***	7.617**	7.615**
	(5.718)	(3.489)	(3.829)	(3.833)	(3.506)	(3.508)
person GDP	−0.651***	−1.343***	−1.590***	−1.554***	−1.224***	−1.236***
	(0.126)	(0.266)	(0.309)	(0.307)	(0.271)	(0.270)
Constant	13.14***	18.62***	18.29***	17.95***	17.39***	17.50***
	(1.472)	(2.732)	(3.176)	(3.158)	(2.775)	(2.768)
Observations	434	434	434	434	434	434
R-squared	0.403	0.961	0.948	0.948	0.960	0.960

Standard errors in parentheses, *** $p < 0.01$, ** $p < 0.05$, * $p < 0.1$

effectively reduce the cost of tax compliance. Standardized and process-oriented tax collection and management is one of the most effective ways to ease financial pressure before the development of new tax sources.

The regression coefficient between scientific expenditure and cultural expenditure is not significant. The possible reason is that cultural expenditure can't play a role in relieving financial pressure, and the effect of scientific expenditure on relieving financial pressure lags behind, which needs to be studied in a longer time line.

5.3 Robustness Test

In order to verify the robustness of the conclusions of this study, the variables are tail-reduced. The regression results in Table 3 show that the regression coefficient of the continuous variable of policy intensity is significantly negative and the regression coefficient of tax collection efficiency is significantly negative after the tail reduction of explanatory variables and control variables, indicating that the "combination of national and local taxes" has a significant impact on the relationship between tax collection intensity and local financial pressure. The robustness test results show that, excluding the abnormal discrete values, there is no significant difference between the basic regression results and DID results, further strengthening the reliability of the basic regression conclusions.

Table 3. Robust Test

VARIABLES		VARIABLES	
TF × post	−49.06*** (17.65)	culture	−10.11*** (3.587)
TF	−67.97*** (11.17)	health	−5.120*** (1.758)
educate	−1.440 (1.034)	person GDP	−0.335*** (0.126)
technology	−10.66*** (2.247)		
Constant		6.670*** (1.297)	
Observations		338	
R-squared		0.978	

6 Conclusions

Taxation is an important tool for local government to organize local revenue and an important component of local fiscal revenue. However, the legislative power of tax revenue is vested in the central government, and the way of tax revenue sharing cannot be changed at will. Local governments can only supplement local fiscal revenue to maintain the provision of local public services by improving the performance of fiscal expenditure, effectively using debt funds and improving the efficiency of tax collection and management. The mandatory and unpaid nature of taxation in turn requires the government to provide matching public services. Among them, improving the efficiency of tax collection and administration can effectively increase the unnecessary waste of tax revenue, thus relieving the local financial pressure to a certain extent.

The regression results show that the local government's choice of ways to ease the financial pressure is related to the regional economic development, the financial expenditure structure also has an impact on the financial pressure, and the "state-land tax merger" as an event impact has a significant effect on the tax collection efficiency of 31 provinces and cities in the country, but this effect does not show regional heterogeneity. The first possible reason is that the narrowing of the financial pressure difference between regions cannot depend entirely on the efficiency of tax collection and administration; Second, the improvement of the efficiency of tax collection and administration will ease the financial pressure with the same intensity nationwide; Third, among the factors that affect the financial pressure, the easing of financial pressure brought by the improvement of tax collection and management efficiency cannot effectively solve the "fiscal expenditure dilemma".

Therefore, the local government should not only start from the port of tax collection and management to ease the local financial pressure, hoping to increase the fiscal revenue by reducing the cost of tax compliance or strict tax enforcement, timely collection of taxes and other "process" links, but should start from the "supply side" or "demand side" to effectively broaden the channels of fiscal revenue, cultivate potential tax sources and improve the efficiency of the use of fiscal funds. At the same time, the local financial expenditure structure should be adjusted accordingly, people's livelihood expenditures should be reasonably arranged, and the demand for public services should be balanced with the need for local financial pressure relief.

Fund Project. Postgraduate Innovation Project of Harbin University of Commerce "Research on the Way out of Land Financial Dependence in Heilongjiang Province". (YJSCX2021-713HSD).

References

1. Yonghui, Z., et al.: Divided into incentives, budget constraints and local government taxation behavior. Economics (quarterly) **19**(01), 1–32 (2022)
2. Congshuai, Y., et al.: Promotion incentives and tax collection-evidence from breakpoint regression. Financ. Econ. **02**, 31–41 (2020)
3. Ping, G., et al.: Has fiscal pressure improved local governments' financial absorptive capacity? Financ. Theory Pract. **43**(02), 82–90 (2022)
4. Hongyou, L., et al.: Local government transition, tax collection and administration and tax radicalization. Econ. Manage. **38**(02), 160–168 (2016)
5. Tai Jie, T., et al.: Local officials' administrative pressure, financial target assessment and enterprise effective tax rate. Econ. Rev. (03), 89–103 (2019)
6. Peiyong, G.: Mystery of China's continuous high-speed tax growth. Econ. Res. (12), 13–23 (2006)

7. Yupeng, S., et al.: Financial pressure and enterprise tax avoidance: an empirical study based on endogenous perspective. Financ. Econ. (08), 22–31 (2020)
8. Baocong, H., et al.: Pressure is Power? Increasing financial pressure and improving enterprise quality and efficiency. Tax Econ. Res. **26**(05), 70–80 (2021)
9. Guangrong, M., et al.: Government size, local governance and corporate tax evasion. World Econ. **35**(06), 93–114 (2012)
10. Weian, L., et al.: Tax avoidance effect of political identity. Financ. Res. **03**, 114–129 (2013)
11. Xiaoguang, C.: Financial pressure, tax collection and administration and regional inequality. China Soc. Sci. (04), 53–70+206 (2016)
12. Deqian, Y., et al.: Financial pressure, the choice of government strategies below the provincial level and the structure of fiscal expenditure. Financ. Res. (08), 47–62 (2021)
13. Xinyu, Z., et al.: Quality effect of local financial pressure on economic development —— empirical evidence from panel data of 282 prefecture-level cities in China. Financ. Res. **06**, 57–71 (2019)
14. Deqiu, C., et al.: Policy uncertainty, efficiency of tax collection and administration and enterprise tax evasion. Manage. World (05), 151–163 (2016)

Efficiency Measurement of Financial Subsidies for Agricultural Insurance and Analysis of Provincial differences–A Study Based on Super-SBM Model and Malmquist Index

Hongmei Wen and Hanying Zhang[✉]

School of Finance Administration, Harbin University of Commerce, Harbin 150028, Heilongjiang, China
939774880@qq.com

Abstract. The efficiency evaluation of financial subsidies for agricultural insurance is of great significance to promote the high-quality development of regional agriculture. Taking the 31 provinces, autonomous regions and municipalities directly under the central government as decision-making units, this paper uses the Super SBM model and Malmquist total factor productivity index to make an empirical quantitative analysis of the efficiency of financial subsidies for agricultural insurance in China from 2017 to 2020. The results show that the overall growth of financial subsidies for agricultural insurance in China has remained stable, while at the provincial level, it has changed to varying degrees in space during the observation period. However, some provinces are still in a state of inefficiency, indicating that there is still much room for improvement in domestic agricultural development. The efficiency of agricultural insurance subsidies shows a spatial pattern of "the East is higher than the middle, and the middle is higher than the west".

Keywords: Efficiency of financial subsidies for agricultural insurance · Super SBM model · Malmquist index

Since 2007, the central government has implemented a financial subsidy policy for agricultural insurance, that is, mainly through the central government and governments at all levels to bear part of the net premium of agricultural insurance for insured farmers, so as to reduce the insurance cost of farmers and mobilize the enthusiasm of farmers to participate in insurance. However, at present, the premium subsidy for agricultural insurance has far exceeded the self-paid premium of farmers. Does such a high proportion of subsidies achieve the expected effect of the policy? How to evaluate the efficiency of agricultural insurance subsidies in China and then seeking a practical way to improve the efficiency of the use of fiscal funds has become a standing problem in the field of agricultural insurance, which will also be discussed in this paper.

At present, the relevant literature on the efficiency of agricultural insurance financial subsidies mainly uses DEA method and its derivative model to study the efficiency of

A. Li et al. (Eds.): 6GN 2022, LNICST 504, pp. 280–289, 2023.
https://doi.org/10.1007/978-3-031-36011-4_25

agricultural insurance financial subsidies in China.Zhao Junyan et al. (2015) and Feng Wenli et al. (2015) respectively used BCC and CCR models to measure and analyze the efficiency of agricultural insurance financial subsidies in China. Wang Ren et al. (2016) used the Three-stage DEA model to calculate the efficiency of financial subsidies for agricultural insurance in China, believing that the overall efficiency is at a high level. Huang Yuanji et al. (2018) used DEA Tobit model to identify inefficient decision-making units, their efficiency values, and analyzed the factors affecting their efficiency. According to the empirical results of the three stages of DEA, Ning Wei et al. (2021) divided provinces and cities into two categories: insufficient efficiency of agricultural insurance subsidies and redundant efficiency of subsidies, and then discussed the improvement direction of agricultural insurance subsidy efficiency according to economic conditions.

Although the above literature uses different methods to calculate the efficiency of financial subsidies for agricultural insurance in China, the traditional DEA models may overestimate the efficiency of decision-making units, and lead to the efficiency value of multiple decision-making units being 1 at the same time. Based on this, to improve the reliability and accuracy of efficiency evaluation, this paper uses Super SBM model and Malmquist total factor productivity index to quantitatively analyze the agricultural insurance subsidy efficiency of 31 provinces, autonomous regions and municipalities directly under the central government (excluding Hong Kong, Macao and Taiwan, the same below).

1 Research Method and Index Selection

1.1 Research Method

To achieve the aim of evaluating the efficiency of agricultural insurance financial subsidy in China more comprehensively, Malmquist index will be used to further analyze the changes in agricultural insurance financial subsidy efficiency in different time periods.

Super SBM Model. Andersen & Petersen (1993) proposed Super Efficiency Model (Super-DEA). Tone (2001) proposed a Slack Based Measure (SBM-DEA) based on relaxation variables. In the SBM model, the proportional improvement of invalidity and the improvement of relaxation variables are considered. Tone (2002) proposed Super SBM model based on SBM model. The Super SBM model is actually a non-radial mode of the Super DEA model. The model considers the relaxation variables involved in the input and output indicators in practical problems, and can avoid the deviation of the results. Therefore, this paper chooses Super SBM model. The model assumes that there are n Decision-Making Units (DMU), which are recorded as $\mathbf{DMU}_j$ (j = 1, 2, …,). Each DMU has m inputs and s outputs, which are recorded as $\mathbf{xi}_j$ (= 1, 2, ⋯ ,) and $\mathbf{yr}_j$(r = 1, 2, ⋯ ,) respectively. The Super SBM model under variable returns to scale can be expressed as:

$$\delta^* = \min \delta = \frac{\frac{1}{m} \sum\limits_{i=1}^{m} \frac{\overline{x_i}}{x_{i0}}}{\frac{1}{s} \sum\limits_{r=1}^{s} \frac{\overline{y_r}}{y_{r0}}} \tag{1}$$

$$\begin{cases} \overline{x_i} \geq \sum_{j=1, j \neq 0}^{n} x_{ij} \lambda_j \\ \overline{y_r} \leq \sum_{j=1, j \neq 0}^{n} y_{rj} \lambda_j \\ \overline{x_i} \geq x_{i0} \\ \overline{y_r} \leq y_{r0} \\ \overline{y} \geq 0 \\ \lambda \geq 0 \text{且} \sum_{j=1, j \neq 0}^{n} \lambda_i = 1 \end{cases}$$

Among them δ^* is the efficiency value of super efficiency SBM, λ is a weight vector.

Malmquist Index Model. In 1953, Sten Malmaquist first proposed the Malmquist index. färe et al.(1992) first used DEA method to calculate Malmquist index and split the index into two directions: one is efficiency change (EC), which mainly reflects the change of input-output ratio; The second is technological change (TC), which mainly reflects the changes in the production frontier of the whole industry.

The value of efficiency change and technology change can be greater than 1, less than 1 or equal to 1, indicating that the efficiency has improved, declined or remained unchanged compared with the previous year. Malmquist index can reflect the impact of time on the efficiency of production units by constructing time series functions.

Assuming that x^t、 y^t and x^{t+1}、 y^{t+1} represent the values of the evaluated DMU_k in periods t and t + 1, respectively, the Malmquist index from period t to t + 1 is expressed as:

$$MI(x^{t+1}, y^{t+1}, x^t, y^t) = \sqrt{\frac{E^t(x^{t+1}, y^{t+1})}{E^t(x^t, y^t)} \frac{E^{t+1}(x^{t+1}, y^{t+1})}{E^{t+1}(x^t, y^t)}} \tag{2}$$

$E^t(x^t, y^t)$ and $E^t(x^{t+1}, y^{t+1})$ are the efficiency values of DMU_k in two periods, then the efficiency change is shown in Eq. (3) and the technical change is shown in Eq. (4):

$$EC = \frac{E^{t+1}(x^{t+1}, y^{t+1})}{E^t(x^t, y^t)} \tag{3}$$

$$TC = \sqrt{\frac{E^t(x^t, y^t)}{E^{t+1}(x^t, y^t)} \frac{E^t(x^{t+1}, y^{t+1})}{E^{t+1}(x^{t+1}, y^{t+1})}} \tag{4}$$

The Malmquist index can be broken down into two parts: efficiency change and technology change:

$$MI = \sqrt{\frac{E^t(x^{t+1}, y^{t+1})}{E^t(x^t, y^t)} \frac{E^{t+1}(x^{t+1}, y^{t+1})}{E^{t+1}(x^t, y^t)}} = \frac{E^{t+1}(x^{t+1}, y^{t+1})}{E^t(x^t, y^t)} \times \sqrt{\frac{E^t(x^t, y^t)}{E^{t+1}(x^t, y^t)} \frac{E^t(x^{t+1}, y^{t+1})}{E^{t+1}(x^{t+1}, y^{t+1})}} \tag{5}$$

$$= EC \times TC$$

1.2 Selection of Evaluation Indicators

In this paper, the central financial subsidy quota and the provincial and below-provincial financial (hereinafter referred to as local financial) subsidy quota are used as input indicators, and the premium income, depth and density of agricultural insurance are used as output indicators. The data are from the official website of the provincial finance department and the statistical yearbook of all the provinces. The indicators are shown in Table 1.

Table 1. Input output indicators of financial subsidies for agricultural insurance.

Index variable	Variable name	Index variable	Variable name
Input variable	Central subsidy quota (x1) Local subsidy quota (x2)	Output variable	Agricultural insurance premium income(y1) Agricultural insurance density(y2) Depth of agricultural insurance (y3)

2 Empirical Analysis of the Efficiency of Financial Subsidies for Agricultural Insurance

2.1 Efficiency Calculation of Agricultural Insurance Financial Subsidy Based on Super SBM Model

This study uses MaxDEA8.21 software, combined with the panel data of 31 provinces, autonomous regions and municipalities directly under the central government from 2017 to 2020, the efficiency of agricultural insurance financial subsidies is calculated based on Efficiency calculation of agricultural insurance financial subsidy based on Super SBM model. The efficiency value and ranking results are shown in Table 2.

Table 2. The calculation results of Super SBM model

DMU	2017		2018		2019		2020	
	value	ranking	value	ranking	value	ranking	value	ranking
BJ	1.3874	2	1.3703	2	1.3950	2	1.2719	2
TJ	1.0546	5	1.1914	3	1.2982	3	1.2172	3
LN	0.9492	15	0.9651	14	0.8826	19	0.8912	17
SH	2.8268	1	2.7306	1	2.9615	1	3.5735	1
JS	1.0432	6	1.0382	4	1.0664	4	1.0711	4
ZJ	0.7364	31	0.7329	31	0.7358	31	0.7335	31
FJ	0.8758	22	0.9312	15	0.9051	15	0.9135	14
SD	1.0259	8	1.0279	5	0.8882	18	0.8870	18
GD	0.8663	23	0.8719	23	0.8597	25	0.8675	23
Eastern mean	1.1962	—	1.2066	—	1.2214	—	1.2696	—
HE	0.9176	19	0.9259	16	0.8914	16	0.9031	15
SX	0.7465	30	0.7483	29	0.7572	29	0.7667	29
JL	0.9219	18	0.9212	18	0.9113	14	0.9216	13
HL	0.9844	13	0.9834	13	0.9739	9	0.9852	10
AH	0.9107	20	0.9114	19	0.8638	24	0.8665	25
JX	0.9586	14	1.0123	8	1.0207	6	1.0276	6
HA	0.9357	17	0.9865	12	0.9466	11	0.9331	11
HB	0.8638	24	0.8787	22	0.8886	17	0.8956	16
HN	0.9951	11	0.9977	10	1.0189	7	1.0101	8
HI	0.9468	16	0.8386	27	0.8679	23	0.8674	24
Central mean	0.9181	—	0.9204	—	0.9140	—	0.9177	—
IM	0.9933	12	0.9904	11	0.9879	8	1.0053	9
GX	0.8463	25	0.8684	25	0.8438	26	0.8473	26
CQ	1.0706	4	0.9259	17	0.9682	10	1.0365	5
SC	1.0384	7	1.0202	6	0.9244	13	0.9239	12
YN	0.7592	29	0.7463	30	0.7532	30	0.7438	30
GZ	0.8463	26	0.8788	21	0.8694	22	0.8691	22
XZ	1.1061	3	1.0014	9	0.9315	12	0.8716	21
SN	0.8275	27	0.8679	26	0.8737	20	0.8768	20
GS	0.7694	28	0.7768	28	0.7914	27	0.7873	27
QH	1.0179	9	0.8691	24	0.7775	28	0.7758	28

(*continued*)

Table 2. (*continued*)

DMU	2017		2018		2019		2020	
	value	ranking	value	ranking	value	ranking	value	ranking
NX	0.9021	21	0.8871	20	0.8728	21	0.8856	19
XJ	1.0130	10	1.0172	7	1.0339	5	1.0270	7
Western average	0.9325	—	0.9041	—	0.8856	—	0.8875	—
Annual average	1.0044	—	0.9972	—	0.9923	—	1.0082	—

As can be seen from Table 2: The efficiency of agricultural insurance financial subsidies in various provinces across the country is quite different. In these four years, the efficiency of subsidies has steadily increased in 13 provinces.7 provinces remained a stable level with not much change in subsidy efficiency, while another 11 provinces had varying degrees of decline in subsidy efficiency. The overall fluctuation of the efficiency of agricultural insurance financial subsidies in China is relatively small, showing a trend of steady development with a slight improvement over the years. The efficiency of agricultural insurance subsidies in the three major regions of China shows obvious differences. On the contrary, the average efficiency in the western region continued to decline, while the average efficiency in the central region fluctuated and remained stable as a whole.

In order to more intuitively observe the spatial characteristics and differences of the efficiency of agricultural insurance financial subsidies in 31 provinces, autonomous regions and municipalities directly under the central government, This paper uses ArcGIS 10.2 software to analyze the spatial pattern of the efficiency of agricultural insurance financial subsidies in 2017 and 2020, respectively, in Fig. 1 and 2.

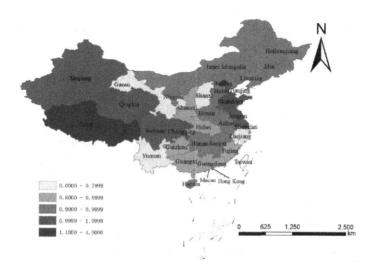

Fig. 1. 2017

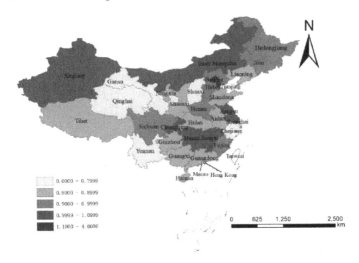

Fig. 2. 2020

2.2 Analysis of Total Factor Productivity Based on Malmquist Index

Using MaxDEA8.21, the Malmquist index of agricultural insurance financial subsidies in 31 provinces, autonomous regions and municipalities directly under the central government from 2017 to 2020 can not only get the efficiency changes in different periods, but also reflect the progress of technology, that is, the movement of production frontier, so as to realize the dynamic analysis of the efficiency of agricultural insurance financial subsidies in various provinces. The specific calculation results and analysis are as follows:

The calculation result of Malmquist total factor index shows the change of the efficiency level of fiscal subsidy policy in these years compared with the previous year. Table 3 clearly reflects the change of Malmquist index of agricultural insurance financial subsidy efficiency in 31 provinces, autonomous regions and municipalities directly under the central government from 2017 to 2020, from 0.982 to 1.040, indicating that the overall production frontier has increased, showing an upward trend.

Malmquist productivity index can be divided into economic efficiency change index (EC) and technological progress efficiency change index (TC). The economic efficiency change index represents the contribution of capital allocation and subsidy scale to the change of efficiency level. The efficiency change index of technological progress represents the contribution of technological and institutional improvement to the change of efficiency level.

According to Table 4, the average total factor productivity of the efficiency of agricultural insurance financial subsidies in various provinces in China from 2017 to 2020 is 1.0112, indicating that the overall premium efficiency level is improving. According to the change rate of economic efficiency of 0.9968 and the efficiency of technological progress of 1.0160, it can be seen that the improvement of the efficiency of financial

Table 3. Malmquist index and sub value of agricultural insurance financial subsidy efficiency

DMU	2017–2018			2018–2019			2019–2020		
	MI	EC	TC	MI	EC	TC	MI	EC	TC
BJ	0.911	0.988	0.922	1.008	1.018	0.990	1.367	0.912	1.499
TJ	0.909	1.130	0.804	1.005	1.090	0.922	0.981	0.938	1.046
LN	1.015	1.017	0.998	1.015	0.914	1.110	1.031	1.010	1.021
SH	1.034	0.966	1.070	0.994	1.085	0.917	1.106	1.207	0.917
JS	1.008	0.995	1.013	1.047	1.027	1.020	1.067	1.004	1.062
ZJ	1.000	0.995	1.005	1.000	1.004	0.996	1.025	0.997	1.028
FJ	0.942	1.063	0.886	0.963	0.972	0.991	0.979	1.009	0.970
SD	1.012	1.002	1.011	1.013	0.864	1.173	1.010	0.999	1.011
GD	1.022	1.006	1.016	1.019	0.986	1.034	1.026	1.009	1.017
HE	1.012	1.009	1.003	1.013	0.963	1.052	1.038	1.013	1.025
SX	1.000	1.002	0.998	1.027	1.012	1.015	1.044	1.013	1.031
JL	1.047	0.999	1.047	1.032	0.989	1.043	1.036	1.011	1.025
HL	1.019	0.999	1.020	1.017	0.990	1.027	1.024	1.012	1.012
AH	1.006	1.001	1.006	1.002	0.948	1.057	1.017	1.003	1.014
JX	1.067	1.056	1.010	1.020	1.008	1.011	1.096	1.007	1.089
HA	1.020	1.054	0.967	1.017	0.960	1.060	1.041	0.986	1.056
HB	1.038	1.017	1.020	1.052	1.011	1.040	1.032	1.008	1.024
HN	1.006	1.003	1.003	1.016	1.021	0.995	1.074	0.991	1.083
HI	0.847	0.886	0.956	1.006	1.035	0.972	1.076	0.999	1.077
IM	1.017	0.997	1.020	1.023	0.997	1.025	1.028	1.018	1.010
GX	1.042	1.026	1.016	1.014	0.972	1.044	1.024	1.004	1.019
CQ	0.754	0.865	0.872	0.998	1.046	0.955	0.986	1.071	0.921
SC	1.003	0.983	1.021	0.979	0.906	1.081	1.015	1.000	1.015
YN	1.002	0.983	1.019	1.042	1.009	1.033	1.007	0.988	1.020
GZ	1.038	1.038	1.000	1.024	0.989	1.035	1.029	1.000	1.029
XZ	0.831	0.905	0.918	0.966	0.930	1.039	0.989	0.936	1.057
SN	1.025	1.049	0.977	1.043	1.007	1.036	1.032	1.004	1.028
GS	1.028	1.010	1.018	1.052	1.019	1.032	1.018	0.995	1.024
QH	0.795	0.854	0.931	0.947	0.895	1.058	1.013	0.998	1.015
NX	0.964	0.983	0.981	0.998	0.984	1.014	1.008	1.015	0.994
XJ	1.018	1.004	1.014	1.022	1.016	1.005	1.016	0.993	1.023
mean value	0.982	0.996	0.985	1.012	0.989	1.025	1.040	1.005	1.037

subsidies for agricultural insurance in China is mainly due to the improvement of the efficiency of technological progress.

Table 4. The average annual Malmquist index and sub value of subsidy efficiency

DMU	EC	TC	MI	DMU	EC	TC	MI
BJ	0.9725	1.1372	1.1059	HB	1.0121	1.0283	1.0407
TJ	1.0523	0.9241	0.9725	HN	1.0051	1.0271	1.0323
LN	0.9803	1.0432	1.0227	HI	0.9734	1.0014	0.9748
SH	1.0857	0.9680	1.0510	IM	1.0041	1.0184	1.0226
JS	1.0089	1.0314	1.0406	GX	1.0006	1.0262	1.0269
ZJ	0.9987	1.0097	1.0084	CQ	0.9937	0.9159	0.9101
FJ	1.0148	0.9489	0.9630	SC	0.9627	1.0390	1.0002
SD	0.9549	1.0647	1.0167	YN	0.9933	1.0239	1.0170
GD	1.0005	1.0222	1.0228	GZ	1.0091	1.0213	1.0306
HE	0.9950	1.0265	1.0214	XZ	0.9238	1.0045	0.9279
SX	1.0089	1.0145	1.0235	SN	1.0197	1.0140	1.0339
JL	0.9999	1.0383	1.0383	GS	1.0078	1.0246	1.0326
HL	1.0003	1.0196	1.0199	QH	0.9154	1.0014	0.9167
AH	0.9839	1.0256	1.0091	NX	0.9940	0.9962	0.9902
JX	1.0237	1.0368	1.0613	XJ	1.0046	1.0140	1.0187
HA	0.9999	1.0277	1.0275				
mean value	0.9968	1.0160	1.0123				

3 Summary

This paper uses Super SBM model and Malmquist index model to comprehensively analyze the efficiency of financial subsidies for agricultural insurance in 31 provinces, autonomous regions and municipalities directly under the central government from static and dynamic perspectives from 2017–2020. The main conclusions are as follows:

Based on the static analysis of Super SBM model, from 2017 to 2020, while the average annual efficiency of agricultural insurance financial subsidies in various provinces in China showed an upward trend of fluctuation as a whole, there was also a periodic decline in 2018 and 2019. It shows that in recent years, although the amount of financial subsidies for agricultural insurance provided by governments at all levels have increased year by year, the financial subsidies for agricultural insurance in China have not reached the optimal allocation of resources. Secondly, the efficiency of financial subsidies for agricultural insurance in China varies significantly between provinces. Significant regional differences are the main characteristics of China's agricultural insurance financial subsidy system at present. The efficiency of the eastern provinces is higher than that of the western provinces, while most of the impoverished population in China are concentrated in the West.

Based on the dynamic analysis of Malmquist index, the Malmquist index of the overall efficiency of agricultural insurance financial subsidies in China has increased year over year, showing an upward trend. The efficiency level of fiscal subsidy policy in most provinces has a clearer growth trend from 2017 to 2020, and the social and economic benefits of premium subsidy policy are better. But there are still a small number of provinces with a Malmquist index less than 1, which may have experienced a decline in efficiency due to declining economies of scale. Local governments also need to adapt to regional conditions.

References

1. Junyan, Z., Xiaosong, J., Yutao, Z., et al.: Comprehensive evaluation of the efficiency of financial subsidies for agricultural insurance in China: Based on DEA Model Agric. Econ. (5), 89–91 (2015)
2. Wenli, F., Xuemei, Y., Yue, B.: Analysis of efficiency and influencing factors of agricultural insurance in China based on DEA Tobit model. Finance Econ. (2), 69–72 (2015)
3. Ren, W., Xixi, Z., Sihan, L.: Research on poverty alleviation efficiency evaluation of agricultural insurance subsidy policy in Hunan Province Based on analytic hierarchy process. J. Hunan Bus. School **23**(02), 123–128 (2016)
4. Yuanji, H., Ren, W., Ying, L.: Analysis of factors affecting the poverty alleviation efficiency of agricultural insurance subsidies based on DEA Tobit panel model - a case study of Hunan Province. Rural Econ. (05), 69–74 (2018)
5. Wei, N., Yanchun, L., Jingxian, Z.: Research on the optimal proportion of agricultural insurance financial subsidy in China -- Analysis Based on Three-stage DEA model. Price Theory Pract. (10), 106–111+194 (2021)
6. Andersen, P., Petersen, N.C.: A procedure for ranking efficient units in data envelopment analysis. Manage. Sci. **39**(10), 1261–1264 (1993)
7. Tone, K.: A slacks -based measure of efficiency in data envelopment analysis. Eur. J. Oper. Res. **130**(3), 498–509 (2001)
8. Tone, K.: A slacks-based measure of super-efficiency in data envelopment analysis. Eur. J. Oper. Res. **143**, 32–41 (2002)
9. Färe, R., Grosskopf, S., Lindgren, B., et al.: Productivity changes in Swedish pharamacies 1980–1989: a non-parametric Malmquist approach. J. Prod. Anal. **3**(1–2), 85 (1992)

Research on the Impact of Digital Economy on Local Tax Revenue—PVAR Model Analysis Based on Chinese Provincial Panel Data

Wang Shuguang and Sun Yifan[✉]

School of Public Finance and Administration, Harbin University of Commerce, Harbin, Heilongjiang 150028, China
1835446218@qq.com

Abstract. The digital economy has been clearly identified as an important means to promote China's economic development in the 14th Five-Year Plan. While promoting regional development, it also affects local tax revenues. Based on the provincial panel data of 30 provinces from 2011 to 2020, this paper constructs an index system to measure the development of provincial digital economy through Internet penetration rate, number of Internet practitioners, Internet-related output, number of mobile Internet users and digital inclusive financial index, and explores the dynamic interaction between digital economy and tax revenue by using PVAR model. The results show that the digital economy has a long-term positive impact on regional tax revenue, but the impact of tax revenue on the digital economy is not significant. It is suggested that local governments should seize the opportunity of the development of the digital economy, conserve tax sources and increase tax revenue on the one hand, and make good use of digital information technology to accelerate the construction of tax information on the other hand.

Keywords: Digital Economy · Tax Revenue · Economic Development

1 Introduction

The digital economy with the core content of 5G, industrial Internet, artificial intelligence, cloud computing, big data and other new generation of information technology research and development and application has gradually become the backbone of promoting high-quality economic growth. At present, China's economic development is in the growth rate shift period, structural adjustment pains period, the early policy digestion period three superimposed stage, emphasizing the steady economic growth, making local taxes subject to certain restrictive effects. At the same time, due to the unprecedented changes in the world and the global pandemic of the new coronavirus epidemic, China's economic and social development environment is more complicated. In this special environment, local taxation is facing tremendous pressure. In the current era of digital economy, digital economy creates growth momentum for local tax revenue by optimizing structure and improving production efficiency. This paper uses empirical methods to test the impact of digital economy on local tax revenue.

A. Li et al. (Eds.): 6GN 2022, LNICST 504, pp. 290–296, 2023.
https://doi.org/10.1007/978-3-031-36011-4_26

2 Variable Description and Data Sources

2.1 Digital Economy Evaluation System

The digital economic evaluation system includes two levels: the first level index and the second level index. The first level index is the digital economy index, which fully reflects the development level of China's digital economy. The secondary indicators include five indicators: Internet penetration rate, number of Internet practitioners, Internet-related output, number of mobile Internet users, and digital inclusive financial index, reflecting the five dimensions of digital economic development in various regions of China. Among them, the number of Internet practitioners with information transmission, software and information technology services in urban units employed persons accounted for the proportion of urban units employed persons. Internet-related output is expressed as the ratio of telecommunications business volume to the year-end resident population. All selected indicators are positive.

2.2 Calculation of Digital Economic Index

Through the principal component analysis method (PCA), the data of the above five indicators are standardized and processed in Dimensionality Reduction. Then we can get the digital economic index of each province, which is recorded as Z. Specifically, in the first step, the data of each index is dimensionless processed by means of averaging, the negative index is reciprocal first. The second step is to determine the weight of each index by PCA, and input with the covariance matrix of the basic index. The third step is to calculate the comprehensive index of the principal components according to the index weight.

The calculation results are shown in Table 1. According to the digital economy index of all provinces (autonomous regions and municipalities), the overall development level of digital economy from 2016 to 2020 is still low, and the regional development level is quite different. The digital economy development level of Beijing, Shanghai, Guangdong, Zhejiang, Jiangsu and other places is far ahead of other regions. However, the development level of digital economy is gradually improving.

Table 1. Digital economy index of 30 provinces in 2016–2020

Provinces	2016	2017	2018	2019	2020
Beijing	4.3670	4.8185	5.7985	6.6143	7.4159
Tianjin	0.8407	1.1953	1.8901	2.4202	3.0750
Hebei	0.4185	0.7310	1.2523	1.7732	2.1312
Shanxi	0.3984	0.6592	1.1112	1.5692	1.9806

(continued)

Table 1. (*continued*)

Provinces	2016	2017	2018	2019	2020
Neimenggu	0.5814	0.9883	1.5899	2.0612	2.4793
Liaoning	0.9990	1.3566	1.7539	2.1649	2.5003
Jilin	0.6343	0.9912	1.4711	1.8882	2.2185
Helongjiang	0.4322	0.8157	1.2021	1.7418	2.2448
Shanghai	2.3334	2.7997	3.6833	4.3915	5.1669
Jiangsu	0.8580	1.1812	1.9004	2.5059	2.7110
Zhejiang	1.3480	1.7514	2.3895	3.1035	3.3507
Anhui	0.0971	0.4350	0.9750	1.5241	1.9597
Fujian	0.9860	1.2887	1.8183	2.2677	2.4709
Jiangxi	-0.0301	0.3457	0.8796	1.4007	1.8246
Shandong	0.5178	0.7915	1.2507	1.6647	2.0156
Henan	0.0521	0.3981	0.9763	1.5385	1.9805
Hubei	0.3951	0.7629	1.3737	2.0549	2.3684
Hunan	0.0384	0.3305	0.8428	1.3871	1.8466
Guangdong	1.5851	1.9981	2.8593	3.3762	3.6290
Guangxi	0.0446	0.3677	1.0360	1.4842	2.0083
Hainan	0.6446	1.0685	1.7429	2.2060	2.5167
Chongqing	0.3927	0.7780	1.3876	1.8934	2.2477
Sichuan	0.5218	0.8583	1.4427	1.9031	2.3951
Guizhou	0.1089	0.5707	1.2740	2.0206	2.5295
Yunnan	0.0592	0.4180	0.9392	1.6011	2.1209
Shanxi	0.7977	1.1694	1.9370	2.4257	2.7851
Gansu	0.0263	0.4388	1.0420	1.6262	2.0404
Qinghai	0.4403	0.8571	1.6173	2.0713	2.5309
Ningxia	0.4966	0.9083	1.5723	2.0238	2.3671
Xinjiang	0.2659	0.4365	1.0197	1.7146	2.3621

2.3 Data Sources

The purpose of this paper is to study the relationship between the digital economy and local tax revenue. Therefore, the tax revenue (tax) and the digital economy index (t) of 30 provinces from 2011 to 2020 are selected as the research samples. Among them, the data of tax revenue are all from the provincial statistical yearbooks. The data used by the provincial digital economy index are from the official website of the National Bureau of Statistics, the China Statistical Yearbook, the China Financial Yearbook, and the China

Urban Statistical Yearbook. For individual missing data, the interpolation method and the trend extension method are used to supplement the integrity.

3 Empirical Analysis

3.1 Model Design

PVAR model is an innovative method of vector auto regression of panel data proposed by Holtz-Eakin in 1988, which has been widely used and optimized in practice. It is a mature method that can truly reflect the dynamic interaction between panel data. The advantage of this method is that it does not need to explore the internal relationship logic between variables in advance, nor does it need to consider the endogenous, exogenous and causal relationship of variables. Instead, all variables are regarded as endogenous variables and put into the model for analysis.

3.2 Stationarity Test of Variables

In order to ensure the robustness of the regression results and avoid the occurrence of "pseudo regression", it is necessary to conduct a stationarity test on the variables before using the PVAR model. LLC test and IPS test are selected. LLC test is for common unit root, while IPS test is for individual unit root. Table 2 shows the results of stationarity test. The test results show that the digital economy (z) and tax revenue (tax) show stable characteristics, and the PVAR model can be established.

Table 2. Variable stationarity test

Variable	LLC Statistic	Prob	IPS Statistic	Prob
Tax	-3.2145	0.0007	7.6921	0.0000
T	-8.2633	0.0000	9.0788	0.0000

Table 3. Determination of Lag Order

Lag	AIC	BIC	HQIC
1	13.918*	14.853*	14.2944
2	15.0732	16.1635	15.5136
3	15.1998	16.4832	15.7199
4	15.7846	17.3161	16.4067
5	14.1311	15.9961	14.8887

Table 4. Variance Decomposition

Periods	Tax	t
1	1	0
2	0.966	0.034
3	0.918	0.082
4	0.878	0.122
5	0.85	0.15
6	0.832	0.168
7	0.822	0.178
8	0.817	0.183

3.3 Determination of Lag Order

In order to perform PVAR estimation, the required optimal lag order needs to be tested. According to AIC, BIC and HQIC information criteria, the optimal lag order of this model is order 1. The results are as follows (Table 3).

3.4 Impulse Response Analysis

1 and 2 in Fig. 1 respectively show the reaction of tax revenue after being impacted by tax revenue and digital economy. It can be seen from the figure that when the tax revenue is impacted by itself, it will form a positive response in the short term, reach the maximum value in the current period, and then decrease rapidly. After the lag of 4 periods, the response value will be stable and tend to zero. When the tax revenue is impacted by the digital economy, it shows the characteristics of rising first and then falling. It reaches the maximum value in the third period, then gradually decreases, always positive, and tends to zero in the long term, indicating that the role of the digital economy on local tax revenue is always positive. With the development of digital economy, the impact on local tax revenue is increased first and then decreased.

3 and 4 in Fig. 1 respectively show the reactions of the digital economy after being impacted by the digital economy and tax revenue. When the digital economy is impacted by itself, it will form a positive response in the short term, and reach the maximum value in the current period, and then rapidly decrease. After it becomes negative, the response value will be stable and tend to zero. This shows that the increase of local tax revenue can bring a positive impact on the digital economy in the short term, but it will soon have a restraining effect.

3.5 Variance Decomposition

As the complementary analysis of impulse response, variance decomposition describes the contribution of impact variables to the changes of variables in the system. As shown in Table 4. Since the decomposition results have not changed much since the 9th period, and

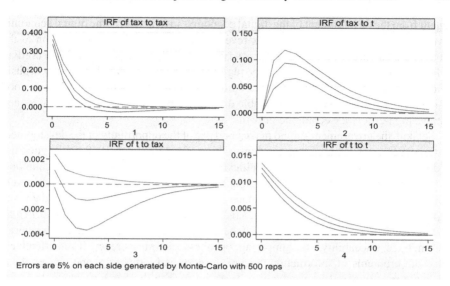

Fig. 1. Impulse response diagram

the variable fluctuation tends to be stable, Table 4 only shows the variance decomposition results of the first 8 periods.

In the variance decomposition of tax revenue, the contribution of digital economy to tax revenue is increasing, and the influence is significant. The contribution of digital economy to tax revenue is 8.2% in the second lag period and 18.3% in the eighth lag period, which indicates that digital economy is an important factor affecting tax revenue.

4   Conclusions and Suggestions

4.1   Conclusion

Based on the provincial-level panel data and using the digital economy index of 30 provinces (autonomous regions and municipalities directly under the Central government) from 2011 to 2020, this paper empirically analyzes the impact of digital economy on local government tax revenue and draws the following conclusions: Digital economy plays a significant role in supporting local tax revenue. This kind of influence effect presents the parabola form which rises first and then decreases; The increase of local tax revenue has a weak effect on the development of local digital economy.

4.2   Suggest

First, the government should make good use of the development of the digital economy to increase local tax revenue. Enhance big data, cloud computing, chain blocks, artificial intelligence and other digital economy core plate support, enhance the level of regional digital economy, it is advantageous to the growth of residents' income and consumption, but also to entrepreneurship and employment market, and let more people benefit from the development of the digital economy, so as to realize the digital economic development lead to the growth of tax revenue. It is necessary to pay attention to the economic characteristics of the region and formulate development policies according to local conditions. Regions with poor regional economic foundation can vigorously develop digital economy and seize development opportunities, while regions with good regional economic foundation can enable digital to empower traditional industries and achieve high-efficiency economic growth.

Second, the government should make good use of the opportunity of the development of digital economy to strengthen the construction of tax information. To make good use of digital information technology, specifically, one is artificial intelligence technology. This technology aims to simulate and expand human intelligence, which can effectively facilitate the collection, analysis and management of tax-related information data, and improve the efficiency of intelligent management of tax data. The second is blockchain technology. It is a distributed shared database, which has the advantages of decentralization, trace, traceability, non-tampering, openness and transparency. It can effectively solve the problems of information closure, forgery and tampering, and can establish a reliable tax coordination mechanism based on it. The third is big data technology. Big data applications can facilitate tax compliance and optimize tax payment services. Through the analysis, mining and application of data information obtained from big data, tax non-compliance behaviors can be effectively identified and tax management risks can be reduced.

References

1. Zijian, C., Yanan, S.: Digital economy, R&D innovation and regional integration: a study based on three Chinese urban agglomerations. Int. J. Econ. Finance Manage. Sci. **10**(3), (2022)
2. Shelepov, A.: The Influence of the G20's digitalization leadership on development conditions and governance of the digital economy. Int. Organ. Res. J. **17**(1), (2022)
3. Qiong, C., Zhaozhi, W.: Research on tax policies to promote the development of digital economy in China. J. Fujian College Financ. Adm. (03), 31–36, (2022)
4. Jingtao, C., Sicong, Z.: An empirical analysis of the impact of digital economy on regional tax revenue distribution in China - based on spatial Durbin model. Tax Res. (06), 13–21 (2022)
5. Hua, A., Qishuang, X., Baoshun, W.: Empirical research on the impact of digital economy on local government tax revenue. Tax Res. (08), 107–112 (2021)

Research on the Influence of Tax Burden on the Research and Development Level of Logistics Enterprises

Shuai Shao[✉]

Harbin University of Commerce, Heilongjiang 150028, China
3134288704@qq.com

Abstract. With the implementation of China's structural tax reduction policy, the taxation environment and mode of the logistics industry have changed. China is also actively responding to a series of problems arising from the rapid economic development. As the logistics industry is a strategic emerging industry in China, its potential development force is very strong. Improving its R&D and innovation level is conducive to occupying the market opportunity. In terms of logistics industry, China has issued a series of preferential tax policies to encourage R&D innovation, which can bring considerable benefits to China's economic development by improving the level of R&D. This paper starts with the definition of logistics industry, R&D level and tax burden, determines the data source as the panel data of listed companies in the logistics industry, discusses the relationship between tax burden and enterprise R&D level, and obtains the empirical results that tax burden is positively related to enterprise R&D level and the relationship is significant, and gives policy recommendations based on this conclusion.

Keywords: Tax burden · Logistics enterprises · Research and development level

1 Introduction

As a productive service industry, logistics industry is one of the important components of the national economy. It runs through production, circulation, consumption and other social reproduction links. Its development plays an important role in promoting regional economic growth and competitiveness. Logistics can be divided into traditional logistics and modern logistics. Now China has put the focus of logistics development on modern logistics, gradually realizing the standardization, intelligence and greening of logistics. In recent years, China's logistics industry has developed rapidly. In 2020, despite the impact of the New Coronary Pneumonia epidemic, the total amount of social logistics in China will still reach 300.1 trillion yuan, an increase of 3.5% year on year. This paper takes the R&D capability of logistics enterprises as a measurement index, and uses the data of listed companies in the logistics industry to analyze the impact of tax burden on the R&D capability of enterprises. It has important practical significance for the government to allocate resources and the development of national economic innovation and

A. Li et al. (Eds.): 6GN 2022, LNICST 504, pp. 297–302, 2023.
https://doi.org/10.1007/978-3-031-36011-4_27

environmental protection. The research of this paper is specific to the listed enterprises in the logistics industry, which provides an important research content for improving the tax burden of promoting the R&D and innovation development of the logistics industry. Through the analysis of this paper, we can see the direction and magnitude of the impact of tax burden on the R&D level of logistics enterprises through data, and provide data support for the subsequent formulation of relevant tax policies in the logistics industry; At the same time, according to the analysis results, the corresponding tax policy reference suggestions are put forward, which can not only promote the economic development, but also enhance the logistics industry's ability to cope with risk challenges.

2 Literature Review

Wang Dongmei and Ju Songdong (2009) [1]; Xi Weiqun (2010) [2] believes that the country's implementation of certain preferential tax policies for logistics enterprises is to help logistics enterprises reduce their comprehensive costs and improve efficiency, while reducing the gap between regions; Meng Xiaobing (2010) [3], based on the practices of other foreign countries, believes that it is necessary for China to reform the tax policy for logistics enterprises and proposes further measures; Li Chuntong and Ma Jieshu (2019) [4] started from the existing tax policies of the government and logistics enterprises, inspected the current situation of China's logistics enterprises, found problems, and proposed corresponding solutions. In a word, different scholars have studied the impact of tax burden on the R&D level of logistics enterprises to varying degrees, but there are still shortcomings, especially qualitative analysis, but lack of quantitative analysis, and more from the overall operation of logistics enterprises, lack of the impact of tax burden on logistics enterprises. In view of this, this paper establishes a model and puts forward assumptions, and finally judges the impact of tax burden on the R&D level of logistics enterprises.

3 An Empirical Study on the Impact of Tax Burden on the R&D Level of Logistics Enterprises

3.1 Data Source and Research Design

Research Hypothesis. At present, there are literatures on tax burden and R&D innovation of enterprises, but the final research results are still different. The existing literature mainly explains how the tax burden affects enterprise innovation through innovation R&D input and innovation R&D output, and draws three conclusions through empirical analysis: positive correlation, negative correlation, and insignificant relationship. Therefore, this paper proposes the following hypothesis: tax burden has a negative impact on the R&D capability of enterprises, that is, the two are negatively correlated.

Source of Samples. This study selects the panel data of listed enterprises in the logistics industry from 2015 to 2020, which approximately represents the development of the entire industry. According to the research experience of previous scholars and the restrictions of the formula used in this paper, and in order to ensure the accuracy and completeness of the data, this paper excludes ST and * ST listed companies, samples with total profits less than 0, samples without R&D personnel and samples with abnormal tax rate. According to the above conditions, a total of 53 samples were finally screened. CSMAR database is the main source of all kinds of data.

Selection of Variables. Enterprise research and innovation level (Rd) is taken as the explanatory variable, the core explanatory variable is tax burden (Tax), and the control variable is enterprise size (Size), asset liability ratio (Lev), and R&D personnel ratio (Rdrp).

Interpreted variable. Research innovation level, through the enterprise research and development innovation investment amount is measured, when to select r&d spending amount through earnings note of r&d, the data is relatively than accounting subjects within the development expenses and other related projects, more can a comprehensive expression of the enterprise in terms of innovation in all input, Will not be affected by depreciation or amortization and other factors, the performance of more real and objective total input.

Core explanatory variables. Tax burden. This paper compares the sum of taxes and surcharges and income taxes in the financial report with the total profit. The larger the value, the heavier the tax burden borne by enterprises.

Control variable. The enterprise scale is evaluated by the natural logarithm of the enterprise's revenue. Scale is generally a key factor that has a greater impact on enterprise innovation, because the use of total assets may bring about collinearity related problems. Therefore, this paper selects the operating revenue as the index to evaluate the enterprise scale. The asset liability ratio reflects the financial structure of the enterprise to a certain extent. It is obtained by comparing the total liabilities and total assets in the balance sheet and reflects the long-term debt capacity of the enterprise. The proportion of R&D personnel is expressed by dividing the total number of R&D personnel by the total number of employees. This proportion can compare the company's emphasis on innovative R&D and measure the innovation strength of the enterprise.

Model Design. This paper selects the panel data of 53 listed enterprises in China's logistics industry from 2015 to 2020, sets the explanatory variable as the tax burden of enterprises, and then sets the explanatory variable as the amount of R&D investment. For the panel data of listed logistics enterprises, a multiple regression analysis is carried out. Drawing on previous scholars' research ideas, this paper has established the following model to test the specific relationship between explanatory variables and explained variables:

$$RD = a + bTax + cSIZE + dLev + eRDRP + \varepsilon$$

3.2 The Empirical Analysis

Descriptive Statistics of Variables. Table 1 describes several variables in terms of minimum value, maximum value, mean value, etc. to show the performance of each variable. According to the panel data descriptive statistical analysis results of 53 samples of listed enterprises in the logistics industry, in terms of the explained variables, the minimum value of enterprises' innovation R&D investment is 8.453 and the maximum value is 23.491, with a large difference, indicating that there is a gap in the investment of listed enterprises in R&D activities. A considerable number of logistics enterprises need to continuously improve their investment in innovation and further improve the overall R&D level. In terms of explanatory variables, the minimum value of tax burden is 0.012, the maximum value is 0.9791, the average value is 0.0485303, and the standard deviation is 0.048702. These values indicate that tax burden has a greater impact on logistics listed enterprises, reflecting to some extent that tax burden affects the R&D investment of logistics listed enterprises. At the same time, there is a very significant individual difference among the sample enterprises, perhaps because of the existence of deferred income tax. In terms of control variables, the average proportion of corresponding R&D personnel is 12.210%, the minimum value is 0.500, and the maximum value is 36.190. This shows that listed enterprises in the logistics industry do not invest too much in R&D innovation. The difference between the maximum and minimum relative values is very obvious, indicating that there is a large gap in the proportion of R&D personnel among listed enterprises. The average value of the corresponding asset liability ratio is 0.516, the standard deviation is 0.536, the minimum value is 0.113, and the maximum value is 0.936. This shows that the overall asset liability ratio of the sample listed enterprises in the logistics industry is within a reasonable range, the gap between different sample listed enterprises is not very obvious, and it is reasonable to have a small number of large differences. The average size of the corresponding enterprises is 22.598, the standard deviation is 1.599, the minimum value is 19.105, and the maximum value is 27.512, which indicates that the size of the sample enterprises is at a level with little difference.

Table 1. Descriptive analysis.

Variable	Observed	Mean	Sd	Min	Max
RD	226	18.85	1.923	8.453	23.491
Tax	226	0.356	0.233	0.012	0.9791
SIZE	226	22.598	1.599	19.105	27.512
Lev	226	0.516	0.536	0.113	0.936
RDRP	226	12.210	8.047	0.500	36.190

Correlation analysis. According to the above correlation analysis, it can be found that the absolute values of coefficients of all variables are between 0 and 0.7, which basically proves that there is no significant multicollinearity problem among these variables, proving that the regression model is effective, and the relationship between variables can be explained by using multiple linear regression. After the specific analysis, it can be seen that the tax burden is inversely proportional to the R&D and innovation investment of enterprises, and the significant level reaches 1%. From the above data, it can be judged that the hypothesis is preliminarily established. There is a positive correlation between R&D investment and the proportion of R&D personnel, indicating that the higher the

R&D investment, the higher the proportion of R&D personnel in the total number of employees. The correlation coefficient between enterprise scale and enterprise R&D investment is positive. It can be concluded that the more R&D funds invested by enterprises, the larger the enterprise scale. The asset liability ratio is significantly negatively related to the R&D investment of enterprises. It is consistent with the business rules of enterprises in the actual market. If the enterprise liabilities increase, the funds invested in R&D will inevitably decrease (Table 2).

Table 2. Correlation Analysis of Variables.

	RD	Tax	Lev	RDRP	SIZE
RD	1.000	1.000			
Tax	−0.604***				
Lev	−0.409***	0.227***	1.000		
RDRP	0.305***	−0.149**	−0.004	1.000	
SIZE	0.687***	0.129*	−0.501***	0.153**	1.000

Note: *, * * and * * * are significant at 10%, 5% and 1% levels respectively.

Regression Result Analysis. The overall R^2 is 0.6893, and the P value is 0.0000, which indicates that the selection of the model parameters is very significant. The correlation coefficient of the explanatory variable Tax is negative, which indicates that the tax burden is inversely related to the enterprise's R&D level. By observing the p value, we can find that the tax burden p value is 0.000, which indicates that the tax burden has a significant impact on the R&D level, and the validation hypothesis is valid. At the same time, it is observed that the coefficient of enterprise scale is positive and p value is 0, and the coefficient of R&D personnel proportion is positive and p value is less than 0.05, indicating that these variables have significant and positive correlation with R&D investment. The correlation coefficient of asset liability ratio is negative, indicating that there is a negative correlation between the asset liability ratio and the enterprise's R&D level (Table 3).

Table 3. Multiple linear regression results of tax burden on enterprise R&D level

RD	Coef	t	P > |t|
Tax	−1.2376	−3.85	0.000
Lev	−0.7518	−1.39	0.165
RDRP	0.0395	4.29	0.000
SIZE	0.9099	17.18	0.000
R-squared	0.6893	AdjR-squared	0.6837
F(4,220)	122.02	Prob > F	0.0000

4 Conclusions and Recommendations

According to the empirical research results, this paper mainly draws the following conclusions: There is an inverse relationship between the level of logistics industry R&D and the tax burden. In short, the value-added tax, enterprise income tax, vehicle purchase tax and other taxes involved in the logistics industry occupy the space of R&D funds to a certain extent, which has a reverse effect on the employment of R&D personnel and the purchase of R&D equipment. Although in the context of structural tax reduction, the tax burden of the logistics industry is still not optimistic.

Based on the above conclusions and the actual situation of the logistics industry, the following suggestions are put forward: First, further increase the scope of deductible projects, include labor, labor and other costs into the deductible scope, and increase the input tax of the logistics industry; Second, we should increase the preferential tax policies, increase the proportion of additional deductions for R&D projects, and solve the improper competition through government regulation to offset the losses of innovation activities under the effects of externalities and market failures; Third, simplify the tax items of the logistics industry, unify the tax rates, unify the tax items and tax rates of all links of the logistics operation, and properly introduce the tax support policies of the logistics industry to help enterprises speed up the equipment update.

References

1. Dongmei, W., Songdong, J.: Analysis on tax burden level of china's logistics industry. China's Circ. Econ. **23**(01), 25–28 (2009)
2. Weiqun, X.: Tax burden and policy orientation of China's logistics industry. Tax Res. **09**, 60–64 (2010)
3. Xiaobing, M.: Using foreign experience to improve China's logistics tax policy. Jiangsu Bus. Rev. **06**, 81–83 (2010)
4. Chuntong, L., Jieshu, M.: Problems and countermeasures of China's logistics tax policy. J. Jishou Univ. (Soc. Sci. Ed.) **40**(S1), 99–101 (2019)

Tax Policy, Technological Innovation and Industrial Structure Upgrading – Based on Mediating Effect Model Test

Shuai Shao[✉] and Yuyang Zhao

Harbin University of Commerce, Harbin 150028, Heilongjiang, China
3134288704@qq.com

Abstract. The tax revenue promotes structure optimization and upgrading is a development path that our country has been actively exploring. Starting from the mediating variable of technological invention, this paper constructs the theoretical analysis framework of tax policy, industrial structure change, and makes time series data to analyze the mediating effect, aiming at characterizing tax policy on industrial structure change. The results show that the macro tax burden has a negative effect on the upgrading of industrial structure and inhibits the upgrading of industrial structure. The macro tax burden has a negative effect on technological upgrading, which restrains the input of technological invention and affects the industrial structure change. There is a quantitative mediating effect of "tax policy-technological innovation-industrial structure upgrading".

Keywords: Tax Policy · Technological Invention · Industrial structure change

1 Introduction

New development pattern is the main melody of the present economic development in our country. The 14th Five-Year Plan points out that we will enhance the modern industrial system, and stick to innovation-driven development. Taxation not only plays a role in ensuring fiscal revenue, but also irreplaceable to the government's macro-regulation of the economy. As one of the means of economic regulation by the government, tax policy has a certain impact on the industrial structure change and technological invention. It could not be ignored that technological innovation is a key node in the process of tax policies on industrial structure changing.

2 Literature Review

An Tiifu (2011) [1] points out that tax revenue promoting the structure and changing optimization of industry is also an important development path that China has been actively exploring. Chen Mingyi et al. (2021) [2] studied enterprises of market economy subject from a micro perspective. From a macro perspective, scholars' research focuses

A. Li et al. (Eds.): 6GN 2022, LNICST 504, pp. 303–310, 2023.
https://doi.org/10.1007/978-3-031-36011-4_28

on two points. The first is the impact of tax competition. Zhang Guoqing and Li Hui (2019) [3] analyzed the impact of total tax competition and tax division competition on the changing of industry under the consideration of spatial impact relationship and industrial structure changing, and also analyzed the regional heterogeneity of the impact relationship. The second is the influence of macro tax burden on industrial structure changing. Gan Xingqiong and Jiang Bingwei (2019) [4] used panel threshold model to focus on the effectiveness of tax on industrial structure changing, and concluded that macro tax burden increase would change from not conducive to industrial structure transformation to conducive to industrial structure transformation. Zhang Xuesheng (2021) [5] studied the relation between government tax competition and industrial structure changing from the perspectives of structure and aggregate, analyzed it and drew conclusion that there were aggregate and structural mediating effects. The research provides a new perspective on the relationship of tax revenue. In the end, scholars focus on the important influence of factors on the changing of industrial structure from many factors that affect the changing of structure. Among them, tax has a beneficial and negative impact on technological innovation. It is worth thinking about whether the effect of preferential tax policies on the upgrading of industrial structure still holds in terms of the overall tax burden. This article will conduct further discussion and research on the intermediary effect of tax policy, the structure and changing optimization of industry, which is based on the time series data of our country from the overall tax policy level of tax reduction and fee reduction.

3   Theoretical Analysis and Research Hypothesis

3.1   The Mechanism of Tax Policy Promoting Invention

The promotion influence of tax policy on technological invention is mainly reflected in tax preferential policy. According to the theory of quasi-public goods, the technological innovation of enterprises has some problems, such as high risk, externality of earnings and asymmetry of information. Li Yingzhou [6] believe that pure market resource allocation cannot achieve the optimal allocation of resources, so the government needs to bear certain risks to make up for the loss of its main body. Tax as a tool of government regulation of the economy, corresponding to the level of technological innovation, the concrete measures include the technology innovation subject to claim additional deduction tax, low tax rates, and a series of preferential measures to further undertake the risk and cost of main body of technical innovation and differentiation, and improve the competition mechanism to ensure the external market environment. From a macro perspective to the market main body tax, in particular, can directly affect the costs and benefits of the business, tax breaks for technology innovation, will be more able to direct its resources more configuration on technology innovation level, to promote innovation is to meet the strategic plan. Thus, the paper raises the following hypotheses:

H1: Preferential tax policies can promote technological innovation by reducing costs and sharing risks.

3.2 The Mechanism of Technological Invention Promoting Industrial Structure Changing

The evaluation standard of whether the industrial construction restructuring is upgraded in the total economic volume to judge whether the industry is upgraded. It is known that the more proportion of high-tech industry, high-end manufacturing industry and other technology-intensive industries and the tertiary industry in the secondary industry, the more perfect the industry. The action system of technological invention on industry restructuring is mainly reflected in two aspects. First, innovation can give birth to a new industrial structure. Kong Qixiang [7] believe that the scientific and technological achievements of a series of technological revolutions in recent years can be transformed into real productivity, and the spillover effect can be improved through industrial integration and agglomeration, thus promoting the change of technology-intensive industries. On the other hand, technological innovation can enhance the change of traditional industries. Thus, this paper comes up with the following hypotheses:

H2: Technological change promotes the restructuring of industrial structure by giving birth to new industrial construction.

To sum up, tax policy can reduce the cost and risk of technological innovation by enterprises through a series of preferential measures, so as to promote enterprises to continuously increase the input, and finally achieve the purpose of technological creation. Under this mechanism path, the increase of tax policy, especially tax preferential policy, can play a certain incentive role in the changing of industrial construction. Therefore, this paper raises the following hypotheses:

H3: Tax policies can finally promote the changing of industrial construction by enhancing technological creation.

4 Research Design

4.1 Index Selection and Data Sources

The paper measures and empirically analyzes the indicators related to the structure and changing optimization of industry. Among them, the tax policy measures through macro tax burden, as the main body of changing of industrial construction is the enterprise, and is the biggest tax factors impact on the business value added tax and enterprise income tax, therefore, this article selects the interpretation of the variable macro tax burden (TP) by value-added tax (VAT) income and the business income taxe in our country tax revenue (CIT), $TP_t = \sum(VAT_t + CIT_t)$

Among them, VAT tax revenue (VAT) is the sum of VAT and business tax revenue, excluding import VAT tax, in order to ensure data integrity and flatness, due to the large difference and different caliber of tax changes before and after the reform in 2016. Business income taxe revenue is the total income tax revenue of domestic and foreign enterprises.

For the measurement and selection of technological innovation indicators, different scholars choose different indicators from different perspectives for measurement. For investment, they include fiscal expenditure in fiscal expenditure, per capita R&D expenditure, and the level of R&D investment. As for output, it includes patents authorized, the amount of R&D institutions, the quantity of colleges and universities, and as for the scale of high-tech industries. Mentioned above, it learns the technological creation, focus on the tax policy on the improvement of the enterprise technology innovation cost and risk, so pay more attention to technology innovation input part of the indicators, using Gu Hongwen [8], such as measuring technology innovation thinking, selection of R&D investment intensity as intermediary variable technology innovation investment (Inn) measure.

In the study of industrial construction upgrading, the paper mainly focuses on the consequence of structure restructuring, that is, whether the industrial structure reaches the predetermined target. Therefore, for the explained variable industrial structure changing (Str), which is specifically expressed as the percentage of the output value.

In addition, aiming at reducing the influence of other socioeconomic variables on the research variables, this paper selects three control variables: level of opening to the outside world (To), urbanization rate (Urb) and government expenditure level (Gc). Among them, the level of openness to the outside world (To) is the scale of the total import and export volume of China to the corresponding year's GDP value; Urbanization rate (Urb) is the scale of urban populations to the whole population in China; Government expenditure level (Gc) is the scale of total fiscal expenditure to GDP value.

Due to the lack of partial data before 2000 and to fit the development of China at the present stage, this paper adopts 21 years of relevant data from 2000 to 2020 to make up the time series data for empirical analysis. To eliminate the time trend, the relevant data are logarithmic processed. The explained variable is the changing of industrial construction, the explanatory variable is the macro tax burden, and the technological invention is the intermediary variable. At the same time, the urbanization rate and the level of government expenditure are taken as the control variables. The specific data content is from China Statistical Yearbook and China Tax Yearbook. Specific indicator selection, basic meaning and descriptive statistics are shown in Table 1 below.

Table 1. Descriptive analysis

Variable	Observed	Mean	Sd	Max	Min
ln-Str	21	4.649	0.176	4.971	4.47
ln-TP	21	10.549	0.832	11.509	8.912
ln-Inn	21	0.513	0.261	0.875	0
ln-To	21	3.778	0.236	4.162	3.456
ln-Urb	21	3.901	0.177	4.157	3.59
ln-Gc	21	3.044	0.152	3.24	2.763

4.2 Model Setting

According to the above analysis, to test the mediating result of technological innovation on the upgrading of industrial construction, this paper explores the intermediary effect of tax policy on the upgrading of industrial construction through the distribution regression method, and constructs the mediating effect model as follows:

$$lnStr_t = \alpha_1 lnTP_t + \alpha_2 CV_t + c_1 + \varepsilon_{1t} \tag{1}$$

$$lnInn_t = \beta_1 lnTP_t + \beta_2 CV_t + c_2 + \varepsilon_{2t} \tag{2}$$

$$lnStr_t = \gamma_1 lnTP_t + \gamma_2 lnInn_t + \gamma_3 CV_t + c_3 + \varepsilon_{3t} \tag{3}$$

In the above three models, the subscript t represents the corresponding year of each variable. At the same time, since the variable is a time series, the logarithmic transformation of every variable is to reduce the influence of heteroscedasticity. Lnstr represents the logarithm of the advanced industrial construction, LnTP expresses the logarithm of the macro tax burden, and LnINN represents the logarithm of the R&D investment intensity. Meanwhile, CV is a series of control variables, ε is a random error term, C is a constant term, and $\beta_1 * \gamma_2$ is the mediating effect transmitted through technological innovation.

5 Empirical Results Analysis

5.1 Main Effect Test

In this paper, Stata14 is used to perform stepwise regression on the pattern, and the return to the results appear in Table 2 below. Through the distribution regression analysis, we can see that the first coefficient α_1 is passive at the conspicuousness level of 1%, showing that the macro tax burden and industrial construction changing have clear negative correlation, that is, with the decrease of the macro tax burden, the standard of industrial construction changing is increasing. At the same time, the coefficient β_1 is negative at the conspicuousness level of 5%, and also shows that the macro tax burden has a conspicuous negative level on technological construction. The negative signs of coefficients β_1, γ_1 and γ_2 also indicate that the mediating effect path of macro tax burden on industrial construction changing is feasible. On the basis of Table 3 and the mediating effect diagram above, it is shown that the value of coefficient α_1 is -0.331, that is, the total effect of macro tax burden on industrial structure upgrading is -0.331. Meanwhile, the coefficient β_1 is conspicuous at 5%, but the coefficient γ_2 is not conspicuous, so it is necessary to further judge whether the mediating effect is conspicuous by Sobel test.

In control variable ways, high-level industrial construction has significantly negative effects in our country, this paper argues that mainly import and export goods is proportional to the second industry development level, with the total increase of import and export goods, the ratio of the third industry of secondary industry will decline. In three steps rate coefficient regression model in the town are significantly positive, the urbanization level of technological invention and upgrade of industrial structure has significant positive effect, this paper argues that the main reason may be brought by the urbanization of the technical level of the abundant human resources to improve and upgrade of industrial structure have a positive impact, Of course, the impact of urban education level needs to be further considered, which will not be repeated here. In model 2, the level of government consumption has a conspicuous positive effect on technological innovation, indicating that the expansion has an active effect on the improvement of technological innovation level.

Table 2. The evaluation results of tax policy on industrial construction changing

variable name	Model1 lnStr	Model2 lnInn	Model3 lnStr
lnTP	(0.0981) −0.331***	(0.114) −0.292**	(0.112) −0.424***
lnInn			−0.317 (0.206)
lnTo	−0.214*** (0.0658)	0.250*** (0.0767)	−0.135 (0.0815)
lnUrb	2.324*** (0.388)	2.016*** (0.452)	2.964*** (0.558)
lnGc	−0.0954 (0.229)	1.192*** (0.267)	0.282 (0.330)
Constant	0.179 (1.123)	−8.842*** (1.308)	−2.624 (2.116)
Observations	21	21	21
R-squared	0.975	0.985	0.978

5.2 Mediating Effect Test

In the analysis of the mediating effect of the structure and changing optimization of industry, it is observed that the coefficient $\gamma 2$ in model 3 in Table 2 is not significant of technological change on the structure and changing optimization of industry, and the coefficient $\beta 1$ is significant, so it is essential to further carry out the Sobel test to judge whether there is a mediating effect. The results can be seen in Table 3 below.

Table 3. Results of Sobel test on the mediating result of tax policy on industrial structure upgrading

	Coef	Std Err	Z	P > |Z|
Sobel	0.09258778	0.07022561	1.318	0.01873586
Goodman-1 (Aroian)	0.09258778	0.07406547	1.25	0.02112702
Goodman-2	0.09258778	0.06616327	1.399	0.01616981
a coefficient	−0.292076	0.114277	−2.55586	0.010593
b coefficient	−0.316999	0.205977	−1.539	0.123804
indirect effect	0.092588	0.070226	1.31843	0.187359
direct effect	−0.424081	0.111733	−3.79549	0.000147
total effect	−0.331493	0.098098	−3.37922	0.000727

As can be seen from Sobel-Goodman test, P value of Goodman-1 (Aroian) coefficient is 0.02112702, indicating that macro tax has a conspicuousness mediating result on industrial structure upgrading at the standard of 5%. It can prove hypothesis H1, H2 and H3. Meanwhile, in the mediating effect test, it can be seen intuitively that the indirect effect is 0.092588, the direct effect is −0.424081, and the total effect is −0.331493. Furthermore, We can calculate that the proportion of indirect effect in total effect (indirect effect/total effect) is −0.27930503, the proportion of indirect effect in direct effect (indirect effect/direct effect) is 0.21832559, and the proportion of total effect in direct effect (total effect/direct effect) is 0.78167441. In conclusion, the decline of macro tax burden is conducive to promoting the structure and changing optimization of industry, and the mediating effect path of "tax policy, technological innovation and industrial structure upgrading" has also been verified.

6 Conclusions and Suggestions

Starting from the mediating variable, the paper constructs the theoretical analysis framework of tax policy, the structure and changing optimization of industry, and uses time series datum to analyze the mediating effect, aiming at characterizing the influence of tax policy on industrial construction changing and its transmission path. In this paper, we should pay attention to the following three aspects:

First, the tax burden has an obvious inhibitory effect on industrial construction changing. As for the process of tax policy reform, we should take care to the reduction of tax burden, the tax burden of micro, small and medium-sized enterprises, which has an obvious impact on the increase of technology input cost and technological innovation risk. Tax incentives should be increased. Second, some time recently, tax reduction and fee reduction" are positive role in reducing the tax burden of enterprises, but pay attention to the proportion between direct tax and indirect tax, reduce the tax burden from the tax structure, save tax costs, improve the scale of direct tax, decrease the scale of indirect tax. Third, invention for the promotion of industrial change is also obvious, but can be seen in the intermediary effect analysis, macro tax burden by influencing the technological innovation, had inhibitory effect on industrial structure upgrade, so in the process of reform of tax policy to incline to the tax policy of technology innovation, especially intensify tax incentives of high and new technology industry.

The national "14th Five-Year Plan" has put forward new guidance and requirements. During tax policy reform, people would still pay attention to the balance between tax burden and tax efficiency. This article is constrained by the limitation of data acquisition and empirical analysis level, and does not analyze the intermediary result of tax policy and industrial construction changing of tax system construction, hoping to deepen the analysis of the influence of tax policy on the structure and changing optimization of industry, in order to provide theoretical reference for our tax policy reform.

Fund project. Philosophy and Social Science Fund of China "Research on the Dynamic Mechanism and Path of High-Quality Development of New Urbanization under the New Pattern of Double Circulation" (22BSH019).

References

1. Tifu, A., Qiang, R.: Tax policies to promote the optimization and upgrading of industrial structure. J. Central Univ. Finan. Econ. **12**, 1–6 (2011)

2. Chen, M., Pang, B., Wang, L.: Effect of tax reduction, Technological Innovation and Industrial Transformation and Upgrading: empirical evidence from listed companies in Yangtze River Delta. Shanghai Econ. Res. **2021**(01), 78–89+128 (2021)

3. Zhang, G., Li, H.: The Impact of tax revenue growth on industrial upgrading: An empirical analysis based on spatial metrology and panel threshold model. J. Yunnan Univ. Finan. Econ. **35**(07), 36–48 (2019)

4. Gan, X., Jiang, B.: Analysis on the effect of tax promotion on industrial structure Transformation in China: Experience from provincial panel data. Tax Res. **12**, 100–105 (2019)

5. Zhang, X.: Local government tax competition, technological innovation and industrial structure upgrading. Finan. Sci. **05**, 46–55 (2021)

6. Li, Y., Chen, F., Fang, L.: Research on tax preferential policies to encourage the development of high-tech enterprises. Sci. Technol. Manage. Res. **29**(09), 54–56 (2009)

7. Sun, Q., Zhou, X.: Scientific and technological innovation and high-quality economic development. J. Peking Univ. (Philos. Soc. Sci.) **57**(03), 140–149 (2020)

8. Jia, H., Zhang, W., Pan, Y.: Scientific and technological innovation, industrial structure upgrading and high-quality economic development. Shanghai Econ. Res. **05**, 50–60 (2021)

Research on the Equalization Level of Public Services Under Urban-Rural Integration Development in Heilongjiang Province Based on Empirical Data Analysis

Xiaofeng Zhang[✉] and Yifan Sun

School of Public Finance and Administration, Harbin University of Commerce, Harbin 150028, Heilongjiang, China
zhxf928@163.com

Abstract. To guarantee equitable access to fundamental public services is of great significance to achieve common prosperity. As China has stepped into a well-off society and lifted the poor out of poverty, the government has proposed a major strategy of countryside revitalization, calling for the integration of city and countryside development, mutual promotion. What is the level of how to ensure equitable access to fundamental public services under integrated city-countryside development? Has it been effectively promoted? On this issue, based on empirical data in Heilongjiang province as an example, using the AHP and entropy method to quantify the standard of the equal fundamental public service between city and countryside areas of HLJ China. Then, the grey correlation model is used to verify the factors that affect the equalization level of fundamental public services in city and countryside areas, and it is demonstrated that various factors in the integrated progress of city and countryside areas promote the equalization of fundamental public service.

Keywords: Integration · Public Service · Equalization Level

1 Einleitung

City-countryside integration is one of the primary ways to deal with Industrial Relations, peasants, city or countryside areas and try to deal with the issue of balance development between city and countryside region in the fresh field. Its purpose is to narrow the gap between city or countryside development and the gap between residents' living standards, rationally allocate public resources between city or countryside areas, and promote the free flow of factors, so as to achieve a fresh type of city-countryside relationship that is fully integrated and prosperous. Ensuring equitable access to fundamental public services refers to ensuring that the fundamental public service related to the most fundamental survival and life of the public can be provided relatively fairly and justly to members of the society. Since fundamental public services are a kind of public goods, the government assumes the main responsibility, and the supply of funds for public services is mainly based on government investment.

A. Li et al. (Eds.): 6GN 2022, LNICST 504, pp. 311–319, 2023.
https://doi.org/10.1007/978-3-031-36011-4_29

The concept of equalization of fundamental public services has been around for chron, and many scholars have studied the equalization level between regions and between city and countryside areas. However, there are still few researches on the standard of balance of fundamental public service in the process of city and countryside integration development. Does the city and countryside integration development further raise the standard of equality of fundamental public service? Do various policies in the city-countryside integration development affect the standard of equality of fundamental public service? Studies on these issues are not yet clear. Based on this situation, this paper analyzes the empirical data of city-countryside integrated development in HLJ China, studies the integration standard of city and countryside fundamental public services in Heilongjiang Province, and analyzes the influence mechanism of integrated development and to ensure more suitable way to fundamental public services in city and countryside areas.

2 Research on Theoretical Mechanisms

City or countryside integrated development includes the coordinated evolution of city and countryside industries, economy, ecology, and institutions. After the gradual integrated development of city and countryside relations, it will greatly improve the conditions for realizing the equalization of fundamental public services in city and countryside places and promote the equalization of fundamental public services in city and countryside places.

Industrial city and countryside integration refers to the coordinated configuration of city and countryside industrial chains to achieve high-quality operation, which usually provides a material basis for the equalization of city and countryside fundamental public services. From the economic aspect, city and countryside integration will increase the economic exchanges between cities and countryside, and make the economic relations become closer, thus providing economic conditions for the equal development of fundamental public services in city or countryside places. From the perspective of institutional integration of city and countryside areas, with the in-depth integration of city and countryside relations, a series of systems to promote city and countryside integration, such as orderly progress in urbanization of migrant agricultural population and incentive system for city talents to move to countryside areas, have been continuously established, creating a good institutional environment to guarantee how to ensure equitable access to basic public services.

Therefore, the process of city and countryside integrated progress will naturally be accompanied by the equal development of fundamental public services, which will narrow the gap between city and countryside areas and improve the industrial, economic, institutional and ecological conditions of city and countryside development. With the deep integration of city and countryside relations, the equal development of fundamental public services is inevitable. Policies and measures in the process of city and countryside integration will also affect the equal level of fundamental public services and promote the balanced development of city and countryside places in fundamental public services.

3   Equalization Level Measurement of Fundamental Public Services

In order to study how to ensure the fair way to fundamental public services under the integration of city and countryside areas, this paper discusses the influencing factors of how to ensure the fair access to fundamental public services in the development of city and countryside integration. The equalization level of fundamental public services should be reasonably quantified first. By collecting relevant data from the statistical yearbook, we measure the balance standard of city and countryside fundamental public services in HLJ China by using subjective AHP and objective entropy method.

3.1   Selection of Indicators

Concerns about availability and data validity, the scientific nature, the objectivity and other principles of the pointer system, in order to comprehensively reflect the public service projects that can best ensure the fundamental survival and living rights of the public, this paper evaluates the equalization level of city and countryside fundamental public service in HLJ China from four dimensions: fundamental education, social insurance, medical care and infrastructure (Table 1).

Table 1.   Indicator System.

Target Layer	Criterion Layer	Index Layer
Equalization of fundamental public services in city and countryside areas	Public Education (B_1)	Per Student Education Expenditure in Secondary Schools (C_1)
		Per Student Education Expenditure in Primary Schools (C_2)
		Teacher-Student Ratio in Secondary Schools (C_3)
		Teacher-Student Ratio in Primary Schools (C_4)
	Social Security (B_2)	Per capita pension expenditure (C_5)
		Coverage of fundamental medical insurance (C_6)
		Proportion of employment number (C_7)
	Medical Treatment and Public Health (B_3)	Number of beds per 10,000 people (C_8)
		Number of hospital technicians per 10,000 people (C_9)
		Number of professional professional doctors per 10,000 people (C_{10})
	Infrastructure Construction (B_4)	rate of water-served population (C_{11})
		rate of gas-used population (C_{12})

3.2 Confirm of Indexes Proportion

In terms of determining the index weight, this paper uses a combination of two methods, namely the subjective weight method and the objective weight way. The AHP way is used to determine the sub-weight, and the entropy way is used to determine the objective weight.

AHP Method. When using the AHP method to determine the index weight, it is necessary to gradually determine the weight according to the relative importance of each index at the same level on the basis of establishing the hierarchical structure model. The steps of AHP to decide the index weight are as follows:

According to the relative importance between the elements, construct a pairwise comparison judgment matrix $A = (a_{ij})_{n \times n}$, where a_{ij} is the value of the pairwise comparison of the importance of the *i-th* row index relative to the *j-th* column index, a_{ij} is the numbers 1–9 and its reciprocal.

Compute the maximum eigenvalue λmax of the judgment matrix A and the normalized eigenvector w.

$$Aw = \lambda_{max} w \tag{1}$$

Consistency check. CR is calculated according to the judgment matrix consistency indicator CI and the given random consistency indicator RI. When the consistency ratio $CR < 0.10$, it indicates that can accept the consistency of the judgment matrix, and the vector w is the corresponding weight of each indicator.

$$CR = \frac{CI}{RI} \tag{2}$$

$$CI = \frac{\lambda max - n}{n - 1} \tag{3}$$

Entropy Method. The entropy method can determine the weight of the evaluation indicator according to the level of difference between the indicator values. Specifically, the greater the entropy value, the smaller the indicator weight; the smaller the entropy value, the greater the index weight. The steps of deciding index weight by entropy way:

Let xij be the surveied cost of the j-th indicator in the i-th appraise object. (i = 1, 2,..., n; j = 1, 2,..., m).

Compute the indicator cost ratio of the *i-th* evaluated object on the *j-th* appraise indicator.

$$P_{ij} = \frac{x_{ij}}{\sum_{i=1}^{n} x_{ij}} \tag{4}$$

Compute the entropy cost of the *j-th* appraise indicator.

$$e_j = -\frac{1}{\ln n} \sum_{i=1}^{n} p_{ij}, \ln(p_{ij}) \tag{5}$$

Compute the different coefficient g_j of the appraise indicator x_j.

$$g_j = 1 - e_j \tag{6}$$

Determination of weight.

$$w_{2j} = g_j / \sum\nolimits_{j=1}^{m} g_j, \; j = 1, 2, \ldots m \tag{7}$$

Determination of the Comprehensive Weight of Indicators. The comprehensive weight of the indicator is obtained by combining the weight w1j obtained by AHP with the weight w2j obtained by entropy method (Table 2).

$$w_j = \frac{1}{2}w_{1j} + \frac{1}{2}w_{2j} \tag{8}$$

Table 2. Comprehensive weight of indicators.

Criterion Layer	Index Layer	w_{1j}	w_{2j}	w_j
B_1	C_1	0.05968	0.03728	0.04848
	C_2	0.04926	0.01347	0.03136
	C_3	0.19187	0.11714	0.15451
	C_4	0.11465	0.03759	0.07612
B_2	C_5	0.09269	0.17061	0.13165
	C_6	0.16127	0.21662	0.18895
	C_7	0.03549	0.06663	0.05106
B_3	C_8	0.08882	0.08669	0.08775
	C_9	0.05650	0.00579	0.03115
	C_{10}	0.02396	0.03708	0.03052
B_4	C_{11}	0.03145	0.00385	0.01765
	$C1_2$	0.09434	0.20725	0.15079

3.3 The Result of the Equalization Index

The city and countryside fundamental equal access to public services level index of Heilongjiang Province can be obtained according to the value of the established fundamental public service equalization index and the weight obtained after subjective and objective analysis. In this paper, the city and countryside fundamental public service balance index can be computed according to the following formula:

$$S = \sum\nolimits_{j=1}^{m} w_j \times x_{ij} \tag{9}$$

That is, when computing the balance index of each fundamental public service, the equalization level is obtained by using the method of weighted sue for peace of the standardizing value of the index and the homologous index weight. In order to remove the impact of dimension on equalization index, it is determined to carry out standardization processing and adopt the method of comparing city data with countryside data (Table 3).

Table 3. Equalization level of city and countryside public services.

Year	Indicator of equalization of public services
2009	0.649783
2010	0.658627
2011	0.705193
2012	0.716655
2013	0.78149
2014	0.779955
2015	0.7611
2016	0.748631
2017	0.6708
2018	0.671545
2019	0.638806

4 Further Analysis: Factors Affecting the Equalization of Fundamental Public Services

4.1 Analysis and Screening of Influencing Factors

To guarantee equitable access to fundamental public services under city-countryside integration is an significant content and key link of city-countryside integrated development. The policy measures implemented during city-countrysidel integrated development are likely to affect the level of balance of fundamental public services. Therefore, the factors affecting how to guarantee equitable access to fundamental public services can be inferred according to the level and characteristics of the balance development of city and countryside fundamental public services in Heilongjiang Province.

Firstly, the scale of fiscal expenditure on fundamental public services affects the overall quality and level of fundamental public services in city and countryside areas. Only with sufficient financial funds can we raise the supply level of fundamental public services and promote to how to guarantee equitable access to fundamental public services under city-countryside areas. Secondly, the policy orientation in the process of city-countrysidel integration development is also a factor affecting the equitable development of fundamental public services in city and countryside areas. It can be proved that the degree of city-countryside equalization in medical and health care and infrastructure in HLJ China is low, and the proportion of city and countryside areas is gradually decreasing. Therefore, it is speculated that when the level of fundamental public services in the whole province is low, the policy will be more biased towards cities. Thirdly, financial support for agriculture and countryside areas will also affect the level of balance of fundamental public services in city and countryside places. With the proposal of the countryside revitalization strategy, the development of agriculture and countryside areas is very important, and the strength of support for agriculture directly affects the supply system of countryside and fundamental public services Fourthly, behind the reform of the tax-sharing system, the financial resources of local governments have weakened, and the growing gap in fiscal revenue and expenditure has also prevented local governments from fully exerting their information advantages and cannot drive the effective provision of fundamental public services in city and countryside areas.

4.2 Grey Relative Analysis

As a method to measure the degree of correlation between factors, grey relational analysis method is used to judge the degree of correlation by comparing the influence of the change of sequence index on the reference sequence index. The fundamental idea of grey incidence analysis is to decide the correlation degree by analyzing the influence of the comparison sequence index on the reference sequence index. The larger the correlation degree is, the stronger the correlation degree between the comparison order and the reference order is; otherwise, the weaker the correlation degree is.

This paper adopts the way of grey incidence analysis to discuss the degree of correlation between the level of how to ensure equitable access to city and countryside fundamental public services or the scale of financial investment, local financial gap, financial support for countryside areas, and government policy bias. Among them, the gap between the amount of fiscal expenditure and income y_1 represents the fiscal gap of the government, the public expenditure on agriculture, countryside places and farmers y_2 represents the government's support to countryside areas, and the fiscal expenditure on education y_3, medical expenditure y_4 and social security expenditure y_5 represents the investment intensity of fiscal funds. Meanwhile, the word frequency ratio of "city" and "countryside" in the government work report y_6 was used to indicate the city-countryside bias of the policy (Table 4).

The steps of grey correlation analysis are as follows:

Set up reference sequence and comparison sequence. The 2009–2019 city and countryside fundamental public service equalization index in Heilongjiang Province is used as the reference sequence $Y_0(k)$ to represent the public service equalization index in the kth year; the factors that affect how to guarantee equitable access to fundamental public services are used as the comparison sequence $Y_i(k)$ to represent the data of the *i-th* influencing factor index in the *k-th* year.

The initial value method was used to standardize the data, and the ratio of the *i-th* data to the data of the first year was obtained.

$$Y_i'(k) = \frac{Y_i(k)}{Y_i(1)} \tag{10}$$

Get the difference sequence and the second order minimum (large) difference.

$$\Delta_i(k) = \left| Y_I'(k) - Y_0'(k) \right| \tag{11}$$

$$\Delta min = \min_i \left[\min_k \left| Y_I'(k) - Y_0'(k) \right| \right] \tag{12}$$

$$\Delta max = \max_i \left[\max_k \left| Y_I'(k) - Y_0'(k) \right| \right] \tag{13}$$

Compute the correlation coefficient ξ_i and the correlation degree r_i. Usually, $\rho = 0.5$

$$\xi_i(k) = \frac{\Delta min + \rho \Delta max}{\Delta_i(k) + \rho \Delta max} \tag{14}$$

$$r_i = \frac{1}{n} \sum \xi_i(k) \tag{15}$$

4.3 Correlation Results

Based on the grey system theory, the degree of correlation between the balance level of city and countryside public services in HLJ China and the financial input, financial support for agriculture, and the financial gap of local authorities under the tax-sharing system can be obtained. The higher the correlation, the greater the impact on how to ensure equitable access to city-countryside fundamental public services.

Table 4. Statistical description of variables.

Variable name		Mean	Std. Dev.	Min	Max
Y_0	y_0	0.70751	0.05335	0.63881	0.78149
Y_i	y_1	571.008	239.517	192.42	881.99
	y_2	2476.08	851.943	1236.12	3748.8
	y_3	479.339	111.520	266.61	573.11
	y_4	651.637	278.726	306.06	1113.27
	y_5	227.974	68.8126	135.18	314.423
	y_6	1.00465	0.29484	0.71875	1.48101

As what shows in Table 5, the correlation between every influencing factor and how to ensure equitable access to basic public services in city and countryside places is between 0.55 and 0.85. It shows that the factors of financial gap, agricultural support and financial expenditure of fundamental public services are all important factors that can affect how to ensure access to fundamental public services in a equitable way in HLJ China.

Table 5. Interdependence coefficients.

index	y_1	y_2	y_3	y_4	y_5	y_6
relational degree	0.71	0.55	0.73	0.75	0.79	0.83

5 Conclusions

Through the quantification of the standard of can affect how to guarantee well access to fundamental public services in Heilongjiang and the analysis of its influencing factors, it can be concluded that the policy measures in the process of city-countryside integration development will indeed affect the standard of how to ensure equitable way to fundamental public services.

The amount of financial input and the bias of policies have the most direct effect on the equalization of fundamental public services. Public service is a social public product, and the government's financial input determines the level of social public service. The government's preference for city and countryside development also directly affects the level of public service equalization between city and countryside areas. If the government's fiscal policy is non-agricultural, the level of fundamental public service in city areas will be better than that in countryside areas. In addition, the financial situation that income does not cover expenditure and the investment in agriculture also affect the standard of how to guarantee equitable way to fundamental public services between city and countryside areas in HLJ China to one certain extent. If the local government's income does not cover its expenditure, it cannot actively guide the realization of the standard of how to guarantee equitable way to fundamental public services. If the importance of village areas is not taken seriously, the gap between city and countryside fundamental public services cannot be eliminated.

Fund Project. Philosophy and Social Science Fund of China "Research on the Dynamic Mechanism and Path of High-Quality Development of New Urbanization under the New Pattern of Double Circulation" (22BSH019); Philosophy and Social Science Fund of Heilongjiang Province "Research on the high-quality development path of county economy in Heilongjiang Province based on the new development concept" (22JYH066).

References

1. Nguyen, L.D., Raabe, K., Grote, U.: Rural-urban migration, household vulnerability, and welfare in Vietnam. World Develop. **71**, 79–93 (2015)
2. Antoon, S.: The role of governments in aligning functional income distribution with full employment. J. Econ. Issues **51**(3), 688–697 (2017)
3. Bairoliya, N., Miller, R.: Social Insurance, Demographics, and Rural-Urban Migration in China. Social Science Electronic Publishing (2020)
4. Belanche, D., Casaló, L.V., Rubio, M.N.: Local place identity: a comparison between residents of rural and urban communities. J. Rural Stud. **82**(1), 242–252 (2021)

Application Research of Electronic Invoice System Based on Blockchain Technology—Taking Shenzhen City as an Example

Xiaofeng Zhang and Shiyu Lu[✉]

School of Finance and Public Administration, Harbin University of Commerce, Harbin, China
lushiyu19971025@163.com

Abstract. This paper starts with the operation principle of blockchain electronic invoice system, the operation effect and development bottleneck in Shenzhen. Based on this, it explains how blockchain technology is integrated into electronic invoices system, analyzes the operation effect of Shenzhen blockchain electronic invoices system, and finally analyzes the bottlenecks in the application of blockchain electronic invoices system of Shenzhen Taxation Bureau based on index construction. Provide experience and reference for improving the application of national electronic invoices system.

Keywords: Blockchain · Electronic invoice system · Application research

1 Introduction

1.1 Blockchain Electronic Invoice System

Blockchain is a chain data structure composed of data blocks connected in sequence according to time sequence, and it is cryptographically guaranteed not to be tampered with and not to be forged. A block is the basic data unit, which aggregates all transaction-related information. The chain structure formed by connecting each block is a blockchain. The latter block includes the ID (identification code) of the previous block, which makes each block. Every block can find the previous node.

Blockchain electronic invoices system have the following advantages: checkable, verifiable, credible, and traceable; data security is guaranteed; closed-loop management of the whole process of invoice circulation, etc. The comparison with traditional invoices system is shown in Table 1:

1.2 Diagram of Shenzhen Blockchain Electronic Invoice System Operation

By reading the literature on the principle of blockchain technology deployment, this paper divides the Shenzhen blockchain electronic invoice system into five layers, namely: hardware layer, blockchain layer, blockchain interface layer, application interface layer and presentation layer. The specific analysis is shown in Fig. 1.

A. Li et al. (Eds.): 6GN 2022, LNICST 504, pp. 320–324, 2023.
https://doi.org/10.1007/978-3-031-36011-4_30

Table 1. The comparison.

project	Blockchain Electronic Invoice system	traditional electronic invoice system
Electronic entry, reimbursement and reporting	can	some can't
tampering risk	low risk	medium to high risk
Is it possible to exchange information	can	no
Is the data traceable?	can	no
Data leakage, forgery risk	low risk	medium to high risk

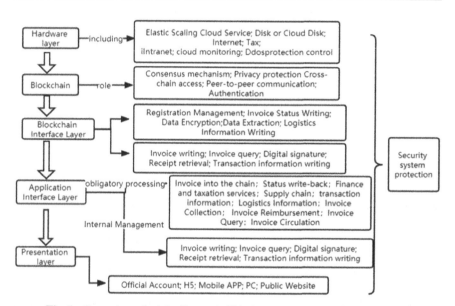

Fig. 1. Operation principle diagram of blockchain electronic invoice system.

2 Analysis of Bottlenecks in the Development of Blockchain Electronic Invoices System in Shenzhen

2.1 Construction of Evaluation Index System

This article cites the relevant data of the "2018 China Blockchain Industry Index Research Report" to analyze and explain the problems existing in the development of Shenzhen's blockchain. In this research report, the blockchain industry index of 32 central cities is ranked and evaluated. In this report, the blockchain evaluation is refined to 5 indicators, namely scale base, financial strength, innovation ability, ecological Environmental and social contribution. Each indicator has corresponding selection basis and secondary and tertiary indicators. The specific indicator framework is shown in Table 2.

Table 2. Index system construction.

first-level indicator	Secondary indicators	three-level indicator
scale basis	Blockchain enterprise scale	Ordinary business
		Leading enterprise
		Listed company
	Blockchain service organization	Investment agency
		industry organization
		Research institute
	Blockchain Industrial Park	Industrial Park
		Entrepreneurship base
		Incubation Park
financial strength	capital investment	investment amount
		Investment frequency
	Financing	Financing Amount
		Financing frequency
	financial performance	Return on investment and financing
Creativity	Blockchain Talent	Number of employees
		Employee quality
		University opens blockchain major
		Professional training institutions
	Blockchain Patent	Patent filed in the year
		patented in the year
	blockchain technology	Newly developed major technologies of the year
		Promoting major technological achievements
	Blockchain top-level design	Number of industry standard documents issued
ecosystem	Policy Environment	Number of dedicated blockchain policies introduced
		Number of policies related to blockchain
	social environment	The city's publicity and education activities and publication of books and periodicals
		Community Activities and Resident Awareness and Participation
	Risk control environment	Regulatory bodies and mechanisms
		case
Social Contributions	Scenario application	Application industry

2.2 Analysis of Results

The According to the importance of different indicators, the corresponding scores are divided and calculated. This paper selects the top 10 cities for citation and analysis. The ranking of each indicator is shown in Table 3.

Table 3. Results Analysis.

	Overall Index (100 points)	scale technology (30 points)	financial strength (20 points)	Creativity (25 points)	ecosystem (15 marks)	Social Contributions (10 points)
Beijing	65.86	19	12.8	13.16	11	9.9
Shanghai	63.24	18.3	12.6	10.54	12.8	9
Hangzhou	63.09	18.45	10.7	10.14	14.8	9
Shenzhen	60.49	16.85	17	12.44	4.9	9.3
Guangzhou	45.27	18.45	6.1	8.52	4.8	7.4
Chengdu	39.18	12.9	3.7	8.18	6.3	8.1
Tianjin	31.23	13.6	0	6.48	6.9	4.2
Guiyang	24.35	11.6	0	2.9	8.8	1.05
Qingdao	22.78	12.65	0	5.68	1.4	3.05
Xi'an	21.7	12.25	0.5	5.1	1.4	2.45
	Overall Index (100 points)	scale technology (30 points)	financial strength (20 points)	Creativity (25 points)	ecosystem (15 marks)	Social Contributions (10 points)

It can be seen from Table 3 that the overall development of blockchain technology in Shenzhen ranks fourth, but the ecological environment and scale foundation, especially the ecological environment, is far behind the top three, and even lags behind the inland areas of Chengdu, Tianjin and Guiyang city.

On the one hand, Shenzhen ranks low in terms of ecological environment indicators, in which policy and environmental issues are particularly prominent. It shows that Shenzhen's support for the development of blockchain is weak in terms of policies, and the relevant policies issued for blockchain are far inferior to other cities. On the other hand, Shenzhen ranks slightly behind in terms of scale-based indicators, showing a backward trend compared with the overall indicators. The most obvious problem is the lack of "blockchain industrial parks", with a score of 0, and Guangzhou's 2.3. Compared with Shanghai's 1.7, the gap is very large. This shows that the development of the blockchain industry in Shenzhen relies almost on the efforts of the enterprises themselves, especially thanks to a large number of Internet giants in Shenzhen, and the policy support is weak.

From the analysis of the above two aspects, it can be seen that one of the factors restricting the development of blockchain electronic invoices system in Shenzhen is that the policy support is not strong enough. The lack of relevant policy documents leads to a poor policy environment for blockchain development. The government does not build blockchain industrial parks, resulting in less policy support for blockchain.

3 Suggestions

3.1 Strengthening Policy Support for Blockchain Technology

The state should introduce corresponding policies to actively support the development of blockchain technology. In terms of finance, blockchain technology companies can be given certain financial subsidies and tax incentives, set more relaxed industry thresholds, and create blockchain industrial parks as blocks. The development of chain technology provides a good environment. In addition, regional governments should actively introduce high-tech companies such as blockchain, use policy dividends to encourage blockchain companies to settle in the local area, develop blockchain technology, and promote the combination of blockchain technology and electronic invoices system.

3.2 Multi-party Cooperation to Build a Blockchain Electronic Invoice System

The state should also introduce relevant policies and systems to strongly support and encourage cooperation between tax authorities and blockchain technology companies. To cultivate and introduce talents in blockchain technology, tax authorities in various regions should actively communicate and communicate with local blockchain high-tech companies, determine cooperation plans, and use the power of enterprises and society to promote the reform of electronic invoices and boost electronic invoices system Develop and complete the innovation and transformation of tax collection and management.

Fund Project. Philosophy and Social Science Fund of Heilongjiang Provincet " Research on high-quality construction of new-type urbanization under the pattern of 'dual circulation'in Heilongjiang Province"(21JYC239); Harbin university of commerce PhD research startup fund"Research on the Fiscal and Taxation Policy of Agricultural Population Citizenization under New Urbanization " (2019DS002); Youth innovative talent project Harbin university of commerce " Research on the fiscal and taxation policy system and mechanism to promote the integrated development of ice and snow tourism and cultural industry in Heilongjiang Province" (2020CX21).

References

1. Feng, P.: Research on the application of blockchain technology in the construction of financial sharing platforms in colleges and universities. Front. Econ. Culture **04**, 45–48 (2022)
2. Li, C., Jiaxi, C.: an analysis of modern tax management mode based on blockchain technology. Finan. Manage. Res. **02**, 70–77 (2022)
3. Xin, D.: Analysis on the application of blockchain electronic invoices system in college reimbursement business. Friends Account. **01**, 157–161 (2022)
4. Miao, S., Zhi, X.: Research on the development strategy of blockchain electronic invoice. Bus. Account. **2021**(15), 87–89 (2021)
5. Geng, J.: Improving the level of tax risk management by applying blockchain technology. J. Hunan Taxation College **34**(02), 29–32.1 (2021)

Design of an Algorithm of Fault Diagnosis Based on the Multiple Source Vibration Signals

Ming Jiang[1(✉)], Zhenyu Xu[2], and Si Li[1]

[1] Harbin Institute of Technology, Harbin 150001, China
mjiang@hit.edu.cn
[2] Hui Zhou Engineering Vocational College, Hui Zhou 516023, China

Abstract. The main application direction of this paper is to diagnose various fault states or normal states of the three kinds of pumps, such as the lubricating oil pump, the centrifugal pump and the hydraulic pump, on the industrial equipment and other equipment. The data processing is performed according to the acceleration signals measured by each sensor in the fault or normal state of the three pumps provided, and the data is divided into a training set and a validation set. The common algorithm of fault diagnosis is adopted, and the one-dimensional convolutional neural network is used as the core to construct the overall framework of fault diagnosis, so as to judge whether the fault is faulty by detecting the single-source vibration signal, and obtain the correct rate of judgment. The two-dimensional convolutional neural network model is first built, and the method of convolutional neural network is used for multi-source information fusion. The vibration signals measured by the acceleration sensors at four different locations are composed of two-dimensional signals and input into the new two-dimensional convolutional neural network. Input the dataset classification into the architecture for architecture training and accuracy analysis, and change the convolutional neural network structure to achieve higher accuracy.

Keywords: Fault diagnosis · Convolutional Neural Network · Multi-source information fusion

1 Introduction

Mechanical fault diagnosis has always been a research hotspot at home and abroad. For a long time, the signal processing methods were used to study the fault types of rotating machinery such as pumps. The specific methods include singular value analysis [1, 2], wavelet transform [3], empirical mode decomposition, etc. There are many machine learning based fault diagnosis methods beyond the limitations of traditional methods, such as K nearest neighbor classification. In recent years, the concept of Convolutional Neural Networks (CNN) [4–8] has been put forward, which has become the most popular fault diagnosis method due to its strong feature extraction ability [9, 10] and the use of deep learning [11]. The aim of this paper is to study whether the pumps of industrial equipment work normally, including oil pumps, centrifugal pumps and hydraulic pumps,

A. Li et al. (Eds.): 6GN 2022, LNICST 504, pp. 325–331, 2023.
https://doi.org/10.1007/978-3-031-36011-4_31

which are necessary for industrial equipment. By measuring their real-time acceleration signals, it can judge whether the pumps on industrial equipment work normally or fail in time. Normal operation is exactly what we want, but if a fault is detected, stop the operation of the industrial equipment in time, and conduct maintenance in time to prevent the industrial equipment from having very serious consequences after operation.

2   One Dimensional CNN Architecture Design, Data Processing and Optimizer Selection

The preliminary design of the architecture of one-dimensional convolutional neural network is completed, which is a key step for the construction of the overall architecture of the subsequent fault diagnosis algorithm. In addition to the construction of one-dimensional convolutional neural network architecture, attention should also be paid to the input data input into the architecture, that is, the processing of data sets. The processing of data sets is very important, including the classification and labeling of data sets. If the data sets are too few or the samples are unbalanced, special processing should also be carried out on the data sets. As with dataset processing, the choice of optimizer is also important.

The basic structure of one-dimensional convolutional neural network always roughly includes convolution layer, pooling layer, activation function layer, Batch Normalization (BN layer), full connection layer and classification layer. For two discrete signals, the definition of convolution is shown in formula (1).

$$f[n] * g[n] = \sum_{m=-\infty}^{+\infty} f[n]g[n-m] \tag{1}$$

The convolution layer, BN layer, activation function layer and pooling layer are preliminarily selected to form a hidden layer structure. The hidden layer structure appears five times repeatedly to achieve more levels of information extraction. Then through the full connection layer and the classification layer, the probability of nine faults is finally output.

Classification of data sets, that is, data sets are divided into training sets and verification sets. Generally speaking, part of the data is used as an "exercise" of the neural network architecture, and part of the data is used as a "self-test". The basic size of each data is $1 \times 4 \times 2048$, which represents one-dimensional data. Each pump has four sensors for measurement, and 1024 points are measured as a group. Each fault type shall be trained by magnitude. The database includes the multiple source vibration signals generated by lubricating oil pump, centrifugal pump and hydraulic pump. The data set is divided into training set and verification set. It is found that the number of samples is moderate, and there is no need to expand the data volume separately. There are about 4000 samples of each type, and the total number of samples reaches 40000, which is enough. The method of directly expanding data sets is adopted to achieve the balance of data sets. The choice of optimizer is very important for the whole convolutional neural network. It determines the speed of training and the final accuracy rate, so it should be carefully selected. In this experiment, the Adam optimizer was selected, which has the following advantages. First of all, the implementation method is relatively simple, the calculation efficiency is high, and the memory requirement is small. This is very important for this experiment, because my computer can't bear the training of optimizer with high memory requirements. Hyperparameters are very interpretative, and usually require no adjustment or little fine-tuning, which also provides convenience for subsequent parameter adjustment. The updating step size is limited to a small range, that is, the initial learning rate will not change significantly. But it can automatically adjust the learning rate slightly to find lower losses faster. The reason why Adam was finally selected is that in the optimizer comparison experiment, Adam has obvious advantages over SGD, another very common optimizer.

3   Training Realization of One-Dimensional Convolutional Neural Network

The basic architecture of one-dimensional convolutional neural network has been built, and its external framework has been implemented. The specific values of internal parameters have not been updated. Then the training of the one-dimensional convolutional neural network is very necessary. After the architecture is designed, the above neural network should be trained. The essence of training is to carry out the weight self optimization process of the back propagation algorithm. The purpose of training is to change the parameters of the neural network as much as possible, so that it can more accurately deal with a class of problems, that is, fault diagnosis classification problem. The content of this chapter is to build a training framework for one-dimensional convolutional neural networks to update the network parameters and minimize the loss of its cost function.

The main content of this part is to train the one-dimensional convolutional neural network model that has been built. The purpose of training is to change the network parameters in the model to make the value of its loss function smaller, which is more accurate in theory. The main function for training needs to be written. After the compilation, the main function is used for actual training to get a training result. First of all, an experiment was carried out on the lack of BN layer. BN layer is added to obtain the fault diagnosis model of single source vibration signal for five rounds. The results show that the loss is very low, and the accuracy has reached more than 95%, which is a very good result. Then the optimization experiment is carried out, and the conclusion that Adam optimizer is better is finally obtained. Finally, the prediction ability of repeated BP units is tested. The test results show that the fault diagnosis architecture composed of full connection layer only has no scientific prediction ability, and is inferior to the hidden layer structure model.

4   Multiple Source Information Fusion Mode Selection and Architecture Optimization

There are four groups of acceleration vibration signals measured by acceleration sensors in the data set, all of which are input into the convolutional neural network. Through multi-source information fusion, the accuracy is further improved and the overall loss is reduced. After multi-source information fusion, a fault diagnosis architecture based on multi-source vibration signals and output fault types is obtained. Theoretically, the accuracy can be improved. However, in order to obtain a more stable accuracy and overall loss, architecture optimization is essential. Only by finding the most suitable structure for pump fault detection can a more reliable fault diagnosis structure be obtained. So we should do a series of experiments to find the optimal solution.

4.1   Selection and Implementation of Multi Source Information Fusion Mode

The basic concepts of multi-source information fusion is based on a variety of similar or heterogeneous information sources, by combining these information sources in time or space according to a certain standard, in order to obtain consistent interpretation of the analyzed object and make the information analysis system have better performance. The experimental data used in this experiment is measured by four different acceleration sensors for each pump, and the four groups of data can be obtained simultaneously, and each group of data can be used for fault diagnosis. According to the analysis, the data layer fusion is selected, that is, multi-source information fusion is carried out at the input. The theoretical method is to combine four groups of one-dimensional acceleration sensor measured vibration signals into a group of two-dimensional input signals at the input. The two-dimensional convolution neural network method is used to process the data and finally obtain the fault diagnosis results.

Single source vibration signals are processed before, and the size of each basic signal is 1×2048, now it forms a two-dimensional input signal, using the method similar to the matrix, before input, the data is spliced to form 4×2048. In the DATASET function, the input dimension is changed to achieve the transformation from one dimension to two dimensions, change the five layer hidden layer structure in the convolutional neural network. The multi-source information fusion in the data layer is realized to improve the accuracy of fault diagnosis and reduce the overall loss.

4.2   Optimization of Learning Rate and Hidden Layer Structure Repetition

Learning rate is the most important artificial parameter in a convolutional neural network. The optimizer has the greatest correlation with the learning rate. The training rounds selected are all 5 rounds. On average, the training time for one round is about 10 min based on the computing power of the personal computer. This experiment sets the learning rate as 3×10^{-2}, 3×10^{-3}, 3×10^{-4}, 3×10^{-5}, and then conduct five rounds of two-dimensional convolutional neural network training at a time. From the trend, only the learning rate is 3×10^{-5}. The total loss of each round is consistent with the downward trend, but the total loss of each round is high.

After optimizing the learning rate, the number of repetitions of the hidden layer structure should be optimized. The initial setting is 5 repetitions. The first convolution core is 64, which is used to identify long chain information, and the last four convolution cores are 3, which is used to identify short chain information. The long convolution kernel can get more overall information, while the short convolution kernel can get more detailed information to analyze detailed differences. In the learning rate experiment, the final result is 3×10^{-3}, 3×10^{-4}. The two learning rates have good learning characteristics, so both of them should be used in the following implementation. When the learning rate is 3×10^{-3}, the 4-layer hidden layer structure is the most appropriate. When the learning rate is 3×10^{-4}, the 3-layer hidden layer structure is the most appropriate. When the learning rate is 3×10^{-4}, the structure and learning rate of the three hidden layers are 3×10^{-3}, the experiment of 4-layer hidden layer structure is repeated to prevent unexpected data. Choose stable and stronger learning through final comparison 3×10^{-4}, the two-dimensional convolutional neural network with three hidden layers is the core of the fault diagnosis architecture.

4.3   Repeat Experiment of Good Model After Special Data Processing

After special processing of the dataset, this paper repeats the experiment again to observe the change of the accuracy and the total loss of the round. By analyzing Fig. 1 and Fig. 2, it can be found that the learning rate is 3×10^{-4}, when the 3-layer hidden layer structure repeats the experiment, the 12 round accuracy rate after data balancing is lower than that without data balancing. When the learning rate is 3×10^{-3}, when the 4-layer hidden layer structure repeats the experiment, after the data is balanced, the accuracy has been significantly improved, and is basically stable at more than 99%.The final selection of fault diagnosis architecture should be based on the data balance, because such architecture can make more balanced judgment, and will not preset which fault rarely occurs. So the learning rate is 3×10^{-3}, a two-dimensional convolutional neural network with good network parameters is trained from a 4-layer hidden layer structure to complete the final fault diagnosis architecture.

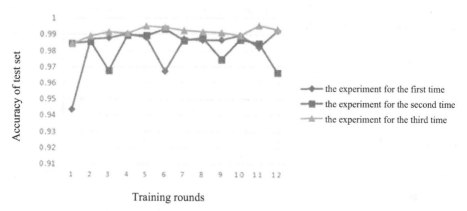

Fig. 1. The 4-layer hidden layer structure repeat experimental verification set accuracy for learning rate of 3×10^{-4}.

4.4   Final Implementation of Fault Diagnosis Network Architecture

In this experiment, Bagging's integration method is used. For trained students, the learning rate is 3×10^{-3}, the 2-dimensional convolutional neural network with 4-layer hidden

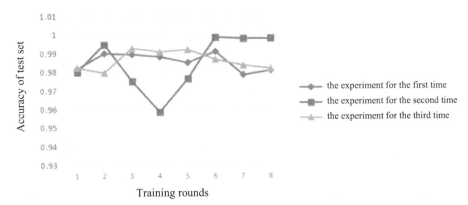

Fig. 2. The 4-layer hidden layer structure repeat experimental verification set accuracy for learning rate of 3×10^{-3}.

layer structure selects the model with high accuracy, and then Bagging is performed once. Two two-dimensional convolutional neural network models Bagging are carried out. The correctness of the verification set of these two convolutional neural networks is 99.852% and 99.805% respectively. After the two models Bagging, the accuracy of the fault diagnosis architecture has reached an amazing 99.945%, which is the first time that this experiment has raised the accuracy to three nines. As the above relatively good results are obtained, Bagging's two-dimensional convolutional neural network model is further improved to five, and the individual accuracy of the three added models is 99.113%, 99.602% and 99.566%. After five models bagging, the accuracy of the fault diagnosis architecture has reached 99.981%.

5   Conclusion

On the basis of single source vibration signal analysis, multi-source information fusion is adopted, and data sets are used as much as possible to improve the accuracy. Various experiments were carried out to optimize the structure of the convolutional neural network and get a better architecture. By adopting Bagging method in integrated learning, a fault diagnosis architecture with the final accuracy of 99.981% is obtained.

References

1. Uzhga-Rebrov, O., Kuleshova, G.: Using Singular Value Decomposition to Reduce Dimensionality of Initial Data Set. In: 2020 61st International Scientific Conference on Information Technology and Management Science of Riga Technical University (ITMS), pp. 1–4 (2020)
2. Zhang, X., Yu, X.: Color image reconstruction based on singular value decomposition of quaternion matrices. In: 2018 2nd IEEE Advanced Information Management, Communicates, Electronic and Automation Control Conference (IMCEC), pp. 2645–2647 (2018)
3. Sornsen, I., Suppitaksakul, C., Kitpaiboontawee, R.: Partial discharge signal detection in generators using wavelet transforms. In: 2021 International Conference on Power, Energy and Innovations (ICPEI), pp. 195–198 (2021)

4. Uçkun, F.A., Özer, H., Nurbaş, E., Onat, E.: Direction finding using convolutional neural networks and convolutional recurrent neural networks. In: 2020 28th Signal Processing and Communications Applications Conference (SIU), 1–4 (2020)
5. Li, G., RangZhuoma, C., Zhijie, C., Chen, D.: Tibetan voice activity detection based on one-dimensional convolutional neural network. In: 2021 3rd International Conference on Natural Language Processing (ICNLP), 129–133 (2021)
6. Zhu, K., Wang, J., Wang, M.: One dimensional convolution neural network radar target recognition based on direct sampling data. In: 2019 IEEE 3rd Information Technology, Networking, Electronic and Automation Control Conference (ITNEC), pp. 76–80 (2019)
7. Chowdhury, T.T., Hossain, A., Fattah, S.A., Shahnaz, C.: Seizure and non-seizure EEG signals detection using 1-D convolutional neural network architecture of deep learning algorithm. In: 2019 1st International Conference on Advances in Science, Engineering and Robotics Technology (ICASERT), pp. 1–4 (2019)
8. Li, Y., Zou, L., Jiang, L., Zhou, X.: Fault diagnosis of rotating machinery based on combination of deep belief network and one-dimensional convolutional neural network. IEEE Access **7**, 165710–165723 (2019)
9. Li, R., Li, K.: The research of multi-source information fusion based on cloud computing. In: 2016 12th International Conference on Computational Intelligence and Security (CIS), pp. 440–443 (2016)
10. Deng, T.: Derivations and relations of various cost functions for all pass phase-equalizing filter Design. In: 2019 IEEE Asia Pacific Conference on Circuits and Systems (APCCAS), pp. 89–92 (2019)
11. Zhang, W., Peng, G., Li, C., et al.: A new deep learning model for fault diagnosis with good anti-noise and domain adaptation ability on raw vibration signals. Sensors MDPI AG **17**(2), 425 (2017)

Author Index

Printed in the United States
by Baker & Taylor Publisher Services